COLLECTED WHEEL PUBLICATIONS

VOLUME 19

NUMBERS 281 – 295

BPS PARIYATTI EDITIONS

BPS Pariyatti Editions
An imprint of Pariyatti Publishing
www.pariyatti.org

© Buddhist Publication Society, 2008

All rights reserved. No part of this book may be used or reproduced in any manner whatsoever without the written permission of BPS Pariyatti Editions, except in the case of brief quotations embodied in critical articles and reviews.

Copies of this book for sale in the Americas only. Although this is an American edition, we have left any British spelling of words unchanged.

First BPS Pariyatti Edition, 2025
ISBN: 978-1-68172-196-5 (Print)
ISBN: 978-1-68172-197-2 (PDF)
ISBN: 978-1-68172-198-9 (ePub)
ISBN: 978-1-68172-199-6 (Mobi)
LCCN: 2018940050

Contents

WH 281   Colonel Olcott
           B. P. Kirthisinghe, M. P. Amarasuriya 1

WH 282   Going for Refuge & Taking the Precepts
to 284   *Bhikkhu Bodhi* 29

WH 285   Buddhism and Social Action
& 286   *Ken Jones* 95

WH 287   Buddhist Stories (from the Dhammapada Commentary, Part I)
to 289   *Eugene Watson Burlingame* 141

WH 290   Buddhism in Psychotherapy
& 291   *Seymour Boorstein, M.D., Olaf G. Deatherage, Ph.D.* 211

WH 292   Buddhist Women at the Time of the Buddha
& 293   *Hellmuth Hecker* 245

WH 294   The Buddhist Layman
& 295   *R. Bogoda, Susan Elbaum Jootla,*
           and M.O'C. Walshe 301

Key to Abbreviations

A	Aṅguttara Nikāya	Paṭis	Paṭisambhidamagga
Ap	Apadāna	Peṭ	Peṭakopadesa
Bv	Buddhavaṃsa	S	Saṃyutta Nikāya
Cp	Cariyāpiṭaka	Sn	Suttanipāta
D	Dīgha Nikāya	Th	Theragāthā
Dhp	Dhammapada	Thī	Therīgāthā
Dhs	Dhammasaṅgaṇī	Ud	Udāna
It	Itivuttaka	Vibh	Vibhaṅga
Ja	Jātaka verses and commentary	Vin	Vinaya-piṭaka
Khp	Khuddakapāṭha	Vism	Visuddhimagga
M	Majjhima Nikāya	Vism-mhṭ	Visuddhimagga Sub-commentary
Mil	Milindapañha	Vv	Vimānavatthu
Nett	Nettipakaraṇa	Nidd	Niddesa

The above is the abbreviation scheme of the Pali Text Society (PTS) as given in the *Dictionary of Pali* by Margaret Cone.

The commentaries, *aṭṭhakathā*, are abbreviated by using a hyphen and an "a" ("-a") following the abbreviation of the text, e.g., *Dīgha Nikāya Aṭṭhakathā* = D-a. Likewise the sub-commentaries are abbreviated by a "ṭ" ("-ṭ") following the abbreviation of the text.

The sutta reference abbreviation system for the four Nikāyas, as is used in Bhikkhu Bodhi's translations is:

AN	Aṅguttara Nikāya	DN	Dīgha Nikāya
MN	Majjhima Nikāya	Sn	Saṃyutta Nikāya
J	Jātaka story	Mv	Mahāvagga (Vinaya Piṭaka)
Cv	Cullavagga (Vinaya Piṭaka)	SVibh	Suttavibhaṅga (Vinaya Piṭaka)

Colonel Olcott

His Service to Buddhism

by
B. P. Kirthisinghe
M. P. Amarasuriya

Copyright © Kandy; Buddhist Publication Society, (1981)

Colonel Olcott

Col. Olcott with Hikkaduve Sumangala

Col. Olcott with a group of monks

The Panadura Debate

Colonel Henry Steele Olcott

The Great American Buddhist by
Dr. Buddhadasa P. Kirthisinghe

Colonel Olcott was an inspiring servant of mankind. He lived in our age and dedicated the later years of his life to Buddhism and the peoples of Asia, particularly those of India and Ceylon. He gave up an affluent life for a simpler and nobler one. He devoted his energies to working for the benefit of the common people. The services rendered to Asia and particularly to the revival of Buddhist cultures are contributions worthy of an honoured place in the pages of Asian history.

Colonel Olcott died on 17th February 1907, at his home in Adyar, near Madras, India, after having served his beloved Asian people for nearly 32 years. The anniversary of his death is celebrated throughout India and south-east Asia and particularly by the people of Ceylon, who have a special veneration for him. As a demonstration of their gratitude, a large photograph of him hangs in most of the Buddhist schools and colleges which he helped to establish in Ceylon.

Colonel Henry Steele Olcott was born on 2nd August 1832, in Orange, New Jersey, U.S.A. After a brilliant school career at the City College of New York, and Columbia University, he became interested in scientific agriculture. He edited a farmers' periodical, and in 1858 he became associated with the *New York Tribune* as the agriculture editor. When the American Civil war broke out in 1861, he gave up his newspaper work and went to the front, where he eventually attained the rank of colonel.

Colonel Olcott served in special capacities in both the Army and Navy Departments. After the conclusion of the War, he was admitted to the Bar of New York State. He became prominent as a lawyer, as well as an investigator of "graft," especially in connection with the scandals in the Mustering and Disbanding Departments. This work required unusual integrity and courage, as his life was constantly threatened.

As a result of his investigations, several malefactors were sent to jail. As a lawyer he had a lucrative practice. Later he was employed by the Government to investigate certain abuses in the Navy Yard. He was appointed by the President in 1878 to report on trade conditions between America, India and Ceylon.

The year 1874 is of special significance in the life of the noble colonel. It was in this year that he was employed by the *New York Sun* to investigate the mystic phenomena which took place at the Eddy Farm in New York. His methods of investigation and his reports made a deep impression on the American public, and the book he wrote called *People of the Other World* sold out rapidly. It was in connection with these investigations that he met Madame H.P. Blavatsky at the Eddy Farm. From then on began a long friendship and collaboration with her which lasted until her death in 1891. During this time Colonel Olcott became interested in oriental religions, especially Buddhism. In 1875, he and Madame Blavatsky founded the Theosophical Society of New York. The main objectives of the society were to establish the nucleus of a universal brotherhood of humanity, to promote the study of comparative religion and philosophy, and to make a systematic investigation of the mystic potencies of life and matter, or what is usually called occultism.

He set out with Madame Blavatsky for India in 1878 to study various religions there, and they arrived in Ceylon on 17th May 1880. Sometime later in the same month both of them embraced Buddhism publicly in Galle, a town 75 miles from Colombo, on the south coast of the island.

What profoundly influenced Colonel Olcott to adopt Buddhism as his religion was his study of the famous public debates that took place in 1873 at Panadura, a small town 20 miles from Ceylon's capital. These debates erupted between incumbent monk Venerable Migettuwatte Gunānanda of Kotahena Temple, Ceylon's greatest orator in modern times, and his adversaries in the Christian priesthood, occasioned by the persecution by Christian missionaries of the Buddhists under the British colonial administration. It is recorded by a *bhikkhu* that Venerable Gunānanda faced the united forces of Christian orthodoxy. So powerful was his eloquence and reasoning in the Panadura controversy, which was intended to bring discredit to the Buddhists, that the tables were turned against Christianity in Ceylon. It was so impressive that no Catholic or Protestant ventured to cross words with Buddhist wisdom. Bhikkhu Sangharakshita states "If at the Panadura controversy Christian fanaticism suffered its first serious repulse, by the ceremony at Galle (where Colonel Olcott and friend embraced Buddhism), Buddhism scored its positive victory, and this victory for Buddhism was won by the founders of the Theosophical Society." They hold him in boundless gratitude.

Therefore the two decades between 1870 and 1890 became a crucial period in the history of modern Ceylon. The four notables in this period were Venerable Migettuwatte Gunānanda, Venerable Hikkaduwe Sri Sumangala, Maha Nayaka Thera of Maligakanda Vidyodaya Pirivena College, Colonel Olcott, and his pupil, the Ven. Anagarika Dharmapāla. Their contributions to the revival of Buddhism, Buddhist culture and Buddhist education will never be forgotten by the Sinhalese Buddhists, who revere their memory.

Colonel Olcott had a deep sympathy for all Asian religions, Hinduism, Islam, etc. When he came in contact with Asians, they became his blood brothers. He lectured on Hinduism, Islam, and Zoroastrianism, and he wanted to equip archaeological expeditions with the aid of the Parsis of Bombay, to go to Persia (Iran) in search of Zoroastrian remains, and particularly to search for their lost scriptures.

When he went to India, the magnificent civilisation of India was in a state of decay. He was the first in India to organise in Bombay, in 1879, a Swadeshi exhibition of Indian manufactures to show the public of India what beautiful objects were being produced by Indian craftsmen. These crafts were slowly being forgotten in India because Indians cared little for them. In short, he stimulated India's awakening after a deep slumber of ages, and the revival of her past glories. This was long before Mahatma Gandhi, who led the Indian masses to freedom. The work of Colonel Olcott later stimulated the formation of the Indian National Congress, which inspired India to produce great leaders and attain her freedom peacefully and with the retention of the friendship of the British people. As a matter of fact, Colonel Olcott's influence was so great on both the elite and the masses of India, that his successor to the presidency of the Theosophical Society, Dr. Annie Besant, an English lady, became the first president of the Indian National Congress at its very inception.

> *This is to certify that on the 19th May 1880 the Founders of the Theosophical Society Madame H. P. Blavatsky and myself took the Panchasila for the first time at Vijayananda Vih from Akmemana Dhammaram Thera.*
>
> *S. Olcott*

On a wall of Vijayananda Vihara, Welliwatta, Galle, was the above in Colonel Olcott's own handwriting. (*"This is to certify that on the 19th May 1880 the Founders of the Theosophical Society Madame H. P. Blavatsky and myself took the Panchasila for the first time at Vijayananda Vihara from Akmemana Dhammarama Thera."*) (See page 3)

In 1879 Colonel Olcott wrote as follows on the first Swadeshi exhibition in India in an old diary:

"On 29th November, an event of much importance occurred: we celebrated with great *éclat* the fourth anniversary of the formation of the Theosophical Society. It was also our first public function of the kind …

"Mr. Wimbridge designed and lithographed an artistic invitation card, inviting our friends to 'attend at the Headquarters, 108 Girgaum Back Road, Bombay, at 8.30 p.m. on the 29th November 1879, a meeting commemorative of the Society's fourth anniversary, the founding of the *Theosophist*, and the opening of the library. There will be addresses and a display of machinery made by native artisans.' Signed by myself as president, and H.P. Blavatsky as corresponding secretary.

"The grounds and the land leading to them from the public road were brilliantly illuminated; arches of flame and pyramids of Indian coloured lamps were placed at the mouth of the lane and the entrance to the compound; Chinese lanterns were hung on wires stretched between the palm trees; an arch of gas jets, spelling the word 'Welcome' lighted up the library façade; the whole ground was spread with striped Indian carpets; 400 chairs were placed for guests; a band of twenty musicians played Indian and foreign airs—among the latter the American national hymn and the scene was altogether beautiful. Far above the palms, the azure, tropical, star-studded sky looked down on us.

"Inside the library building, tables and walls were covered with exhibits of indigenous work in brass, ivory, sandalwood, steel; the marble mosaics of Agra, the lovely shawls and soft woollen stuffs of Kashmir, hand-woven muslins from Dacca and elsewhere, cutlery from Pandharpur, and work from the Baroda School of Arts. The Dewan of Cutch, the enlightened Mr. Manibhai Jashbai, sent a complete collection of arms and some of the famous silver work of that state.

"About 500 invited guests—the best known and most respected in Bombay—were present. Addresses were made by Messrs. Gopal Rao Hari Deshmukh (as chairman); Naoroji Fundunji, a beloved Parsi statesman; Kashinath Trimbaknath Telang, subsequently a Justice of the Bombay High Court; Shantaram Narayan, a most respected Maratha lawyer; Nurshunker Lalshunker, the 'Guzerati poet', and myself. Altogether, it was a most appropriate and encouraging help to our Indian career. The Europeans present expressed themselves charmed with the industrial display, and gave deserved praise to Vishram Jetha's mechanical exhibits."

The noble colonel decried the Indian caste system, which was one of the causes of the downfall of the great Indian civilisation. He made every effort to get India to forbid this much-abused social system, which culminated in its being banned in the new Indian constitution.

He founded schools for the outcastes in South India. Colonel Olcott stipulated that no school fees should be charged; that the school hours were to be convenient for the occupations of the domestic servants and others who might seek education; that no Christian or other proselytism was to be permitted; Tamil (reading, writing and correct spelling) as well as arithmetic, English speaking and Hindustani speaking were to be taught.

Colonel Olcott departed for Europe on the 14th May 1894, but he left full instructions with Mr. S. Ryder, a European Theosophist, for supervising the erection of the building (a mere mud-walled, half-open, palmyra-thatched structure, like most Indian village schoolhouses) and its management until his return. The school was opened in June 1894, and appropriately named "The Olcott Free School."

The success of the experiment is reported by its manager in the *Madras Mail*, 1896. He wrote: "The free education offered by Colonel Olcott is now so well appreciated that we shall soon have to refuse further admission of pupils for want of room. The movement is becoming so popular that I believe it would be comparatively easy to gather several thousand pariah boys and girls into free schools in Madras and its suburbs alone."

In 1898 a second school named the "H.P.B. Memorial Free School" was founded at Kodambakam, and in 1899 a third school named the "Damodar Free School" was opened at Teynampet. In 1901 Colonel Olcott made an appeal to his countrymen in a letter to the *Record-Herald* of Chicago, for funds for extending this work, and in September 1901 a fourth school was opened at Mylapore. It was named after the great South Indian yogi, Tiruvalluvar, himself a *panchama*. The fifth and last school was opened on the 1st May 1906, at Krishnampet, five miles from Adyar, outside the city limits, and named the "Besant Free School."

In 1925, owing to financial difficulties, it was found impossible to carry on work in all the schools, and on 6th January 1926, the three schools within the municipal area of the city of Madras were transferred as gifts with all their property, such as buildings, books, furniture, etc., to the Corporation of Madras.

The transference of these three schools was facilitated by the fact that there had been passed a law for free elementary education to be provided from taxes. This had never existed up to this time in India. The two schools managed today by the Olcott Panchama School Committee are outside the municipal limits of the city of Madras, and therefore could not be taken over by the city. They lie within the district of Chingleput, but the District Board has, owing to lack of funds, refused to take them over.

The Panchama Schools organised by Colonel Olcott secured very early the services of Miss Sarah E. Palmer, B.Sc., of Wisconsin, U.S.A., who volunteered to come for this special work. Miss Palmer introduced for the first time into elementary schools in Madras the ideals of the kindergarten, and these five schools for outcaste children became in many ways more advanced in their methods than the schools in the city for caste children. Teachers from these latter schools constantly visited the Panchama Schools to observe the new methods. Miss Palmer returned home in 1931 after many years of service to these and other schools conducted by Colonel Olcott.

Colonel Olcott's reform movement has been greatly assisted by the expansion of the Theosophical Headquarters at Adyar. A large number of boys of these schools, as they grew up, found employment as servants at Adyar, the European and American residents invariably so employing them, and giving them such training as has enabled them, when not employed at Adyar, to find places among Europeans in the city of Madras. While among caste people there is still objection to employing them as domestic servants, even this objection has greatly lessened among many Hindu residents and visitors at Adyar. Colonel Olcott's work has now affected a larger field, and the very name "depressed classes" is tending to disappear.

He assisted them also in becoming acquainted with Buddhism, and a certain number of panchamas (a so-called low caste) in Madras became Buddhists (a tradition already existed among them that once they had been Buddhists). At any rate, as Buddhists, they became a little less "untouchable."

It is recorded in history that the Emperor Asoka sent his own son and daughter to Ceylon for Buddhist missionary work in the 3rd century B.C. With the adoption of Buddhism as the state religion, the Sinhalese civilisation of Ceylon blossomed into its golden period. But when Colonel Olcott came to Ceylon in 1880, this great civilisation was in a decadent state. He found on his arrival that there were only three Buddhist schools in this Buddhist country. The education system was dominated and dictated by the Christian churches, which discriminated against the Buddhists and compelled them not only to go to Christian schools, but also to get marriage certificates only in Christian churches. It was a time when Buddhists were frightened and ashamed to call themselves Buddhists openly, due to fear of economic persecution by the missionaries. Colonel Olcott revolted against this prejudice. He therefore started the Buddhist educational movement and founded the Colombo branch of the Buddhist Theosophical Society, with the cooperation of local Buddhists. In a remarkable way, all the high Buddhist monks of the island gathered around and received him with much warmth, so that he was the envy of other Europeans who lived secluded and isolated from the native people. He became one of the oppressed Buddhists who fought for their rights.

Quite a unique document was granted to Colonel Olcott from the principal chief priests of Buddhism in Ceylon, to empower him to admit converts to Buddhism. By immemorial tradition the action of becoming a Buddhist consists of a statement of belief in the Three Refuges—Buddha, Dhamma and Saṅgha—and pledging oneself to observe the Pancha Sīla, the Five Precepts. This profession of faith is constantly reiterated, so whenever any Buddhist goes to a Buddhist temple to offer flowers before the image of the Lord Buddha, it is customary for him to repeat the vows before he enters the shrine. Usually he goes to a Buddhist monk and asks "to be given the Refuges and the Precepts." The monk then says the ancient Pāli words phrase by phrase, and the layman repeats them after him.

Till the giving of this commission to Colonel Olcott, no Buddhist layman ever considered himself authorised, as are the monks, to give the Pancha Sīla. But it was just this unusual privilege that was given to Colonel Olcott, by this document which is deposited in Adyar. Of the chief priests who signed it, the best known are Hikkaduwe Sri Sumangala, the chief priest of Adam's Peak and principal of Vidyodaya College, Colombo, and W. Subhuti, another learned chief priest who was the instructor of the Pāli scholar T.W. Rhys Davids.

Colonel Olcott, together with Anagarika Dharmapāla of Ceylon, were pioneers in the Buddhist revival movement in India and Ceylon. They worked together in the development of Ceylon's educational movement. They travelled from village to village on foot and in bullock cart, exhorting the people to live Buddhist lives, and collecting funds. Principally to the credit of

Colonel Olcott there are about 12 large colleges and over 400 Buddhist schools in the island, which have now been handed over to the government under the recent nationalisation act.

In 1883 a savage attack was made by the Christians on a Buddhist procession in Colombo, and rioting ensued. Colonel Olcott was invited by the Buddhists to assist them in their difficulties, and he became practically their champion in the redress of their grievances. Fortunately the governor of Ceylon at the time was Sir Arthur Gordon, later Lord Stanmore, whom Colonel Olcott found greatly sympathetic, due to his broad-mindedness, and also because he was somewhat interested in occultism and comparative religion. It was at an interview with the governor on 10th February 1884, that Colonel Olcott obtained a promise from him that the Buddhists should have their sacred day, the birthday of the Lord Buddha, declared a public holiday. The significance of this can scarcely be realised today. In 1883, Christian Protestant missionaries completely dominated the island. Only Christian holidays were recognised by the government as public holidays. Several instances happened, such as Buddhist boys in Christian schools absenting themselves from school on certain Buddhist festivals, being punished by the headmaster for their absence. This particularly happened to certain boys at the Vesak festival of 1883. When, therefore, Colonel Olcott, as the result of his work, obtained for the Buddhists a public holiday on their chief festival, the natural result was that later both the Hindus and the Muslims obtained the same right from the government. Colonel Olcott went as the representative of the Buddhists to interview the Colonial Secretary in London, and was able to put the Buddhist view of affairs before him.

One of the first things Colonel Olcott did while organising the Ceylon educational system was to compose a Buddhist catechism, so that Buddhists could teach their children. This Buddhist Catechism, which was endorsed by the chief priest Sumangala, was one of the most striking contributions to the resuscitation of Buddhism. The Catechism was first published in Sinhalese on 24th July 1881, and later in English and several other languages. As this Catechism was too advanced for some of the children, a simpler, more elementary one was prepared by Rev. C.W. Leadbeater, a British collaborator of the colonel. Colonel Olcott's Catechism has now gone through 44 English editions, and probably more in Sinhalese; and that of Rev. C.W. Leadbeater in Sinhalese (up to 1914) through 21 editions of Part I, and 18 editions of Part II.

At this point Colonel Olcott felt the need for a symbol to rally the local Buddhists. To meet this need, he designed a flag for the Buddhists from the aura that shone around the head of the Buddha. The first five stripes of the flag are blue, yellow, red, white, pink; the sixth colour is a mixture of the five, but for design, it has been broken up into its constituents.

The colonel's flag, in the course of time, came to symbolise the unity of all Buddhists. It was accepted as the international Buddhist flag by the World Fellowship of Buddhists which met in Ceylon in 1950 for the first time, and its acceptance was further confirmed at the conference in Japan in 1952. From then on, it came into use on a world-wide scale, and is now being used in nearly 60 countries, in festivities, particularly on the celebration of the birthday of the Buddha.

Colonel Olcott travelled widely in the East and in Europe on lecture tours. He was also associated with the revival of Buddhism in Japan, and visited that country twice. On his first visit in 1888, he gave 70 lectures, and on his second visit in 1890 he brought the Mahāyāna Buddhists of Japan, Korea, China and Viet-Nam into closer cooperation with the Theravāda Buddhists of India, Burma, Ceylon, Thailand, Cambodia and Laos, by calling their attention to the fundamental principles of Buddhism which are common to all schools and sects. Thereby he established a common platform for all Buddhists, whether of the Northern or the Southern school. It was one of the most remarkable and statesmanlike contributions of Colonel Olcott.

The following fourteen items of belief which were accepted as fundamental principles in both the Southern and Northern sections of Buddhism in 1891 by their authoritative committees, to whom they were submitted by Colonel Olcott personally, have such historical importance that they were added to the last edition of the Buddhist Catechism as an appendix. It has been reported that the chief lamas of the Mongolian Buddhist monasteries declared to Prince Ouchtomsky, the learned Russian orientalist, after the document was translated to them, that they accept every one of the propositions as drafted, with the one exception that the date of the Buddha is by them believed to have been some thousands of years earlier than the one given by Colonel Olcott. This surprising fact had not hitherto come to the prince's knowledge. Could it be that the Mongolian Saṅgha confused the real epoch of Sakyamuni with that of his alleged predecessor? Be this as it may, it is a most encouraging fact that the whole Buddhist world may now be said to have united at least in accepting the Fourteen Propositions.

Colonel Olcott's Fourteen Fundamental Buddhist Beliefs

1. Buddhists are taught to show the same tolerance, forbearance, and brotherly love to all men, without distinction; and an unswerving kindness towards the members of the animal kingdom.
2. The universe was evolved, not created; and it functions according to law, not according to the caprice of any god.
3. The truths upon which Buddhism is founded are natural. They have, we believe, been taught in successive *kalpas*, or world-periods, by certain illuminated beings called Buddhas, the name Buddha meaning "Enlightened."
4. The fourth teacher in the present *kalpa* was Sakyamuni, or Gautama Buddha, who was born in a royal family in India about 2,500 years ago. He is a historical personage and his name was Siddhartha Gautama.
5. Sakyamuni taught that ignorance produces desire, unsatisfied desire is the cause of rebirth, and rebirth the cause of sorrow. To get rid of sorrow, therefore, it is necessary to escape rebirth, it is necessary to extinguish desire; and to extinguish desire, it is necessary to destroy ignorance.
6. Ignorance fosters the belief that rebirth is a necessary thing. When ignorance is destroyed the worthlessness of every such rebirth, considered as an end in itself, is perceived, as well as the paramount need of adopting a course of life by which the necessity for such repeated rebirth, can be abolished. Ignorance also begets the illusive and illogical idea that there is only one existence for man, and the other illusion that this one life is followed by a state of unchangeable pleasure or torment.

7. The dispersion of all this ignorance can be attained by the persevering practice of an all-embracing altruism in conduct, development of intelligence, wisdom in thought, and destruction of desire for the lower personal pleasures.
8. The desire to live being the cause of rebirth, when that is extinguished rebirths cease, and the perfected individual attains by meditation that highest state of peace called Nirvāna.
9. Sakyamuni taught that ignorance can be dispelled and sorrow removed by the knowledge of the Four Noble Truths, that is,
    i. Existence is misery;
    ii. The cause productive of misery is the desire ever-renewed of satisfying oneself, without being able ever to secure that end;
    iii. The destruction of that desire, or the estranging of oneself from it;
    iv. The means of obtaining this destruction of desire. The means which he pointed out are called the Noble Eightfold Path, that is, Right Belief, Right Thought, Right Speech, Right Action, Right Means of Livelihood, Right Exertion, Right Remembrance, Right Meditation.
10. Right Meditation leads to spiritual enlightenment, or the development of that Buddha-like faculty which is latent in every man.
11. The essence of Buddhism, as summed up by the Tathāgata (Buddha) himself, consists in: desisting from all evil; acquiring virtue; purifying the heart.
12. The universe is subject to a natural causation known as Karma. The merits and demerits of a being in his past existence determine his condition in the present one. Each man, therefore, has prepared the causes of the effect which he now experiences.
13. The obstacles to the attainment of good Karma may be removed by the observance of the following precepts, which are embraced in the moral code of Buddhism: (1) kill not; (2) steal not; (3) indulge not in forbidden sexual pleasure; (4) lie not; (5) take no intoxicating or stupefying drugs or liquor. Five other precepts which need not be enumerated here

should be observed by those who would attain more quickly than the average layman the release from misery and rebirth.
14. Buddhism discourages superstitious credulity. Gautama Buddha taught it to be the duty of a parent to have his child educated in science and literature. He also taught that no one should believe what is spoken by any sage, written in any book, or affirmed by tradition, unless it accords with reason.

This was drafted as a common platform upon which all Buddhists can agree, and signed by H.S. Olcott. The document then closed with the following endorsements.

Respectfully submitted for the approval of the high priests of the nations which we severally represent, in the Buddhist conference held at Adyar, Madras, on the 8th, 9th, 10th, 11th and 12th of January 1891 (A.B. 2434).

Japan	Kozen Gunaratana, Chiezo Tokuzawa
Burma	U Hmoay Tha Aung
Ceylon	Dhammapala Hevavitarana
The Maghs of Chittagong	Krishna Chandra Chowdry, by his appointed Proxy, Maung Tha Dwe.

Burma

Approved on behalf of the Buddhists of Burma, this 3rd day of February 1891 (A.B. 2434):
 Tha-tha-na-baing Sayadawgyi; Aung Myi Shwebōn Sayadaw; Me-ga-waddy Sayadaw; Hmat-Khaya Sayadaw; Hti-lin Sayadaw; Myadaung Sayadaw; Hla-Htwe Sayadaw; and sixteen others.

Ceylon

Approved on behalf of the Buddhists of Ceylon on this 25th day of February 1891 (A.B. 2434):
Yatawatte Chandajoti, high priest of Asgiri Vihara at Kandy.
(Sd.) Yatawatta
Hikkaduwe Sri Sumangala, high priest of Adam's Peak and the district of Colombo.
(Sd.) H. Sumangala

Suriyagoda Sonuttara, librarian of the oriental library at the Temple of the Tooth Relic at Kandy.
(Sd.) S. Sonuttara
    Dhammalankara, high priest.
(Sd.) W. Dhammalankara
    Waskaduwe Subhuti, high priest.
(Sd.) W. Subhuti

Japan

Accepted as included within the body of Northern Buddhism.

Shaku Genyu	(Shingon Shu)
Fukuda Nichiye	(Nichiren Shu)
Sanada Seyke	(Zen Shu)
Ito Quan Shyu	(Zen Shu)
Takehana Hakuyo	(Jodo Shu)
Kono Rioshin	(Ji-Shu Shu)
Kiro Ki-Ko	(Jodo Seizan Shu)
Harutani Shinsho	(Tendai Shu)
Manabe Shun-myo	(Shingon Shu)

Chittagong

Accepted for the Buddhists of Chittagong.

Nagawa Parvata Viharadhipati Guna Megu Wini-Lankara, Harbing, Chittagong, Bengal.

Adyar Oriental Library

Colonel Olcott established the Adyar Oriental Library in 1886. It has become one of the famous oriental institutions of the world, and during the course of his life, he collected and preserved rare Sanskrit, Pāli, Tibetan, Burmese and Sinhalese manuscripts which were fast becoming unavailable. The institution was dedicated to the revival of ancient learning, and its connection with the great religions of India.

In this library there are over 17,584 palm-leaf manuscripts. Today, there is a large staff of Indian and Western-trained workers in charge of the library. Copies of these manuscripts are made in the library and are available to other oriental libraries of the world. The sign of Theosophy in the hall, which is based on the word of the Buddha, is the seal of the society, with its motto, "There is no religion higher than truth."

H.G. Wells, writing in his *Outline of History*, states, "For eight and twenty years, Asoka worked sanely for the real needs of men. Amidst the tens of thousands of names of monarchs that crowd the columns of history, their majesties, and graciousnesses, and serenities and royal highnesses and the like, the name of Asoka shines and shines almost alone, a star. From the Volga to Japan, his name is still honoured. China, Tibet and even India, though it has left his doctrine, preserve the tradition of his greatness. More living men cherish his memory today than have ever heard the names of Constantine or Charlemagne."

It can be safely asserted that the name of Colonel Olcott is honoured in Hindu-Buddhist Asia from India and Ceylon to Japan, more than that of any other American who has lived in Asia. Ceylon's educational system, the international Buddhist flag and Adyar Oriental Library stand today as living monuments to his greatness.

Shortly after his death, the new president of the Theosophical Society, Annie Besant, reported: "When he was lying dead in his Adyar home, the flag which he had devised, and which had been accepted by the Buddhist nations—that and the American flag—covered his corpse, and were carried with it to the burning place."

Olcott's Last Message

"To my beloved brethren in the physical body: I bid you farewell. In memory of me, carry on the grand work of proclaiming and living the brotherhood of religions.

"To my beloved brothers on the higher planes: I greet you and come to you, and implore you to help me to impress on all men on earth that 'there is no religion higher than truth', as the Buddhists say and that in the brotherhood of religions lie the peace and progress of humanity."

2nd February 1907, H.S. Olcott

Colonel Olcott and the Buddhist Revival in Sri Lanka

M. P. Amarasuriya

Right from the time that the first European races landed in Sri Lanka, at the beginning of the 16th century, attempts were made to replace the culture of the Sinhalas with that of Europe. In this movement it was the missionaries that played the most prominent part. They were, of course, well intentioned, but, unfortunately for us, they came to Sri Lanka with the deep-rooted idea that the Sinhalas were a primitive people and that their religion—which represented the high-water level of their civilisation—was something that should be combated whenever and wherever possible and with every available means. The process of eradication thus started continued for many decades, and the defeatist mentality of the Sinhalas, which was the direct consequence of the missionary campaign, became more and more pronounced. It was at the depth of this decline that the people awoke to the sense of the abject humiliation and deep degradation under which they lived. The religion had somehow been kept alive in the recesses of monasteries, and it was from those that there arose men of outstanding ability, of knowledge and wisdom, to kindle into flames the sparks that lay smouldering.

A fighter was needed to supply the dynamic energy; the hour produced the man. He was Ven. Migettuwatte Gunānanda. There is an unauthenticated story that as a layman he had joined a class for the training of catechists held by a Christian clergyman, a well-known Sinhala scholar, the Rev. C. Alwis. Whatever the truth of this story may be, Ven. Migettuwatte seems to have spent several years in a thorough reading of Christian books and also the works of critics of Christianity. He entered the *saṅgha* at Kotahena temple and started battle with the missionaries. He published numerous pamphlets, leaflets and books in defence of Buddhism, meeting the charges that were being urged against it; but he went further. He also started a counter-campaign, carrying war into the enemies' camp. He was a man of ceaseless activity, he toured the country from end to end in the Sinhala districts, sometimes addressing several meetings a day, and thousands flocked to hear him wherever be went. Olcott described him as the most brilliant polemic orator of the island, the terror of the missionaries, a middle-aged shaven monk of full medium stature, with a very intellectual head, the boldest, most brilliant and powerful champion of Sinhalese Buddhism.

A well-known missionary, Rev. S. Langden, wrote to the *Ceylon Friend* in September 1873, after hearing Migettuwatte speak, "There is that in his manner as he rises to speak which puts one in mind of some orators at home. He showed a consciousness of power with the people. (His) voice ... is of great compass and has a clear ring about it. His action is good and the long yellow robe thrown over one shoulder helps to make it impressive. His power of persuasion shows him to be a born orator."

Migettuwatte's activities culminated in the famous Panadura controversy held in August 1873. It was a historic occasion. Rev. David de Silva led the Christian side, supported by a galaxy of very learned clergymen. Migettuwatte had on his side the most eminent *bhikkhus* of the day—Hikkaduwe Sumangala, Bulatgama Dhammālankara, Potuwila Indajoti, Koggala Sanghatissa and Weligama Sri Sumangala, to mention only a few. The controversy ended in an undoubted victory for the Buddhists, both factual and, what was far more important, moral. The Christians had been challenged and met face to face and had been convincingly defeated. John Capper of the *Ceylon Times* (later *The Times of Ceylon*) published in book-form a full account of the historic controversy, with the speeches of the protagonists on either side, translated into English. This book had an unexpectedly wide circulation both in Europe and in America.

A copy fell into the hands of a brilliant American, Colonel Henry Steele Olcott. He became interested in religion, and in 1875 he abandoned his very lucrative practice at the bar. In the same year he founded, with a few friends, the Theosophical Society. In 1878 he and his colleagues came out to India to study the religious systems of the country, and from there to Sri Lanka to study Buddhism and to meet the great fighter who had become the "terror of missionaries." Olcott's fame had preceded him to Sri Lanka, and when his ship was berthed in Galle on the 17th

May 1880, a tumultuous welcome awaited him. Earlier, the ship had touched at Colombo and with prophetic vision Olcott had written in his diary, on the day before reaching Colombo, "New and great responsibilities are to be faced: momentous issues hang on the result of this visit."

The days after his arrival with Madame Blavatsky, the pair were admitted to the Buddhist faith, by taking the Five Precepts at Vijayananda Temple in Galle. From Galle, Olcott and his colleagues proceeded to Colombo. It was a real triumphant march. Arriving in Colombo, in addition to the numerous lectures and public meetings, Olcott had several private conferences with the Buddhist leaders, both bhikkhus and laymen, and as a result, at a home called Red Cliff on Slave Island, on 17th June 1880, the Colombo branch of the Theosophical Society (called the Buddhist Theosophical Society) was founded with about forty members. Its object was "the promotion of Buddhism by guarding it from the attacks of those who propagate other religions, by strengthening Buddhists in their faith and in the practice of Buddhist morals, and by the spreading and teaching of Buddhist doctrines."

During the course of his stay in the island, Olcott travelled widely. Wherever he went, welcome was widespread and spontaneous. He was deeply moved and made up his mind to do all he could to help Buddhists in Sri Lanka regenerate themselves. Sri Lanka always had a soft corner in his heart. "Ah! lovely Lanka," he wrote in his Diary Leaves many years later, "how doth thy sweet image rise before me as I write the story of my experiences among thy dusky children, of my success in warming their hearts to revere their incomparable religion and its holiest founder. Happy the karma that brought me to thy shores."

From the very start Olcott gathered round him a band of most able and enthusiastic workers. He became their "guide, philosopher and friend." He indicated in unmistakable terms the steps that were necessary to transform the new-found enthusiasm into practical shape, so as to achieve real and lasting results. He was a man of indomitable will, no obstacle could stand in his way. Antagonist propaganda only gave him greater strength, and even government opposition which he encountered in no small measure, only made him redouble his efforts. Even the attempt made on his life by some Christian fanatics served to increase his enthusiasm.

He put his finger at once on the weakest spot in the Buddhist position. He insisted that Buddhists should take the education of their children into their own hands. At the time of his arrival in Sri Lanka, there were only two Buddhist schools on the island; one at Dodanduwa started by the Ven. Piyaratana Thera and the other at Panadura, conducted by a local Buddhist society under the supervision of Ven. Gunaratana Nayaka Thera. The total attendance at both schools was 246. At this time there were 805 Christian schools with an attendance of 78,086 children, a very large percentage of whom were born of non-Christian parents. The Buddhist schools had, after many years, received a grant from Government of Rs. 532 whereas the grant of the Christian schools in the same year amounted to Rs. 174,420.

Olcott threw himself heart and soul into the fight for the establishment of Buddhist schools everywhere. He was most anxious that the Buddhist educational movement should primarily be a movement of the people, by the people and for the people, that it should grow from the soil, and that its roots should reach deep down into the peoples' lives. He wished to link it up with a national revival in which the people should be taught to take pride in their language, their customs and their noble culture. He himself gave of his time and services and even money, freely, generously. But he never dictated plans or lines of action. He allowed those who took up the work to find their own feet with him watching in the background only, to struggle, to make mistakes or, even, to quarrel. He wanted them to taste of the joys of achievement of success gained, of battles fought and won. When money was needed, he often went himself as a beggar, begging-bowl in hand.

The first "Buddhist Fancy Bazaar" was held on 23rd December 1883, and it is recorded that at the start there was opposition from the Buddhists for this type of collection. Later these "Fancy Bazaars" became a regular feature of Buddhist activities, and goods were for sale from lands overseas—Thailand and Burma, England and America.

On the full moon day of Wesak 1881, Olcott inaugurated at Kelaniya Temple a Buddhist National Fund for the "general promotion of religious and secular education of Buddhist children and the dissemination of Buddhist literature." The first cheque (Rs. 100) was handed to Olcott immediately after his speech by R.A. Mirando, who up to the time of his untimely death continued to be a great worker in the Buddhist cause. By 1886 the Buddhist National Fund had collected Rs. 13,000. Olcott also did many things to rouse the people's enthusiasm; he suggested the necessity for a public holiday on Wesak Day and helped in getting it for the Buddhists. He emphasised the need for a headquarters building for the new movement, and got the Buddhists to purchase it in May 1885.

He suggested the importance of propaganda and the establishment of a newspaper. The result was the *Sarasavi Sandaresa*, started in December 1889; it brought a new spirit into Sinhalese writing, a fine style, elegant and yet popular, which created a new era in Sinhala literature. The *Sandaresa* soon became an institution to be reckoned with. The editor was merciless in his exposure of corruption and snobbishness among members of the public service who had got accustomed to give themselves the air of petty *rajas*. Government officials raised the cry of sedition against the editor and spoke of "a new danger to the peace and prosperity of the island." Their allies in the British press made editorial demands for the stern suppression of the growing tendency towards the creation of a seditious "native" press. But the editor was undaunted. He established contact with enlightened journalists and public men in England and the local government found it impossible to suppress him. *The Buddhist* was later started as an English supplement to the *Sandaresa* and published by the B.T.S. till it was handed over to the Y.M.B.A. (Young Men's Buddhist Association) in 1918. The first editor of *The Buddhist* was C.W. Leadbeater. He was followed in succession by Mudaliyar L.C. Wijesinghe, the famous translator of the *Mahāvamsa*, A.E. Bultjens, D.B. Jayatilaka and W.A. de Silva, all of whom made their mark in the Buddhist renaissance movement in more ways than one, and worked wholeheartedly for its success.

Experience had shown Olcott that not only the children and the laity but even many Buddhist bhikkhus were ignorant of the fundamentals of their religion. He tried without success to get a Buddhist bhikkhu to compile a Buddhist catechism. Olcott therefore took it upon himself during his second visit to do the job, writing at odd moments during his travels, lectures and other activities.

His idea was to produce an elementary handbook on lines similar to those used so effectively by Christian sects. To fit himself for the task this indefatigable American read 10,000 pages of Buddhist books in English and French translations. After the manuscript of the catechism was completed Olcott got it approved by the Ven. Hikkaduwe Sumangala, head of Vidyodaya Pirivena.

The Sinhala and English versions appeared simultaneously on 24th July 1881, and it became a textbook in the schools and found its way into every Sinhala family. Olcott, noting that the book had been translated into 20 different languages, commented that "from a grain of mustard seed has developed a giant tree."

These various activities roused opposition, as might be expected, from all quarters. In official eyes the Buddhist educational movement was the offspring of a factious opposition which had to be crushed out of existence. Repressive measures were often adopted; more often discriminatory regulations were arbitrarily imposed to put handicaps upon Buddhist activities. One such was the "quarter mile" clause, by which no Buddhist school could be registered unless it happened to be more than a quarter of a mile away from an existing Christian school, even in villages where there was not a single Christian family. And, what was worse, the regulation was brought into operation with retrospective effect: Another was the denial of the use of the tom-tom and other music in Buddhist processions, whereas no such restrictions were placed upon either the Hindus or the Muslims.

In the Easter Day riots of 1883, a peaceful procession of Buddhists was severely manhandled at Kotahena, and murder was committed, yet the apathy of the officials towards Buddhists was so marked that hardly any attempt was made to bring offenders to book. This roused the Buddhists to a sense of their insecurity, and they were constrained to set up an organisation known as the Buddhist Defence Committee to protect their own interests and to secure the redress of certain glaring grievances. This committee persuaded Colonel Olcott to proceed to London on their behalf, and to interview the Secretary of State for the Colonies. Olcott accepted the commission on the stipulation that "under no circumstances could he receive any remuneration whatsoever for his services."

Olcott's visit to the Colonial Office was fruitful in many ways. He was successful in getting Buddhist registrars of marriages appointed in various places, so that Buddhists could have their marriages solemnised without the necessity of a church ceremony. The Christian oath which even the Buddhists took in court was given up as affirmation. Buddhist holidays appeared in the official calendar and the Buddhists began to celebrate Vesak as a festival of lights.

The missionaries looked upon the movement at first with contemptuous indifference and with a metaphorical shrug of the shoulder. Then they began to take notice of it and referred to it as "the so-called Buddhist revival." By 1889 the position, from their point of view, was not quite satisfactory. In an appeal issued in that year, they asked for prayers and the assistance of the faithful: "We need these prayers and this help to enable us to cope successfully with the forces of the enemy that are spreading all around us. Buddhism is multiplying its agents and activities in opposing the progress of the Gospel of our Lord Jesus Christ."

In 1902 the success of Buddhist work prompted the Church Missionary Society to pass a resolution not to employ any Christian in their schools who had at any time served in Buddhist schools. By 1903 their complaints were louder against "the conducting of preaching campaigns (by Buddhists) to draw away the children placed under our care by their parents. Many children have been withdrawn and have cost us loss in the matter of government grants." That same year the Rev. (afterwards Canon) G.B. Ekanayake writing in *East and West* did not hesitate to admit that "the current of Christian concession had been effectively stemmed by the Buddhist revival." "The barrenness of missionary effort calls for energetic action," he urged. The Roman Catholics adopted a rather strange and amusing attitude. The following is an extract from the *Ceylon Catholic Messenger* of 20th May 1881: "The Theosophists cannot in any case be worse than the sectarian missionaries, and if Colonel Olcott can induce the Buddhists to establish schools of their own, as he is trying to do, he will be doing us a service; because if the Buddhists could have their own denominational schools as we have ours, they would put a stop to the dishonesty now practised by sectarian missionaries of obtaining government money for proselytising purposes under the pretext of grants-in-aid of education."

The progress made by the Buddhist educational movement in its early years, in the face of these numerous drawbacks was indeed remarkable. On 13th February 1881, the first Buddhist Sunday school was started at the Society's premises in Maliban Street. From May that year, C.W. Leadbeater, who had come to Sri Lanka with Olcott, was in charge of the Sunday school. On 1st November 1886, the same school in Pettah was converted into the Pettah Buddhist English School, which later became Ānanda College. The school started with 37 pupils with Leadbeater as honorary headmaster. It is significant of the conditions of the times that at the public meeting held on 23rd October 1886 to inaugurate this venture, the invitations sent out contained words prominently printed in Sinhala to the effect that "on this occasion no collection whatsoever will be made." Leadbeater records that on the memorable Sunday, just before school was started, *kiribath* and other delicacies were served. In the first year the Buddhist English School earned the very handsome grant-in-aid of Rs. 359. By 1899 there were 194 Buddhist schools with 15,490 children and of these 92 had been registered. At that time the Roman Catholics had 30,425 children in their schools, the Wesleyans 22,808 and the C.M.S. 14,110. The grant received by the Buddhists was Rs. 27,430, while the expenditure incurred by the B.T.S. was Rs. 34,000, in addition to Rs. 15,000 spent by local managers and local committees.

Mention must be made, with due respect and gratitude, to early workers who gave of their best in the cause which brought them no glory or power, but only the satisfaction of having done their duty by their religion and their country. It would be impossible to give anything like a complete list. Some names have already been mentioned. But in the annals of the Buddhist educational movement, when its early career comes to be adequately recorded, tribute must surely be paid to other giants as well, like J.W. Bowles-Daly and Marie Musaeus Higgins, pioneers of Buddhist education in Ceylon; A.E. Bultjens, most distinguished alumnus of that very distinguished school, St. Thomas College; Dharmapala, missionary and fire-eater, yet the hardest working of the early workers, indefatigable, indomitable, nationalist, the value of whose services in numerous fields of activity, we have not fully recognised; Andrew Perera, B.T.S.'s first president;

Muhandiram Dharma Gunawardena; John R. de Silva, secretary of the Buddhist Defence Committee; William de Abrew, Harry Dias, J. Munasinghe, C. Don Bastian and last, but not the least, C.P. Gunawardene, most lovable and self-effacing of men. None knew how much the Society owed its success to him, especially in its darker days when its very existence was threatened.

Olcott was in many ways eminently suited to lead the Buddhists of Sri Lanka. He was a distinguished scholar who had at one time been offered the chair of Scientific Agriculture by the University of Athens. He had served on the staff of a leading American newspaper as a journalist. On the outbreak of the Civil War he had joined the Northern army as an officer, and had a brilliant military record. His ability and integrity had been recognised and he had been appointed special commissioner for the War Department as well. Back in civilian life he had been called to the Bar and had built up a lucrative practice. He and Madame Blavatsky had already founded the Theosophical Society. The Buddhists in Sri Lanka could have found no better champion of their cause.

Before Olcott said goodbye to Sri Lanka he was able to see the fulfilment of the hopes he had had on the eve of his first landing on these shores. Of the many facets of his work, his achievement in the sphere of education is the brightest. There were, when he left Sri Lanka, three first-class Buddhist colleges and two hundred schools to the credit of his movement.

Momentous indeed were the results of Olcott's visit, and in the old *Diary Leaves* he reviewed for posterity his contribution in the following words. "For now we see the splendid harvest that has come from the sowing of the seed, schools springing up everywhere; 20,000 Buddhist children rescued from hostile religious teachers; religion reviving, and the prospect brightening every year."

Going for Refuge & Taking the Precepts

by
Bhikkhu Bodhi

Copyright © Kandy; Buddhist Publication Society, (1981)

Preface

The first two steps in the process of becoming a lay disciple of the Buddha are the going for refuge (*saraṇa gamana*) and the undertaking of the five precepts (*pañca-sīla-samādāna*). By the former step a person makes the commitment to accept the Triple Gem—the Buddha, the Dhamma, and the Saṅgha—as the guiding ideals of his life, by the latter he expresses his determination to bring his actions into harmony with these ideals through right conduct. The following two tracts were written for the purpose of giving a clear and concise explanation of these two steps. Though they are intended principally for those who have newly embraced the Buddha's teaching they will probably be found useful as well by long-term traditional Buddhists wanting to understand the meaning of practices with which they are already familiar and also by those who want to know what becoming a Buddhist involves.

In order to keep our treatment compact, and to avoid the intimidating format of a scholastic treatise, references to source material in the tracts themselves have been kept to a minimum. Thus we here indicate the sources upon which our account has drawn. *Going for Refuge* is based primarily upon the standard commentarial passage on the topic, found with only minor variations in the *Khuddakapāṭha Aṭṭhakathā* (*Paramatthajotika*), the *Dīghanikāya Aṭṭhakathā* (*Sumaṅgalavilāsinī*), and the *Majjhimanikāya Aṭṭhakathā* (*Papañcasūdanī*). The first has been translated by Ven. Bhikkhu Ñāṇamoli in *Minor Readings and the Illustrator* (London: Pali Text Society, 1960), the third by Ven. Nyanaponika Thera in his *The Threefold Refuge* (B.P.S., Wheel No. 76).

The tract *Taking the Precepts* relies principally upon the commentarial explanations of the training rules in the *Khuddakapāṭha Aṭṭhakathā*, referred to above, and to the discussion of the courses of *kamma* in the *Majjhimanikāya* (commentary to No. 9, *Sammādiṭṭhi-sutta*). The former is available in English in Ven. Ñāṇamoli's *Minor Readings and Illustrator,* the latter in *Right Understanding,* Discourse and Commentary on the *Sammādiṭṭhi-sutta,* translated by Bhikkhu Soma (Sri Lanka: Bauddha Sahitya Sabha, 1946). Another useful work on the precepts was *The Five*

Precepts and the Five Ennoblers by HRH Vajirañāṇavarorasa, a late Supreme Patriarch of Thailand (Bangkok: Mahamakut Rajavidyalaya Press, 1975). Also consulted was the section on the courses of karma in Vasubandhu's *Abhidharmakoṣa* and its commentary, a Sanskrit work of the Sarvāstivāda tradition.

—Bhikkhu Bodhi

Going for Refuge

The Buddha's teaching can be thought of as a kind of building with its own distinct foundation, stories, stairs, and roof. Like any other building the teaching also has a door, and in order to enter it we have to enter through this door. The door of entrance to the teaching of the Buddha is the going for refuge to the Triple Gem—that is, to the Buddha as the fully enlightened teacher, to the Dhamma as the truth taught by him, and to the Saṅgha as the community of his noble disciples. From ancient times to the present the going for refuge has functioned as the entranceway to the dispensation of the Buddha, giving admission to the rest of the teaching from its lowermost story to its top. All those who embrace the Buddha's teaching do so by passing through the door of taking refuge, while those already committed regularly reaffirm their conviction by making the same threefold profession:

Buddhaṃ saraṇaṃ gacchāmi

I go for refuge to the Buddha;

Dhammaṃ saraṇaṃ gacchāmi

I go for refuge to the Dhamma;

Saṅghaṃ saraṇaṃ gacchāmi

I go for refuge to the Saṅgha.

As slight and commonplace as this step might seem, especially in comparison with the lofty achievements lying beyond, its importance should never be underestimated, as it is this act which imparts direction and forward momentum to the entire practice of the Buddhist path. Since the going for refuge plays such a crucial role it is vital that the act be properly understood both in its own nature and in its implications for future development along the path. To open up the process of going for refuge to the eye of inner understanding, we here present an examination of the process in terms of its most significant aspects. These will be dealt with under the following eight headings: the reasons for taking refuge; the existence of a refuge; the identification of the refuge objects; the act of going for refuge; the function of going for refuge, methods of going for refuge; the corruption and breach of the going for refuge; and the similes for the refuges.

I. The Reasons for Taking Refuge

When it is said that the practice of the Buddha's teaching starts with taking refuge, this immediately raises an important question. The question is: "What need do we have for a refuge?" A refuge is a person, place, or thing giving protection from harm and danger. So when we begin a practice by going for refuge, this implies that the practice is intended to protect us from harm and danger. Our original question as to the need for a refuge can thus be translated into another question: "What is the harm and danger from which we need to be protected?" If we look at our lives in review we may not see ourselves exposed to any imminent personal danger. Our jobs may be steady, our health good, our families well-provided for, our resources adequate, and all this we may think gives us sufficient reason for considering ourselves secure. In such a case the going for refuge becomes entirely superfluous.

To understand the need for a refuge we must learn to see our position as it really is; that is, to see it accurately and against its total background. From the Buddhist perspective the human situation is similar to an iceberg: a small fraction of its mass appears above the surface, the vast substratum remains below, hidden out of view. Owing to the limits of our mental vision our insight fails to penetrate beneath the surface crust, to see our situation in its underlying depths. But there is no need to speak of what we cannot see; even what is immediately visible to us we rarely perceive with accuracy. The Buddha teaches that cognition is subservient to wish. In subtle ways concealed from ourselves, our desires condition our perceptions, twisting them to fit into the mould they themselves want to impose. Thus our minds work by way of selection and exclusion. We take note of those things agreeable to our pre-conceptions; we blot out or distort those that threaten to throw them into disarray.

From the standpoint of a deeper, more comprehensive understanding, the sense of security we ordinarily enjoy comes to view as a false security sustained by unawareness and the mind's capacity for subterfuge. Our position appears impregnable only because of the limitations and distortions of our outlook. The real way to safety, however, lies through correct insight, not through wishful thinking. To reach beyond fear and danger we must sharpen and widen our vision. We have to pierce through the deceptions that lull us into a comfortable complacency, to take a straight look down into the depths of our existence, without turning away uneasily or running after distractions. When we do so, it becomes increasingly clear that we move across a narrow footpath at the edge of a perilous abyss. In the words of the Buddha we are like a traveller passing through a thick forest bordered by a swamp and precipice; like a man swept away by a stream, seeking safety by clutching at reeds; like a sailor crossing a turbulent ocean; or like a man pursued by venomous snakes and murderous enemies. The dangers to which we are exposed may not always be immediately evident to us. Very often they are subtle, camouflaged, difficult to detect. But though we may not see them straightaway the plain fact remains that they are there all the same. If we wish to get free from them we must first make the effort to recognize them for what they are. This, however, calls for courage and determination.

On the basis of the Buddha's teaching, the dangers that make the quest for a refuge necessary can be grouped into three general classes: (1) the dangers pertaining to the present life; (2) those pertaining to future lives; and (3) those pertaining to the general course of existence. Each of these in turn involves two aspects: (A) an objective aspect which is a particular feature of the world; and (B) a subjective aspect which is a corresponding feature of our mental constitution. We will now consider each of these in turn.

1. The dangers pertaining to the present life

A. *Objective aspect.* The most obvious danger confronting us is the sheer fragility of our physical body and its material supports. From the moment we are born we are subject to disease, accident and injury. Nature troubles us with disasters such as earthquakes and floods, societal existence with crime, exploitation, repression and the threat of war. Events on the political, social, and economic fronts rarely pass very long without erupting into crisis. Attempts at reform and revolution always wind up repeating the same old story of stagnation, violence and consequent disillusionment. Even in times of relative tranquillity the order of our lives is never quite perfect. Something or other always seems to be getting out of focus. Snags and predicaments follow each other endlessly.

Even though we might be fortunate enough to escape the serious adversities there is one we cannot avoid. This is death. We are bound to die, and with all our wealth, expertise and power we still stand helpless before our inevitable mortality. Death weighs upon us from the time we are born. Every moment brings us closer to the inescapable. As we are drawn along, feeling secure in the midst of our comforts, we are like a man walking across a frozen lake, believing himself safe while the ice is cracking underfoot.

The dangers hanging over us are made even more problematic by their common feature of uncertainty. We have no knowledge when they will take place. If we knew calamity were going to hit, we could at least prepare in advance to resign ourselves stoically. But we do not enjoy even this much edge on the future. Because we lack the benefit of foreknowledge our hopes stand up straight, moment after moment, coupled with a vague presentiment that any second, in a flash, they can suddenly be dashed to pieces. Our health might be stricken down by illness, our business fail, our friends turn against us, our loved ones die—we do not know. We can have no guarantee that these reversals will not come upon us. Even death is only certain in that we can be sure it will strike. Exactly when it will strike still remains uncertain.

B. *Subjective aspect.* The adversities just sketched are objective features built into the world's constitution. On the one side there are calamity, crisis and predicament, on the other the radical uncertainty pervading them. The subjective aspect of the danger pertaining to the present life consists in our negative response to this twofold liability.

The element of uncertainty tends to provoke in us a persistent disquietude running beneath our surface self-assurance. At a deep interior level we sense the instability of our reliances, their transience and vulnerability to change, and this awareness produces a nagging apprehensiveness which rises at times to a pitch of anxiety. The source of our disquietude we may not always be able to pinpoint, but it remains lurking in the undercurrent of the mind—an unlocalized fear that our familiar supports will suddenly be stripped away, leaving us without our usual frame of reference.

This anxiety is sufficient disturbance in itself. Yet often our fears are confirmed. The course of events follows a pattern of its own, independent of our will, and the two do not necessarily coincide. The world throws up illness, loss and death, which strike when the time is ripe. When the course of events clashes with our will the outcome is pain and dissatisfaction. If the conflict is small we become angry, upset, depressed, or annoyed; if it is great we undergo anguish, grief, or despair. In either case a fundamental disharmony emerges from the cleavage between desire and the world, and the result, for us, is suffering.

The suffering that arises is not significant solely in itself. It has a symptomatic value, pointing to some more deeply grounded malady underlying it. This malady lies in our attitude towards the world. We operate out of a mental frame built up of expectations, projections and demands. We expect reality to conform to our wishes, to submit to our mandates, to confirm our preconceptions, but this it refuses to do. When it refuses we meet pain and disappointment, born from the conflict between expectation and actuality. To escape this suffering one of the two must change, our will or the world. Since we cannot alter the nature of the world to make it harmonize with our will, the only alternative is to change ourselves, by putting away attachment and aversion towards the world. We have to relinquish our clinging, to stop hankering and grasping, to learn to view the fluctuation of events with a detached equanimity free from the swing of elation and dejection.

The mind of equanimity, poised beyond the play of worldly opposites, is the highest safety and security, but to gain this equanimity we stand in need of guidance. The guidance available cannot protect us from objective adversity. It can only safeguard us from the dangers of a negative response—from anxiety, sorrow, frustration, and despair. This is the only protection possible, and because it grants us this essential protection such guidance can be considered a genuine refuge.

This is the first reason for going for refuge—the need for protection from negative reactions to the dangers besetting us here and now.

2. The dangers pertaining to future lives

A. *Objective aspect.* Our liability to harm and danger does not end with death. From the perspective of the Buddha's teaching the event of death is the prelude to a new birth and thus the potential passageway to still further suffering. The Buddha teaches that all living beings bound by ignorance and craving are subject to rebirth. So long as the basic drive to go on existing stands intact, the individualized current of existence continues on after death, inheriting the impressions and dispositions accumulated in the previous life. There is no soul to transmigrate from one life to the next, but there is an ongoing stream of consciousness which springs up following death in a new form appropriate to its own dominant tendencies.

Rebirth, according to Buddhism, can take place in any of six realms of becoming. The lowest of the six is the hells—regions of severe pain and torment where evil actions receive their due expiation. Then comes the animal kingdom where suffering prevails and brute force is the ruling power. Next is the realm of "hungry ghosts" (*petavisaya*), shadowy beings afflicted with strong desires they can never satisfy. Above them is the human world, with its familiar balance of happiness and suffering, virtue and evil. Then comes the world of the demi-gods (*asuras*), titanic beings obsessed by jealousy and ambition. And at the top stands the heavenly worlds inhabited by the *devas* or gods.

The first three realms of rebirth—the hells, the animal kingdom, and the realm of ghosts—together with the asuras, are called the "evil destinations" (*duggati*) or "planes of misery" (*apāyabhūmi*). They receive these names because of the preponderance of suffering found in them. The human world and the heavenly worlds are called, in contrast, the "happy destinations" (*sugati*) since they contain a preponderance of happiness. Rebirth in the evil destinations is considered especially unfortunate not only because of the intrinsic suffering they involve, but for another reason as well. Rebirth there is calamitous because escape from the evil destinations is extremely difficult. A fortunate rebirth depends on the performance of meritorious actions, but the beings in the evil destinations find little opportunity to acquire merit; thence the suffering in these realms tends to perpetuate itself in a circle very difficult to break. The Buddha says that if a yoke with a single hole was floating at random on the sea, and a blind turtle living in the sea were to surface once every hundred years, the likelihood of the turtle pushing his neck through the hole in the yoke would be greater than that of a being in the evil destinations regaining human status. For these two reasons—because of their inherent misery and because of the difficulty of escaping from them—rebirth in the evil destinations is a grave danger pertaining to the future life, from which we need protection.

B. *Subjective aspect.* Protection from a fall into the plane of misery cannot be obtained from others. It can only be obtained by avoiding the causes leading to an unfortunate rebirth. The cause for rebirth into any specific plane of existence lies in our *kamma*, that is, our willed actions and volitions. Kamma divides into two classes, the wholesome and the unwholesome. The former are actions motivated by detachment, kindness, and understanding, the latter are actions motivated by greed, hatred and delusion. These two classes of *kamma* generate rebirth into the two general planes of existence: wholesome *kamma* brings rebirth into the happy destinations, unwholesome *kamma* brings rebirth into the evil destinations.

We cannot obliterate the evil destinations themselves; they will continue on as long as the world itself endures. To avoid rebirth in these realms we can only keep watch over ourselves, by controlling our actions so that they do not spill over into the unwholesome courses leading to a plunge into the plane of misery. But to avoid generating unwholesome *kamma* we need help, and that for two principal reasons.

First, we need help because the avenues of action open to us are so varied and numerous that we often do not know which way to turn. Some actions are obviously wholesome or unwholesome, but others are difficult to evaluate, throwing us into perplexity when we run up against them. To choose correctly we require guidance—the clear indications of one who knows the ethical value of all actions and the pathways leading to the different realms of being.

The second reason we need help is because, even when we can discriminate right from wrong, we are often driven to pursue the wrong against our better judgment. Our actions do not always follow the counsel of our dispassionate decisions. They are often impulsive, driven by irrational urges we cannot master or control. By yielding to these drives we work our own harm even while helplessly watching ourselves do so. We have to gain mastery over our mind, to bring our capacity for action under the control of our sense of higher wisdom. But this is a task which requires discipline. To learn the right course of discipline we need the instructions of one who understands the subtle workings of the mind and can teach us how to conquer the obsessions which drive us into unhealthy, self-destructive patterns of behaviour. Because these instructions and the one who gives them help protect us from future harm and suffering, they can be considered a genuine refuge.

This is the second reason for going for refuge—the need to achieve mastery over our capacity for action so as to avoid falling into the evil destinations in future lives.

3. The dangers pertaining to the general course of existence

A. *Objective aspect.* The perils to which we are exposed are immensely greater than those just discussed. Beyond the evident adversities and misfortunes of the present life and the risk of a fall into the plane of misery, there is a more fundamental and comprehensive danger running through the entire course of worldly existence. This is the intrinsic unsatisfactoriness of *saṃsāra*. *Saṃsāra* is the cycle of becoming, the round of birth, aging and death, which has been revolving through beginningless time. Rebirth does not take place only once, leading to an eternity in the life to come. The life-process repeats itself over and over, the whole pattern spelling itself out again and total with each new turn: each single birth issues in decay and death, each single death gives way to a new birth. Rebirth can be fortunate or miserable, but wherever it occurs no halt is made to the revolution of the wheel. The law of impermanence imposes its decree upon the entire domain of sentient life; whatever arises must eventually cease. Even the heavens provide no outlet; life there also ends when the *kamma* that brought a heavenly birth is exhausted, to be followed by a re-arising in some other plane, perhaps in the miserable abodes.

Because of this pervasive transience, all forms of conditioned existence appear to the eye of wisdom as essentially *dukkha*, unsatisfactory or suffering. None of our supports and reliances is exempt from the necessity to change and pass away. Thence what we resort to for comfort and enjoyment is in reality a concealed form of suffering; what we rely on for security is itself exposed to danger; what we turn to for protection itself needs to be protected. Nothing that we want to hold to can be held onto forever, without perishing: "It is crumbling away, it is crumbling away, therefore it is called 'the world.'"

Youth issues in old age, health in sickness, life in death. All union ends in separation, and in the pain that accompanies separation. But to understand this situation in its full depth and gravity we must multiply it by infinity. From time without beginning we have been transmigrating through the round of existence, encountering the same experiences again and again with vertiginous frequency: birth, aging, sickness and death, separation and loss, failure and frustration. Repeatedly we have made the plunge into the plane of misery; times beyond counting we have been animal, ghost, and denizen of hell. Over and over we have experienced suffering, violence, grief, despair. The Buddha declares that the amount of tears and blood we have shed in the course of our saṃsāric wandering is greater than the waters in the ocean; the bones we have left behind could form a heap higher than the Himalaya mountains. We have met this suffering countless times in the past, and as long as the causes of our cycling in *saṃsāra* are not cut off we risk meeting more of the same in the course of our future wandering.

B. *Subjective aspect.* To escape from these dangers there is only one way of release: to turn away from all forms of existence, even the most sublime. But for the turning away to be effective we must cut off the causes that hold us in bondage to the round. The basic causes that sustain our wandering in *saṃsāra* lie within ourselves. We roam from life to life, the Buddha teaches, because we are driven by a profound insatiable urge for the perpetuation of our being. This urge the Buddha calls *bhava-taṇhā*, the craving for existence. While craving for existence remains operative, even if only latently, death itself is no barrier to the continuation of the life-process. Craving will bridge the vacuum created by death, generating a new form of existence determined by the previously accumulated storage of *kamma*. Thus craving and existence sustain each other in succession. Craving brings forth a new existence; the new existence gives the ground for craving to resume its search for gratification.

Underlying this vicious nexus which links together craving and repeated existence is a still more primordial factor called "ignorance" (*avijjā*). Ignorance is a basic unawareness of the true nature of things, a beginningless state of spiritual unknowing. The unawareness operates in two distinct ways: on one side it obscures correct cognition, on the other it creates a net of cognitive and perceptual distortions. Owing to ignorance we see beauty in things that are really repulsive, permanence in the impermanent, pleasure in the unpleasurable, and selfhood in selfless, transient, unsubstantial phenomena. These delusions sustain the forward drive of craving. Like a donkey chasing a carrot suspended from a cart, dangling before its face, we rush headlong after the appearances of beauty, permanence, pleasure and selfhood, only to find ourselves still empty-handed, more tightly entangled in the saṃsāric round.

To be freed from this futile and profitless pattern it is necessary to eradicate the craving that keeps it in motion, not merely temporarily but permanently and completely. To eradicate craving, the ignorance which supports it has to be dislodged, for as long as ignorance is allowed to weave its illusions the ground is present for craving to revive. The antidote to ignorance is wisdom (*paññā*). Wisdom is the penetrating knowledge which tears aside the veils of ignorance in order to "see things as they really are." It is not mere conceptual knowledge, but an experience that must be generated in ourselves; it has to be made direct, immediate and personal. To arouse this wisdom we need instruction, help, and guidance—someone who will teach us what we must understand and see for ourselves, and the methods by which we can arouse the liberating wisdom that will cut the cords binding us to repeated becoming. Since those who give this guidance, and the instructions themselves, provide protection from the perils of transmigration, they can be considered a genuine refuge.

This is the third reason for going for refuge—the need for deliverance from the pervasive unsatisfactoriness of *saṃsāra*.

II. The Existence of a Refuge

To realize that the human situation impels the search for a refuge is a necessary condition for taking refuge, but is not in itself a sufficient condition. To go for refuge we must also become convinced that an effective refuge actually exists. But before we can decide on the existence of a refuge we first have to determine for ourselves exactly what a refuge is.

The dictionary defines "refuge" as a shelter or protection from danger and distress, a person or place giving such protection, and an expedient used to obtain such protection. This tallies with the explanation of the Pali word *saraṇa*, meaning "refuge", which has come down in the Pali commentaries. The commentaries gloss the word *saraṇa* with another word meaning "to crush" (*hiṃsati*), explaining that "when people have gone for refuge, then by that very going for refuge it crushes, dispels, removes, and stops their fear, anguish, suffering, risk of unhappy rebirth and defilement."[1] These explanations suggest two essential qualifications of a refuge. (1) First, a refuge must be itself beyond danger and distress. A person or thing subject to danger is not secure in itself, and thus cannot give security to others. Only what is beyond fear and danger can be confidently relied upon for protection. (2) Second, the purported refuge must be accessible to us. A state beyond fear and danger that is inaccessible is irrelevant to our concerns and thus cannot function as a refuge. In order for something to serve as a refuge it must be approachable, capable of giving protection from danger.

From this abstract determination of the qualifications of a refuge we can return to the concrete question at hand. Does there exist a refuge able to give protection from the three types of dangers delineated above: from anxiety, frustration, sorrow and distress in the present life; from the risk of an unhappy destination after death; and from continued transmigration in *saṃsāra*? The task of working out an answer to this question has to be approached cautiously. We must recognize at once that an objectively verifiable, publicly demonstrable answer cannot be given. The existence of a refuge, or the specification of a particular refuge, cannot be proven logically in an irrefutable manner binding on all. The most that can be done is to adduce cogent grounds for believing that certain persons or objects possess the qualifications of a refuge. The rest depends upon faith, a confidence born out of trust, at least until that initial assent is transformed into knowledge by means of direct experience. But even then the verification remains inward and personal, a matter of subjective appropriation rather than of logical proof or objective demonstration.

From the Buddhist perspective there are three refuges which together make available complete protection from danger and distress. These three are the Buddha, the Dhamma, and the Saṅgha. The three are not separate refuges each sufficient in itself; rather they are interrelated members of a single effective

---

1. *Khuddakapāṭha-Aṭṭhakathā: Saraṇagatānaṃ ten'eva saraṇagamanena bhayaṃ santāsaṃ dukkhaṃ duggatiṃ parikilesaṃ hiṃsati vidhamati niharati nirodheti.*

refuge which divides into three by way of a distinction in the characteristics and functions of its members. Why such a distinction is necessary becomes clear if we consider the order in which the three are presented.

The Buddha comes first because he is a person. Since we are persons we naturally look to another person for guidance, inspiration, and direction. When it is ultimate deliverance that is at stake, what we look for in the first place is a person who has himself reached complete freedom from danger and can lead us to the same state of safety. This is the Buddha, the enlightened one, who comes first in the triad for the reason that he is the person who discovers, achieves, and proclaims the state of refuge. In the second place, we need that state of refuge itself, beyond fear and danger; we need a path leading to this goal; and we need a set of instructions guiding us along the path. This is the Dhamma, which as we will see has this threefold denotation. Then, in the third place, we need persons who began like ourselves—as ordinary people troubled by afflictions—and by following the way taught by the guide, reached the state of safety beyond fear and danger. This is the Saṅgha, the community of spiritual persons who have entered the path, realized the goal, and can now teach the path to others.

Within the triad, each member works in harmony with the other two to make the means of deliverance available and effective. The Buddha serves as the indicator of refuge. He is not a saviour who can bestow salvation through the agency of his person. Salvation or deliverance depends upon us, upon our own vigour and dedication in the practice of the teaching. The Buddha is primarily a teacher, an expounder of the path, who points out the way we ourselves must tread with our own energy and intelligence. The Dhamma is the actual refuge. As the goal of the teaching, the Dhamma is the state of security free from danger; as the path it is the means for arriving at the goal; and as the verbal teaching it is the body of instructions describing the way to practise the path. But to make effective use of the means at our disposal we need the help of others who are familiar with the path. Those who know the path make up the Saṅgha, the helpers in finding refuge, the union of spiritual friends who can lead us to our own attainment of the path.

This triadic structure of the three refuges can be understood with the aid of a simple analogy. If we are ill and want to get well we need a doctor to diagnose our illness and prescribe a remedy; we need medicine to cure our illness; and we need attendants to look after our requirements. The doctor and attendants cannot cure us. The most they can do for us is to give us the right medicine and make sure that we take it. The medicine is the actual remedy which restores our health. Similarly, when seeking relief from suffering and distress, we rely on the Buddha as the physician who can find out the cause of our illness and show us the way to get well; we rely on the Dhamma as the medicine which cures our afflictions; and we rely on the Saṅgha as the attendants who will help us take the medicine. To get well we have to take the medicine. We can't just sit back and expect the doctor to cure us all by himself. In the same way, to find deliverance from suffering, we have to practise the Dhamma, for the Dhamma is the actual refuge which leads to the state of deliverance.

III. Identification of the Objects of Refuge

The fruitfulness of the act of taking refuge is proportional to the depth and precision with which we understand the nature of the refuge-objects. Therefore these objects have to be identified with precision and correctly understood. Each refuge-object has a double layer of signification, one concrete and mundane, the other intangible and supramundane. The two are not entirely distinct, but intermesh in such a way that the former acts as a vehicle for the latter. An examination of each refuge in turn will make clear what their twofold signification is and how they interfuse.

1. The Buddha

The Buddha as refuge can be considered first. On one level the word "Buddha" refers to a particular figure—the man Siddhattha Gotama who lived in India in the fifth century B.C. When we take refuge in the Buddha, we take refuge in this person, for he is the teacher of the Dhamma and the historical founder of Buddhism. However, in going to him for refuge, we do not take refuge in him merely in his concrete particularity. We rely upon him as the Buddha, the enlightened one, and this has a significance transcending the limits of what can be given by empirical, historical fact. What enables the Buddha to function as a refuge is his actualization of a supramundane attainment. This attainment is the state of Buddhahood or perfect enlightenment, a state which has been realized by other persons in the past and will be realized again in the future. Those who realize this state are Buddhas. When we take refuge in the Buddha we rely upon him as a refuge because he embodies this attainment in himself. It is his Buddhahood that makes the Buddha a refuge.

But what is the Buddhahood of the Buddha? In brief the Buddhahood of the Buddha is the sum total of the qualities possessed by that person named Gotama which make him a Buddha. These qualities can be summed up as the abandonment of all defects and the acquisition of all virtues.

The defects abandoned are the defilements (*kilesa*) together with their residual impressions (*vasana*). The defilements are afflictive mental forces which cause inner corruption and disturbance and motivate unwholesome actions. Their principle members are greed, hatred, and delusion; from these all the secondary defilements derive. In the Buddha these defilements have been abandoned totally, completely, and finally. They are abandoned *totally* in that all defilements have been destroyed with none remaining. They are abandoned *completely* in that each one has been destroyed at the root, without residue. And they have been abandoned *finally* in that they can never arise again in the future.

The virtues acquired by the Buddha are very numerous, but two stand out as paramount: great wisdom (*mahāpaññā*) and great compassion (*mahākaruṇā*). The great wisdom of the Buddha has two aspects—extensiveness of range and profundity of view. Through the extensive range of his wisdom the Buddha understands the totality of existent phenomena; through his profundity of view he understands the precise mode of existence of each phenomenon.

The Buddha's wisdom does not abide in passive contemplation but issues in great compassion. Through his great compassion the Buddha comes forth to work for the welfare of others. He takes up the burden of toiling for the good of sentient beings, actively and fearlessly, in order to lead them to deliverance from suffering.

When we go for refuge to the Buddha we resort to him as the supreme embodiment of purity, wisdom and compassion, the peerless teacher who can guide us to safety out of the perilous ocean of *saṃsāra*.

2. The Dhamma

The Dhamma too involves a double reference. At the elementary level the word "Dhamma" signifies the teaching of the Buddha—the conceptually formulated, verbally expressed set of doctrines taught by or deriving from the historical figure Gotama. This teaching, called "the transmission" (*āgama*), is contained in the *Tipiṭaka* or three collections of scripture and in the commentaries and expository works which explain them. The three collections are the *Vinayapiṭaka*, the *Suttapiṭaka*, and the *Abhidhammapiṭaka*. The *Vinayapiṭaka* collects together all the monastic rules and regulations detailing the discipline for Buddhist monks and nuns. The *Suttapiṭaka* contains the discourses of the Buddha expounding his doctrine and the practice of his path. The *Abhidhammapiṭaka* presents an exposition of the sphere of actuality from the standpoint of a precise philosophical understanding which analyzes actuality into its fundamental constituting elements and shows how these elements lock together through a network of conditional relations.

The verbally transmitted Dhamma contained in the scriptures and commentaries serves as the conduit to a deeper level of meaning communicated through its words and expressions. This is the Dhamma of actual achievement (*adhigama*), which comprises the path (*magga*) and the goal (*attha*). The goal—*Nibbāna*—is the final end of the teaching, the complete cessation of suffering, the unconditioned state outside and beyond the round of impermanent phenomena making up *saṃsāra*. This goal is to be reached by a specific path, a course of practice bringing its attainment, namely the noble eightfold path—right views, right intentions, right speech, right action, right livelihood, right effort, right mindfulness, and right concentration. The path divides into two stages, a mundane path and a supramundane path. The mundane path is the course of application developed when its factors are cultivated in daily life and in periods of intensified practice. The supramundane path is a state of wisdom-consciousness that arises when all the requisite conditions for realization are fully matured, usually at the peak of intensified practice. This path actually represents a stage in the experience of enlightenment, having the dual function of realizing *Nibbāna* and eradicating defilements.

The supramundane path comes only in momentary breakthroughs which, when they occur, effect radical transformations in the structure of the mind. These breakthroughs are four in number, called the four paths. The four divide according to their ability to cut the successively subtler "fetters" causing *saṃsāra*. The first path, the initial breakthrough to enlightenment, is the path of stream-entry (*sotāpattimagga*), which eradicates the fetters of ego-affirming views, doubt, and clinging to rites and wrong observances. The second, called the path of the once-returner (*sakadāgāmimagga*), does not cut off any fetters but weakens their underlying roots. The third, the path of the non-returner (*anāgāmimagga*), eliminates the fetters of sensual desire and ill-will. And the fourth, the path of arahatship (*arahattamagga*), eradicates the five remaining fetters—desire for existence in the spheres of fine material and immaterial being, conceit, restlessness, and ignorance. Each path-moment is followed immediately by several moments of another supramundane experience called fruition (*phala*), which comes in four stages corresponding to the four paths. Fruition marks the enjoyment of the freedom from defilement effected by the preceding path-moment. It is the state of release or experiential freedom which comes when the fetters are broken.

Earlier it was said that the Dhamma is the actual refuge. In the light of the distinctions just drawn this statement can now be made more precise. The verbal teaching is essentially a map, a body of instructions and guidelines. Since we have to rely on these instructions to realize the goal, the teaching counts as an actual refuge, but it is so in a derivative way. Thus we can call it an actual but indirect refuge. The mundane path is direct, since it must be practised, but because it serves principally as preparation for the supramundane path its function is purely provisional; thus it is an actual and direct but provisional refuge. The supramundane path apprehends *Nibbāna*, and once attained leads irreversibly to the goal; thence it may be called an actual, direct, and superior refuge. However, even the supramundane path is a conditioned phenomenon sharing the characteristic of impermanence common to all conditioned phenomena. Moreover, as a means to an end, it possesses instrumental value only, not intrinsic value. Thus its status as a refuge is not ultimate. Ultimate status as a refuge belongs exclusively to the goal, to the unconditioned state of *Nibbāna*, which therefore among all three refuges can alone be considered the refuge which is actual, direct, superior, and ultimate. It is the final resort, the island of peace, the sanctuary offering permanent shelter from the fears and dangers of saṃsāric becoming.

3. The Saṅgha

At the conventional or mundane level the Saṅgha signifies the Bhikkhu-Saṅgha, the order of monks. The Saṅgha here is an institutional body governed by formally promulgated regulations. Its doors of membership are open to any candidate meeting the required standards. All that is needed to enter the Saṅgha is to undergo ordination according to the procedure laid down in the *Vinaya*, the system of monastic discipline.

Despite its formal character, the order of monks fulfils an indispensable role in the preservation and perpetuation of the Buddha's dispensation. In an unbroken lineage extending back over twenty-five hundred years, the monastic order has served as the custodian of the Dhamma. The mode of life it makes possible permits it to exercise this function. The Buddha's dispensation, as we suggested, possesses a twofold character; it is a path of practice leading to liberation from suffering, and also a distinctive set of doctrines embedded in scriptures expounding the details of this path. The Saṅgha bears the responsibility for maintaining both aspects of the dispensation. Its members assume the burden of continuing the tradition of practice with the aim of showing that the goal can be realized and deliverance attained. They also take up the task of preserving the doctrines, seeing to it that the scriptures are taught and transmitted to posterity free from distortion and misinterpretation. For these reasons the institutional Saṅgha is extremely vital to the perpetuation of the Buddha's teaching.

However, the order of monks is not itself the Saṅgha which takes the position of the third refuge. The Saṅgha which serves as refuge is not an institutional body but an unchartered spiritual community comprising all those who have achieved penetration of the innermost meaning of the Buddha's teaching. The Sangha-refuge is the ariyan Saṅgha, the noble community, made up exclusively of ariyans, persons of superior spiritual stature. Its membership is not bound together by formal ecclesiastical ties but by the invisible bond of a common inward realization. The one requirement for admission is the attainment of this realization, which in itself is sufficient to grant entrance.

Though the way of life laid down for the monastic order, with its emphasis on renunciation and meditation, is most conducive to attaining the state of an ariyan, the monastic Saṅgha and the ariyan Saṅgha are not coextensive. Their makeup can differ, and that for two reasons: first, because many monks—the vast majority in fact—are still worldlings (*puthujjana*) and thence cannot function as a refuge; and second, because the ariyan Saṅgha can also include laymen. Membership in the ariyan Saṅgha depends solely on spiritual achievement and not on formal ordination. Anyone—layman or monk—who penetrates the Buddha's teaching by direct vision gains admission through that very attainment itself.[2]

The membership of the ariyan Saṅgha comprises eight types of persons, which unite into four pairs. The first pair consists of the person standing on the path of stream-entry and the stream-enterer, who have entered the way to deliverance and will attain the goal in a maximum of seven lives; the second pair is the person standing on the path of the once-returner and the once-returner, who will return to the human world only one more time before reaching the goal; the third pair is the person standing on the path of the non-returner and the non-returner, who will not come back to the human world again but will take rebirth in a pure heavenly world where he will reach the final goal; and the fourth pair is the person standing on the path of arahatship and the *arahat*, who has expelled all defilements and cut off the ten fetters causing bondage to *saṃsāra*.

---

2. It should be remarked that although the ariyan Saṅgha can include lay persons, the word "Saṅgha" is never used in the Theravada Buddhist tradition to include the entire body of practitioners of the teaching. In ordinary usage the word signifies the order of monks. Any extension beyond this would tend to be considered unjustified.

The eight persons can be divided in another way into two general classes. One class consists of those who, by penetrating the teaching, have entered the supramundane path to liberation but still must practise further to arrive at the goal. These include the first seven types of ariyan persons, who are collectively called "trainees" or "learners" (*sekha*) because they are still in the process of training. The second class comprises the arahats, who have completed the practice and fully actualized the goal. These are called "beyond training" (*asekha*) because they have no further training left to undertake.

Both the learners and the arahats have directly understood the essential import of the Buddha's teaching for themselves. The teaching has taken root in them, and to the extent that any work remains to be done, they no longer depend on others to bring it to its consummation. By virtue of this inner mastery, these individuals possess the qualifications needed to guide others towards the goal. Hence the ariyan Saṅgha, the community of noble persons, can function as a refuge.

IV. The Act of Going for Refuge

To enter the door to the teaching of the Buddha it is not enough merely to know the reference of the refuge-objects. The door of entrance to the teaching is the going for refuge to the Buddha, the Dhamma, and the Saṅgha. To understand what the refuge-objects mean is one thing, to go to them for refuge is another, and it is the going for refuge alone that constitutes the actual entrance to the dispensation.

But what is the going for refuge? At first glance it would seem to be the formal commitment to the Triple Gem expressed by reciting the formula of refuge, for it is this act which marks the embracing of the Buddha's teaching. Such an understanding, however, would be superficial. The treatises make it clear that the true going for refuge involves much more than the reciting of a pre-established formula. They indicate that beneath the verbal profession of taking refuge there runs concurrently another process that is essentially inward and spiritual. This other process is the mental commitment to the taking of refuge.

The going for refuge, as defined by the commentaries, is in reality an occasion of consciousness: "It is an act of consciousness devoid of defilements, (motivated) by confidence in and reverence for (the Triple Gem), taking (the Triple Gem) as the supreme resort."[3] That the act is said to be "devoid of defilements" stresses the need for sincerity of aim. Refuge is not pure if undertaken with defiled motivation—out of desire for recognition, pride, or fear of blame. The only valid motivation for taking refuge is confidence and reverence directed towards the Triple Gem. The act of consciousness motivated by confidence and reverence occurs "taking the Triple Gem as the supreme resort" (*pārāyana*). That the Triple Gem is taken as the "supreme resort" means that it is perceived as the sole source of deliverance. By turning to the threefold refuge as supreme resort, the going for refuge becomes an act of opening and self-surrender. We drop our defences before the objects of refuge and open ourselves to their capacity to help. We surrender our ego, our claim to self-sufficiency, and reach out to the refuge-objects in the trust that they can guide us to release from our confusion, turmoil, and pain.

Like any other act of consciousness the going for refuge is a complex process made up of many factors. These factors can be classified by way of three basic faculties: intelligence, volition, and emotion. To bring the act of going for refuge into clearer focus we will take the mental process behind the outer act, divide it by way of these faculties, and see how each contributes to its total character. That is, we will examine the going for refuge as an act of intelligence, will, and emotion.

Before doing this, however, one word of caution is necessary. Any particular phenomenon represents far more than is immediately visible even to a deeply probing inspection. A seed, for example, has a much greater significance than the grain of organic matter that meets the eye. On one side it collects into itself the entire history of the trees that went into its making; on the other it points beyond to the many potential trees locked up in its hull. Similarly the act of consciousness involved in taking refuge represents the crystallization of a vast network of forces

---

3. *Tappasādataggarutahi vihataviddhaṃsitakileso tappārāyanatākārappavatto cittuppādo saraṇagamanaṃ.*

extending backwards, forwards, and outwards in all directions. It simultaneously stands for the many lines of experience converging upon its formation out of the dim recesses of the past, and the potential for future lines of development barely adumbrated in its own immediate content. This applies equally to the act of taking refuge as a whole and to each of its constituting factors: both the whole and its parts must be seen as momentary concretions with a vast history, past and future, hidden from our sight. Therefore what emerges out of an analytical scrutiny of the refuge-act should be understood to be only a fraction of what the act implies by way of background and future evolution.

Turning to the act of taking refuge itself, we find in the first place that it is an act of understanding. Though inspired by reverence and trust, it must be guided by vision, by an intelligent perceptivity which protects it from the dangers of blind emotion. The faculty of intelligence steers the act of refuge towards the actualization of its inner urge for liberation. It distinguishes the goal from the distractions, and prevents the aspirant from deviating from his quest for the goal to go in pursuit of futile ends. For this reason we find that in the formulation of the noble eightfold path, right view is given first. To follow the path we must see where it leads from, where it goes, and the steps that must be taken to get from the one point to the other.

In its initial form the faculty of intelligence involved in taking refuge comprehends the basic unsatisfactoriness of existence which makes reliance on a refuge necessary. Suffering has to be seen as a pervasive feature infecting our existence at its root, which cannot be eliminated by superficial palliatives but only by a throughgoing treatment. We must come to see further that the causes of our dissatisfaction and unrest lie within ourselves, in our clinging, craving, and delusions, and that to get free from suffering we must follow a course which extinguishes its causes.

The mind also has to grasp the reliability of the refuge-objects. Absolute certainty as to the emancipating power of the teaching can only come later, with the attainment of the path, but already at the outset an intelligent conviction must be established that the refuge-objects are capable of providing help. To this end the Buddha has to be examined by investigating the records of his life and character; his teaching searched for contradictions and irrationalities; and the Saṅgha approached to see if it is worthy of trust and confidence. Only if they pass these tests can they be considered dependable supports for the achievement of our ultimate aim.

Intelligence comes into play not only with the initial decision to take refuge, but throughout the entire course of practice. The growth of understanding brings a deeper commitment to the refuges, and the deepening of the inner refuge facilitates the growth of understanding. The climax of this process of reciprocal development is the attainment of the supramundane path. When the path arises, penetrating the truth of the teaching, the refuge becomes irreversible, for it has been verified by direct experience.

The going for refuge is also an act of volition. It results from a voluntary decision free from coercion or outside pressures. It is a choice that must be *aparappaccaya*, "not compelled by others." This freely chosen act brings about a far-reaching restructuring of volition. Whereas previously the will might have been scattered among a multitude of interests and concerns, when the taking of refuge gains ascendancy the will becomes ordered in a unified way determined by the new commitment. The spiritual ideal comes to the centre of the inner life, expelling the less crucial concerns and relegating the others to a position subordinate to its own direction. In this way the act of refuge brings to the mind a harmonization of values, which now ascend to and converge upon the fundamental aspiration for deliverance as the guiding purpose of all activity.

The act of taking refuge also effects a deep-seated reversal in the movement of the will. Before refuge is taken, the will tends to move in an outward direction, pushing for the extension of its bounds of self-identity. It seeks to gain increasing territory for the self, to widen the range of ownership, control and domination. When refuge is sought in the teaching of the Buddha the ground is laid for this pattern to be undermined and turned around. The Buddha teaches that our drive for self-expansion is the root of our bondage. It is a mode of craving, of grasping and clinging, leading headlong into frustration and despair. When this is understood the danger in egocentric seeking comes to the surface and the will turns in the opposite direction, moving towards renunciation and detachment. The objects of clinging are gradually relinquished, the sense of "I" and "mine" withdrawn from the objects to which it has attached itself. Ultimate deliverance is now seen to lie, not in the extension of the ego to the limits of infinity, but in the utter abolition of the ego-delusion at its base.

The third aspect of going for refuge is the emotional. While going for refuge requires more than emotional fervour, it also cannot come to full fruition without the inspiring upward pull of the emotions. The emotions entering into the refuge act are principally three: confidence, reverence, and love. Confidence (*pasada*) is a feeling of serene trust in the protective power of the refuge-objects, based on a clear understanding of their qualities and functions. Confidence gives rise to reverence (*garava*), a sense of awe, esteem, and veneration born from a growing awareness of the sublime and lofty nature of the Triple Gem. Yet this reverence does not remain cool, formal, and aloof. As we experience the transforming effect of the Dhamma on our life, reverence awakens (*pema*). Love adds the element of warmth and vitality to the spiritual life. It kindles the flame of devotion, coming to expression in acts of dedicated service by which we seek to extend the protective and liberative capacity of the threefold refuge to others.

V. The Function of Going for Refuge

The going for refuge is the door of entrance to the teaching of the Buddha. It functions in the context of the teaching as the entranceway to all the practices of the Buddhist discipline. To engage in the practices in their proper setting we have to enter them through the door of taking refuge, just as to go into a restaurant and have a meal we have to enter through the door. If we merely stand outside the restaurant and read the menu on the window we may come away with a thorough knowledge of the menu but not with a satisfied appetite. Similarly, by merely studying and admiring the Buddha's teaching we do not enter upon its practice. Even if we abstract certain elements of practice for our personal use without first taking refuge, our efforts cannot count as the actual practice of the Buddha's teaching. They are only practices derived from the teaching, or practices in harmony with the teaching, but so long as they are not conjoined with a mental attitude of taking refuge in the Triple Gem they have not yet become the practice of the Buddha's teaching.

To bring out the significance of going for refuge we can consider a contrast between two individuals. One meticulously observes the moral principles embedded in the five precepts (*pañcasīla*). He does not formally undertake the precepts in the context of Buddhist ethical practice but spontaneously conforms to the standards of conduct they enjoin through his own innate sense of right and wrong; that is, he follows them as part of natural morality. We might further suppose that he practises meditation several hours a day, but does this not in the framework of the Dhamma but simply as a means to enjoy peace of mind here and now. We can further suppose that this person has met the Buddha's teaching, appreciates it and respects it, but does not feel sufficiently convinced to acknowledge its truth or find himself impelled to go for refuge.

On the other hand let us suppose there is another person whose circumstances prevent perfect observance of the precepts and who cannot find leisure for practising meditation. But though he lacks these achievements, from the depths of his heart, with full sincerity, understanding, and dedication of purpose he has gone for refuge to the Triple Gem. Comparing these two persons we can ask whose mental attitude is of greater long-term spiritual value—that of the person who without going for refuge observes the moral principles embedded in the five precepts and practises meditation several hours a day, or that of the other person who cannot accomplish these practices but has sincerely gone for refuge to the Buddha, Dhamma, and Saṅgha. No clear pronouncement on this case is found in the *suttas* and commentaries, but enough indication is given to support an intelligent guess. On this basis we would say that the mental attitude of the second person, who has gone for refuge with clear understanding and sincerity of heart, is of greater long-term spiritual value. The reason for such a judgment is as follows.

As a result of his moral and meditative practices the first individual will enjoy peace and happiness in his present life, and will accumulate merit which will lead to a favourable rebirth in the future. However, when that merit ripens, it will become exhausted and expend its force without leading to further spiritual development. When the fortunate rebirth resulting from the merit comes to an end, it will be followed by rebirth in some other plane, as determined by stored-up *kamma*, and the person will continue to revolve in the cycle of existence. His virtuous undertakings do not contribute directly to the transcending of the saṃsāric round.

On the other hand the person who has sincerely gone for refuge to the Triple Gem, without being capable of higher practices, still lays the foundation for spiritual progress in future lives merely by his heartfelt act of seeking refuge. Of course he has to reap the results of his *kamma* and cannot escape them by taking refuge, but all the same the mental act of going for refuge, if it is truly the focus of his inner life, becomes a powerful positive *kamma* in itself. It will function as a link tending to bring him into connection with the Buddha's dispensation in future lives, thereby aiding his chances for further progress. And if he fails to reach deliverance within the dispensation of the present Buddha it will very likely lead him to the dispensations of future Buddhas, until he eventually reaches the goal. Since this all comes about through the germination of that mental act of going for refuge, we can understand that the taking of refuge is very essential.

The importance of going for refuge can be further gauged through a textual simile comparing faith to a seed. Since faith is the motivating force behind the act of refuge, the analogy may be transferred to the refuge-act itself. We explained earlier that the mental act of going for refuge calls into play three cardinal faculties—understanding, will, and emotion. These three faculties are already present even in that very simple, basic act of seeking refuge, contained there as seeds with the potential to develop into the flowers and fruits of the Buddhist spiritual life. The understanding that leads a man to go for refuge—the understanding of the danger and fearfulness of saṃsāric existence—this is the seed for the faculty of wisdom which eventually issues in direct penetration of the four noble truths. The element of volition is the seed for the will to renunciation—the driving force that impels a man to renounce his craving, enjoyments, and egoistic clingings in order to go forth in search of liberation. It functions as well as the seed for the practice of right effort, the sixth factor of the noble eightfold path, by which we strive to abandon unwholesome impure mental states and to cultivate the wholesome and pure states. Devotion and reverence for the Triple Gem—these become the seed for the germination of "unwavering confidence" (*aveccapasāda*), the assurance of a noble disciple whose confidence in the Buddha, Dhamma, and Saṅgha can never be shaken by any outside force. In this way the simple act of going for refuge serves as the threefold seed for the development of the higher faculties of right understanding, right effort, and unshakeable confidence. From this example we can again understand the taking of refuge to be very essential.

VI. The Methods of Going for Refuge

The methods of going for refuge divide into two general kinds: the superior or supramundane going for refuge and the common or mundane going for refuge. The supramundane going for refuge is the going for refuge of a superior person, that is, of an ariyan disciple who has reached the supramundane path leading irreversibly to *Nibbāna*. When such a person goes for refuge to the Triple Gem, his going for refuge is a superior refuge, unshakeable and invincible. The ariyan person can never again, through the remainder of his future births (which amount to a maximum of only seven), go for refuge to any other teacher than the Buddha, to any other doctrine than the Dhamma, or to any other spiritual community than the Saṅgha. The Buddha says that the confidence such a disciple places in the Triple Gem cannot be shaken by anyone in the world, that it is firmly grounded and immovable.

The common way of going for refuges is the way in which ordinary persons, the vast majority below the ariyan plane, go for refuge to the Triple Gem. This can be subdivided into two types: the initial going for refuge and the recurrent going for refuge.

The initial going for refuge is the act of formally going for refuge for the first time. When a person has studied the basic principles of the Buddha's teaching, undertaken some of its practices, and become convinced of its value for his life, he may want to commit himself to the teaching by making an outer profession of his conviction. Strictly speaking, as soon as there arises in his mind an act of consciousness which takes the Buddha, Dhamma, and Saṅgha as his guiding ideal, that person has gone for refuge to the Triple Gem and become a Buddhist lay disciple (*upāsaka*). However, within the Buddhist tradition it is generally considered to be insufficient under normal circumstances to rest content with merely going for refuge by an internal act of dedication. If one has sincerely become convinced of the truth of the Buddha's teaching, and wishes to follow the teaching, it is preferable, when possible, to conform to the prescribed way of going for refuge that has come down in the Buddhist tradition. This way is to receive the three refuges from a bhikkhu, a Buddhist monk who has taken full ordination and remains in good standing in the monastic Order.

After one has decided to go for refuge, one should seek out a qualified monk—one's own spiritual teacher or another respected member of the Order—discuss one's intentions with him, and make arrangements for undergoing the ceremony. When the day arrives, one should come to the monastery or temple bringing offerings such as candles, incense, and flowers for the shrine room and a small gift for the preceptor. After making the offerings, one should, in the presence of the preceptor, join the palms together in respectful salutation (*añjali*), bow down three times before the image of the Buddha, and pay respects to the Buddha, Dhamma, and Saṅgha, as represented by the images and symbols in the shrine. Then, kneeling in front of the shrine, one should request the bhikkhu to give the three refuges. The bhikkhu will reply: "Repeat after me" and then recite:

Buddhaṃ saraṇaṃ gacchāmi
Dhammaṃ saraṇaṃ gacchāmi
Saṅghaṃ saraṇaṃ gacchāmi

> I go for refuge to the Buddha.
> I go for refuge to the Dhamma.
> I go for refuge to the Saṅgha.

Dutiyampi Buddhaṃ saraṇaṃ gacchāmi

> A second time I go for refuge to the Buddha.

Dutiyampi Dhammaṃ saraṇaṃ gacchāmi

> A second time I go for refuge to the Dhamma.

Dutiyampi Saṅghaṃ saraṇaṃ gacchāmi

> A second time I go for refuge to the Saṅgha.

Tatiyampi Buddhaṃ saraṇaṃ gacchāmi
   A third time I go for refuge to the Buddha.
Tatiyampi Dhammaṃ saraṇaṃ gacchāmi
   A third time I go for refuge to the Dhamma.
Tatiyampi Saṅghaṃ saraṇaṃ gacchāmi
   A third time I go for refuge to the Saṅgha.

The candidate should repeat each line after the bhikkhu. At the end the bhikkhu will say: *Saraṇagamanaṃ sampuṇṇaṃ,* "The going for refuge is completed." With this, one formally becomes a lay follower of the Buddha, and remains such so long as the going for refuge stands intact. But to make the going for refuge especially strong and definitive, the candidate may confirm his acceptance of the refuge by declaring to the monk: "Venerable sir, please accept me as a lay disciple gone for refuge from this day forth until the end of my life." This phrase is added to show one's resolution to hold to the three refuges as one's guiding ideal for the rest of one's life. Following the declaration of the refuges, the bhikkhu will usually administer the five precepts, the ethical observances of abstaining from taking life, stealing, sexual misconduct, false speech, and intoxicants. These will be discussed below in the second half of this paper.

By undergoing the formal ceremony of taking refuge, one openly embraces the teaching of the Buddha and becomes for the first time a self-declared follower of the Master. However, going for refuge should not be an event which occurs only once in a lifetime and then is allowed to fade into the background. Going for refuge is a method of cultivation, a practice of inner development which should be undertaken regularly, repeated and renewed every day as part of one's daily routine. Just as we care for our body by washing it each morning, so we should also take care of our mind by implanting in it each day the fundamental seed for our development along the Buddhist path, that is, the going for refuge. Preferably the going for refuge should be done twice each day, with each refuge repeated three times; but if a second recitation is too difficult to fit in, as a minimum one recitation should be done every day, with three repetitions of each refuge.

The daily undertaking of the refuges is best done in a shrine room or before a household altar with a Buddha-image. The actual recitation should be preceded by the offering of candles, incense, and possibly flowers. After making the offerings one should make three salutations before the Buddha-image and then remain kneeling with the hands held out palms joined. Before actually reciting the refuge formula it may be helpful to visualize to oneself the three objects of refuge arousing the feeling that one is in their presence. To represent the Buddha one can visualize an inspiring picture or statue of the Master. The Dhamma can be represented by visualizing, in front of the Buddha, three volumes of scripture to symbolize the Tipiṭaka, the three collections of Buddhist scriptures. The Dhamma can also be represented by the *dhammacakka*, the "wheel of Dhamma," with its eight spokes symbolizing the noble eightfold path converging upon *Nibbāna* at the hub; it should be bright and beautiful, radiating a golden light. To represent the Saṅgha one can visualize on either side of the Buddha the two chief disciples, Sāriputta and Moggallāna; alternatively, one can visualize around the Buddha a group of monks, all of them adepts of the teaching, arahats who have conquered the defilements and reached perfect emancipation.

Generating deep faith and confidence, while retaining the visualized images before one's inner eye, one should recite the refuge-formula three times with feeling and conviction. If one is undertaking the practice of meditation it is especially important to recite the refuge-formula before beginning the practice, for this gives needed inspiration to sustain the endeavour through the difficulties that may be encountered along the way. For this reason those who undertake intensive meditation and go off into solitude preface their practice, not with the usual method of recitation, but with a special variation: *Ahaṃ attānaṃ Buddhassa niyyātemi Dhammassa Saṅghassa*, "My person I surrender to the Buddha, Dhamma, and Saṅgha." By surrendering his person and life to the Triple Gem the yogin shields himself against the obstacles which might arise to impede his progress and safeguards himself against egoistic clinging to the attainments he might reach. However, this variation on the refuge-formula should not be undertaken lightly, as its consequences are very serious. For ordinary purposes it is enough to use the standard formula for daily recitation.

VII. Corruptions and Breach of the Refuge

Corruptions of the refuge are factors that make the going for refuge impure, insincere, and ineffective. According to the commentaries there are three factors that defile the going for refuge—ignorance, doubt, and wrong views. If one does not understand the reasons for going for refuge, the meaning of taking refuge, or the qualities of the refuge-objects, this lack of understanding is a form of ignorance which corrupts the going for refuge. Doubt corrupts the refuge insofar as the person overcome by doubt cannot settle confidence firmly in the Triple Gem. His commitment to the refuge is tainted by inner perplexity, suspicion, and indecision. The defilement of wrong views means a wrong understanding of the act of refuge or the refuge-objects. A person holding wrong views goes for refuge with the thought that the refuge-act is a sufficient guarantee of deliverance; or he believes that the Buddha is a god with the power to save him, or that the Dhamma teaches the existence of an eternal self, or that the Saṅgha functions as an intercessory body with the ability to mediate his salvation. Even though the refuge act is defiled by these corruptions, as long as a person regards the Triple Gem as his supreme reliance his going for refuge is intact and he remains a Buddhist follower. But though the refuge is intact, his attitude of taking refuge is defective and has to be purified. Such purification can come about if he meets a proper teacher to give him instruction and help him overcome his ignorance, doubts, and wrong views.

The breach of the refuge means the breaking or violation of the commitment to the threefold refuge. A breach of the refuge occurs when a person who has gone for refuge comes to regard some counterpart to the three refuges as his guiding ideal or supreme reliance. If he comes to regard another spiritual teacher as superior to the Buddha, or as possessing greater spiritual authority than the Buddha, then his going for refuge to the Buddha is broken. If he comes to regard another religious teaching as superior to the Dhamma, or resorts to some other system of practice as his means to deliverance, then his going for refuge to the Dhamma is broken. If he comes to regard some spiritual community other than the ariyan Saṅgha as endowed with supramundane status, or as occupying a higher spiritual level than the ariyan Saṅgha, then his going for refuge to the Saṅgha is broken. In order for the refuge-act to remain valid and intact, the Triple Gem must be recognized as the exclusive resort for ultimate deliverance: "For me there is no other refuge, the Buddha, Dhamma, and Saṅgha are my supreme refuge."[4]

Breaking the commitment to any of the three refuge-objects breaks the commitment to all of them, since the effectiveness of the refuge-act requires the recognition of the interdependence and inseparability of the three. Thus by adopting an attitude which bestows the status of a supreme reliance upon anything outside the Triple Gem, one cuts off the going for refuge and relinquishes one's claim to be a disciple of the Buddha, Dhamma and Saṅgha.[5] In order to become valid once again the going for refuge must be renewed, preferably by confessing one's lapse and then by once more going through the entire formal ceremony of taking refuge.

VIII. The Similes for the Refuges

In the traditional Indian method of exposition, no account or treatment of a theme is considered complete unless it has been illustrated by similes. Therefore we conclude this explanation of going for refuge with a look at some of the classical similes for the objects of refuge. Though many beautiful similes are given in the texts, from fear of prolixity we here limit ourselves to four.

The first simile compares the Buddha to the sun, for his appearance in the world is like the sun rising over the horizon. His teaching of the true Dhamma is like the net of the sun's rays spreading out over the earth, dispelling the darkness and cold of the night, giving warmth and light to all beings. The Saṅgha is like the beings for whom the darkness of night has been dispelled, who go about their affairs enjoying the warmth and radiance of the sun.

---

4. *Natthi me saraṇaṃ aññaṃ Buddho (... Dhammo ... Saṅgho) me saraṇaṃ varaṃ*—traditional Buddhist devotional stanzas.
5. Though the traditional literature always explains the breach of the refuge as occurring though a change of allegiance, it would seem that a complete loss of interest in the Triple Gem and the feeling that reliance on a refuge is not necessary would also break the commitment to the threefold refuge.

The second simile compares the Buddha to the full moon, the jewel of the night-time sky. His teaching of the Dhamma is like the moon shedding its beams of light over the world, cooling off the heat of the day. The Saṅgha is like the persons who go out in the night to see and enjoy the refreshing splendour of the moonlight.

In the third simile the Buddha is likened to a great rain cloud spreading out across the countryside at a time when the land has been parched with a long summer's heat. The teaching of the true Dhamma is like the downpour of the rain, which inundates the land giving water to the plants and vegetation. The Saṅgha is like the plants—the trees, shrubs, bushes, and grass—which thrive and flourish when nourished by the rain pouring down from the cloud.

The fourth simile compares the Buddha to a lotus flower, the paragon of beauty and purity. Just as a lotus grows up in a muddy lake, but rises above the water and stands in full splendour unsoiled by the mud, so the Buddha, having grown up in the world, overcomes the world and abides in its midst untainted by its impurities. The Buddha's teaching of the true Dhamma is like the sweet perfumed fragrance emitted by the lotus flower, giving delight to all. And the Saṅgha is like the host of bees who collect around the lotus, gather up the pollen, and fly off to their hives to transform it into honey.

Taking the Precepts

Going for refuge to the Triple Gem—the Buddha, the Dhamma, and the Saṅgha—is the door of entrance to the Buddha's teaching. To enter the teaching we have to pass through this door, but once we have made the initial commitment by taking refuge it is necessary to go further and to put the teaching into actual practice. For the Buddha's teaching is not a system of salvation by faith. It is essentially a path leading to *Nibbāna*, the end of suffering. At the outset we need a certain degree of faith as the incentive for entering the path, but progress towards the goal depends primarily upon our own energy and intelligence in following the path through each of its successive stages. The teaching takes the attainment of deliverance away from every external resort and places it into our own hands. We have to realize the goal for ourselves, within ourselves, by working upon ourselves with the guidance of the Buddha's instructions.

The path to liberation that the Buddha points to is the threefold training in moral discipline (*sīla*), concentration (*samādhi*), and wisdom (*paññā*). These three divisions of the path rise up each in dependence upon its predecessor—concentration upon moral discipline and wisdom upon concentration. The foundation for the entire path, it can be seen, is the training in moral discipline. Because this first section of the path plays such a pivotal role it is vitally important for the serious practitioner to obtain a clear understanding of its essential meaning and the way it is to be practised. To aid the development of such an understanding we here present an explanation of the training in *sīla* or moral discipline, giving special attention to its most basic form as the observance of the five precepts (*pañcasīla*). The subject will be dealt with under the following headings: (i) the essential meaning of *sīla*; (ii) the five precepts individually explained; (iii) the eight precepts; (iv) the benefits of *sīla*; (v) the undertaking of *sīla*; (vi) the breach of *sīla*; and (vii) the similes for *sīla*.

I. The Essential Meaning of Sīla

The Pali word for moral discipline, *sīla,* has three levels of meaning: (1) inner virtue, i.e., endowment with such qualities as kindness, contentment, simplicity, truthfulness, patience, etc.; (2) virtuous actions of body and speech which express those inner virtues outwardly; and (3) rules of conduct governing actions of body and speech designed to bring them into accord with the ethical ideals. These three levels are closely intertwined and not always distinguishable in individual cases. But if we isolate them, *sīla as inner virtue* can be called the aim of the training in moral discipline, *sīla as purified actions of body and speech* the manifestation of that aim, and *sīla as rules of conduct* the systematic means of actualizing the aim. Thus *sīla as inner virtue* is established by bringing our bodily and verbal actions into accord with the ethical ideals, and this is done by following the rules of conduct intended to give these ideals concrete form.

The Buddhist texts explain that *sīla* has the characteristic of harmonizing our actions of body and speech. *Sīla* harmonizes our actions by bringing them into accord with our own true interests, with the well-being of others, and with universal laws. Actions contrary to *sīla* lead to a state of self-division marked by guilt, anxiety, and remorse. But the observance of the principles of *sīla* heals this division, bringing our inner faculties together into a balanced and centred state of unity. *Sīla* also brings us into harmony with other men. While actions undertaken in disregard of ethical principles lead to relations scarred by competitiveness, exploitation, and aggression, actions intended to embody such principles promote concord between man and man—peace, cooperation, and mutual respect. The harmony achieved by maintaining *sīla* does not stop at the social level, but leads our actions into harmony with a higher law—the law of *kamma,* of action and its fruit, which reigns invisibly behind the entire world of sentient existence.

The need to internalize ethical virtue as the foundation for the path translates itself into a set of precepts established as guidelines to good conduct. The most basic set of precepts found in the Buddha's teaching is the *pañcasīla,* the five precepts, consisting of the following five training rules:

1. the training rule of abstaining from taking life;
2. the training rule of abstaining from taking what is not given;
3. the training rule of abstaining from sexual misconduct;
4. the training rule of abstaining from false speech; and
5. the training rule of abstaining from fermented and distilled intoxicants which are the basics for heedlessness.

These five precepts are the minimal ethical code binding on the Buddhist laity. They are administered regularly by the monks to the lay disciples at almost every service and ceremony, following immediately upon the giving of the three refuges. They are also undertaken afresh each day by earnest lay Buddhists as part of their daily recitation.

The precepts function as the core of the training in moral discipline. They are intended to produce, through methodical practice, that inner purity of will and motivation which comes to expression as virtuous bodily and verbal conduct. Hence the equivalent term for precept, *sikkhāpada*, which means literally "factor of training," that is, a factor of the training in moral discipline. However, the formulation of ethical virtue in terms of rules of conduct meets with an objection reflecting an attitude that is becoming increasingly widespread. This objection, raised by the ethical generalist, calls into question the need to cast ethics into the form of specific rules. It is enough, it is said, simply to have good intentions and to let ourselves be guided by our intuition as to what is right and wrong. Submitting to rules of conduct is at best superfluous, but worse tends to lead to a straightjacket conception of morality, to a constrictive and legalistic system of ethics.

The Buddhist reply is that while moral virtue admittedly cannot be equated flatly with any set of rules, or with outward conduct conforming to rules, the rules are still of value for aiding the development of inner virtue. Only the very exceptional few can alter the stuff of their lives by a mere act of will. The overwhelming majority of men have to proceed more slowly, with the help of a set of stepping stones to help them gradually cross the rough currents of greed, hatred, and delusion. If the process of self-transformation which is the heart of the Buddhist path begins with moral discipline, then the concrete manifestation of this discipline is in the lines of conduct represented by the five precepts, which call for our adherence as expedient means to self-transformation. The precepts are not commandments imposed from without, but principles of training each one takes upon himself through his own initiative and endeavours to follow with awareness and understanding. The formulas for the precepts do not read: "Thou shalt abstain from this and that." They read: "I undertake the training rule to abstain from the taking of life," etc. The emphasis here, as throughout the entire path, is on self-responsibility.

The precepts engender virtuous dispositions by a process involving the substitution of opposites. The actions prohibited by the precepts—killing, stealing, adultery, etc.—are all motivated by unwholesome mental factors called in Buddhist terminology the "defilements" (*kilesa*). By engaging in these actions knowingly and willingly we reinforce the grip of the defilements upon the mind to the point where they become our dominant traits. But when we take up the training by observing the precepts we then put a brake upon the current of unwholesome mental factors. There then takes place a process of "factor substitution" whereby the defilements are replaced by wholesome states which become increasingly more deeply ingrained as we go on with the training.

In this process of self-transformation the precepts draw their efficacy from another psychological principle, the law of development through repetition. Even though at first a practice arouses some resistance from within, if it is repeated over and over with understanding and determination, the qualities it calls into play pass imperceptibly into the makeup of the mind. We generally begin in the grip of negative attitudes, hemmed in by unskilful emotions. But if we see that these states lead to suffering and that to be free from suffering we must abandon them, then we will have sufficient motivation to take up the training designed to counter them. This training starts with the outer observance of *sīla*, then proceeds to internalize self-restraint through meditation and wisdom. At the start to maintain the precepts may require special effort, but by degrees the virtuous qualities they embody will gather strength until our actions flow from them as naturally and smoothly as water from a spring.

The five precepts are formulated in accordance with the ethical algorithm of using oneself as the criterion for determining how to act in relation to others. In Pali the principle is expressed by the phrase *attānaṃ upamaṃ katvā,* "consider oneself as similar to others and others as similar to oneself." The method of application involves a simple imaginative exchange of oneself and others. In order to decide whether or not to follow a particular line of action, we take ourselves as the standard and consider what would be pleasant and painful for ourselves. Then we reflect that others are basically similar to ourselves, and so, what is pleasant and painful to us is also pleasant and painful to them; thus just as we would not want others to cause pain for us, so we should not cause pain for others. As the Buddha explains:

> In this matter the noble disciple reflects: 'Here am I, fond of my life, not wanting to die, fond of pleasure and averse from pain. Suppose someone should deprive me of my life, it would not be a thing pleasing or delightful to me. If I, in my turn, were to deprive of his life one fond of life, not wanting to die, one fond of pleasure and averse from pain, it would not be a thing pleasing or delightful to him. For that state which is not pleasant or delightful to me must be not pleasant or delightful to another: and a state undear and unpleasing to me, how could I inflict that upon another?' As a result of such reflection he himself abstains from taking the life of creatures and he encourages others so to abstain, and speaks in praise of so abstaining.
>
> Saṃyuttanikāya 55, No. 7

This deductive method the Buddha uses to derive the first four precepts. The fifth precept, abstaining from intoxicants, appears to deal only with my relation to myself, with what I put into my own body. However, because the violation of this precept can lead to the violation of all the other precepts and to much further harm for others, its social implications are deeper than is evident at first sight and bring it into range of the same method of derivation.

Buddhist ethics, as formulated in the five precepts, is sometimes charged with being entirely negative. It is criticized on the ground that it is a morality solely of avoidance lacking any ideals of positive action. Against this criticism several lines of reply can be given. First of all it has to be pointed out that the five precepts, or even the longer codes of precepts promulgated by the Buddha, do not exhaust the full range of Buddhist ethics. The five precepts are only the most rudimentary code of moral training, but the Buddha also proposes other ethical codes inculcating definite positive virtues. The *Maṅgala Sutta*, for example, commends reverence, humility, contentment, gratitude, patience, generosity, etc. Other discourses prescribe numerous family, social, and political duties establishing the well-being of society. And behind all these duties lie the four attitudes called the "immeasurables"—loving-kindness, compassion, sympathetic joy, and equanimity.

But turning to the five precepts themselves, some words have to be said in defence of their negative formulation. Each moral principle included in the precepts contains two aspects—a negative aspect, which is a rule of abstinence, and a positive aspect, which is a virtue to be cultivated. These aspects are called, respectively, *vāritta* (avoidance) and *cāritta* (positive performance). Thus the first precept is formulated as abstaining from the destruction of life, which in itself is a *vāritta*, a principle of abstinence. But corresponding to this, we also find in the descriptions of the practice of this precept a *cāritta*, a positive quality to be developed, namely compassion. Thus in the *suttas* we read: "The disciple, abstaining from the taking of life, dwells without stick or sword, conscientious, full of sympathy, desirous of the welfare of all living beings." So corresponding to the negative side of abstaining from the destruction of life, there is the positive side of developing compassion and sympathy for all beings. Similarly, abstinence from stealing is paired with honesty and contentment, abstinence from sexual misconduct is paired with marital fidelity in the case of lay people and celibacy in the case of monks, abstinence from falsehood is paired with speaking the truth, and abstinence from intoxicants is paired with heedfulness.

Nevertheless, despite this recognition of a duality of aspect, the question still comes up: if there are two sides to each moral principle, why is the precept worded only as an abstinence? Why don't we also undertake training rules to develop positive virtues such as compassion, honesty, and so forth?

The answer to this is twofold. First, in order to develop the positive virtues we have to begin by abstaining from the negative qualities opposed to them. The growth of the positive virtues will only be stunted or deformed as long as the defilements are allowed to reign unchecked. We cannot cultivate compassion while at the same time indulging in killing, or cultivate honesty while stealing and cheating. At the start we have to abandon the unwholesome through the aspect of avoidance. Only when we have secured a foundation in avoiding the unwholesome can we expect to succeed in cultivating the factors of positive performance. The process of purifying virtue can be compared to growing a flower garden on a plot of uncultivated land. We don't begin by planting the seeds in expectation of a bountiful yield. We have to start with the duller work of weeding out the garden and preparing the beds. Only after we have uprooted the weeds and nourished the soil can we plant the seeds in the confidence that the flowers will grow healthily.

Another reason why the precepts are worded in terms of abstinence is that the development of positive virtues cannot be prescribed by rules. Rules of training can govern what we have to avoid and perform in our outer actions but only ideals of aspiration, not rules, can govern what develops within ourselves. Thus we cannot take up a training rule to always be loving towards others. To impose such a rule is to place ourselves in a double bind since inner attitudes are just simply not so docile that they can be determined by command. Love and compassion are the fruits of the work we do on ourselves inwardly, not of assenting to a precept. What we can do is to undertake a precept to abstain from destroying life and from injuring other beings. Then we can make a resolution, preferably without much fanfare, to develop loving-kindness, and apply ourselves to the mental training designed to nourish its growth.

One more word should be added concerning the formulation of the precepts. Despite their negative wording, even in that form the precepts are productive of tremendous positive benefits for others as well as for oneself. The Buddha says that one who abstains from the destruction of life gives immeasurable safety and security to countless living beings. How the simple observance of a single precept leads to such a result is not immediately obvious but calls for some thought. Now by myself I can never give immeasurable safety and security to other beings by any program of positive action. Even if I were to go on protest against all the slaughterhouses in the world, or to march against war continuously without stopping, by such action I could never stop the slaughter of animals or ensure that war would come to an end. But when I adopt for myself the precept to abstain from the destruction of life, then by reason of that precept I do not intentionally destroy the life of any living being. Thus any other being can feel safe and secure in my presence; all beings are ensured that they will never meet harm from me. Of course even then I can never ensure that other living beings will be absolutely immune from harm and suffering, but this is beyond anyone's power. All that lies within my power and the sphere of my responsibility are the attitudes and actions that emanate from myself towards others. And as long as these are circumscribed by the training rule to abstain from taking life, no living being need feel threatened in my presence, or fear that harm and suffering will come from me.

The same principle applies to the other precepts. When I undertake the precept to abstain from taking what is not given, no one has reason to fear that I will steal what belongs to him; the belongings of all other beings are safe from me. When I undertake the precept to abstain from sexual misconduct, no one has reason to fear that I will try to transgress against his wife. When I undertake the precept to abstain from falsehood, then anyone who speaks with me can be confident that they will hear the truth; my word can be regarded as trustworthy and reliable even in matters of critical importance. And because I undertake the precept of abstaining from intoxicants, then one can be assured that the crimes and transgressions that result from intoxication will never be committed by myself. In this way, by observing the five precepts I give immeasurable safety and security to countless beings simply through these five silent but powerful determinations established in the mind.

II. The Five Precepts

1. The First Precept: Abstinence from Taking Life

The first of the five precepts reads in Pali, *Pāṇātipātā-veramaṇī-sikkhāpadaṃ samādiyāmi*; in English, "I undertake the training rule to abstain from taking life." Here the word *pana*, meaning that which breathes, denotes any living being that has breath and consciousness. It includes animals and insects as well as men, but does not include plants as they have only life but not breath or consciousness. The word "living being" is a conventional term, an expression of common usage, signifying in the strict philosophical sense the life faculty (*jīvitindriya*). The word *atipāta* means literally striking down, hence killing or destroying. Thus the precept enjoins abstinence (*veramaṇī*) from the taking of life. Though the precept's wording prohibits the killing of living beings, in terms of its underlying purpose it can also be understood to prohibit injuring, maiming, and torturing as well.

The Pali Buddhist commentaries formally define the act of taking life thus: "The taking of life is the volition of killing expressed through the doors of either body or speech, occasioning action which results in the cutting off of the life faculty in a living being, when there is a living being present and (the perpetrator of the act) perceives it as a living being."[6]

The first important point to note in this definition is that the act of taking life is defined as a volition (*cetanā*). Volition is the mental factor responsible for action (*kamma*); it has the function of arousing the entire mental apparatus for the purpose of accomplishing a particular aim, in this case, the cutting off of the life faculty of a living being. The identification of the transgression with volition implies that the ultimate responsibility for the act of killing lies with the mind, since the volition that brings about the act is a mental factor. The body and speech function merely as doors for that volition, i.e., as channels through which the volition of taking life reaches expression. Killing is classified as a bodily deed since it generally occurs via the body, but what

---

6. *Khuddakapāṭha Aṭṭhakathā* (Khp-a), p. 26.

really performs the act of killing is the mind using the body as the instrument for actualizing its aim.

A second important point to note is that killing need not occur directly through the body. The volition to take life can also express itself through the door of speech. This means that the command to take life, given to others by way of words, writing, or gesture, is also considered a case of killing. One who issues such a command becomes responsible for the action as soon as it achieves its intention of depriving a being of life.

A complete act of killing constituting a full violation of the precept involves five factors: (1) a living being; (2) the perception of the living being as such; (3) the thought or volition of killing; (4) the appropriate effort; and (5) the actual death of the being as a result of the action. The second factor ensures that responsibility for killing is incurred only when the perpetrator of the act is aware that the object of his action is a living being. Thus if we step on an insect we do not see, the precept is not broken because the perception or awareness of a living being is lacking. The third factor ensures that the taking of life is intentional. Without the factor of volition there is no transgression, as when we kill a fly while intending simply to drive it away with our hand. The fourth factor holds that the action must be directed to the taking of life, the fifth that the being dies as a result of this action. If the life faculty is not cut off, a full violation of the precept is not incurred, though in harming or injuring living beings in any way, its essential purpose will be violated.

The taking of life is distinguished into different types by way of its underlying motivation. One criterion for determining the motivation is the defilement principally responsible for the action. Acts of killing can originate from all three unwholesome roots—from greed, hatred, and delusion. As the immediate cause concomitant with the act of killing, hatred together with delusion function as the root, since the force which drives the act is the impulse to destroy the creature's life, a form of hatred. Any of the three unwholesome roots, however, can serve as the impelling cause or decisive support (*upanissaya paccaya*) for the act, operating over some span of time. Though greed and hatred are always mutually exclusive at a single moment, the two can work together at different moments over an extended period to occasion the taking of life. Killing motivated primarily by greed is seen in such cases as killing in order to gain material benefits or high status for oneself, to eliminate threats to one's comfort and security, or to obtain enjoyment as in hunting and fishing for sport. Killing motivated by hatred is evident in cases of vicious murder where the motive is strong aversion, cruelty, or jealousy. And killing motivated by delusion can be seen in the case of those who perform animal sacrifices in the belief that they are spiritually wholesome or who kill followers of other religions with the view that this is a religious duty.

Acts of taking life are differentiated by way of their degree of moral gravity. Not all cases of killing are equally blameworthy. All are unwholesome, a breach of the precept, but the Buddhist texts make a distinction in the moral weight attached to different kinds of killing. The first distinction given is that between killing beings with moral qualities (*guṇa*) and killing beings without moral qualities. For all practical purposes the former are human beings, the latter animals, and it is held that to kill a fellow human being is a more serious matter ethically than to kill an animal. Then within each category further distinctions are drawn. In the case of animals the degree of moral gravity is said to be proportional to the size of the animal, to kill a larger animal being more blameworthy than to kill a smaller one. Other factors relevant to determining moral weight are whether the animal has an owner or is ownerless, whether it is domestic or wild, and whether it has a gentle or a vicious temperament. The moral gravity would be greater in the former three alternatives, less in the latter three. In the killing of human beings the degree of moral blame depends on the personal qualities of the victim, to kill a person of superior spiritual stature or one's personal benefactors being more blameworthy than to kill a less developed person or one unrelated to oneself. The three cases of killing selected as the most culpable are matricide, parricide, and the murder of an *arahat*, a fully purified saint.

Another factor determinative of moral weight is the motivation of the act. This leads to a distinction between premeditated murder and impulsive killing. The former is murder in cold blood, intended and planned in advance, driven either by strong greed or strong hatred. The latter is killing which is not planned in advance, as when one person kills another in a fit of rage or in self-defence. Generally, premeditated murder is regarded as a graver transgression than impulsive killing, and the motivation of hatred as more blameworthy than the motivation of greed. The presence of cruelty and the obtaining of sadistic pleasure from the act further increase its moral weight.

Other factors determinative of moral gravity are the force of the defilements accompanying the act and the amount of effort involved in its perpetration, but limitations of space prohibit a full discussion of their role.

2. The Second Precept: Abstinence from Taking What Is Not Given

The second precept reads: *Adinnādānā-veramaṇī-sikkhāpadaṃ samādiyāmi*, "I undertake the training rule to abstain from taking what is not given." The word *adinna*, meaning literally "what is not given," signifies the belongings of another person over which he exercises ownership legally and blamelessly (*adaṇḍāraho anupavajjo*). Thus no offence is committed if the article taken has no owner, e.g., if logs are taken to make a fire or stones are gathered to build a wall. Further, the other person has to have possession of the article taken legally and blamelessly; that is, he has to have the legal right over the article and also has to be blameless in his use of it. This latter phrase apparently becomes applicable in cases where a person gains legal possession of an article but does so in an improper way or uses it for unethical purposes. In such cases there might be legitimate grounds for depriving him of the item, as when the law requires someone who commits a misdemeanour to pay a fine or deprives a person of some weapon rightfully his which he is using for destructive purposes.

The act of taking what is not given is formally defined thus: "Taking what is not given is the volition with thievish intent arousing the activity of appropriating an article belonging to another legally and blamelessly in one who perceives it as belonging to another."[7] As in the case of the first precept the transgression here consists ultimately in a volition. This volition can commit the act of theft by originating action through body or speech; thus a transgression is incurred either by taking something

---

7. Khp-a, p. 26.

directly by oneself or else indirectly, by commanding someone else to appropriate the desired article. The fundamental purpose of the precept is to protect the property of individuals from unjustified confiscation by others. Its ethical effect is to encourage honesty and right livelihood.

According to the commentaries, for a complete breach of the precept to be committed five factors must be present: (1) an article belonging to another legally and blamelessly; (2) the perception of it as belonging to another; (3) the thought or intention of stealing; (4) the activity of taking the article; and (5) the actual appropriation of the article. By reason of the second factor there is no violation in taking another's article if we mistakenly perceive it as our own, as when we might confuse identical-looking coats, umbrellas, etc. The third factor again provides a safeguard against accidental appropriation, while the fifth asserts that to fall into the class of a transgression the action must deprive the owner of his article. It is not necessary that he be aware that his possession is missing, only that it be removed from his sphere of control even if only momentarily.

Taking what is not given can be divided into many different kinds of violation. We might mention some of the most prominent. One is *stealing*, that is, taking what is not given, secretly, without the knowledge of the owner, as in housebreaking, a midnight bank theft, pick-pocketing, etc. Another type is *robbery*, taking what is not given by force, either by snatching someone's belongings away from him or by compelling him to hand them over by means of threats. A third type is *fraudulence*, laying false claims or telling lies in order to gain someone else's possessions. Still another is *deceit*, using deceptive means to deprive someone of an article or to gain his money as when storekeepers use false weights and measures or when people produce counterfeit bills for use.

The violation of this precept need not amount to a major crime. The precept is subtle and offers many opportunities for its breach, some of them seemingly slight. For example, transgression will be incurred when employees take goods belonging to their employers, pocketing small items to which they have no right with the thought that the company will not miss them; when using another's telephone to make long-distance calls without his consent, letting him cover the bill; in bringing articles into a country without declaring them to customs in order to avoid paying duty on them; in idling away time on the job for which one is being paid in the expectation that one has been working diligently; in making one's employees work without giving them adequate compensation, etc.

By way of its underlying roots, the act of taking what is not given can proceed either from greed or hatred, both being coupled with delusion. Stealing by reason of greed is the obvious case, but the offence can also be driven by hatred. Hatred functions as the motive for stealing when one person deprives another of an article not so much because he wants it for himself as because he resents the other's possession of it and wants to make him suffer through its loss.

The degree of blame attached to acts of stealing is held to be determined by two principal factors, the value of the article taken and the moral qualities of the owner. In stealing a very valuable article the degree of blame is obviously greater than in stealing an article of little worth. But where the value of the article is the same the blameworthiness of the action still varies relative to the individual against whom the offence is committed. As determined by this factor, stealing from a person of high virtuous qualities or a personal benefactor is a more serious transgression than stealing from a person of lesser qualities or from an unrelated person. This factor, in fact, can be even more important than the cash value of the object. Thus if someone steals an alms-bowl from a meditative monk, who needs the bowl to collect his food, the moral weight of the act is heavier than that involved in cheating a racketeer out of several thousand dollars, owing to the character of the person affected by the deed. The motivation behind the action and the force of the defilements are also determinative of the degree of moral gravity, hatred being considered more culpable than greed.

3. The Third Precept: Abstinence from Misconduct in regard to Sense Pleasures

The third precept reads: *Kāmesu micchācārā veramaṇī sikkhapadaṃ samādiyāmi,* "I undertake the training rule to abstain from misconduct in regard to sense pleasures." The word *kāma* has the general meaning of sense pleasure or sensual desire, but the commentaries explain it as sexual relations (*methuna-samācāra*), an interpretation supported by the *suttas*. *Micchācāra* means wrong modes of conduct. Thus the precept enjoins abstinence from improper or illicit sexual relations.

Misconduct in regard to sense pleasures is formally defined as "the volition with sexual intent occurring through the bodily door, causing transgression with an illicit partner".[8] The primary question this definition elicits is: who is to qualify as an illicit partner? For men, the texts list twenty types of women who are illicit partners. These can be grouped into three categories: (1) a woman who is under the protection of elders or other authorities charged with her care, e.g., a girl being cared for by parents, by an older brother or sister, by other relatives, or by the family as a whole; (2) a woman who is prohibited by convention, that is, close relatives forbidden under family tradition, nuns and other women vowed to observe celibacy as a spiritual discipline, and those forbidden as partners under the law of the land; and (3) a woman who is married or engaged to another man, even one bound to another man only by a temporary agreement. In the case of women, for those who are married any man other than a husband is an illicit partner. For all women a man forbidden by tradition or under religious rules is prohibited as a partner. For both men and women any violent, forced, or coercive union, whether by physical compulsion or psychological pressure, can be regarded as a transgression of the precept even when the partner is not otherwise illicit. But a man or woman who is widowed or divorced can freely remarry according to choice.

The texts mention four factors which must be present for a breach of the precept to be incurred: (1) an illicit partner, as defined above; (2) the thought or volition of engaging in sexual union with that person; (3) the act of engaging in union; and (4) the acceptance of the union. This last factor is added for the purpose of excluding from violation those who are unwillingly forced into improper sexual relations.

The degree of moral gravity involved in the offence is determined by the force of the lust motivating the action and the qualities of the person against whom the transgression is committed. If the transgression involves someone of high spiritual

---

8. *Majjhimanikāya Aṭṭhakathā*, Vol. I, p. 202 (Burmese ed.).

qualities, the lust is strong, and force is used, the blame is heavier than when the partner has less developed qualities, the lust is weak, and no force is used. The most serious violations are incest and the rape of an *arahat* (or arahatess). The underlying root is always greed accompanied by delusion.

4. The Fourth Precept: Abstinence from False Speech

The fourth precept reads: *Musāvādā veramaṇī sikkhapadaṃ samādiyāmi,* "I undertake the training rule to abstain from false speech." False speech is defined as "the wrong volition with intent to deceive, occurring through the door of either body or speech, arousing the bodily or verbal effort of deceiving another."[9] The transgression must be understood as intentional. The precept is not violated merely by speaking what is false, but by speaking what is false with the intention of representing that as true; thus it is equivalent to lying or deceptive speech. The volition is said to arouse bodily or verbal action. The use of speech to deceive is obvious, but the body too can be used as an instrument of communication—as in writing, hand signals, and gestures—and thus can be used to deceive others.

Four factors enter into the offence of false speech: (1) an untrue state of affairs; (2) the intention of deceiving another; (3) the effort to express that, either verbally or bodily; and (4) the conveying of a false impression to another. Since intention is required, if one speaks falsely without aiming at deceiving another, as when one speaks what is false believing it to be true, there is no breach of the precept. Actual deception, however, is not needed for the precept to be broken. It is enough if the false impression is communicated to another. Even though he does not believe the false statement, if one expresses what is false to him and he understands what is being said, the transgression of speaking falsehood has been committed.

The motivation for false speech can be any of the three unwholesome roots. These yield three principal kinds of falsehood: (1) false speech motivated by greed, intended to increase one's gains or promote one's status or that of those dear to oneself; (2) false speech motivated by hatred, intended to destroy the welfare of others or to bring them harm and suffering; and (3) false

---

9. Khp-a, p. 26.

speech of a less serious kind, motivated principally by delusion in association with less noxious degrees of greed or hatred, intended neither to bring special benefits to oneself nor to harm others. Some examples would be lying for the sake of a joke, exaggerating an account to make it more interesting, speaking flattery to gratify others, etc.

The principal determinants of the gravity of the transgression are the recipient of the lie, the object of the lie and the motivation of the lie. The recipient is the person to whom the lie is told. The moral weight of the act is proportional to the character of this person, the greatest blame attaching to falsehoods spoken to one's benefactors or to spiritually developed persons. The moral weight again varies according to the object of the lie, the person the lie affects, being proportional to his spiritual qualities and his relation to oneself in the same way as with the recipient. And thirdly, the gravity of the lie is contingent on its motivation, the most serious cases being those with malicious intent designed to destroy the welfare of others. The worst cases of false speech are lying in a way that defames the Buddha or an *arahat*, and making false claims to have reached a superior spiritual attainment in order to increase one's own gains and status. In the case of a bhikkhu this latter offence can lead to expulsion from the Saṅgha.

5. The Fifth Precept: Abstinence from Intoxicating Drinks and Drugs

The fifth precept reads: *Surāmerayamajja-pamādaṭṭhānā-veramaṇī-sikkhāpadaṃ samādiyāmi*, "I undertake the training rule to abstain from fermented and distilled intoxicants which are the basis for heedlessness." The word *meraya* means fermented liquors, *sura* liquors which have been distilled to increase their strength and flavour. The word *majja*, meaning an intoxicant, can be related to the rest of the passage either as qualified by *surāmeraya* or as additional to them. In the former case the whole phrase means fermented and distilled liquors which are intoxicants, in the latter it means fermented and distilled liquors and other intoxicants. If this second reading is adopted the precept would explicitly include intoxicating drugs used non-medicinally, such as the opiates, hemp, and psychedelics. But even on the first reading the precept implicitly proscribes these drugs by way of its guiding purpose, which is to prevent heedlessness caused by the taking of intoxicating substances.

The taking of intoxicants is defined as the volition leading to the bodily act of ingesting distilled or fermented intoxicants.[10] It can be committed only by one's own person (not by command to others) and only occurs through the bodily door. For the precept to be violated four factors are required: (1) the intoxicant; (2) the intention of taking it; (3) the activity of ingesting it; and (4) the actual ingestion of the intoxicant. The motivating factor of the violation is greed coupled with delusion. No gradations of moral weight are given. In taking medicines containing alcohol or intoxicating drugs for medical reasons, no breach of the precept is committed. There is also no violation in taking food containing a negligible amount of alcohol added as a flavouring.

This fifth precept differs from the preceding four in that the others directly involve a man's relation to his fellow beings while this precept ostensibly deals solely with a person's relation to himself—to his own body and mind. Thus whereas the first four precepts clearly belong to the moral sphere, a question may arise whether this precept is really ethical in character or merely hygienic. The answer is that it is ethical, for the reason that what a person does to his own body and mind can have a decisive effect on his relations to his fellow men. Taking intoxicants can influence the ways in which a man interacts with others, leading to the violation of all five precepts. Under the influence of intoxicants a man who might otherwise be restrained can lose self-control, become heedless, and engage in killing, stealing, adultery, and lying. Abstinence from intoxicants is prescribed on the grounds that it is essential to the self-protection of the individual and for establishing the well-being of family and society. The precept thus prevents the misfortunes that result from the use of intoxicants: loss of wealth, quarrels and crimes, bodily disease, loss of reputation, shameless conduct, negligence, and madness.

The precept, it must be stressed, does not prohibit merely intoxication but the very use of intoxicating substances. Though occasional indulgences may not be immediately harmful in isolation, the seductive and addictive properties of intoxicants are

---

10. Khp-a., p. 26.

well known. The strongest safeguard against the lure is to avoid them altogether.

III. The Eight Precepts

Beyond the five precepts Buddhism offers a higher code of moral discipline for the laity consisting of eight precepts (*aṭṭhasīla*). This code of eight precepts is not entirely different in content from the fivefold code, but includes the five precepts with one significant revision. The revision comes in the third precept, where abstaining from sexual misconduct is changed to abstaining from incelibacy. The third precept of the eightfold set thus reads: *Abrahmacariyā veramaṇī sikkhāpadaṃ samādiyāmi*, "I undertake the training rule to abstain from incelibacy." To these basic five three further precepts are added:

(6) *Vikālabhojanā-veramaṇī-sikkhāpadaṃ samādiyāmi*, "I undertake the training rule to abstain from eating beyond the time limit," i.e., from mid-day to the following dawn.

(7) *Nacca-gīta-vādita visūkadassana-māla-gandha-vilepana-dharaṇa-maṇḍana-vibhūsanaṭṭhāṇā-veramaṇī-sikkhāpadaṃ samādiyāmi*, "I undertake the training rule to abstain from dancing, singing, instrumental music, unsuitable shows, and from wearing garlands, using scents, and beautifying the body with cosmetics."

(8) *Uccāsayana-mahāsayanā-veramaṇī-sikkhāpadaṃ samādiyāmi*, "I undertake the training rule to abstain from high and luxurious beds and seats."

There are two ways in which these precepts are observed—permanently and temporarily. Permanent observance, far the less common of the two, is undertaken generally by older people who, having completed their family duties, wish to deepen their spiritual development by devoting the later years of their life to intensified spiritual practice. Even then it is not very widespread. Temporary observance is usually undertaken by lay people either on Uposatha days or on occasions of a meditation retreat. Uposatha days are the new moon and full moon days of the lunar month, which are set aside for special religious observances, a custom absorbed into Buddhism from ancient Indian custom going back even into the pre-Buddhistic period of Indian history. On these days lay people in Buddhist countries often take the eight precepts, especially when they go to spend the Uposatha at a temple or monastery. On these occasions the undertaking of the eight precepts lasts for a day and a night. Then, secondly, on occasions of retreat lay people take the eight precepts for the duration of their retreat, which might last anywhere from several days to several months.

The formulation of two distinct ethical codes follows from the two basic purposes of the Buddhist moral discipline. One is the fundamental ethical purpose of putting a brake on immoral actions, actions which are harmful either directly or indirectly to others. This purpose falls into the province of the fivefold code of precepts, which deals with the restraint of actions that cause pain and suffering to others. In enjoining abstinence from these unwholesome actions, the five precepts also protect the individual from their undesirable repercussions on himself—some immediately visible in this present life, some coming to manifestation only in future lives when the *kamma* they generate bears its fruit. The other purpose of the Buddhist training in moral discipline is not so much ethical as spiritual. It is to provide a system of self-discipline which can act as a basis for achieving higher states of realization through the practice of meditation. In serving this purpose the code functions as a kind of ascesis, a way of conduct involving self-denial and renunciation as essential to the ascent to higher levels of consciousness. This ascent, culminating in *Nibbāna* or final liberation from suffering, hinges upon the attenuation and ultimate eradication of craving, which with its multiple branches of desire is the primary force that holds us in bondage. To reduce and overcome craving it is necessary to regulate not only the deleterious types of moral transgressions but also modes of conduct which are not harmful to others but still give vent to the craving that holds us in subjection.

The Buddhist code of discipline expounded in the eight precepts represents the transition from the first level of moral discipline to the second, that is, from *sīla* as a purely moral undertaking to *sīla* as a way of ascetic self-training aimed at progress along the path to liberation. The five precepts also fulfil this function to some extent, but they do so only in a limited way, not as fully as the eight precepts. With the eight precepts the ethical code takes a pronounced turn towards the control of desires which are not socially harmful and immoral. This extension of the training focuses upon desires centering around the physical body and its concerns. The change of the third precept to abstinence from incelibacy curbs the sexual urge, regarded in itself not as a moral evil but as a powerful expression of craving that has to be held in check to advance to the higher levels of meditation. The three new precepts regulate concern with food, entertainment, self-beautification, and physical comfort. Their observance nurtures the growth of qualities essential to the deeper spiritual life—contentment, fewness of wishes, modesty, austerity, renunciation. As these qualities mature, the defilements are weakened, aiding the effort to reach attainment in serenity and insight.

IV. The Benefits of Sīla

The benefits *sīla* brings to the one who undertakes it can be divided into three classes: (1) the benefits pertaining to the present life; (2) the benefits pertaining to future lives; and (3) the benefit of the ultimate good. These we will discuss in turn.

1. Benefits pertaining to the present life

At the most elementary level, the observance of the five precepts protects one from coming into trouble with the law, ensuring immunity from temporal punishment at least with regard to those actions covered by the precepts. Killing, stealing, adultery, bearing false testimony, and irresponsible behaviour caused by drunkenness being offences punishable by law, one who undertakes the five precepts avoids the penalties consequent upon these actions by abstaining from the actions which entail them.

Further temporal benefits accrue through the observance of the precepts. Following the precepts helps to establish a good reputation among the wise and virtuous. At a more inward level it leads to a clear conscience. Repeated violations of the basic principles of ethics, even if they escape detection, still tend to create a disturbed conscience—the pain of guilt, uneasiness, and remorse. But maintaining the precepts results in freedom from remorse, an ease of conscience that can evolve into the "bliss of blamelessness" (*anavajjasukha*) when we review our actions and realize them to be wholesome and good. This clarity of conscience fosters another benefit—the ability to die peacefully, without fear or confusion. At the time of death the various actions we have regularly performed in the course of life rise to the surface of the mind, casting up their images like pictures upon a screen. If unwholesome actions were prevalent, their weight will predominate and cause fear at the approach of death, leading to a confused and painful end. But if wholesome actions were prevalent in the course of life, the opposite will take place: when death comes we will be able to die calmly and peacefully.

2. Benefits pertaining to future lives

According to the Buddha's teaching the mode of rebirth we take in our next existence is determined by our *kamma*, the willed actions we have performed in this present existence. The general principle governing the working of the rebirth process is that unwholesome *kamma* leads to an unfavourable rebirth, wholesome *kamma* to a favourable rebirth. More specifically, if the *kamma* built up by breaking the five precepts becomes the determining cause of the mode of rebirth it will conduce to rebirth in one of the four planes of misery—the hells, the realm of tormented spirits, the animal world, or the world of the asuras. If, as a result of some wholesome *kamma*, a person who regularly breaks the five precepts should take rebirth as a human being, then when his unwholesome *kamma* matures it will produce pain and suffering in his human state. The forms this suffering takes correspond to the transgressions. Killing leads to a premature death, stealing to loss of wealth, sexual misconduct to enmity, false speech to being deceived and slandered by others, and the use of intoxicants to loss of intelligence.

The observance of the five precepts, on the other hand, brings about the accumulation of wholesome *kamma* tending to rebirth in the planes of happiness, i.e., in the human or heavenly worlds. This *kamma* again, coming to maturity in the course of the life, produces favourable results consonant in nature with the precepts. Thus abstaining from the taking of life leads to longevity, abstaining from stealing to prosperity, abstaining from sexual misconduct to popularity, abstaining from false speech to a good reputation, and abstaining from intoxicants to mindfulness and wisdom.

3. The benefits of the ultimate good

The ultimate good is the attainment of *Nibbāna*, deliverance from the round of rebirths, which can be achieved either in the present life or in some future life depending on the maturity of our spiritual faculties. *Nibbāna* is attained by practicing the path leading to deliverance, the noble eightfold path in its three stages of moral discipline, concentration, and wisdom. The most fundamental of these three stages is moral discipline or *sīla*, which begins with the observance of the five precepts. The undertaking of the five precepts can thus be understood to be the first actual step taken along the path to deliverance and the indispensable foundation for the higher attainments in concentration and wisdom.

Sīla functions as the foundation for the path in two ways. First the observance of *sīla* promotes a clear conscience, essential to the development of concentration. If we often act contrary to the precepts our actions tend to give rise to remorse, which will swell up to the surface of the mind when we sit in meditation, creating restlessness and feelings of guilt. But if we act in harmony with the precepts our minds will be imbued with a bliss and clarity of conscience which allows concentration to develop easily. The observance of the precepts conduces to concentration in a second way: it rescues us from the danger of being caught in a crossfire of incompatible motives disruptive of the meditative frame of mind. The practice of meditation aimed at serenity and insight requires the stilling of the defilements. But when we deliberately act in violation of the precepts our actions spring from the unwholesome roots of greed, hatred and delusion. Thus in committing such actions we are arousing the defilements while at the same time, when sitting in meditation, we are striving to overcome them. The result is inner conflict, disharmony, a split right through the centre of our being, obstructing the unification of the mind needed for meditative attainment.

At the outset we cannot expect to eliminate the subtle forms of the defilements all at once. These can only be tackled later, in the deeper stages of meditation. In the beginning we have to start by stopping the defilements in their coarser modes of occurrence, and this is achieved by restraining them from reaching expression through the channels of body and speech. Such restraint is the essence of *sīla*. We therefore take up the precepts as a form of spiritual training, as a way of locking in the defilements and preventing them from outward eruptions. After they have been shut in and their effusions stopped we can then work on eliminating their roots through the development of concentration and wisdom.

V. The Undertaking of Sīla

The Buddhist tradition recognizes three distinct ways of observing the precepts. One is called immediate abstinence (*sampattavirati*), which means abstaining from unwholesome actions naturally through an ingrained sense of conscience resulting either from an innately keen ethical disposition or from education and training. The second is called abstinence through undertaking (*samādana-virati*), which means abstaining as a result of having undertaken rules of training with a determination to follow those rules as guidelines to right action. The third way is called abstinence through eradication (*samuccheda-virati*), which means abstaining from the transgressions covered by the precepts as a result of having cut off the defilements out of which transgressions arise.

For purposes of self-training Buddhism emphasizes the importance of the second type of abstinence. Immediate abstinence is seen as praiseworthy in itself but not sufficient as a basis for training since it presupposes the prior existence of a strong conscience, which is not a reality in the overwhelming majority of men. In order to develop the mental strength to resist the upsurge of the defilements it is essential to undertake the precepts by a deliberate act of will and to form the determination to observe them diligently.

There are two ways of formally undertaking the five precepts, the initial and the recurrent, corresponding to the two ways of going for refuge. The initial undertaking takes place immediately after the initial going for refuge. When the aspirant receives the three refuges from a bhikkhu in a formal ceremony, this will then be followed by the administering of the five precepts, the monk reciting each of the precepts in turn and the lay disciple repeating them after him. If there is no monk available to administer the refuges and precepts, the aspirant can take them upon himself by a strong and fixed mental resolution, preferably doing so before an image of the Buddha. The presence of a monk is not necessary but is generally desired to give a sense of the continuity of the lineage.

The undertaking of the precepts is not a one-shot affair to be gone through once and then dropped off into the storage bank of memories. Rather, like the going for refuge the precepts should be undertaken repeatedly, preferably on a daily basis. This is the recurrent undertaking of the precepts. Just as the disciple repeats the three refuges each day to strengthen his commitment to the Dhamma, so he should recite the five precepts immediately after the refuges in order to express his determination to embody the Dhamma in his conduct. However, the practice of *sīla* is not to be confused with the mere recitation of a verbal formula. The recitation of the formula helps reinforce one's will to carry out the training, but beyond all verbal recitations the precepts have to be put into practice in day-to-day life, especially on the occasions when they become relevant. Undertaking the precepts is like buying a ticket for a train: the purchase of the ticket permits us to board the train but does not take us anywhere by itself. Similarly, formally accepting the precepts enables us to embark upon the training, but after the acceptance we have to translate the precepts into action.

Once we have formed the initial determination to cultivate *sīla*, there are certain mental factors which then help to protect our observance of the precepts. One of these is mindfulness (*sati*). Mindfulness is awareness, constant attention and keen observation. Mindfulness embraces all aspects of our being—our bodily activities, our feelings, our states of mind, our objects of thought. With sharpened mindfulness we can be aware exactly what we are doing, what feelings and states of mind are impelling us towards particular courses of action, what thoughts form our motivations. Then, by means of this mindfulness, we can avoid the unwholesome and develop the wholesome.

Another factor which helps us maintain the precepts is understanding (*paññā*). The training in moral discipline should not be taken up as a blind dogmatic submission to external rules, but as a fully conscious process guided by intelligence. The factors of understanding give us that guiding intelligence. To observe the precepts properly we have to understand for ourselves which kinds of actions are wholesome and which are unwholesome. We also have to understand the reason why—why they are wholesome and unwholesome, why the one should be pursued and the other abandoned. The deepening of understanding enables us to see the roots of our actions, i.e., the mental factors from which they spring, and the consequences to which they lead, their long-term effects upon ourselves and others. Understanding expands our vision not only into consequences, but also into alternatives, into the different courses of action offered by any objective situation. Thence it gives us knowledge of the various alternatives open to us and the wisdom to choose some in preference to others.

A third factor that helps in maintaining the precepts is energy (*viriya*). The training in right conduct is at base a way of training the mind, since it is the mind that directs our actions. But the mind cannot be trained without effort, without the application of energy to steer it into wholesome channels. Energy works together with mindfulness and understanding to bring about the gradual purification of *sīla*. Through mindfulness we gain awareness of our states of mind; through understanding we can ascertain the tendencies of these states, their qualities, roots and consequences; then through energy we strive to abandon the unwholesome and to cultivate the wholesome.

The fourth factor conducive to the training in *sīla* is patience (*khanti*). Patience enables us to endure the offensive actions of others without becoming angry or seeking retaliation. Patience also enables us to endure disagreeable circumstances without dissatisfaction and dejection. It curbs our desires and aversions, restraining us from transgressions through greedy pursuits or violent reprisals.

Abstinence through eradication (*samuccheda-virati*), the highest form of observing the precepts, comes about automatically with the attainment of the state of an ariyan, one who has reached direct realization of the Dhamma. When the disciple reaches the stage of stream-entry (*sotāpatti*), the first of the ariyan stages, he becomes bound to reach full liberation in a maximum of seven more lives. He is incapable of reverting from the course of forward progress towards enlightenment. Simultaneously with his attainment of stream-entry the disciple acquires four inalienable qualities, called the four factors of stream-entry (*sotāpattiyaṅga*). The first three are unshakable faith in the Buddha, the Dhamma, and the Saṅgha. The fourth is completely purified *sīla*. The noble disciple has cut off the defilements which motivate transgressions of the precepts. Thus he can never deliberately violate the five precepts. His observance of the precepts has become "untorn, unrent, unblotched, unmotiled, liberating, praised by the wise, not clung to, conducive to concentration."

VI. The Breach of Sīla

To undertake the precepts is to make a determination to live in harmony with them, not to ensure that one will never break them. Despite our determination it sometimes happens that due to carelessness or the force of our conditioning by the defilements we act contrary to the precepts. The question thus comes up as to what to do in such cases.

One thing we should not do if we break a precept is to let ourselves become ridden by guilt and self-contempt. Until we reach the planes of liberation it is to be expected that the defilements can crop up from time to time and motivate unwholesome actions. Feelings of guilt and self-condemnation do nothing to help the matter but only make things worse by piling on an overlay of self-aversion. A sense of shame and moral scrupulousness are central to maintaining the precepts but they should not be allowed to become entangled in the coils of guilt.

When a breach of the precepts takes place there are several methods of making amends. One method used by monks to gain exoneration in regard to infringements on the monastic rules is confession. For certain classes of monastic offences a monk can gain clearance simply by confessing his transgression to another monk. Perhaps with suitable modifications the same procedure could be applied by the laity, at least with regard to more serious violations. Thus if there are a number of lay people who are earnestly intent on following the path, and one falls into a breach of a precept, he can confess his lapse to a Dhamma friend, or, if one is not available, he can confess it privately before an image of the Buddha. It must be stressed, however, that confession does not aim at gaining absolution. No one is offended by the ethical lapse, nor is there anyone to grant forgiveness. Also, confession does not abrogate the *kamma* acquired by the transgression. The *kamma* has been generated by the deed and will produce its due effect if it gains the opportunity. The basic purpose of confession is to clear the mind of the remorse bearing upon it as a consequence of the breach. Confession especially helps to prevent the concealment of the lapse, a subtle manoeuvre of the ego used to bolster its pride in its own imagined perfection.

Another method of making amends is by retaking the five precepts, reciting each precept in turn either in the presence of a monk or before an image of the Buddha. This new undertaking of the precepts can be reinforced by a third measure, namely, making a strong determination not to fall into the same transgression again in the future. Having applied these three methods one can then perform more virtuous actions as a way of building up good *kamma* to counteract the unwholesome *kamma* acquired through the breach of the precept. Kamma tends to produce its due result and if this tendency is sufficiently strong there is nothing we can do to blot it out. However, *kamma* does not come to fruition always as a matter of strict necessity. Kammic tendencies push and tug with one another in complex patterns of relationship. Some tend to reinforce the results of others, some to weaken the results, some to obstruct the results. If we build up wholesome *kamma* through virtuous actions, this pure *kamma* can inhibit the unwholesome *kamma* and prevent it from reaching fruition. There is no guarantee that it will do so, since *kamma* is a living process, not a mechanical one. But the tendencies in the process can be understood, and since one such tendency is for the wholesome to counteract the unwholesome and hinder their undesired results, a helpful power in overcoming the effects of breaking the precepts is the performance of virtuous actions.

VII. The Similes for Sīla

The texts illustrate the qualities of *sīla* with numerous similes, but as with the three refuges we must again limit ourselves to only a few. *Sīla* is compared to a stream of clear water, because it can wash off the stains of wrong actions which can never be removed by the waters of all other rivers. *Sīla* is like sandalwood, because it can remove the fever of the defilements just as sandalwood (according to ancient Indian belief) can be used to allay bodily fever. Again, *sīla* is like an ornament made of precious jewels because it adorns the person who wears it. It is like a perfume because it gives off a pleasant scent, the "scent of virtue," which unlike ordinary perfume travels even against the wind. It is like moonbeams because it cools off the heat of passion as the moon cools off the heat of the day. And *sīla* is like a staircase because it leads upwards by degrees—to higher states of future existence in the fortunate realms, to the higher planes of concentration and wisdom, to the supernormal powers, to the paths and fruits of liberation, and finally to the highest goal, the attainment of *Nibbāna*.

Buddhism and Social Action

An Exploration
by
Ken Jones

WHEEL PUBLICATION NO. 285/286

Copyright © Kandy; Buddhist Publication Society, (1981)

Acknowledgments

I am grateful to Mr. Paul Ingram who, as the then editor, published the original, very much abbreviated, version of this paper in the Buddhist Society's journal *The Middle Way* (Vol. 54, No. 2 Summer 1979, 85–88). My thanks are also due to the Ven. Nyanaponika Mahathera who encouraged me to develop my ideas further. For these, however, I must accept sole responsibility.

Ken Jones

Part One: The Fundamentals

1.1 Buddhism and the new global society

It is the manifest suffering and folly in the world that invokes humane and compassionate social action in its many different forms. For Buddhists this situation raises fundamental and controversial questions. And here, also, Buddhism has implications of some significance for Christians, humanists and other non-Buddhists.

By 'social action' we mean the many different kinds of action intended to benefit mankind. These range from simple individual acts of charity, to teaching and training, organised kinds of service, 'Right Livelihood' in and outside the helping professions, and through various kinds of community development as well as to political activity in working for a better society.

Buddhism is a pragmatic teaching which starts from certain fundamental propositions about how we experience the world and how we act in it. It teaches that it is possible to transcend this sorrow-laden world of our experience and is concerned first and last with ways of achieving that transcendence. What finally leads to such transcendence is what we shall call Wisdom. The enormous literature of Buddhism is not a literature of revelation and authority. Instead, it uses ethics and meditation, philosophy and science, art and poetry to point a Way to this Wisdom. Similarly, Buddhist writing on social action, unlike secular writings, makes finite proposals which must ultimately refer to this Wisdom, but which also are arguable in terms of our common experience.

In the East, Buddhism developed different schools or 'traditions,' serving the experiences of different cultures, ranging from Sri Lanka through Tibet and Mongolia to Japan. Buddhism may thus appear variously as sublime humanism, magical mysticism, poetic paradox and much else. These modes of expression, however, all converge upon the fundamental teaching, the 'perennial Buddhism.' This pamphlet is based upon the latter, drawing upon the different oriental traditions to present the teachings in an attempt to relate them to our modern industrial society.

From the evidence of the Buddha's discourses, or *suttas*, in the Dīgha Nikāya, it is clear that early Buddhists were very much concerned with the creation of social conditions favourable to the individual cultivation of Buddhist values. An outstanding example of this, in later times, is the remarkable 'welfare state' created by the Buddhist emperor Asoka (B.C. 274–236). Walpola Rāhula stated the situation—perhaps at its strongest—when he wrote that "Buddhism arose in India as a spiritual force against social injustices, against degrading superstitious rites, ceremonies and sacrifices; it denounced the tyranny of the caste system and advocated the equality of all men; it emancipated woman and gave them complete spiritual freedom" (Rāhula, 1978). The Buddhist scriptures do indicate the general direction of Buddhist social thinking, and to that extent they are suggestive for our own times. Nevertheless it would be pedantic, and in some cases absurd, to apply directly to modern industrial society social prescriptions detailed to meet the needs of a social order which flourished twenty-three centuries ago. The Buddhist householder of the Sigālovāda Sutta[1] experienced a different way of life from that of a computer consultant in Tokyo or an unemployed black youth in Liverpool. And the conditions which might favour their cultivation of the Middle Way must be secured by correspondingly different—and more complex—social, economic and political strategies.

It is thus essential to attempt to distinguish between perennial Buddhism on the one hand and, on the other, the specific social prescriptions attributed to the historical Buddha which related the basic, perennial teaching to the specific conditions of his day. We believe that it is unscholarly to transfer the scriptural social teaching uncritically and without careful qualification to modern societies, or to proclaim that the Buddha was a democrat and an internationalist. The modern terms 'democracy' and 'internationalism' did not exist in the sense in which we understand them in the emergent feudal society in which the Buddha lived. Buddhism is ill-served in the long run by such special pleading. On the other hand, it is arguable that there are democratic and internationalist implications in the basic Buddhist teachings.

---

1. Translated in The Wheel No. 14, *Everyman's Ethics*.

In the past two hundred years society in the West has undergone a more fundamental transformation than at any period since Neolithic times, whether in terms of technology or the world of ideas. And now in the East while this complex revolution is undercutting traditional Buddhism, it is also stimulating oriental Buddhism; and in the West it is creating problems and perceptions to which Buddhism seems particularly relevant. Throughout its history Buddhism has been successively reinterpreted in accordance with different cultures, whilst at the same time preserving its inner truths. Thus has Buddhism spread and survived. The historic task of Buddhists in both East and West in the twenty-first century is to interpret perennial Buddhism in terms of the needs of industrial men and women in the social conditions of their time, and to demonstrate its acute and urgent relevance to the ills of that society. To this great and difficult enterprise Buddhists will bring their traditional boldness and humility. For certainly this is no time for clinging to dogma and defensiveness.

1.2 Social action and the problem of suffering

In modern Western society, humanistic social action in its bewildering variety of forms is seen both as the characteristic way of relieving suffering and enhancing human well-being and, at the same time, as a noble ideal of service and self-sacrifice by humanists of all faiths. Buddhism, however, is a humanism in that it rejoices in the possibility of a true freedom as something inherent in human nature. For Buddhism, the ultimate freedom is to achieve full release from the root causes of all suffering: greed, hatred and delusion, which clearly are also the root causes of all social evils. Their grossest forms are those which are harmful to others. To weaken, and finally eliminate them in oneself, and, as far as possible, in society, is the basis of Buddhist ethics. And here Buddhist social action has its place.

The experience of suffering is the starting point of Buddhist teaching and of any attempt to define a distinctively Buddhist social action. However, misunderstanding can arise at the start, because the Pali word *dukkha*, which is commonly translated simply as 'suffering,' has a much wider and more subtle meaning. There is, of course, much gross, objective suffering in the world (*dukkha-*

dukkha), and much of this arises from poverty, war, oppression and other social conditions. We cling to our good fortune and struggle at all costs to escape from our bad fortune.

This struggle may not be so desperate in certain countries which enjoy a high material standard of living spread relatively evenly throughout the population. Nevertheless, the material achievements of such societies appear somehow to have been 'bought' by social conditions which breed a profound sense of insecurity and anxiety, of restlessness and inner confusion, in contrast to the relatively stable and ordered society in which the Buddha taught.

Lonely, alienated industrial man has unprecedented opportunities for living life 'in the context of equipment,' as the philosopher Martin Heidegger so aptly put it. He has a highly valued freedom to make meaning of his life from a huge variety of more or less readily available forms of consumption or achievement—whether career building, home making, shopping around for different world ideologies (such as Buddhism), or dedicated social service. When material acquisition palls, there is the collection of new experiences and the clocking up of new achievements. Indeed, for many their vibrating busyness becomes itself a more important self-confirmation than the goals to which it is ostensibly directed. In developing countries to live thus, 'in the context of equipment,' has become the great goal for increasing numbers of people. They are watched sadly by Westerners who have accumulated more experience of the disillusion and frustration of perpetual non-arrival.

Thus, from the experience of social conditions there arises both physical and psychological suffering. But more fundamental still is that profound sense of unease, of anxiety or *angst,* which arises from the very transience (*anicca*) of life (*viparināma-dukkha*). This angst, however conscious of it we may or may not be, drives the restless search to establish a meaningful self-identity in the face of a disturbing awareness of our insubstantiality (*anattā*). Ultimately, life is commonly a struggle to give meaning to life— and to death. This is so much the essence of the ordinary human condition and we are so very much inside it, that for much of the time we are scarcely aware of it. This existential suffering is the distillation of all of the various conditions to which we have referred above—it is the human condition itself.

Buddhism offers to the individual human being a religious practice, a Way, leading to the transcendence of suffering. Buddhist social action arises from this practice and contributes to it. From suffering arises desire to end suffering. The secular humanistic activist sets himself the endless task of satisfying that desire, and perhaps hopes to end social suffering by constructing utopias. The Buddhist, on the other hand, is concerned ultimately with the transformation of desire. Hence he contemplates and experiences social action in a fundamentally different way from the secular activist. This way will not be readily comprehensible to the latter, and has helped give rise to the erroneous belief that Buddhism is indifferent to human suffering. One reason why the subject of this pamphlet is so important to Buddhists is that they will have to start here if they are to begin to communicate effectively with non-Buddhist social activists. We should add, however, that although such communication may not be easy on the intellectual plane, at the level of feelings shared in compassionate social action experienced together, there may be little difficulty.

We have already suggested one source of the widespread belief that Buddhism is fatalistic and is indifferent to humanistic social action. This belief also appears to stem from a misunderstanding of the Buddhist law of Karma. In fact, there is no justification for interpreting the Buddhist conception of karma as implying quietism and fatalism. The word *karma* (Pali: *kamma*) means volitional action in deeds, words and thoughts, which may be morally good or bad. To be sure, our actions are conditioned (more or less so), but they are not inescapably determined. Though human behaviour and thought are all too often governed by deeply ingrained habits or powerful impulses, still there is always the potentiality of freedom—or, to be more exact, of a relative freedom of choice. To widen the range of that freedom is the primary task of Buddhist mind training and meditation.

The charge of fatalism is sometimes supported by reference to the alleged 'social backwardness' of Asia. But this ignores the fact that such backwardness existed also in the West until comparatively recent times. Surely this backwardness and the alleged fatalistic acceptance of it stem from specific social and political conditions, which were too powerful for would-be reformers to contend with. But apart from these historic facts, it must be stressed here that the Buddha's message of compassion is certainly not indifferent to human suffering in any form; nor do Buddhists think that social misery cannot be remedied, at least partly. Though Buddhist realism does not believe in the Golden Age of a perfect society, nor in the permanence of social conditions, yet Buddhism strongly believes that social imperfections can be reduced by the reduction of greed, hatred and ignorance, and by compassionate action guided by wisdom.

From the many utterances of the Buddha illustrative of our remarks, two may be quoted here:

> "He who has understanding and great wisdom does not think of harming himself or another, nor of harming both alike. He rather thinks of his own welfare, of that of others, of that of both, and of the welfare of the whole world. In that way one shows understanding and great wisdom."
>
> Aṅguttara Nikāya (*Gradual Sayings*) Fours, No. 186

> "By protecting oneself (e.g. morally), one protects others; by protecting others, one protects oneself."
>
> Saṃyutta Nikāya (*Kindred Sayings*), 47;
> Satipaṭṭhāna Samy., No. 19

In this section we have introduced the special and distinctive quality of Buddhist social action. In the remainder of Part One we shall explore this quality further, and show how it arises naturally and logically from Buddhist teaching and practice.

1.3 The weight of social karma

Individual karmic behaviour patterns are created by the struggles of the individual human predicament. They condition the behaviour of the individual and, in traditional Buddhist teaching, the subsequent rounds of birth and rebirth. We suggest, however, that this karmic inheritance is also expressed as social karma. Specific to time and place, different social cultures arise, whether of a group, a community, a social class or a civilisation. The young are socialised to their inherited culture. Consciously and unconsciously they assimilate the norms of the approved behaviour—what is good, what is bad, and what is 'the good life' for that culture.

The social karma—the establishment of conditioned behaviour patterns—of a particular culture is and is not the aggregate of the karma of the individuals who comprise the culture. Individuals share common institutions and belief systems, but these are the results of many different wills, both in the past and the present, rather than the consequence of any single individual action. It is, however, individual karmic action that links the individual to these institutions and belief systems. Each individual is a light-reflecting jewel in Indra's net, at the points where time and space intersect. Each reflects the light of all and all of each. This is the mysticism of sociology or the sociology of mysticism!

Human societies, too, suffer the round of birth and rebirth, of revolution and stability. Each age receives the collective karmic inheritance of the last, is conditioned by it, and yet also struggles to refashion it. And within each human society, institutions, social classes and subcultures, as well as individuals, all struggle to establish their identity and perpetuate their existence.

Capitalist industrial society has created conditions of extreme impermanence, and the struggle with a conflict-creating mood of dissatisfaction and frustration. It would be difficult to imagine any social order for which Buddhism is more relevant and needed. In these conditions, egotistical enterprise, competitive conflict and the struggle for status become great social virtues, while, in fact, they illustrate the import of the three root-causes of suffering—greed, hatred, and delusion.

"These cravings," argues David Brandon, "have become cemented into all forms of social structures and institutions. People who are relatively successful at accumulating goods and social position wish to ensure that they remain successful ... Both in intended and unintended ways they erect barriers of education, finance and law to protect their property and other interests ... These structures and their protective institutions continue to exacerbate and amplify the basic human inequalities in housing, health care, education and income. They reward and encourage greed, selfishness, and exploitation rather than love, sharing and compassion. Certain people's life styles, characterised by greed and over-consumption, become dependent on the deprivation of the many. The oppressors and oppressed fall into the same trap of continual craving" (Brandon, 1976, 10–11).

It should be added that communist revolution and invasion have created conditions and social structures which no less, but differently, discourage the spiritual search.

Thus we see that modern social organisation may create conditions of life which not only give rise to 'objective,' non-volitionally caused suffering, but also tend to give rise to 'subjective,' volitionally caused karmic suffering, because they are more likely to stimulate negative karmic action than do other kinds of social organisation. Thus, some of us are born into social conditions which are more likely to lead us into following the Buddhist way than others. An unskilled woman factory worker in a provincial industrial town is, for example, less likely to follow the Path than a professional person living in the university quarter of the capital city. A property speculator, wheeling and dealing his samsaric livelihood anywhere is perhaps even less likely than either of them to do so. However, all three may do so. Men and women make their own history, but they make it under specific karmic conditions, inherited from previous generations collectively, as well as individually. The struggle is against nurture, as well as nature, manifested in the one consciousness. "The present generation are living in this world under great pressure, under a very complicated system, amidst confusion. Everybody talks about peace, justice, equality but in practice it is very difficult. This is not because the individual person is bad but because the overall environment, the pressures, the circumstances are so strong, so influential" (Dalai Lama, 1976, p. 17).

In short, Buddhist social action is justified ultimately and above all by the existence of social as well as individual karma. Immediately it is simply concerned with relieving suffering; ultimately, in creating social conditions which will favour the ending of suffering through the individual achievement of transcendent wisdom. But is it enough, to take a beautiful little watering can to a flower dying in sandy, sterile soil? This will satisfy only the waterer. But if we muster the necessary ploughs, wells, irrigation systems and organised labour, what then will become of the spiritual life amongst all this busyness and conflict? We must next consider this fundamental question.

1.4 Is not a Buddhist's prime task to work on him- or herself? Answer: YES and NO

Buddhism is essentially pragmatic. Buddhism is, in one sense, something that one does. It is a guide to the transformation of individual experience. In the traditional Buddhist teaching, the individual sets out with a karmic inheritance of established volitions, derived from his early life, from earlier lives and certainly from his social environment, a part of his karmic inheritance. Nevertheless, the starting point is the individual experiencing of life, here and now.

Our train of argument began with the anxiety, the profound sense of unease felt by the individual in his naked experience of life in the world when not masked by busyness, objectives, diversions and other confirmations and distractions. Buddhism teaches that all suffering—whether it be anxiety, or more explicitly karmic, brought-upon-ourselves-suffering, or 'external' suffering, accidental and inevitable through war, disease, old age and so on—arises ultimately from the deluded belief in a substantial and enduring self. In that case, what need has the individual Buddhist for concern for other individuals, let alone for social action since his prime task is to work on himself in order to dissolve this delusion? Can he only then help others?

The answer to these questions is both yes and no. This does not mean half-way between yes and no. It means yes and no. It means that the answer to these fundamental questions of Buddhist social action cannot ultimately be logical or rational. For the Buddhist Middle Way is not the middle between two extremes, but the Middle Way which transcends the two extremes in a 'higher' unity.

Different traditions of Buddhism offer different paths of spiritual practice. But all depend ultimately upon the individual becoming more deeply aware of the nature of his experience of the world, and especially of other people and hence of himself and of the nature of this self. "To learn the way of the Buddha is to learn about oneself. To learn about oneself is to forget oneself. To forget oneself is to experience the world as pure object—to let fall one's own mind and body and the self-other mind and body" (Zen Master Dogen, *Shobogenzo*). Meditation both reveals and ultimately calms and clarifies the choppy seas and terrifying depths of the underlying emotional life. All the great traditions of spiritual practice, Buddhist and non-Buddhist, emphasise the importance of periods of withdrawal for meditation and reflection. Their relative importance is not our present concern. However, in all Buddhist traditions the training emphasises a vigilant mindfulness of mental feelings in the course of active daily life, as well as in periods of withdrawal. It also advocates the parallel development of habitual forms of ethical behaviour (*sīla*).

"We need not regard life as worth [either] boycotting or indulging in. Life situations are the food of awareness and mindfulness ... We wear out the shoe of *saṃsāra* by walking on it through the practice of meditation" (Chogyam Trungpa, 1976, p. 50). The same message comes across forcefully in the Zen tradition: "For penetrating to the depths of one's true nature ... nothing can surpass the practice of Zen in the midst of activity ... The power of wisdom obtained by practising Zen in the world of action is like a rose that rises from the fire. It can never be destroyed. The rose that rises from the midst of flames becomes all the more beautiful and fragrant the nearer the fire rages" (Zen Master Hakuin, 1971, p. 34).

It is open to us, if we wish, to extend our active daily life to include various possible forms of social action. This offers a strong immediate kind of experience to which we can give our awareness practice. Less immediately, it serves to fertilize our meditation— 'dung for the field of bodhi.' Thirdly, it offers wider opportunities for the cultivation of *sīla*—the habituation to a selfless ethic.

The above remarks are about taking social action. They refer to the potential benefits of social action for individual practice. They are less 'reasons' for social action than reasons why a Buddhist should not desist from social action. The mainspring of Buddhist social action lies elsewhere; it arises from the heart of a ripening compassion, however flawed it still may be by ego needs. This is giving social action, with which we shall be concerned in the next section.

Social action as a training in self-awareness (and compassionate awareness of others) may be a discipline more appropriate to some individual temperaments, and, indeed, to some cultures and times, than to others. We are not concerned with advocating it for all Buddhists, but simply to suggesting its legitimacy for such as choose to follow it. For Buddhism has always recognised the diversity of individual temperaments and social cultures that exist, and has offered a corresponding diversity of modes of practice.

1.5 Buddhist social action as heartfelt paradox

As we have noted, the significance of social action as mindfulness training is, of course, incidental to that profound compassionate impulse which more or less leads us to seek the relief of the suffering of others. Our motives may be mixed, but to the extent that they are truly selfless they do manifest our potential for Awakening and our relatedness to all beings.

Through our practice, both in the world and in withdrawn meditation, the delusion of a struggling self becomes more and more transparent, and the conflicting opposites of good and bad, pain and pleasure, wealth and poverty, oppression and freedom are seen and understood in a Wisdom at once serene and vigilant. This Wisdom partakes of the sensitivity of the heart as well as the clarity of thought.

In this Wisdom, in the words of R.H. Blyth, things are beautiful—but not desirable; ugly—but not repulsive; false—but not rejected. What is inevitable, like death, is accepted without rage; what may not be, like war, is the subject of action skilful and the more effective because, again, it is not powered and blinded by rage and hate. We may recognize an oppressor and resolutely act to remove the oppression, but we do not hate him. Absence of hatred, disgust, intolerance or righteous indignation within us is itself a part of our growth towards enlightenment (*bodhi*).

Such freedom from negative emotions should not be mistaken for indifference, passivity, compromise, loving our enemy instead of hating him, or any other of these relativities. This Wisdom transcends the Relativities which toss us this way and that. Instead, there is an awareness, alert and dispassionate, of an infinitely complex reality, but always an awareness free of despair, of self-absorbing aggression, or of blind dogma, an awareness free to act or not to act. Buddhists have their preferences, and in the face of such social cataclysms as genocide and nuclear war, they are strong preferences, but they are not repelled into quietism by them. What has been said above has to be cultivated to perfection by one following the Bodhisattva ideal. We are inspired by it, but very few of us can claim to live it. Yet we shall never attain the ideal by turning our backs upon the world and denying the compassionate Buddha nature in us that reaches out to suffering humanity, however stained by self love those feelings may be. Only through slowly 'wearing out the shoe of saṃsara' in whatever way is appropriate to us can we hope to achieve this ideal, and not through some process of incubation.

This Great Wisdom (*prajñā*) exposes the delusion, the folly, sometimes heroic, sometimes base, of human struggle in the face of many kinds of suffering. This sense of folly fuses with the sense of shared humanity in the form of compassion (*karuṇā*). Compassion is the everyday face of Wisdom.

In individual spiritual practice though, some will incline to a Way of Compassion and others to a Way of Wisdom, but finally the two faculties need to be balanced, each complementing and ripening the other.

> He who clings to the Void
> And neglects Compassion
> Does not reach the highest stage.
> But he who practises only Compassion
> Does not gain release from the toils of existence.
>
> Saraha, 1954

To summarise, Buddhist or non-Buddhist, it is our common humanity, our 'Buddha nature,' that moves us to compassion and to action for the relief of suffering. These stirrings arise from our underlying relatedness to all living things, from being brothers and sisters one to another. Buddhist spiritual practice, whether at work or in the meditation room, ripens alike the transcendental qualities of Compassion and Wisdom.

Social action starkly confronts the actor with the sufferings of others and also confronts him with his own strong feelings which commonly arise from such experience, whether they be feelings of pity, guilt, angry partisanship or whatever. Social action is thus a powerful potential practice for the follower of the Way, a 'skilful means' particularly relevant to modern society.

Finally, it is only some kind of social action that can be an effective and relevant response to the weight of social karma which oppresses humanity and which we all share.

Part Two: The Action

2.1 Giving and helping

All social action is an act of giving (*dāna*), but there is a direct act which we call charitable action, whether it be the UNESCO Relief Banker's Order or out all night with the destitutes' soup kitchen. Is there anything about Buddhism that should make it less concerned actively to maintain the caring society than is Christianity or humanism? "Whoever nurses the sick serves me," said the Buddha. In our more complex society, does this not include the active advancement and defence of the principles of a national health service?

The old phrase 'as cold as charity' recalls the numerous possibilities for self-deception in giving to others and in helping them. Here is opportunity to give out goodness in tangible form, both in our own eyes and those of the world. It may also be a temptation to impose our own ideas and standards from a position of patronage. David Brandon, who has written so well on the art of helping, reminds us that "respect is seeing the Buddha nature in the other person. It means perceiving the superficiality of positions of moral authority. The other person is as good as you. However untidy, unhygienic, poor, illiterate and bloody-minded he may seem, he is worthy of your respect. He also has autonomy and purpose. He is another form of nature" (Brandon, 1976, p. 59).

There are many different ways in which individual Buddhists and their organisations can give help and relieve suffering. However, 'charity begins at home.' If a Buddhist group or society fails to provide human warmth and active caring for all of its members in their occasional difficulties and troubles—though always with sensitivity and scrupulous respect for privacy—where then is its Buddhism? Where is the Saṅgha?

In our modern industrial society there has been, on the one hand, a decline in personal and voluntary community care for those in need and, on the other, too little active concern for the quality and quantity of institutional care financed from the public purse that has to some extent taken its place. One facet of this which may be of particular significance for Buddhists is a failure to recognize adequately and provide for the needs of the dying. In recent years there has been a growing awareness of this problem in North America and Europe, and a small number of hospices have been established by Christian and other groups for terminally ill people. However, only a start has been made with the problem. The first Buddhist hospice in the West has yet to be opened. And, less ambitiously, the support of regular visitors could help many lonely people to die with a greater sense of dignity and independence in our general hospitals.

2.2 Teaching

Teaching is, of course, also a form of giving and helping. Indeed, one of the two prime offences in the Mahayana code of discipline is that of withholding the wealth of the Dharma from others. Moreover, teaching the Dharma is one of the most valuable sources of learning open to a Buddhist.

Here we are concerned primarily with the teaching of the Dharma to newcomers to Buddhism, and with the general publicising of Buddhism among non-Buddhists.

Buddhism is by its very nature lacking in the aggressive evangelising spirit of Christianity or Islam. It is a pragmatic system of sustained and systematic, self-help practice, in which the teacher can do no more than point the way and, together with fellow Buddhists, provide support, warmth and encouragement in a long and lonely endeavour. There is here no tradition of instant conversion and forceful revelation, for the enlightenment experience, however sudden, depends upon a usually lengthy period of careful cultivation. Moreover, there is a tolerant tradition of respect for the beliefs and spiritual autonomy of non-Buddhists.

Nevertheless, a virtue may be cultivated to a fault. Do we not need to find a middle way between proselytizing zeal and aloof indifference? Does not the world cry out for a Noble Truth that 'leads to the cessation of suffering'? The task of teaching the Dharma also gives individual Buddhists an incentive to clarify their ideas in concise, explicit everyday terms. And it requires them to respond positively to the varied responses which their teaching will provoke in others.

It will be helpful to treat the problem on two overlapping levels, and to distinguish between (a) publicising the Dhamma, and (b) introductory teaching for enquirers whose interest has thus been awakened.

At both the above levels, activity is desirable both by a central body of some kind and by local groups (in many countries there will be several central bodies, representing different traditions and tendencies). The central body can cost-effectively produce for local use introductory texts and study guides, speakers' notes, audiocassettes, slide presentations and 'study kits' combining all of these different types of material. It has the resources to develop correspondence courses such as those run by the Buddhist Society in the United Kingdom which offer a well-tried model. And it will perhaps have sufficient prestige to negotiate time on the national radio and television network.

Particularly in Western countries there are strong arguments for organisations representing the different Buddhist traditions and tendencies to set up a representative Buddhist Information and Liaison Service for propagating fundamental Buddhism and some first introductions to the different traditions and organisations. It would also provide a general information clearing house for all the groups and organisations represented. It could be financed and controlled through a representative national Buddhist council which, with growing confidence between its members and between the different Buddhist organisations which they represented, might in due course take on additional functions. Certainly in the West there is the prospect of a great many different Buddhist flowers blooming, whether oriental or new strains developed in the local culture. This is to be welcomed, but the kind of body we propose will become a necessity to avoid confusion for the outsider and to work against any tendency to sectarianism of a kind from which Buddhism has been relatively free.

Local groups will be able to draw upon the publicity and teaching resources of national centres and adapt these to the needs of local communities. Regular meetings of such groups may amount to no more than half a dozen people meeting in a private house. Sensitively handled it would be difficult to imagine a better way of introducing a newcomer to the Dharma. Such meetings are worthy of wide local publicity. A really strong local base exists where there is a resident Buddhist community of some kind, with premises convenient for meetings and several highly committed workers. Unfortunately, such communities will, understandably, represent a particular Buddhist tradition or tendency, and this exclusiveness may be less helpful to the newcomer than a local group in which he or she may have the opportunity to become acquainted with the different Buddhist traditions represented in the membership and in the programme of activity.

In many countries the schools provide brief introductions to the world's great religions. Many teachers do not feel sufficiently knowledgeable about introducing Buddhism to their pupils and may be unaware of suitable materials even where these do exist. There may be opportunities here for local groups, and certainly the Information Service suggested above would have work to do here.

Finally, the method of introductory teaching employed in some Buddhist centres leaves much to be desired both on educational grounds and as Buddhist teaching. The Buddha always adapted his teaching to the particular circumstances of the individual learner; sometimes he opened with a question about the enquirer's occupation in life, and built his teaching upon the answer to this and similar questions. True learning and teaching has as its starting point a problem or experience posed by the learner, even if this be no more than a certain ill-defined curiosity. It is there that teacher and learner must begin. The teacher starts with the learner's thoughts and feelings and helps him or her to develop understanding and awareness. This is, of course, more difficult than a standard lecture which begins and ends with the teacher's thoughts and feelings, and which may in more senses than one leave little space for the learner. It will also exclude the teacher from any learning.

It follows that unless the teacher is truly inspiring, the 'Dharma talk' is best used selectively: to introduce and stimulate discussion or to summarise and consolidate what has been learnt. Dharma teachers must master the art of conducting open discussion groups, in which learners can gain much from one another and can work through an emotional learning situation beyond the acquisition of facts about Buddhism. Discussion groups have become an important feature of many lay Buddhist and social action organisations in different parts of the world.

They are the heart, for example, of the Japanese mass organisation Rissho Kosei Kai, which explores problems of work, the family and social and economic problems.

2.3 Political action: the conversion of energy

Political power may manifest and sustain social and economic structures which breed both material deprivation and spiritual degradation for millions of men and women. In many parts of the world it oppresses a wide range of social groupings—national and racial minorities, women, the poor, homosexuals, liberal dissidents, and religious groups. Ultimately, political power finds its most terrible expression in war, which reaches now to the possibility of global annihilation.

For both the oppressors and the oppressed, whether in social strife or embattled nations, karmic delusion is deepened. Each group or nation emphasizes its differences, distinguishing them from its opponents; each projects its own shortcomings upon them, makes them the repository of all evil, and rallies round its own vivid illusions and blood-warming hates. Collective hating, whether it be the raised fist, or prejudice concealed in a quiet community, is a heady liquor. Allied with an ideology, hate in any form will not depart tomorrow or next year. Crowned with delusive idealism, it is an awesome and murderous folly. And even when victory is achieved, the victors are still more deeply poisoned by the hate that carried them to victory. Both the revolution and the counter-revolution consume their own children. Buddhism's 'Three Fires' of delusion (*moha*), hatred and ill-will (*dosa*), and greed and grasping (*lobha*), surely burn nowhere more fiercely.

Contrariwise, political power may be used to fashion and sustain a society whose citizens are free to live in dignity and harmony and mutual respect, free of the degradation of poverty and war. In such a society of good heart all men and women find encouragement and support in making, if they will, the best use of their human condition in the practice of wisdom and compassion. This is the land of good karma—not the end of human suffering, but the beginning of the end, the Bodhisattva-land, the social embodiment of *sīla*.

This is not to be confused with the belief common among the socially and politically oppressed that if power could be seized (commonly by an elite claiming to represent them), then personal, individual, 'ideological' change will inevitably follow. This absolutely deterministic view of conditioning (which Marx called 'vulgar Marxism'), is as one-sided as the idea of a society of 'individuals' each struggling with only his own personal karma in a private bubble, hermetically sealed off from history and from other people.

Political action thus involves the Buddhist ideal of approaching each situation without prejudice but with deserved circumspection in questions of power and conflict, social oppression and social justice. These social and political conflicts are the great public samsaric driving energies of our life to which an individual responds with both aggression and self-repression. The Buddha Dharma offers the possibility of transmuting the energies of the individual into Wisdom and Compassion. At the very least, in faith and with good heart, a start can be made.

Buddhists are thus concerned with political action, firstly, in the direct relief of non-volitionally caused suffering now and in the future, and, secondly, with the creation of social karmic conditions favourable to the following of the Way that leads to the cessation of volitionally caused suffering and the creation of a society of a kind which tends to the ripening of wisdom and compassion rather than the withering of them. In the third place, political action, turbulent and ambiguous, is perhaps the most potent of the 'action meditations.'

It is perhaps because of this potency that some Buddhist organisations ban political discussion of any kind, even at a scholarly level, and especially any discussion of social action. There are circumstances in which this may be a sound policy. Some organisations and some individuals may not wish to handle such an emotionally powerful experience which may prove to be divisive and stir up bad feeling which cannot be worked upon in any positive way. This division would particularly tend to apply to 'party politics.' On the other hand, such a discussion may give an incomparable opportunity to work through conflict to a shared wisdom. Different circumstances suggest different 'skilful means,' but a dogmatic policy of total exclusion is likely to be ultimately unhelpful.

In this connection it is worth noting that any kind of social activity which leads to the exercise of power or conflict may stir up 'the fires' in the same way as overtly political activity. Conflict within a Buddhist organisation is cut from the same cloth as conflict in a political assembly and may be just as heady, but the Buddhist context could make such an activity a much more difficult and delusive meditation subject. The danger of dishonest collusion may be greater than that of honest collusion (to borrow one of the Ven. Sangharakshita's aphorisms). The dogmatism and vehemence with which some Buddhists denounce and proscribe all political involvement is the same sad attitude as the dogmatism and vehemence of the politicians which they so rightly denounce.

To be lost in revolution or reform or conservatism is to be lost in *saṃsara* and the realm of the angry warrior, deluded by his power and his self-righteousness. To turn one's back upon all this is to be lost in an equally false idea of nirvana—the realm of gods no less deluded by spiritual power and righteousness; "You do not truly speak of fire if your mouth does not get burnt."

Effective social action on any but the smallest scale will soon involve the Buddhist in situations of power and conflict, of 'political' power. It may be the power of office in a Buddhist organisation. It may be the unsought-for leadership of an action group protesting against the closing of an old people's day-care centre. It may be the organising of a fund-raising movement to build a Buddhist hospice for care of the dying. It may be membership of a local government council with substantial welfare funds. It may be joining an illegal dissident group. In all these cases the Buddhist takes the tiger—his own tiger—by the tail. Some of the above tigers are bigger than others, but all are just as fierce. Hence a Buddhist must be mindful of the strong animal smell of political power and be able to contain and convert the valuable energy which power calls up. A sharp cutting edge is given into his hands. Its use we must explore in the sections which follow.

2.4 Buddhist political theory and policy

Buddhism and politics meet at two levels—theory and practice. Buddhism has no explicit body of social and political theory comparable to its psychology or metaphysics. Nevertheless, a Buddhist political theory can be deduced primarily from basic Buddhism, from Dharma. Secondarily, it can be deduced from the general orientation of scriptures which refer explicitly to a bygone time. We have already argued, however, that this can be done only in a limited and qualified way.

Whatever form it may take, Buddhist political theory like other Buddhist 'theory' is just another theory. As it stands in print, it stands in the world of the conditioned; it is of *saṃsara*. It is its potential, its spiritual implications, which make it different from 'secular' theory. When skilfully practised, it becomes a spiritual practice. As always, Buddhist 'theory' is like a label on a bottle describing the contents which sometimes is mistaken for the contents by zealous label-readers. In that way we can end up with a lot of politics and very little Buddhism.

This is not to decry the value of a Buddhist social and political theory—only its misuse. We have only begun to apply Buddhism as a catalyst to the general body of Western social science and most of the work so far has been in psychology. Such work in allied fields could be extremely helpful to Buddhists and non-Buddhists alike.

The writings of some Buddhists from Sri Lanka, Burma and elsewhere offer interesting examples of attempts to relate Buddhism to nationalism and Marxism (not to be confused with communism). Earlier in the century Anāgārika Dharmapāla stressed the social teaching of the Buddha and its value in liberating people from materialistic preoccupations. U Nu, the eminent Burmese Buddhist statesman, argued that socialism follows naturally from the ethical and social teachings of the Buddha, and another Burmese leader, U Ba Swe, held that Marxism is relative truth, Buddhism absolute truth. This theme has been explored more recently in Trevor Ling's book *Buddha, Marx and God*, (2nd ed., Macmillan, London 1979) and Michal Edwardes's *In the Blowing out of a Flame* (Allen & Unwin 1976). Both are stimulating and controversial books. E.F. Schumacher's celebrated book *Small is Beautiful* (Blond & Briggs, London 1973) has introduced what he terms 'Buddhist economics' and its urgent relevance in the modern world to many thousands of non-Buddhists. Of this we shall say more in a later section on the Buddhist 'good society.'

Buddhist social and political theory and policy can only be mentioned in passing in this pamphlet, although we have earlier introduced the idea of 'social karma' as of central importance. We are, instead, concerned here with problems and questions arising in the practice of social and political work by Buddhists and the nature of that work.

2.5 Conflict and partisanship

The Buddhist faced with political thought, let alone political action, is straightaway plunged into the turbulent stream of conflict and partisanship and right and wrong.

Let the reader, perhaps prompted by the morning newspaper, select and hold in his mind some particular controversial public issue or public figure. Now, how does your Buddhism feel, please? (No, not what does your Buddhism think!) How does it feel when, again, some deeply held conviction is roughly handled at a Buddhist meeting or in a Buddhist journal? "The tears and anguish that follow arguments and quarrels," said the Buddha, "the arrogance and pride and the grudges and insults that go with them are all the result of one thing. They come from having preferences, from holding things precious and dear. Insults are born out of arguments and grudges are inseparable from quarrels" (Kalahavivāda-sutta, trans. H. Saddhatissa, 1978, para. 2). Similarly, in the words of one of the Zen patriarchs: "The conflict between longing and loathing is the mind's worst disease" (Seng Ts'an, 1954).

In all our relationships as Buddhists we seek to cultivate a spirit of openness, cooperation, goodwill and equality. Nonetheless, we may not agree with another's opinions, and, in the final analysis, this divergence could have to do even with matters of life and death. But hopefully we shall be mindful and honest about how we think and how we feel, and how our opponent thinks and feels. In such controversies, are we each to confirm our own ego? Or each to benefit from the other in the search for wise judgment? Moreover, in the words of the Dalai Lama, "when a person criticises you and exposes your faults, only then are you able to discover your faults and make amends. So your enemy is your greatest friend because he is the person who gives you the test you need for your inner strength, your tolerance, your respect for others ... Instead of feeling angry with or hatred towards such a person, one should respect him and be grateful to him" (Dalai Lama, 1976, p. 9). We are one with our adversary in our common humanity; we are two in our divisive conflict. We should be deluded if we were to deny either—if we were to rush either to compromise or to uncompromising struggle. Our conflict and our humanity may be confirmed or denied at any point along that line of possibilities which links the extremes, but ultimately it will be resolved in some other, less explicit sense. Sangharakshita expresses this paradox in his observation that "it is not enough to sympathize with something to such an extent that one agrees with it. If necessary, one must sympathize to such an extent that one disagrees" (Sangharakshita, 1979, p. 60).

Zen Master Dogen has advised, "When you say something to someone, he may not accept it, but do not try to make him understand it rationally. Don't argue with him; just listen to his objections, until he himself finds something wrong with them." Certainly we shall need much time and space for such wisdom and compassion as may inform us in such situations. If we do fight, may our wisdom and compassion honour both our adversary and ourselves, whether in compromise, victory or defeat.

And so,

"On how to sing
The frog school and the skylark school
Are arguing."

Shiki, 1958, p. 169

2.6 Ambiguity, complexity, uncertainty

Our 'Small Mind' clings to delusions of security and permanence. It finds neither of these in the world where, on the contrary, it experiences a sense of ambiguity, complexity and uncertainty which it finds intolerable, and which make it very angry when it is obliged to confront them. 'Small Mind' prefers to see social, economic and political phenomena in terms of black and white, or 'Left and Right.' It likes to take sides, and it clings to social dogmas both sophisticated and simple. ("The rich/poor are always selfish/idle.")

To the extent that we have achieved 'Big Mind' we perceive with equanimity what 'Small Mind' recoils from as intolerable. We are freer to see the world as it is in all the many colours of the rainbow, each merging imperceptibly into the next. In place of clinging to a few black, white and grey compartments, scrutiny is freed, encouraged by the Buddha's discriminating and differentiating attitude (Vibhajjavāda; see Wheel: No. 238/240, Aṅguttara Anthology, Part III, pp. 59 ff.).

We shall not be surprised then that the personal map which guides the Wise through social and political realities may turn out to be disturbingly unconventional. Their reluctance readily to 'take sides' arises not from quietism or an attachment to compromise or a belief in the 'unreality' of conflict, as is variously the case with those guided by mere rules. On the contrary, they may not even sit quietly, throwing soothing generalisations into the ring, as is expected of the religious. This seemingly uncomfortable, seemingly marginal stance simply reflects a reality which is experienced with equanimity.

However, it does not require much equanimity to discover the deeper truths which underlie many current conventional truths. Conventional politics, for example, run from 'left' to 'right,' from radicals through liberals and conservatives to fascists. But this is much too simple. Some radicals are, for example, as dogmatic and authoritarian in practice as fascists, and to their ultimate detriment they hate no less mightily. And, again, some conservatives are equally dogmatic because of an awareness of the subtle, organic nature of society and hence the danger of attempts at 'instant' restructuring.

Similarly an ideology such as Marxism may be highly complex but has been conveniently oversimplified even by quite well educated partisans, both those 'for' and those 'against' the theory. The present Dalai Lama is one of those who have attempted to disentangle 'an authentic Marxism,' which he believes is not without relevance to the problems of a feudal theocracy of the kind that existed in Tibet, from "the sort one sees in countless countries claiming to be Marxist," but which are "mixing up Marxism and their national political interests and also their thirst for world hegemony" (Dalai Lama, 1979).

The Wise person sees clearly because he does not obscure his own light; he does not cast the shadow of himself over the situation. However, even an honest perception of complexity commonly paralyses action with "Yes, that's all very well, but ... On the other hand it is also true that ..." Contemplative wisdom is a precious thing, but true Wisdom reveals itself in positive action—or 'in-action.' Though a person may, through Clear

Comprehension of Purpose (*satthaka-sampajañña*), keep loyal to the social ideal, his Clear Comprehension of (presently absent) Suitability may counsel in-action, or just 'waiting.'

In a social action situation the complexity and ambiguity to which we refer above is strongly felt as ethical quandary, uncertainty as to what might be the best course of action. Even in small organisations all power is potentially corrupting; the power wielder is soon lost in a thicket of relative ethics, of means and ends confused, of greater and lesser evils, of long-term and short-term goals. This is not a 'game.' It is the terrible reality of power, wealth and suffering in the world, and the confusion of good and delusion. It cannot be escaped; it can only be suffered through. We cannot refuse life's most difficult problems because we have not yet attained to Wisdom. We simply have to do our mindful and vigilant best, without guilt or blame. That is all we have to do.

2.7 Violence and non-violence

The First Precept of Buddhism is to abstain from taking life. But it must be made clear that the Buddhist 'Precepts' are not commandments; they are 'good resolutions,' sincere aspirations voluntarily undertaken. They are signposts. They suggest to us how the truly Wise behave, beyond any sense of self and other.

Evil springs from delusion about our true nature as human beings, and it takes the characteristic forms of hatred, aggression and driving acquisitiveness. These behaviours feed upon themselves and become strongly rooted, not only in individuals but in whole cultures. Total war is no more than their most spectacular and bloody expression. In Buddhism the cultivation of *sīla* (habitual morality) by attempting to follow the Precepts is an aspiration towards breaking this karmic cycle. It is a first step towards dissolving the egocentricity of headstrong wilfulness, and cultivating heartfelt awareness of others. The Precepts invite us to loosen the grip, unclench the fist, and to aspire to open-handedness and open-heartedness. Whether, and to what extent, he keeps the Precepts is the responsibility of each individual. But he needs to be fully aware of what he is doing.

The karmic force of violent behaviour will be affected by the circumstances in which it occurs. For example, a 'diminished responsibility' may be argued in the case of conscripts forced to kill by an aggressive government. And there is surely a difference between wars of conquest and wars of defence. Ven. Walpola Rāhula describes a war of national independence in Sri Lanka in the 2nd century BC conducted under the slogan "Not for kingdom but for Buddhism," and concludes that "to fight against a foreign invader for national independence became an established Buddhist tradition, since freedom was essential to the spiritual as well as the material progress of the community" (Rāhula, 1978, p. 117). We may deplore the historic destruction of the great Indian Buddhist heritage in the middle-ages, undefended against the Mongol and Muslim invaders. It is important to note, however, that "according to Buddhism there is nothing that can be called a 'just war'—which is only a false term coined and put into circulation to justify and excuse hatred, cruelty, violence and massacre" (Rāhula, 1967, p. 84).

It is an unfortunate fact, well documented by eminent scholars such as Edward Conze and Trevor Ling, that not only have avowedly Buddhist rulers undertaken violence and killing, but also monks of all traditions in Buddhism. Nonetheless, Buddhism has no history of specifically religious wars, that is, wars fought to impose Buddhism upon reluctant believers.

Violence and killing are deeply corrupting in their effect upon all involved, and Buddhists will therefore try to avoid direct involvement in violent action or in earning their living in a way that, directly or indirectly, does violence. The Buddha specifically mentioned the trade in arms, in living beings and flesh.

The problem is whether, in today's 'global village,' we are not all in some degree responsible for war and violence to the extent that we refrain from any effort to diminish them. Can we refrain from killing a garden slug and yet refrain, for fear of 'political involvement,' from raising a voice against the nuclear arms race or the systematic torture of prisoners of conscience in many parts of the world?

These are questions which are disturbing to some of those Buddhists who have a sensitive social and moral conscience. This is understandable. Yet, a well-informed Buddhist must not forget that moral responsibility, or karmic guilt, originate from a volitional and voluntary act affirming the harmful character of the act. If that affirmation is absent, neither the responsibility for the act, nor karmic guilt, rest with those who, through some form of pressure, participate in it. A slight guilt, however, might be involved if such participants yield too easily even to moderate pressure or do not make use of 'escape routes' existing in these situations. But failure to protest publicly against injustice or wrongdoings does not necessarily constitute a participation in evil. Voices of protest should be raised when there is a chance that they are heard. But 'voices in the wilderness' are futile, and silence, instead, is the better choice. It is futile, indeed, if a few well-meaning heads try to run against walls of rock stone that may yield only to bulldozers. It is a sad fact that there are untold millions of our fellow-humans who do affirm violence and use it for a great variety of reasons (though not 'reasonable reasons'!). They are unlikely to be moved by our protests or preachings, being entirely obsessed by diverse fanaticisms or power urges. This has to be accepted as an aspect of existential suffering. Yet there are still today some opportunities and nations where a Buddhist can and should work for the cause of peace and for reducing violence in human life. No efforts should be spared to convince people that violence does not solve problems or conflicts.

The great evil of violence is its separation unto death of us and them, of 'my' righteousness and 'your' evil. If you counter violence with violence you will deepen that separation through thoughts of bitterness and revenge. The Dhammapada says: "Never by hatred is hatred appeased, but it is appeased by kindness. This is an eternal truth" (I, 5). Buddhist non-violent social action (*avihiṃsa, ahiṃsa*) seeks to communicate, persuade and startle by moral example. "One should conquer anger through kindness, wickedness through goodness, selfishness through charity, and falsehood through truthfulness" (Dhammapada, XVII, 3).

The Buddha intervened personally on the field of battle, as in the dispute between the Sakyas and Koliyas over the waters of the Rohiṇī. Since that time, history has provided us with a host of examples of religiously inspired non-violent social action, skilfully adapted to particular situations. These are worthy of deep contemplation.

Well known is Mahatma Gandhi's non-violent struggle against religious intolerance and British rule in India, and also the Rev. Martin Luther King's black people's civil rights movement in the United States. A familiar situation for many people today is the mass demonstration against authority, which may be conducted either peacefully or violently. As Robert Aitken Gyoun Roshi has observed, "the point of disagreement, even the most fundamental disagreement, is still more superficial than the place of our common life." He recalls the case of a friend who organised an anti-nuclear demonstration at a naval base passing through a small town in which virtually every household had at least one person who gained his livelihood by working at the base. Consequently, when the friend visited every single house before the demonstration he hardly expected to win the people over to his cause. But he did convince them that he was a human being who was willing to listen to them and who had faith in them as human beings. "When we finally had our demonstration, with four thousand people walking through this tiny community, nobody resisted us, nobody threw rocks. They just stood and watched" (*The Ten Directions,* Los Angeles Zen Centre, 1 (3) Sept. 1980, p. 6).

And yet again, situations may arise in which folly is mutually conditioned, but where we must in some sense take sides in establishing the ultimate responsibility. If we do not speak out then, we bow only to the conditioned and accept the endlessness of suffering and the perpetuation of evil karma. The following lines were written a few days after Archbishop Oscar Romero, of the Central American republic of El Salvador, had been shot dead on the steps of his chapel. Romero had roundly condemned the armed leftist rebel factions for their daily killings and extortions. However, he also pointed out that these were the reactions of the common people being used as "a production force under the management of a privileged society ... The gap between poverty and wealth is the main cause of our trouble ... And sometimes it goes further: it is the hatred in the heart of the worker for his employer ... If I did not denounce the killings and the way the army removes people and ransacks peasants' homes I should be acquiescing in the violence" (*Observer* newspaper (London), 30 March, 1980).

Finally there is the type of situation in which the truly massive folly of the conflict and of the contrasting evils may leave nothing to work with and there is space left only for personal sacrifice to bear witness to that folly. Such was the choice of the Buddhist monks who burnt themselves to death in the Vietnam war—surely one of the most savage and despairing conflicts of modern times, in which a heroic group of Buddhists had for some time struggled in vain to establish an alternative 'third force.'

2.8 The good society

The social order to which Buddhist social action is ultimately directed must be one that minimises non-volitionally caused suffering, whether in mind or body, and which also offers encouraging conditions for its citizens to see more clearly into their true nature and overcome their karmic inheritance. The Buddhist way is, with its compassion, its equanimity, its tolerance, its concern for self-reliance and individual responsibility, the most promising of all the models for the New Society which are an on offer.

What is needed are political and economic relations and a technology which will:

(a) Help people to overcome ego-centredness, through cooperation with others, in place of either subordination and exploitation or the consequent sense of 'righteous' struggle against these things.

(b) Offer to each a freedom which is conditional only upon the freedom and dignity of others, so that individuals may develop a self-reliant responsibility rather than being the conditioned animals of institutions and ideologies (see *Buddhism and Democracy*, Bodhi Leaves No. B. 17).

The emphasis should be on the undogmatic acceptance of a diversity of tolerably compatible material and mental 'ways,' whether of individuals or of whole communities. There are no short cuts to utopia, whether by 'social engineering' or theocracy. The good society towards which we should aim should simply provide a means, an environment, in which different 'ways,' appropriate to different kinds of people, may be cultivated in mutual tolerance and understanding. A prescriptive commonwealth of saints is totally alien to Buddhism.

(c) The good society will concern itself primarily with the material and social conditions for personal growth, and only secondarily and dependently with material production. It is noteworthy that the 14th Dalai Lama, on his visit to the West in 1973, saw "nothing wrong with material progress provided man takes precedence over progress. In fact it has been my firm belief that in order to solve human problems in all their dimensions we must be able to combine and harmonise external material progress with inner mental development." The Dalai Lama contrasted the "many problems like poverty and disease, lack of education" in the East with the West, in which "the living standard is remarkably high, which is very important, very good." Yet he notes that despite these achievements there is "mental unrest," pollution, overcrowding, and other problems. "Our very life itself is a paradox, contradictory in many senses; whenever you have too much of one thing you have problems created by that. You always have extremes and therefore it is important to try and find the middle way, to balance the two" (Dalai Lama, 1976, pp. 10, 14, 29).

(d) E.F. Schumacher has concisely expressed the essence of Buddhist economics as follows:

"While the materialist is mainly interested in goods, the Buddhist is mainly interested in liberation. But Buddhism is 'The Middle Way' and therefore in no way antagonistic to physical well-being ... The keynote of Buddhist economics is simplicity and non-violence. From an economist's point of view, the marvel of the Buddhist way of life is the utter rationality of its pattern—amazingly small means leading to extraordinarily satisfying results" (Schumacher, 1973, p. 52).

Schumacher then outlines a 'Buddhist economics' in which production would be based on a middle range technology yielding on the one hand an adequate range of material goods (and no more), and on the other a harmony with the natural environment and its resources. (See also Dr. Padmasiri de Silva's pamphlet *The Search for a Buddhist Economics,* in the series, Bodhi Leaves, No. B. 69).

The above principles suggest some kind of diverse and politically decentralised society, with co-operative management and ownership of productive wealth. It would be conceived on a human scale, whether in terms of size and complexity of organisation or of environmental planning, and would use modern technology selectively rather than being used by it in the service of selfish interests. In Schumacher's words, "It is a question of finding the right path of development, the Middle Way, between materialist heedlessness and traditionalist immobility, in short, of finding 'Right Livelihood.'"

Clearly, all the above must ultimately be conceived on a world scale. "Today we have become so interdependent and so closely connected with each other that without a sense of universal responsibility, irrespective of different ideologies and faiths, our very existence or survival would be difficult" (Dalai Lama, 1976, pp. 5, 28). This statement underlines the importance of Buddhist internationalism and of social policy and social action conceived on a world scale.

The above is not offered as some kind of blueprint for utopia. Progress would be as conflict-ridden as the spiritual path of the ordinary Buddhist—and the world may never get there anyway. However, Buddhism is a very practical and pragmatic kind of idealism, and there is, as always, really no alternative but to try.

2.9 Organising social action

A systematic review of the different kinds of Buddhist organisation for social action which have appeared in different parts of the world is beyond the scope of this pamphlet. Some considerable research would be required and the results would merit at least a separate pamphlet.

Later we shall introduce three contrasting movements which are, in some sense or other, examples of Buddhist social action. Each is related more or less strongly to the particular social culture in which it originated, and all should therefore be studied as illustrative examples-in-context and not necessarily as export models for other countries. They are, however, very suggestive, and two of the three have spread beyond their country of origin.

But first, let us identify some issues for an organisational approach to social action.

2.9a Maintaining balance

Social action needs to be organised and practised in such a way as to build upon its potential for spiritual practice and to guard against its seductions. Collective labour with fellow-Buddhists raises creative energy, encourages positive attitudes and engenders a strong spirit of fellowship. The conflicts, disagreements, obstacles, and discouragements which will certainly be met along the way offer rich meditation experiences and opportunity for personal growth, so long as a scrupulous mindfulness is sustained.

The meditator will learn as much about himself in a contentious meeting as he will in the meditation hall. Both kinds of experience are needed, and they complement one another. Social action is a great ripener of compassion (for self as well as for others), out of the bitterness of the experiences which it commonly offers. Yet, like nothing else, it can stir up the partisan emotions and powerfully exult the opinionated ego. The busy, patronising evangelist not only gives an undercover boost to his own ego; he also steals another person's responsibility for himself. However, these dangers are, comparatively speaking, gross and tangible when set against the no less ego-enhancing seduction of Other-Worldliness and dharma-ridden pietism. Such 'spiritual materialism,' as Chogyam Trungpa calls it, has long been recognised as the ultimate and most elusive kind of self-deception which threatens the follower of the spiritual path.

The seduction lies in being carried away by our good works, in becoming subtly attached to the new goals and enterprises we have set ourselves, so that no space is left in our busily structured hours in which some saving strength of the spirit can abide. Here is opportunity to learn how to dance with time—"the river in which we go fishing," as Thoreau called it, instead of neatly packaging away our lives in it, or letting it dictate us. And in committee lies the opportunity of slowly turning the hot, lusty partisanship of self-opinionated confirmation into the kind of space and dialogue in which we can communicate, and can even learn to love our most implacable opponents.

It is therefore important that both the individual and the group set aside regular periods for meditation, with periods of retreat at longer intervals. It is important also that experiences and the feel of the social action project should as far as possible be shared openly within the Buddhist group.

In our view, the first social action of the isolated Buddhist is not to withhold the Dharma from the community in which he or she lives. However modest one's own understanding of the Dharma, there is always some first step that can be taken and something to be learnt from taking that step. Even two or three can be a greater light to one another, and many forms of help are often available from outside such as working together through a correspondence course, for example, or listening to borrowed audiocassettes.

For the reasons given earlier it is important that social action projects should, where possible, be undertaken by a Buddhist group rather than each individual 'doing his own thing.' And since the Buddhist group will, in most Western countries, be small and isolated, it is important that the work be undertaken in cooperation with like-minded non-Buddhists. This will both use energies to better effect since social action can be very time- and energy-consuming, and create an even better learning situation for all involved. Forms of social action which are high on explicit giving of service and low on conflict and power situations will obviously be easier to handle and to 'give' oneself to, though still difficult in other respects. For example, organising and participating in a rota of visits to lonely, long-stay hospital patients would contrast, in this respect, with involvement in any kind of local community development project.

2.9b Spiritual centres: example and outreach

In this section we are concerned with the significance of Buddhist residential communities both as manifestations and examples of the 'good society' and as centres of social outreach (mainly, though not solely, in the form of teaching the Dharma). We may distinguish four possible kinds of activity here.

In the first place, any healthy spiritual community does, by its very existence, offer to the world a living example not only of the Good Life but also of the Good Society. Certain spiritual values are made manifest in its organisation and practice in a way not possible in print or in talk. On the other hand, the purely contemplative and highly exclusive community can do this only in some limited, special and arguable sense.

In the second place, where the members of such a community undertake work as a community in order to sustain their community economically ('Right Livelihood'), then to that extent the community becomes a more realistic microcosm of what has to be done in the wider world and a more realistic model and example of how it might best be done.

Thirdly, such communities are commonly teaching and training communities. This may be so in formal terms, in that they offer classes and short courses and also longer periods of training in residence, in which the trainees become veritable community members. And it may be true in terms of the 'openness' of the community to outsiders who wish for the present to reserve their formal commitment, but who wish to open up their communication with the community through some participation in work, ritual, teaching, meditation.

Fourthly, the community might involve itself in various kinds of outside community service, development or action beyond that of teaching, and beyond the necessarily commercial services which may sustain the community's 'Right Livelihood.' Examples might be running a hospice for the terminally ill, providing an information and advice centre on a wide range of personal and social problems for the people of the local community, and assisting—and maybe leading—in various aspects of development of a socially deprived local community. The spiritual community thus becomes more strongly a community within a community. In this kind of situation would the spiritual community draw strength from its service to the social, the 'lay' community, creating an upward spiral of energy? Or would the whole scheme founder through the progressive impoverishment and corruption of the spiritual community in a vicious downward spiral?

In the Eastern Buddhist monastic tradition the first and third aspects (above) are present. In contrast to Christian monasticism, monks are not necessarily expected to be monks for life, and the monasteries may have an important function as seminaries and as long and short stay teaching and training centres. On the other hand, economically such communities are commonly strongly sustained by what is predominantly a Buddhist society. In the West there are now similar communities in all the main Buddhist traditions. Although these are to some extent sustained also by lay Buddhist contributions, their income from training and teaching fees may be important. And whether it is or not, it is clear that their actual and potential training and teaching role is likely to be very important in non-Buddhist societies in which there is a growing interest in Buddhism. A good example is the Manjusri Institute in the United Kingdom, which is now seeking official recognition for the qualifications which it awards, and which could eventually become as much part of the national education system as, say, a Christian theological college. Such an integration of Buddhist activity into the pattern of national life in the West is, of course, most welcome, and opens up many new opportunities for making the Dharma more widely understood.

The above developments may be compared with the communities which form the basis of the Friends of the Western Buddhist Order (FWBO). In these, our second aspect (above), that of Right Livelihood, is found, in addition to the first and third.

The FWBO was founded in 1967 in the United Kingdom by the Ven. Maha Sthavira Sangharakshita, a Londoner who spent twenty years in India as a Buddhist monk and returned with the conviction that the perennial Buddhism always expresses itself anew in each new age and culture. The FWBO is concerned with building what it calls the 'New Society' in the minds and practice of its members. Opening the FWBO's London Buddhist Centre, Ven. Sangharakshita was reported as saying that the New Society was a spiritual community composed of individuals who are "truly human beings: self-aware, emotionally positive people whose energies flow freely and spontaneously, who accept responsibility for their own growth and development, in particular by providing three things: firstly, a residential spiritual community; secondly, a co-operative Right Livelihood situation; and thirdly a public centre, offering classes, especially in meditation" (Marichi, 1979).

The FWBO does in fact follow a traditional Mahayana spiritual practice, but within this framework it does have, as the quotation above suggests, a strong Western flavour. This owes much to the eleven co-operatives by which many of the eighteen autonomous urban communities support themselves. These businesses are run by teams of community members as a means of personal and group development. They include a printing press, graphic design business, photographic and film studio, metalwork forge, and shops and cafes.

Membership of the communities (which are usually single sex) varies between four and thirty people, and often the community members pool their earnings in a 'common purse.' The FWBO comprises Order members, Mitras (who have made some initial commitment) and Friends (supporters in regular contact). Each community is autonomous and has its own distinctive character. Attached to communities are seven Centres, through which the public are offered talks, courses and instruction in meditation. Regular meetings of Chairmen of Centres and other senior Order members, supported by three central secretariats, are planned for the future, but it is not intended to abridge the autonomy of the constituent communities, each of which is a separately registered legal body.

The FWBO is growing very rapidly, not only in the United Kingdom but also overseas, with branches in Finland, the Netherlands, New Zealand, Australia, the USA, and, interestingly, in India, where a sustained effort is being made to establish centres.

2.9c Community services and development

We refer in this section to the fourth aspect distinguished early in the previous section 2.9b, namely, various possible kinds of service and support which may be given by organised Buddhists to the local community in which they live. The FWBO does not undertake this kind of activity (see previous section for examples), and in fact there do not appear to be any major examples of it in the West.

Arguably if this kind of work is undertaken at all, it might more likely be initiated by a non-residential 'lay' Buddhist group, whose members as householders and local workers may have strong roots in their town or neighbourhood. As an example of what can be achieved by a relatively small group of this kind, we quote the following (from *The Middle Way*, 54 (3) Autumn 1979, p. 193):

"The Harlow Buddhist Society has recently opened Dana House, a practical attempt to become involved with the ordinary people of the town and their problems. The new centre ... has four regular groups using it. The first is an after-care service for those who have been mentally or emotionally ill. The centre is there for those in need of friendship and understanding. The second group is a psychotherapy one, for those with more evident emotional problems. It is run by an experienced group leader and a psychologist who can be consulted privately. The third group is a beginners' meditation class based on the concept of 'Right Understanding.' The fourth group is the Buddhist group, which is not attached to any particular school of Buddhism.

"Peter Donahoe writes: 'We have endeavoured to provide a centre which can function in relation to a whole range of different needs, a place of charity and compassion, where all are welcomed regardless of race, colour, sex or creed, welcomed to come to terms with their suffering in a way which is relative to each individual.'"

However, on the whole, it is only in the East, in societies in which Buddhist culture is predominant or important, that there are sufficiently committed Buddhists to play a part in extensive community service and development projects. For example, in Japan there are several such movements and we shall refer in the next section to one example—Soka Gakkai, a movement which also plays a number of other roles. We must first, however, turn our attention to a pre-eminent example of a Buddhist-inspired movement for community development, the Sarvodaya Shramadana Movement of Sri Lanka.

'Sarvodaya' means 'awakening of all' and 'Shramadana' means 'sharing of labour,' making a gift of time, thought and energy. This well describes what is basically a village self-help movement, inspired by Buddhist principles and founded in 1958 as part of a general national awakening. It is now by far the largest non-governmental, voluntary organisation in Sri Lanka.

The Movement learned in its earliest days how very important non-economic factors are in community development, and its projects combine spiritual-cultural with socioeconomic development. "One important element that cannot be improved upon in Buddhist villages in particular is the unique place of the temple and the Buddhist monk, the one as the meeting place, the other as the chief exponent of this entire process." (All quotations here are from the pamphlet *Ethos and Work Plan*, published by the Movement.) Founded on traditional culture, Sarvodaya Shramadana is ultimately "a non-violent revolutionary movement for changing man and society." At the same time it aims to retain the best in the traditional social and cultural fabric of the community.

Village development projects are undertaken on the initiative of the villagers themselves. To begin with, the community is made aware of the historic causes that led to the impoverishment and disintegration of the community and of its cultural and traditional values. Economic regeneration is only possible if there is a restoration of social values within the village. It is emphasised that the community itself must take the initiative in removing obstacles to development and in learning the new skills needed to carry through a change of programme. The volunteers brought in to help serve only as a catalyst. Action is focussed initially on Shramadana Camps in which villagers and outside volunteers work together upon some community project such as a road or irrigation channel. The experience of such Camps helps to develop a sense of community. Local leaders, working through village groups of farmers, of youth, of mothers and others, emerge to take increasing responsibility for a more or less comprehensive development programme. This may include preschool care for the under-fives, informal education for adults, health care programmes, and community kitchens, with cooperation with State agencies as appropriate. By 1980, Sarvodaya was reaching 3,500 villages and was running 1,185 pre-schools.

Essential to these community development programmes is Sarvodaya Shramadana's system of Development Education programmes, operating through six Institutes and through the Gramodaya centres, each of which co-ordinates development work in some twenty to thirty villages. The movement also provides training in self-employment for the youth who compose the largest sector of the unemployed. Although the main thrust of activity has been in rural areas, the Movement is also interested in urban community development where conditions are favourable and there is local interest.

The main material support for the movement comes from the villagers themselves, although financial and material assistance has also been received from overseas.

It is argued that the basic principles of Sarvodaya Shramadana can be adapted to developed as well as to developing countries, and Sarvodaya groups are already active in West Germany, the Netherlands, Japan and Thailand. "The rich countries also have to help to change their purely materialistic outlook and strike a balance, with spiritual values added to the materialistic values of their own communities so that together all can build a new One World social order."

2.9d Political action and mass movements

Although there may be exceptional circumstances in certain countries, as a general rule there are strong arguments against Buddhist groups explicitly aligning themselves with any political party. It is not just that to do so would be irrelevantly divisive. As we have noted in section 2.6 (above), there are deeper, underlying social and political realities which cross-cut the conventional political spectrum of left, right and centre.

Nevertheless, Buddhism, like other great religious systems, inevitably has political implications. To some extent these seem to be relatively clear, and in other senses they are arguable and controversial. Religion has its own contribution to make to politics and, ultimately, it is the only contribution to politics that really matters. It has failed both politically and as a religion if it falls either into the extreme of being debased by politics or of rejecting any kind of political involvement as a kind of fearful taboo. The fear of creating dissension among fellow Buddhists is understandable, but if Buddhists cannot handle conflict in a positive and creative way, then who can?

On closer examination we shall find that it is not 'politics' that requires our vigilance so much as the problems of power and conflict inherent in politics. Indeed, a better use of the term 'political' would be to describe any kind of power and conflict situation. In this sense a Buddhist organisation may be more intensely and unhappily 'political' in managing its spiritual and practical affairs than if and when its members are discussing such an 'outside' matter as conventional politics. Indeed, any such discussion of social and political questions may be banned by a Buddhist society which may be in fact intensely political in terms of underlying power and conflict with which its members have not really come to terms. All kinds of organisations have problems of power and conflict and derive their positive dynamism from the good management of these, but the dangers of self-delusion seem to be greater in religious bodies.

When we meet Buddhists and get to know them, we find that even when they do not express explicit opinions on political and social matters, it is clear from other things they say that some are inclined to a conservative 'establishment' stance, some are of a radical inclination, and others more dissident still. Since the diversities of THIS and THAT exist everywhere else in the conditioned world, even Buddhists cannot pretend to exclude themselves from such disturbing distinctions. This is not really in question. What is in question is their ability to handle their differences openly and with Buddhist maturity. And, as we have tried to show earlier, this maturity implies a progressive diminution of emotional attachment to views about THIS and THAT, so that we no longer need either in order to sustain our identity in the world and have in some sense transcended our clinging by a higher understanding. We still carry THIS or THAT, but lightly and transparently and manageably—without ego-weight. If we did not still carry them, how could we feel the Compassion for *saṃsara,* for ourselves as well as others?

Alan Watts wrote a suitably controversial little pamphlet on this subject, entitled *Beat Zen, Square Zen and Zen* (City Lights Books, San Francisco, 1959). The following passage may be found helpful to our present discussion; what the author has to say about Zen is surely no less applicable to Buddhism as a whole. Watts argues that the Westerner who wishes to understand Zen deeply "must understand his own culture so thoroughly that he is no longer swayed by its premises unconsciously. He must really have come to terms with the Lord God Jehovah and with his Hebrew-Christian conscience so he can take it or leave it without fear or rebellion. He must be free of the itch to justify himself. Lacking this, his Zen will be either 'beat' or 'square,' either a revolt from the culture and social order or a new form of stuffiness and respectability. For Zen is above all the liberation of the mind from conventional thought and this is something utterly different from rebellion against convention, on the one hand, or adapting foreign conventions, on the other."

In the West, individual Buddhists have been particularly attracted to pacifist, disarmament, and environmentalist movements and parties. These movements have profound concerns, which, arguably, undercut the expediencies of conventional party politics. On the other hand, are they not made the more attractive by a certain political innocence, as yet uncorrupted and unblessed by the realities of power? And do they not also underestimate the karma of power and property?

However, in Western and other non-Buddhist countries Buddhist political action of any kind is little more than speculative. Buddhists are few in number, and their energies are necessarily fully occupied with learning and teaching. Teaching is the major form of social action and we have already discussed certain social action implications of the spiritual community. Social action at most verges upon certain possible kinds of service to the wider community or even participation in community development. We have already suggested the merit of such enterprises. But as to politics, using the word conventionally, in the West and at the present time, that can be no more than a matter for discussion in Buddhist groups. As always, individual Buddhists and perhaps informal groups will decide for themselves about political action or inaction.

However, in countries where there are strong Buddhist movements, well rooted in society, some kind of political stance and action seems unavoidable and, indeed, logical and natural, though conventional party political alignments may generally be avoided.

For example, Sarvodaya Shramadana's success at the higher levels of village self-development depends on "the extent that unjust economic arrangements such as ownership of means of production, e.g., land in the hands of a few, administrative system and political power structures, are changed in such a way that the village masses become the true masters of their own selves and their environment. That the present government has gone very far in this direction is amply demonstrated when one examines the radical measures that have already been taken" (Sarvodaya Shramadana pamphlet *Ethos and Work Plan,* p. 31).

Large and explicitly Buddhist movements fill a variety of different roles, from the devotional to the so-called 'New Religions' which have become particularly important in Japan in the post-war period. (Some mention has already been made of the small discussion groups which are a notable feature of Rissho-Kosei-Kai—the 'Society for Establishing Righteousness and Family Relations'.) With their strong emphasis on pacifism, brotherly love, and mutual aid, these organisations have done much to assist the recovery of the Japanese people from the trauma of military aggression and the nuclear explosions which terminated it.

Soka Gakkai (literally, 'Value Creation Society') is perhaps the most striking of these Japanese Buddhist socio-political movements. It is a lay Buddhist organisation with over fifteen million adherents, associated with the Nichiren-Sho-Shu sect.

Soka Gakkai has an ambitious education and cultural programme, and has founded its own university, high school and hospital. It also has a political party, Komeito—the 'Clean Government Party,' which as early as 1967 returned twenty-five parliamentary candidates to the Japanese lower house, elected with five percent of the national vote. The party has continued to play an important part in Japanese political life, basing itself on "the principles of Buddhist democracy" and opposition to rearmament. Soka Gakkai is a populist movement, militant, evangelical and well organised, pledged to "stand forever on the side of the people" and to "devote itself to carrying out the movement for the human revolution" (President Daisaku Ikeda). More specifically, its political achievements have included a successful confrontation with the mine owners of Hokkaido.

Attitudes to Soka Gakkai understandably differ widely. It has been criticised by some for its radicalism and by others for its conservatism; certainly it has been criticised on the grounds of dogmatism and aggressiveness. Certainly it is imbued with the nationalist fervour of Nichiren, the 13th century Buddhist monk who inspired it. Although it has some claims to missionary work in other countries, Soka Gakkai appears to have a more distinctive national flavour than the other social action groups we have looked at and to be less suitable for export.

2.9e 'Universal Responsibility and the Good Heart'

Elsewhere we have already quoted the words of the Dalai Lama emphasising the active global responsibility of Buddhists, and the importance above all of what he calls 'Universal Responsibility and the Good Heart.' In all countries will be found non-Buddhists, whether religionists or humanists, who share with us a non-violent, non-dogmatic and non-sectarian approach to community and world problems, and with whom Buddhists can work in close cooperation and with mutual respect. This is part of the 'Good Heart' to which the Dalai Lama refers. "I believe that the embracing of a particular religion like Buddhism does not mean the rejection of another religion or one's own community. In fact it is important that those of you who have embraced Buddhism should not cut yourself off from your own society; you should continue to live within your own community and with its members. This is not only for your sake but for others' also, because by rejecting your community you obviously cannot benefit others, which actually is the basic aim of religion" (Dalai Lama, 1976).

Mr Emilios Bouratinos and his colleagues of the Buddhist Society of Greece have framed certain farsighted proposals for the 'rehumanisation of society' which have Buddhist inspiration but which seek to involve non-Buddhist ideological groups with the aim of reaching some common ground with them on the organisation of society. Mr. Bouratinos argues that Buddhists should address themselves "to all people somehow inspired from within—whether they be religionists or not. This is indispensable, for we Buddhists are a tiny minority in the West and yet we must touch the hearts of many if this world is to survive in some meaningful fashion" (Letter to the author, 25 May 1980).

Conclusion

Certainly in the West many Buddhists will maintain that it is necessary to take one step at a time, and that for the present our individual and collective action must go into the inner strengthening of our faith and practice. They would doubtlessly agree on the importance of teaching the Dharma, which we have characterised as one of the important forms of social action, but they would argue that the seduction of other kinds of social action, and the drain of energy, are greater than the opportunities which it can afford for "wearing out the shoe of *saṃsāra*." They would argue that the best way to help other people is by personal example.

This pamphlet concedes some possible truth to the above position but also offers a wide range of evidence to the contrary, to which in retrospect the reader may now wish to return. Whatever we may feel about it, certainly the debate is a worthwhile one since, as we have seen, it points to the very heart of Buddhism—the harmony, or creative equilibrium, of Wisdom and Compassion. And as in all worthwhile debates, the disagreement, and, still more, the possible sense of disagreeableness which it engenders, offers each of us a valuable meditation.

The needs and aptitudes of individuals differ, and our debate will also appear differently to readers in different countries with different cultural backgrounds. Though we are brothers and sisters to one another, as Buddhists each must light his or her own way. To the enquiring reader who has little knowledge of Buddhism and yet who has managed to stay with me to the end, I offer my apologies if I have sometimes seemed to forget him and if my explanations have proved inadequate. For:

> "This is where words fail: for what can words tell
> Of things that have no yesterday, tomorrow or today?"
>
> Tseng Ts'an

To a world knotted in hatreds and aggression and a host of follies, grand and mean, heroic and base, Buddhism offers a unique combination of unshakable equanimity and a deeply compassionate practical concern. And so may we tread lightly through restless experience, riding out defeats and discouragements, aware always of the peace at the heart of things, of the freedom that is free of nothing.

References

Brandon, David, *Zen and the Art of Helping*, Routledge & Kegan Paul, 1976.

Chogyam Trungpa, *The Myth of Freedom and the Way of Meditation*, Shambhala, 1976.

Chuang Tzu, *The Way of Chuang Tzu*, trans. Thomas Merton, Unwin Books, 1970.

Conze, Edward, *Buddhism*, 2nd ed., Cassirer, 1974.

Dalai Lama, H.H.XIV, *Universal Responsibility and the Good Heart*, Dharamsala (Library of Tibetan works), 1976.

Dalai Lama, H.H.XIV, reported in *Tibetan Review*, April 1979, and quoted from Reuter (Paris) News Report, 21st March 1979.

Hakuin, Zen Master, *The Zen Master Hakuin*, trans. P.B. Yampolsky, Columbia University Press, 1971.

Marichi, *Authority and the Individual*, FWBO Newsletter No. 41, Winter 1979, 13.

Rahula, Walpola, *What the Buddha Taught*, 2nd ed., Gordon Fraser, 1967.

Rahula, Walpola, *Zen and the Taming of the Bull: Essays*, Gordon Fraser, 1978.

Saddhatissa, H., trans., *Kalahavivada-sutta* (*Sutta-Nipata*), Buddhist Quarterly, 11(1), 1978, 1–3.

Sangharakshita, M.S., *Peace is a Fire*, Windhorse Publications, 1979.

Saraha, *Treasury of Songs* (*Doha Kosha*), in Conze, E., ed. *Buddhist Texts*, Cassirer, 1954.

Schumacher, E.F., *Small is Beautiful: a Study of Economics as if People Mattered*, Blond & Briggs, 1973.

Seng Ts'an, *On Trust in the Heart,* in Conze, E., ed. *Buddhist Texts*, Cassirer, 1954 (trans. Arthur Waley).

Shiki, *Haiku*, in Henderson, Harold, *An Introduction to Haiku*, Doubleday, 1958.

Buddhist Stories

From the Dhammapada Commentary

Part I

Translated from the Pāli by
Eugene Watson Burlingame

Selected and revised by
Bhikkhu Khantipālo

Copyright © Kandy; Buddhist Publication Society, (1982)

Publisher's Note

This anthology has been compiled from Eugene Watson Burlingame's classic translation of the background stories from the Dhammapada Commentary, *Buddhist Legends.* Originally published in the Harvard Oriental Series, *Buddhist Legends* has been maintained in print since 1969 by the Pali Text Society. With the latter's permission, the Buddhist Publication Society issues this selection of these stories in booklet form in the Wheel Series, edited and arranged by Bhikkhu Khantipālo. The publisher gratefully acknowledges the kindness of the Pali Text Society for granting permission to publish this anthology. Readers who would like to obtain the complete three-volume collection of Buddhist Legends may contact the Pali Text Society or inquire from bookshops specializing in Asian literature.

Introduction

This book comprises Buddhist stories which have been selected from the old commentary to the Dhammapada. This anthology of fifty-six stories represents only a small part of the very large original work, which in its complete translation fills three large volumes. The stories selected here are perhaps among the best, and they will be those most appealing to us at a time more than two thousand years after their origin.

The Dhammapada (Dhp.) itself is the best known of all the collections of the Buddha's sayings, for it has been translated many times into English and into many other languages of the East and the West. It consists of 423 verses arranged into twenty-six chapters. A few of these verses were spoken as pairs and, more rarely, three or more of them were uttered by the Buddha together. Most are single stanzas which sum up the Dhamma that was necessary at that particular time.

No one knows how the Dhammapada was compiled. A great many of its verses are found elsewhere in the Pāli Canon, but a few are peculiar to this collection. Why these particular verses were formed into what we now call the Dhammapada is not clear, but we know that other Buddhist schools had Dhammapadas of their own which varied a good deal from the Pāli version.

If all the stories go back to the Buddha's days (which is unlikely, though the traditional view), then the collection could have been made for teaching purposes since many of the tales are both absorbing and instructive. But the random arrangement of the Dhp. itself points to a time when the Buddha's words were orally transmitted and when a more logical rearrangement would have been difficult. Yet there is some order indeed, for the first verses point to the very heart of the Buddha's Teaching:

"Mental states are forerun by mind,
Mind is chief, mind-made are they ..."

The last chapter of verses on the *arahant*, the person who is of supreme worth since without any defilements, gives one a clear picture of the final goal reached in this world by patient effort and perseverance. But in between there is a mixture of verses and topics which are arranged more for ease of memorization than anything else.

It is likely that many of the Dhammapada stories do record events that happened in the Buddha's time, for they often quote from the Suttas or are based on them. In the latter case they always amplify the rather sparse accounts found in the Suttas. Sometimes the process of embroidery can be clearly seen, as when teachings or classifications not known during the Buddha's lifetime are attributed to him or to that period. Examples of this are the mention of the Three Piṭakas (the "baskets" into which the Buddha's words were arranged), which probably began to be compiled from the time of the First Council onwards; and mention of the two duties (*dhura*) for monks and nuns, that is, either scholarship (which meant oral repetition of the Buddha's words to pass them on to the next generation of students) or meditation—a dichotomy not clearly found in the Buddha's time. Many other examples could be given.

Some of the stories have no counterparts in the Suttas and we do not know where they came from. But as some of them are good stories, well told, conveying the taste of Dhamma, they have been included here. "The Weaver's Daughter" (No. 24) and the next tale of "A Certain Layman" are noteworthy examples.

The Dhammapada Commentary as we have it now was written down by the great Buddhaghosa and his pupils, nearly fifteen hundred years ago. They converted the collections of stories as found in old Sinhalese, together with the word-commentary explaining the verses, into Pāli, which even a thousand years after the Buddha was still a *lingua franca*. In that language it has remained, preserved on palm-leaf manuscripts, until modern times. The whole work has always been used as an enjoyable and easy text for novices learning the Pāli language.

After this brief sketch of the history of the Dhp. stories it might be a good idea to give some hints on how to read them and how not to. They come from a culture far separated from us in time, though if we live in a Buddhist country the "distance" is not so great. However, modern Western-type education is based on very different assumptions from those which lie behind the world of the Dhp. stories, a fact which may make some of them difficult to understand. Stories which I felt would not have much impact now, or which might easily lead to misunderstandings, have been left out of this selection. Even so, the ancient commentators did not hesitate to embroider them with the strange and marvellous, sometimes in the middle of an otherwise straightforward account. In this case I have included the tale thinking that its teaching will be remembered while the embroidery can be forgotten. The purpose of the stories, after all, is to illustrate the Dhamma and to provide memorable incidents which will serve as a pattern for one's own Dhamma practice. If this is forgotten (as seems to have been the case in later collections of Buddhist legends), then the marvellous takes over and the Dhamma teaching disappears. So when reading these stories it is the Dhamma which is important, not whether the incident concerned really happened. The old commentators were not concerned with history or whether precisely these words were spoken or those things done, but they preserved and passed on these stories as examples: either as warnings of what should not be done, or as encouragements for Dhamma practice. This emphasis needs to be remembered, otherwise a reader with a critical mind, thinking, "That's impossible," will miss the real point of the story.

It is recommended that these stories be read and re-read so that they stick in the mind. When they can be remembered easily, one has then a store of Dhamma to carry around which can be related to everyday life. For oneself and for other people to whom one may relate them, they can convey "the taste of Dhamma."

When these stories are related in Buddhist countries during sermons in temples or at Dhamma-study classes, they are not repeated word for word as found in the Dhp. Commentary. Though their main features are unaltered, by being told orally they vary a great deal in the amount of detail included. Here they are presented as the text gives them, but some of the details may not be appropriate to repeat when retelling them. However, care should be taken that the story is not distorted, and even more care taken to see that the Dhp. verse which is the Buddha's word is not incorrectly quoted.

These stories, as the reader will see, range from the comic to the tragic. Indeed, some of the longest, not included here, have all the material for extended drama and have been used as dramatic presentations of the Dhamma. But however amusing or disturbing, the message is always that *kamma has its appropriate results*. Actually there is no real tragedy in the Western sense of this word because what is painful is also impermanent. Though one may be afflicted in this life, one's suffering cannot continue forever. Past life stories are quite common in the Dhp. Commentary and are often related by the Buddha to account for some attainment of happiness or misery in the lives of the people with whom he came into contact.

What is reproduced in these pages is a partly revised version of E.W. Burlingame's translation, entitled *Buddhist Legends*. The revision of these stories was undertaken at the behest of Ven. Nyanaponika Mahāthera. I have left much of the translator's work as it is found in the complete translation: his English style is excellent and his renderings usually very accurate. However, in reading through that three-volume work, a few question marks were inserted into the margins where the meaning was not clear. These points I have cleared up after consulting the Pali Text Society's edition of the Dhp. Commentary. Also, as the translation was made more than fifty years ago, some of the renderings of terms have now been more accurately translated. Generally I have followed the suggestions of the *Buddhist Dictionary* of Ven. Nyanatiloka Mahāthera, and those of Ven. Ñāṇamoli Thera in his various books.

I have used my own verse translation of the stanzas of the Dhammapada to replace the prose renderings in the original translation. It now only remains for me to give thanks to the late I.B. Horner, President of the Pali Text Society, for permission to base this book on the complete translation of the Dhp. Commentary published by the Society. Hopefully, this selection will whet the appetite and lead more people to read the entire work.

Bhikkhu Khantipālo

Part I
Making Good Kamma

1. *The Story of Magha*

BY HEEDFULNESS DID MAGHA GO TO THE LORDSHIP OF THE GODS ... This instruction was given by the Teacher while in residence at a summer-house near Vesālī with reference to Sakka, king of gods.[1]

Story of the Present: Mahāli's Question

A Licchavi prince named Mahāli, who lived at Vesālī, hearing the Teacher recite the Suttanta entitled Sakka's Questions,[2] thought to himself, "The Supremely Enlightened One has described the great glory of Sakka. Has the Teacher seen Sakka? Or has he not seen Sakka? Is the Teacher acquainted with Sakka? Or is he not acquainted with Sakka? I will ask him."

So the Licchavi prince Mahāli drew near to where the Exalted One was, and having drawn near, saluted the Exalted One and sat down on one side.[3] And having sat down on one side, the Licchavi prince Mahāli spoke thus to the Exalted One: "Reverend sir, has the Exalted One seen Sakka, king of gods?"—"Yes, Mahāli, I have indeed seen Sakka, king of gods."—"Reverend sir, it must certainly have been a counterfeit of Sakka; for, reverend sir, it is a difficult matter to see Sakka, king of gods."—"Nevertheless, Mahāli, I know Sakka; I know what qualities made him Sakka; I know by the cultivation of what qualities Sakka attained to the state of Sakka.

"Mahāli, in a previous state of existence Sakka, king of gods, was a human being, a prince named Magha: therefore is he called Maghavā. Mahāli, in a previous state of existence Sakka, king of

---

1. Sakka was the ruler of the gods in the Tāvatiṃsa heaven, the realm of the Thirty-three, one of the celestial realms in the sensual sphere.
2. See *Sakka's Questions* (BPS Wheel No. 10).
3. The portion of the story from this sentence through the verses is found at Saṃyutta Nikāya 11:3.

gods, was a human being who in a previous state of existence gave gifts (*pure dānaṃ adāsi*); therefore he is called Purindada. Mahāli, in a previous state of existence Sakka, king of gods, was a human being who gave alms assiduously (*sakkaccaṃ*); therefore is he called Sakka. Mahāli, in a previous state of existence Sakka, king of gods, was a human being who gave a dwelling-place (*āvasathā*); therefore is he called Vāsava. Mahāli, in a previous state of existence Sakka, king of gods, was a human being who could think of as many as a thousand things (*sahassaṃ atthaṃ*) in an instant: therefore is he called Sahassakkha. Mahāli, Sakka, king of gods, has an asura maiden named Sujātā for his wife; therefore is he called Sujampati. Mahāli, Sakka, king of gods, bears sway as lord and master over the gods of the Thirty-three; therefore is he called King of Gods. Mahāli, Sakka, king of gods, in a previous state of existence as a human being took upon himself and fulfilled seven vows. Because he took upon himself and fulfilled these seven vows, Sakka attained to the state of Sakka.

"Now what were the seven? 'So long as I live, may I be the support of my mother and father. So long as I live, may I honour my elders. So long as I live, may I speak gentle words. So long as I live, may I never give way to back-biting. So long as I live, may I live the life of a householder with heart free from taint of avarice, generous in renunciation of what is mine, with open hand, delighting in liberality, attentive to petitions, delighting in the distribution of alms. So long as I live, may I speak the truth. So long as I live, may I be free from anger. Should anger spring up within me, may I quickly get rid of it.' Mahāli, Sakka, king of gods, in a previous state of existence took upon himself and fulfilled these seven vows. Because he took upon himself and fulfilled these seven vows, Sakka attained to the state of Sakka."

> If a man support his mother and father,
> If he honour his elders in the household,
> If he be gentle and friendly in conversation,
> If he avoid backbiting,
> If he steadfastly put away avarice,
> If he be truthful, if he conquer anger,
> Such a man the gods of the Thirty-three
> Call a good man.

When the Teacher said, "This, Mahāli, was what Sakka did in his previous existence as Prince Magha," Mahāli, desiring to hear the whole story of his conduct, asked the Teacher, "Reverend sir, how did Prince Magha conduct himself?"—"Well then," said the Teacher, "listen." So saying, he related the following story.

Story of the Past: How Magha Became Sakka

In times long past a prince named Magha lived in the village of Macala in the kingdom of Magadha. One day he went to the place where the business of the village was carried on, removed with his foot the dust from the place where he stood, and having made a comfortable place for himself, stood there. Thereupon another struck him with his arm, pushed him aside, and took his place. But instead of becoming angry at the man, he made another comfortable place for himself and stood there. Thereupon another struck him with his arm, pushed him away, and took his place. But neither did he allow himself to become angry at this man; he merely made another comfortable place for himself and stood there. In like manner one man after another came out of his house, struck him with his arm, and pushed him away from the place which he had cleared for himself.

The prince thought to himself, "All these men appear to be pleased. Since this work of mine conduces to the happiness of men, it must be a meritorious work." So on the following day he took a spade and cleared a space as big as a threshing-floor, whereupon all the men came and stood there. In cold weather he built a fire to warm them, so that the place became a favourite resort for all. Then he thought to himself, "It behooves me to take upon myself the task of making the road smooth and even." So early in the morning he started out to make the road smooth and even, cutting down and removing all the branches of trees that needed to be removed. Thus did he spend his time.

Another man saw him and said to him, "Master, what are you doing?" He replied, "Master, I am treading the path that leads to heaven."—"I also am your companion."—"Be my companion, master; heaven is a pleasant place for many." Seeing these two, a third man asked the same question, received the same answer, and joined them; then a fourth, then a fifth, until finally there were thirty-three. All these men worked together with spades and axes and made the road smooth and even for a distance of one or two leagues. The village headman saw them and thought to himself, "These men are all following the wrong occupation. If they would only fetch fish and flesh from the forest, or indulge in strong drink, or do something else of the sort, I should make something by it." So he sent for them and asked them, "What is it you are doing?"—"Treading the path to heaven, master."—"That is no proper occupation for men living the lives of laymen. What you should do is to bring fish and flesh from the forest, indulge in strong drink, and have a general good time." But they refused to follow his suggestion, and the more he urged them, the more firmly they refused to do as he suggested.

Finally the village headman became angry. "I will destroy them," said he. So he went to the king and said to him, "Your majesty, I see a band of thieves going about committing depredations." The king replied, "Go and catch them and bring them before me." So the village headman arrested the thirty-three youths and took them before the king. Without instituting an inquiry into their conduct, the king gave the following order: "Cause them to be trampled to death by an elephant." Thereupon Magha admonished his companions as follows, "Friends, we have no refuge but love. Therefore let your hearts be tranquil. Cherish anger towards no one. Let your hearts be full of love for the king and the village headman and the elephant that tramples you under his feet." The thirty-three youths followed the admonition of their leader. Such was the power of their love that the elephant dared not approach them.

When the king heard of this, he said, "If the elephant sees so many men, he will not venture to trample them under his feet. Have the men covered with heavy matting, and then order the elephant to trample them." So the village headman had the men covered with heavy matting and drove the elephant forwards to trample them. But when the elephant was yet a long way off, he turned round and went back. When the king heard what had happened, he thought to himself, "There must be some reason for this." So he caused the thirty-three youths to be brought before him and asked them, "Friends, is there anything which you have failed to receive at my hands?"—"Your majesty, what do you mean?"—"I am informed that you are a band of thieves and that you rove about the forest committing depredations."—"Your majesty, who said that?"—"Friends, the village headman so informed me."

"Your majesty, it is not true that we are thieves. The fact is, we are clearing a path to heaven for ourselves, and we do this and that. The village headman tried to persuade us to adopt an evil mode of life, and when we refused to follow his suggestions, he became angry at us and determined to destroy us. That is why he said this about us."—"Friends, this animal knows your good qualities; but I, who am a man, was unable to discern them. Pardon me." So saying, the king made the village headman their slave, together with his children and wife, gave them a riding-elephant, and presented that village to them to do with as they saw fit. Thought the thirty-three youths, "Even in this life the advantage to be derived from the performance of work of merit is clearly to be seen." And mounting the elephant by turns, they rode about the village.

As they went about the village, they took counsel together, saying, "It is our duty to perform yet more abundant works of merit. What shall we do?" Thereupon the following thought occurred to them, "Let us build at the crossing of the four highways a rest-house for the multitude, making it secure and strong." So they summoned a builder and ordered him to build a hall for them. And because desire for women had departed from them, they resolved to give women no share in the building of the hall.

Now there were four women living in Magha's house named Joy, Thoughtful, Goodness, and Wellborn. Goodness went secretly to the builder, gave him a bribe, and said to him, "Brother, give me the principal share in the building of this hall."—"Very well," replied the builder, agreeing to her proposal. Accordingly he first marked a tree out of which to make a pinnacle, felled it, and laid it aside to season.

Then he hewed it and planed it and bored it, and having fashioned it in the form of a pinnacle, carved the following inscription on it: "This is the Hall of Goodness." Having so done, he wrapped it in a cloth and laid it aside.

Now when he had completed the hall and the day came to erect the pinnacle, he said to the thirty-three youths, "Noble sirs, there is something we have forgotten."—"What is it, sir?"—"A pinnacle."—"Let us procure one."—"It is impossible to make one out of a freshly hewn tree. We should procure for a pinnacle a tree felled long ago and laid away to season."—"What had we best do under the circumstances?"—"If in anybody's house there is a completed pinnacle which has been laid away to season and which is for sale, that is the thing for you to search for." So they searched everywhere, and finding what they wanted in the house of Goodness, offered her a thousand pieces of money for it. But they were unable to secure it for the price they offered. Said Goodness, "If you will give me a share in the building of the hall, I will give you the pinnacle." But they replied, "We have resolved to give women no share in the building of this hall." Thereupon the builder said to them, "Noble sirs, what are you doing? With the exception of the world of Brahmā, there is no place from which women are excluded. Take the pinnacle, for if you do, our work will speedily be finished."—"Very well," said they. So they took the pinnacle and completed the hall. And they divided the hall into three parts, reserving one chamber for kings, another for the poor, and another for the sick.

Then the thirty-three youths built thirty-three seats, and having so done, gave the following orders to the elephant, "If a visitor comes and sits down in a seat, take him and lodge him in the house of whoever built and owns that seat. It then becomes the duty of the owner of that seat to see that his guest's feet and back are rubbed, to provide him with food both hard and soft, and with lodging; to perform for him, in fact, all the duties of hospitality." Accordingly, whenever a visitor came, the elephant would take him and conduct him to the house of the owner of the seat in which he had sat, and the owner of the seat would on that day perform for him all the duties of hospitality.

Magha planted an ebony-tree near the hall and built a stone seat at the foot of the ebony-tree. All those who entered the hall looked at the pinnacle, read the inscription, and said, "This is the Hall of Goodness." The names of the thirty-three youths did not appear.

Joy thought to herself, "The youths who built this hall resolved to deprive us of a share in the building thereof. But Goodness by her own cleverness obtained a share. I also ought to do something. What can I do?" Thereupon the following thought occurred to her, "Those who come to the hall should be provided with water for drinking and water for bathing. I will have a place dug for a pool." Accordingly Joy caused a bathing-pool to be built.

Thoughtful thought to herself, "Goodness has given a pinnacle, and Joy has caused a bathing-pool to be built. What can I do?" Thereupon the following thought occurred to her, "After those who come to the hall have drunk water and bathed they should be decked with garlands when they are ready to depart. I will cause a flower garden to be laid out." So Thoughtful caused a beautiful flower garden to be laid out. So many and so various were the flowers that grew therein that it was impossible for anyone to say, "Such and such a flower-bearing or fruit-bearing tree does not grow in this garden."

Now Wellborn thought to herself, "I am the daughter of the brother of the mother of Magha and likewise the wife of Magha. The merit of the work he has wrought accrues to me only, and the merit of the work I have wrought accrues to him only." Accordingly she did nothing but spend her time adorning herself.

Thus did Magha minister to his mother and father, honour his elders in the household, speak the truth, avoid harsh words, avoid backbiting, put away avarice, and not become angry. Even thus did he fulfill the seven precepts, as it is said:

> If a man support his mother and father,
> If he honour his elders in the household,
> If he be gentle and friendly in conversation,
> If he avoid backbiting,
> If he steadfastly put away avarice,
> If he be truthful, if he conquer anger,
> Such a man the gods of the Thirty-three
> Call a good man.

Having attained so praiseworthy a state, Magha, upon reaching the end of the term of life allotted to him, was reborn in the world of the Thirty-three as Sakka, king of gods. His companions were likewise reborn there. The builder was reborn as the god Vissakamma.[4]

---

4. Celestial architect or engineer-in-chief of the heavenly world.

Now at that time there were asuras dwelling in the world of the Thirty-three, and when they learnt that new gods had been reborn there, they prepared celestial drink for them.[5] But Sakka gave orders to his retinue that no one should drink it. The asuras, however, drank freely and became intoxicated. Thereupon Sakka thought to himself. "Why should I share my kingdom with these deities?" Then, giving a sign to his retinue, he caused them to pick up the asuras by the heels and fling them into the great ocean. So the asuras fell headlong into the ocean. By the power of their merit there sprang up at the foot of Mount Sineru the palace of the asuras and the tree that is called pied trumpet-flower.

When the conflict between the gods and the asuras was over and the asuras had been defeated, there came into existence the city of the Thirty-three. The distance from the eastern gate to the western gate was ten thousand leagues, and the distance from the southern gate to the northern gate was the same. Now this city was provided with a thousand gates and was adorned with gardens and pools, and in the midst thereof, as the fruit of the building of the hall, there arose a palace called the Palace of Victory. Its height was seven hundred leagues, and it was decked with banners three hundred leagues long. On staffs of gold were banners of jewels, and on staffs of jewels were banners of gold; on staffs of coral were banners of pearls, and on staffs of pearls were banners of coral; on staffs of the seven precious stones were banners of the seven precious stones. Such was the palace that arose as the fruit of the building of the hall; a thousand leagues was its height, and it was composed of the seven precious stones.

As the result of the planting of the ebony-tree, there arose the coral-tree, a hundred leagues in circumference. As the result of the building of the stone seat, there came into existence at the foot of the coral-tree the Yellowstone Throne, of a reddish yellow colour like that of the jasmine flower, sixty leagues in length, fifty leagues in breadth, and fifteen leagues thick. When Sakka sits down on this throne, half its mass sinks into the ground; when he rises, it is all above ground. The elephant was reborn as god Erāvaṇa. There are no animals in the world of the gods; so when he went into

---

5. The asuras are the perennial enemies of the gods, frequently engaging them in battle.

the garden to play, he would quit his form as a god and become the elephant Erāvaṇa, a hundred and fifty leagues in size. For the thirty-three youths, Erāvaṇa created thirty-three vessels, each two or three quarters of a league around.

In the centre of all, Erāvaṇa created for Sakka a vessel called Beautiful. It was thirty leagues in circumference, and above it was a canopy, twelve leagues in size, made entirely of precious stones. At regular intervals about the canopy there arose banners a league in length, made entirely of the seven precious stones. And from the lower edge of each banner depended a row of tinkling bells, which, when they were shaken by the gentle wind, gave forth sweet music like the mingled strains of the music of the five kinds of instruments or the singing of the celestial choir. In the centre of the pavilion a jewelled couch a league in length was prepared for Sakka. There Sakka reclined in state. Erāvaṇa created thirty-three vessels for the thirty-three gods. Each vessel bore seven tusks, each fifty leagues long; each tusk bore seven lotus-tanks; each lotus-tank bore seven lotus-plants; each lotus-plant bore seven flowers; each flower, seven leaves; and on each leaf danced seven celestial nymphs. Thus on all sides round about for a space of fifty leagues there were dancing assemblies poised on elephants' tusks. Such was the glory in the enjoyment of which lived Sakka, king of gods.

When Goodness died, she was also reborn there. And at the same time there came into existence Goodness, the meeting hall of the gods, nine hundred leagues in extent, the most charming of all places. Here, on the eighth day of the month, the Dhamma is preached. Even today, when men behold a charming place, they say, "It is like Goodness, the meeting hall of the gods." When Joy died, she also was reborn there. And at the same time there came into existence a lotus-tank called Joy, five hundred leagues in extent. When Thoughtful died, she also was reborn there. And at the same time there came into existence Thoughtful's creeper-grove, five hundred leagues in extent. There they conduct the gods whose prognostics have appeared,[6] till they are overcome by

---

6. There are five signs of the impending death of a god: their garlands wither, their clothes become soiled, they sweat profusely, their radiance fades, and they become uneasy.

confusion. But when Wellborn died, she was reborn as a crane in a certain mountain cave.

Sakka surveyed his wives and considered within himself, "Goodness has been reborn here and likewise Joy and Thoughtful. Now where has Wellborn been reborn?" Perceiving that she had been reborn as a crane in a mountain-cave, he thought to himself, "Because she did no work of merit, the foolish girl has been reborn as an animal. It is my duty to have her perform some work of merit and bring her here." So saying, he laid aside his proper form, and assuming a disguise, he went to her and asked, "What are you doing here?"—"But, master, who are you?"—"I am your husband, Magha."—"Where were you reborn, husband?"—"I was reborn in the heaven of the Thirty-three. Do you know where your companions were reborn?"—"No, husband, I do not."—"They also were reborn in the heaven of the Thirty-three as my wives. Should you like to see your companions?"—"How can I get there?" Said Sakka, "I will carry you." Placing her in the palm of his hand, he carried her to the realm of the gods and set her free on the bank of the lotus-tank named Joy. Then he said to the other three, "Should you like to see your companion Wellborn?"—"Sire, where is she?"—"On the bank of the lotus-tank named Joy." So the three went and looked at her. "Alas!" they cried out, "See what has been the result of the noble woman's spending her life in adorning herself! Look now at her beak! Look at her feet! Look at her legs! She presents a beautiful appearance indeed!" Thus did they ridicule her. Having so done, they departed.

Sakka went once more to her and said, "Did you see your companions?"—"Yes," replied Wellborn, "I saw them. They ridiculed me and then went their way. Take me back again." So Sakka took her back again, set her free in the water, and then asked her, "Did you see their celestial glory?"—"Yes, sire, I did."—"You also should employ such means as will enable you to obtain rebirth there."—"Sire, what shall I do?"—"If I admonish you, will you keep my admonition?"—"Yes, sire, I will keep your admonition." So Sakka taught her the Five Precepts. Having so done, he said to her, "Be zealous in keeping the precepts," and departed.

Thenceforth she sought after and ate only such fish as had died a natural death. After a few days had passed, Sakka determined to test her. So he went, and taking the form of a fish, lay down on the surface of the sand, pretending to be dead. When she saw the fish, thinking that it was dead, she took it in her beak. Just as she was about to swallow the fish, it wriggled its tail. The instant she discovered the fish was alive she released it in the water. Sakka waited a little while, and then lay down before her on his back once more. Again thinking it was a dead fish, she took it in her beak. But just as she was about to swallow the fish, it moved the tip of its tail. The instant she saw the fish move its tail she knew it was alive, and therefore let it go. When Sakka had thus tested her three times and had satisfied himself that she was keeping the precepts faithfully, he revealed his identity to her and said, "I came here for the purpose of testing you. You are keeping the precepts faithfully. If you continue thus faithfully to keep them, before long you will be reborn as one of my wives. Be heedful." Having spoken thus, he departed.

Thenceforth she used for food either fish that had died a natural death or none at all. After only a few days had passed, she shrivelled up and died, and solely as the fruit of her virtuous conduct was reborn at Benares as the daughter of a potter. When she was about fifteen or sixteen years old, Sakka considered within himself, "Where has she been reborn?" Perceiving that she had been reborn at Benares as the daughter of a potter, he said to himself, "I ought now to go to her."

So filling a cart with the seven kinds of precious stones disguised as cucumbers, he drove into the city of Benares. "Come, get cucumbers!" he cried, as he entered the street. But when people came to him with coins in their hands, he said, "I do not part with my cucumbers for a price."—"On what terms do you part with them, then?" the people asked him. "I give them to the woman that keeps the precepts," he replied. "Master, what do you mean by 'precepts'? Are they black or brown or of some other colour?"—"You don't even know what precepts are; much less will you keep them. I will give my cucumbers to the woman who keeps the precepts."

"Master, there is a potter's daughter who is always going about saying, 'I keep the precepts.' Give them to her." The potter's daughter said to him, "Very well, master, give them to me."— "Who are you?"—"I am a maiden that has never failed to keep the precepts."—"For you alone have I brought these," said Sakka. And driving his cart to her house, he presented to her, in the guise of cucumbers, celestial treasure which cannot be taken away by others. And making his identity known to her, he said, "Here is wealth sufficient for you to live on. Keep the Five Precepts unbroken." So saying, he departed.

At the end of her existence as a potter's daughter she was reborn in the world of the asuras as the daughter of Vepacitti, king of asuras, a bitter enemy of Sakka. Since she had kept the precepts in two successive existences, she was fair of form, her skin was of a golden hue, and she was endowed with beauty and comeliness the like of which had never been seen. Vepacitti, king of asuras, said to all the asura princes who sought her in marriage, "You are not fit to marry my daughter." Having thus refused to give her in marriage to any of the asura princes, he said, "My daughter shall choose for herself such a husband as she sees fit." So saying, he assembled the host of asuras, and placing a garland of flowers in the hand of his daughter, said to her, "Choose for yourself a husband who suits you."

At that moment Sakka looked to see where she had been reborn. Perceiving what was taking place, he assumed the form of an aged asura and went and stood in the outer circle of the assembled company. The daughter of Vepacitti looked this way and that. Suddenly, because in a previous state of existence she had lived with Sakka, she was overwhelmed as by a mighty torrent by the power of the love for him which sprang up within her. And crying out, "He is my husband!" she threw the garland of flowers over his head. Said the asuras, "For a long time our king has been unable to find a husband suitable for his daughter. Now, however, he has found one. This fellow is old enough to be his daughter's grandfather." And they departed, hanging their heads with shame.

Sakka took her by the hand, cried out, "I am Sakka," and flew up into the air. The asuras exclaimed, "We have been fooled by Old Sakka," and started up in pursuit. Mātali the charioteer brought up the chariot called Chariot of Victory and stopped by the way. Thereupon Sakka assisted his bride to mount and set out for the city of the gods. Now when they reached the Forest of Silk-cotton Trees, the garuḍa fledglings, hearing the sound of the chariot and fearing they would be crushed to death, cried out.

When Sakka heard their cries, he asked Mātali, "What are they that are crying?"—"Garuḍa birds, sire."—"Why are they crying?"—"They hear the sound of the chariot and fear they will be crushed to death."—"Let not so numerous a host perish, crushed by the impact of the chariot, because of me alone. Cause the chariot to turn back." Thereupon Mātali gave the sign with the lash to the thousand Sindh horses and caused the chariot to turn back.

When the asuras saw that the chariot had turned back, they said, "Old Sakka started out in flight from the city of the asuras, but has just caused his chariot to turn back. Doubtless he has received reinforcements." And turning back, the asuras entered the city of the asuras by the same road by which they had come out and nevermore lifted up their heads. Sakka bore the asura maiden Wellborn to the city of the gods and installed her as the chief of twenty-five million celestial nymphs.

One day Wellborn asked Sakka for a boon, saying, "Great king, in this world of the gods I have neither mother nor father nor brother nor sister; therefore please take me with you wherever you go."—"Very well," replied Sakka, promising to do for her as she had asked. Thenceforth, when the tree that is called pied trumpet-flower blooms, the asuras cry out, "Now is the time when our heavenly coral-tree blooms," and straightway they sally forth to attack Sakka. Therefore Sakka posts a guard to defend the nāgas in the sea below, and likewise affords protection to the supaṇṇas and the kumbhaṇḍas and the yakkhas, and likewise to the Four Great Kings. And over all, for the purpose of averting disaster, he places before the gates of the city of the gods images of Indra bearing the thunderbolt in his hands. When the asuras, after defeating the nāgas and the other supernatural beings, approach the city of the gods and see the images of Indra, they cry out, "Sakka has made a sally," and flee away (*End of Story of the Past*).

"Thus, Mahāli, Prince Magha adopted the way of heedfulness. Because he was so heedful, he obtained such sovereignty so exalted and came to rule over the two worlds of the gods.[7] Heedfulness is praised by the Buddhas and by others likewise. For it is through heedfulness that all attain the higher attainments, both those that

---

7. The Four Great Kings and the Thirty-three gods.

are worldly and those that transcend all worlds." So saying, he pronounced the following stanza:

30. Heedfulness is always praised,
Heedlessness is ever blamed;
By heedfulness did Magha go
To the lordship of the gods.

2. The Old Brahmin and His Sons

THE TUSKER DHANAPĀLAKA NAMED ... This instruction was given by the Teacher while he was in residence at Sāvatthī with reference to the sons of a certain brahmin who had reached the decrepitude of old age.

The story goes that there lived in Sāvatthī a certain brahmin who had four sons and whose wealth amounted to eight hundred thousand pieces of money. When his sons reached marriageable age, he arranged marriages for them and gave them four hundred thousand pieces of money. After the sons had married, the brahmin's wife died, whereupon the sons took counsel together, saying, "If this brahmin marries again, the family fortune will be divided among his wife's children and there will be nothing left of it. Come then! Let us succour our father and win his favour." Accordingly they waited upon him faithfully, providing him with the choicest food and the finest clothes, rubbing his hands and feet, and performing all of the other duties.

One day they went to wait upon him and found that he had fallen asleep, although it was broad daylight. As soon as he awoke, they rubbed his hands and his feet, and while thus engaged, spoke to him of the disadvantage of living in separate houses. Said they, "We will wait upon you after this manner so long as you live; give us the rest of your wealth also." In compliance with their request the brahmin gave each of them a hundred thousand more. He kept nothing for himself but his under and upper garments; all the rest of his wealth and possessions he divided into four portions and handed over to his sons.

For a few days his eldest son ministered to his needs. One day, however, as he was returning to the house of his eldest son after his bath, his daughter-in-law, who stood at the gate, saw him and said to him, "Did you give your eldest son a hundred or a thousand pieces of money more than you gave your other sons? You certainly gave each of your sons two hundred thousand pieces of money. Do you not know the way to the house of any of your other sons?" The brahmin answered angrily, "Perish, vile woman!" and went to the house of his second son. But in a few days he was driven from the house of his second son as he had been from the house of the first, and in like manner from the houses of his two youngest sons. Finally he found himself without a single house he could enter.

Thereupon he retired from the world and became a monk of the Paṇḍaraṅga Order,[8] begging his food from door to door. In the course of time he became worn out by old age, and his body withered away as a result of the poor food he ate and the wretched quarters in which he was obliged to sleep. One day, after he had returned from his begging rounds, he lay down on his back and fell asleep. When he awoke from sleep and sat up and surveyed himself and reflected that there was no one of his sons to whom he might go for refuge, he thought to himself, "They say that the monk Gotama has a countenance that does not frown, a face that is frank and open, that his manner of conversing is pleasant, and that he greets strangers in a kind and friendly way. Possibly if I go to the monk Gotama, I shall receive a friendly greeting." So adjusting his under and upper garments, taking his alms bowl, and grasping his staff, he went to the Exalted One, even as it is said:[9]

Now a certain brahmin, a man who had formerly possessed wealth and social position, clad in rough garments, drew near to where the Exalted One was, and having drawn near, sat down respectfully on one side. And as he sat respectfully on one side, the Exalted One greeted him in a pleasant manner and said this to him, "How comes it, brahmin, that you are rough and clad in rough garments?"—"Sir Gotama, I have four sons living in this world, but instigated by their wives, they have driven me out of their houses."—"Well then, brahmin, learn these stanzas thoroughly, and when the people are gathered together in the hall and your sons are gathered together with them, recite them before the assembled company:

---

8. A non-Buddhist sect.
9. Saṃyutta Nikāya 7:14.

"They at whose birth my heart was glad,
They for whose being much I longed,
They, instigated by their wives,
Are as a dog that drives off swine.

Wicked and worthless they say to me,
'Dear father' or 'Dear Dad' again:
Demons are they in guise of sons
Forsaking me in my old age;
Just as a worn-out useless horse
Is no longer led to its food
So is the father of these fools;
Though old, he begs at others' doors.

Better in truth the staff for me
Than sons who are disobedient.

It serves to drive off savage bulls
And likewise keeps off savage dogs.

It goes before me in the dark
And in the deeps it steadies me,
And by the power of this staff
Having slipped, I stand up again."

The brahmin, taught by the Teacher, learned these stanzas by heart. On the day appointed for the brahmins to assemble, the sons of the brahmin pushed their way into the hall, dressed in their costliest garments, adorned with all their jewels, and sat down on a costly seat in the midst of the brahmins. Thereupon the brahmin said to himself, "Now is my opportunity." So he entered the hall, made his way into the midst of the assemblage, lifted up his hand, and said, "I desire to recite certain stanzas to you; please listen to me."—"Recite them, brahmin; we are listening." So the brahmin stood there and recited the stanzas which he had learned from the Teacher.

Now at that time this was the law of mankind: *If any devour the substance of mother and father, and support not mother and father, he shall be put to death.* Therefore the sons of that brahmin fell at their father's feet and begged him to spare their lives, saying, "Dear father, spare our lives!" Out of the softness of a father's heart the brahmin said, "Sirs, do not kill my sons; they will support me." The men said to his sons, "Sirs, if from this day you do not take proper care of your father, we will kill you." The sons, thoroughly frightened, seated their father in a chair, raised the chair with their own hands, and carried their father home. They anointed the body of their father with oil, flying this way and that in their haste, bathed him, employing perfumes and aromatic powders, and having so done, summoned their wives and said to them, "From this day forth you are to take proper care of our father; if you neglect this duty, we shall punish you." And they set the choicest dishes before him.

As the result of the wholesome food which the brahmin was given to eat and the comfortable quarters in which he slept, strength came back to him after a few days and his senses were refreshed. As he surveyed his person, he thought to himself, "I have gained this success through the monk Gotama." So desiring to make him a present, he took a pair of cloths and went to the Exalted One, and after exchanging friendly greetings, took his seat respectfully on one side. Then he laid the pair of cloths at the feet of the Exalted One, and said to him, "Sir Gotama, we brahmins desire that a teacher shall receive the offering which is his due; may my lord Gotama, my teacher, accept the offering which is due to him as a teacher." Out of compassion for the brahmin, the Teacher accepted the present which he had brought, and taught Dhamma to him. At the conclusion of the sermon the brahmin was established in the Refuges. Thereupon the brahmin said to the Teacher, "Sir Gotama, my sons provide me regularly with four meals; two of these I give to you." The Teacher replied, "That is well, brahmin; but we shall go only to such houses as we please." So saying, he dismissed him.

The brahmin went home and said to his sons, "Dear sons, the monk Gotama is my friend, and I have given him two of the meals with which you regularly provide me. When he arrives, be not heedless of your duty."—"Very well," replied his sons, promising to do as he said. On the following day the Teacher set out on his alms round and stopped at the door of the house of the brahmin's eldest son. When the brahmin's eldest son saw the Teacher, he took his bowl, invited him into the house, seated him on a costly couch, and gave him the choicest foods. On the succeeding days the Teacher went to the houses of the other sons in order, and all of them provided hospitable entertainment for him in their houses.

One day when a holiday was at hand, the eldest son said to his father, "Dear father, in whose honour shall we make merry?" The brahmin replied, "The monk Gotama is my friend, and I know no others."—"Well then, invite him for tomorrow with his five hundred monks." The brahmin did so. So on the following day the Teacher came to the house with his attendant monks. The house was smeared with fresh cow dung and decked in festive array. The brahmin provided seats within the house for the Order of Monks presided over by the Buddha, and served them with rich porridge sweetened with honey and with the choicest foods, both hard and soft. In the course of the meal the brahmin's four sons sat down before the Teacher and said to him, "Sir Gotama, we care tenderly for our father; we never neglect him. Just look at him!" The Teacher replied, "You have done well. Wise men of old likewise cared tenderly for their mother and father." So saying, he related in detail the Mātuposaka Nāgarāja Jātaka (Jāt. No. 455), in which the story is told of how the *sallakī*-tree and the *kuṭaja*-plant grew up and blossomed in the absence of the elephant. Having so done, he pronounced the following stanza:

324. The tusker Dhanapālaka named,
 Pungent rut exuding, uncontrolled,
 Bound, he does not eat a mouthful,
 The tusker mourns the elephant-wood.

Word Commentary

Dhanapāla: At this time the king of Kāsi sent an elephant-trainer to a charming elephant-grove and caused an elephant to be taken captive; this is the name of the elephant. *Pungent but exuding*: acrid juice; for in the rutting season the root of the elephant's ear bursts. As a rule, when trainers try to subdue elephants at this time with hook or spear or lance, the elephants become fierce. But this elephant was excessively fierce; therefore it is said: *Pungent rut exuding, uncontrolled/Bound, he does not eat a mouthful.* When by command of the king this elephant was led, bound to the elephant-stable and made to stand in a place screened with a curtain of many colours, decked with festoons, and garlands, overhung with a variegated canopy, although the king himself offered him food of various choice flavours and fit for a king, he refused to eat. It is with reference to his entrance into the elephant-stable that the words are employed. *Bound, he does not eat a mouthful,/The tusker mourns the elephant-wood*: No matter how delightful the place in which he lodged, nevertheless he remembered the elephant-wood. Now his (blind) mother, who remained in the forest, suffered greatly by reason of separation from her son. Her son thought to himself, "I am not fulfilling the obligation of a son to succour his mother. What do I care for this food?" Thus he remembered only the solemn obligation resting upon a son to succour his mother. Now inasmuch as it was possible for him to fulfill this obligation only by being in the elephant-grove, therefore it is said: *The tusker mourns the elephant-wood.*

As the Teacher related this Jātaka, detailing his own deed in a previous state of existence, his hearers shed floods of tears, and by reason of the softness of their hearts became fully attentive. Thus did the Exalted One, knowing full well what would be of advantage to them, proclaim the Truths and teach the Dhamma. At the conclusion of the lesson the brahmin, together with his sons and daughters-in-law, was established in the fruit of stream-entry.

3. *A Certain Brahmin*

BY GRADUAL PRACTICE FROM TIME TO TIME ... This instruction was given by the Teacher while he was in residence at Jetavana in Sāvatthī with reference to a certain brahmin.

The story goes that early one morning this brahmin went out of the city, stopped at the place where the monks put on their robes, and stood and watched them as they put on their robes.[10] Now this place was thickly overgrown with grass. As one of the monks put on his robe, the edge of the robe dragged through the grass and became wet with drops of dew. Thought

---

10. This means that they had the lower robe on already but carried the upper robe folded until they reached the city when it (and the outer robe of patches if it had been instituted at this time) was put on over both shoulders for entering an inhabited area.

the brahmin, "The grass should be cleared away from this place." So on the following day he took his mattock, went there, cleared the place and made it as clean and smooth as a threshing-floor. The day after, he went to that place again. As the monks put on their robes, he observed that the edge of the robe of one of the monks dropped to the ground and dragged in the dust. Thought the brahmin, "Sand should be sprinkled here." So he brought sand and sprinkled it on the ground.

Now one day before breakfast the heat was intense. On this occasion he noticed that as the monks put on their robes, sweat poured from their bodies. Thought the brahmin, "Here I ought to cause a shelter to be erected." Accordingly he caused a shelter to be erected. Again one day, early in the morning, it rained. On this occasion also, as the brahmin watched the monks, he noticed that their robes were wetted by the drops of rain. Thought the brahmin, "Here I ought to cause a hall to be erected." So there he caused a hall to be erected. When the hall was finished, he thought to himself, "Now I will hold a festival in honour of the completion of the hall." Accordingly he invited the Order of Monks presided over by the Buddha, seated the monks within and without the hall, and gave alms.

At the conclusion of the meal he took the Teacher's bowl to permit him to pronounce the words of thanksgiving. "Reverend sir," said he, "as I stood in this place when the monks were putting on their robes and watched them, I saw this and that, and I did this and that." And beginning at the beginning, he told the Teacher the whole story. The Teacher listened to his words and then said, "Brahmin, a wise man by doing good works, time after time, little by little, gradually removes the stains of his own evil deeds." So saying, he pronounced the following stanza:

239. By gradual practice from time to time,
    Little by little let the sage
    Blow off his own blemishes
    Just as a smith with silver.

4. *The Bondswoman Puṇṇā*

FOR THOSE WHO ARE EVER VIGILANT ... This instruction was given by the Teacher while he was in residence on Mount Vulture Peak with reference to Puṇṇā, a bondswoman of the treasurer of Rājagaha.

The story goes that one day they gave her much rice to pound. She pounded away until late at night, lighting a lamp to work by; finally she became very weary and, in order to rest, stepped outside and stood in the wind with her body moist with sweat. Now at that time the Venerable Dabba Mallaputta was the one who allotted lodgings to the monks. Having listened to the Dhamma, he then lighted his finger so that he might show the monks the way to their respective lodgings, and preceding them, he created, by power of meditation, a light for them.

The light enabled Puṇṇā to see the monks making their way along the mountain. She thought to herself, "As for me, I am oppressed by my own discomfort, and so, even at this time, am unable to sleep. Why is it that the reverend monks are unable to sleep?" Having considered the matter, she came to the following conclusion, "It must be that some monk who resides there is sick, or else is suffering from the bite of some reptile." So when it was dawn, she took some rice-flour, placed it in the palm of her hand, moistened it with water, and having thus mixed a chapatti, cooked it over a bed of charcoal. Then, saying to herself, "I will eat it on the road leading to the bathing-place on the river," she placed the chapatti in a fold of her dress, and taking a water-pot in her hand, set out for the bathing-place on the river.

The Teacher set out on the same path, intending likewise to enter that village for alms. When Puṇṇā saw the Teacher, she thought to herself, "On other days when I have seen the Teacher, I have had no alms to give him, or if I have had alms to give him, I have not seen him; today, however, not only do I meet the Teacher face to face, but I have alms to give him. If he would accept this chapatti without considering whether the food is of inferior or superior quality, I would give it to him." So setting her water-pot down on one side, she saluted the Teacher and said to him, "Reverend sir, accept this coarse food and bestow your blessing upon me."

The Teacher looked at the Elder Ānanda, whereupon the elder drew a bowl out from under a fold of his robe and presented it to the Teacher. The Teacher held out the bowl and received therein the offering of the chapatti. When Puṇṇā had placed the chapatti in the Teacher's bowl, she bowed down to him respectfully and said to him, "Reverend sir, may the Truth which you have beheld be of avail to me also." The Teacher replied, "So be it." And remaining standing as before, he pronounced the words of thanksgiving. Thereupon Puṇṇā thought to herself, "Although the Teacher bestowed on me a blessing as he took my chapatti, yet he will not eat it himself. He will doubtless keep it until he has gone a little way and will then give it to a crow or a dog. Then he will go to the house of some king or prince and make a meal of choice food."

Thought the Teacher to himself, "What was the thought in the mind of this woman?" Perceiving what was in her mind, the Teacher looked at the Elder Ānanda and intimated that he wished to sit down. The elder spread out a robe and offered the Teacher a seat. The Teacher sat down outside the city and ate his breakfast. The deities squeezed out nectar, food proper to gods and men alike throughout the circle of the worlds, even as one squeezes a honeycomb, and imparted it to the Teacher's food. Puṇṇā stood looking on. At the conclusion of the Teacher's breakfast the elder gave him water. When the Teacher had finished his breakfast, he addressed Puṇṇā and said, "Puṇṇā, why have you blamed my disciples?"—"I do not blame your disciples, reverend sir."—"Then what did you say when you saw my disciples?"

"Reverend sir, the explanation is very simple. I thought to myself: 'As for me, I am oppressed by my own discomfort, and so am unable to sleep. Why is it that the reverend monks are unable to sleep? It must be that some monk who resides there is sick, or else is suffering from the bite of some reptile.' " The Teacher listened to her words and then said to her, "Puṇṇā, in your own case it is because you are afflicted with discomfort that you are unable to sleep. But my disciples are assiduously watchful and therefore they do not sleep." So saying, he pronounced the following stanza:

226. For those who are ever vigilant
And train themselves by night and day,
Upon Nibbāna ever intent,
Their pollutions are eradicated.

At the conclusion of the lesson Puṇṇā, even as she stood there, was established in the fruit of stream-entry; the assembled company also profited by the lesson.

The Teacher, having eaten the chapatti which Puṇṇā made of rice-flour and cooked over a bed of coals, returned to the monastery. Thereupon the monks began a discussion in the Hall of Truth:

"Brethren, how hard it must have been for the Supremely Enlightened One to eat the chapatti of rice-flour which Puṇṇā cooked over a bed of coals and gave him!" At that moment the Teacher drew near and asked them, "Monks, what are you discussing now as you sit here all gathered together?" When they told him, he said, "Monks, this is not the first time I have eaten red-rice powder which she gave me; the same thing happened to me in a previous state of existence also." And the Teacher related the Kuṇḍakasindhavapotaka Jātaka in detail (Jāt. No. 254).

5. *Treasurer Catfoot*

DO NOT DISREGARD MERIT, SAYING ... This instruction was given by the Teacher while he was in residence at Jetavana with reference to Treasurer Catfoot, Biḷālapādaka.

For once upon a time the residents of Sāvatthī banded themselves together and gave alms to the Order of Monks presided over by the Buddha. Now one day the Teacher, in rejoicing (with their merits), spoke as follows, "Lay disciples, here in this world one man himself gives, but does not urge others to give; in the various places where he is reborn, such a man receives the blessing of wealth but not the blessing of a following. A second man does not himself give, but urges others to give; in the various places where he is reborn, such a man receives the blessing of a following but not the blessing of wealth. A third man neither himself gives nor urges others to give; in the various places where he is reborn such a man receives neither the blessing of wealth nor the blessing of a following. Lastly, a man both himself gives and urges others to give; in the various places where he is reborn, such a man receives both the blessing of wealth and the blessing of a following."

Now a certain wise man who stood listening to the Teacher's discourse on the Dhamma thought to himself, "This is indeed a wonderful thing! I will straightaway perform works of merit leading to both of these blessings." Accordingly he arose and said to the Teacher, as the latter was departing, "Reverend sir, accept our offering of food tomorrow."—"But how many monks do you need?"—"All the monks you have, reverend sir." The Teacher graciously consented to come. Then the layman entered the village and went here and there, proclaiming, "Women and men, I have invited the Order of Monks presided over by the Buddha for tomorrow's meal. Give rice and whatever else is needed for making rice-porridge and other kinds of food, each providing for as many monks as his means permit. Let us do all the cooking in one place and give alms in common."

Now a certain treasurer, seeing that the layman had come to the door of his shop, became angry and thought to himself, "Here is a layman who, instead of inviting as many monks as he could himself accommodate, is going about urging the entire village to give alms." And he said to the layman, "Fetch the vessel you brought with you." The treasurer took grains of rice in three fingers, and presented them to the layman similarly with different kinds of pulses. Ever after that the treasurer bore the name Catfoot, Biḷālapāda. Likewise in presenting ghee and jaggery to the layman, he placed a little pot in the layman's vessel and dribbled out his offering drop by drop into one corner, giving him only a very little.

The lay disciple placed together the offerings which the rest presented to him, but placed apart by themselves the offerings of the treasurer. When the treasurer saw the layman do this, he thought to himself, "Why does he place apart by themselves the offerings I have presented to him?" In order to satisfy his curiosity, he sent a serving-boy with orders to follow the layman, saying to the serving-boy, "Go find out what he does with my offerings." The layman took the offerings with him, and saying, "May the treasurer receive a rich reward," put two or three grains of rice into the porridge and cakes, distributing beans and drops of oil and jaggery-pellets in all the vessels. The serving-boy returned and told the treasurer what the layman had done. When the treasurer heard his report, he thought to himself, "If the layman blames me in the midst of the assembled company, I will strike him and kill him the moment he takes my name upon his lips."

On the following day, therefore, the treasurer hid a knife in a fold of his undergarment and went and stood waiting at the refectory. The layman escorted into the refectory the Order of Monks presided over by the Buddha, and then said to the Exalted One, "Reverend sir, at my suggestion the populace has presented these offerings to you. All those persons whom I urged to give have given rice and other provisions according to their respective ability. May all of them receive a rich reward." When the treasurer heard this, he thought to himself, "I came here with the intention of killing the layman in case he took my name upon his lips by way of blame; in case, for example, he said, 'So and so took a pinch of rice and gave it to me.' But instead of so doing, this layman has included all in his request for a blessing, both those who measured out their gifts in pint-pots and those who took pinches of food and gave, saying, 'May all receive a rich reward.' If I do not ask so good a man to pardon me, punishment from the king will fall upon my head!" And straightaway the treasurer prostrated himself before the layman's feet and said, "Pardon me, master."—"What do you mean?" asked the layman. Thereupon the treasurer told him the whole story.

The Teacher, seeing this act, asked the steward of the offerings, "What does this mean?" Thereupon the layman told him the whole story, beginning with the incidents of the previous day. Then the Teacher asked the treasurer, "Is his story correct, treasurer?"—"Yes, reverend sir." Then said the Teacher, "Disciple, one should never regard a good deed as a small matter and say, 'It is a mere trifle.' One should never regard lightly an offering given to a Buddha, or to the Order of Monks presided over by the Buddha, and say of it, 'It is a mere trifle.' For wise men who do works of merit, in the course of time, become filled with merit, even as a water-vessel which stands uncovered becomes filled with water." So saying, he showed the connection, and teaching the Dhamma, pronounced the following stanza:

122. Do not disregard merit, saying:
'That will not come to me'—
For by the falling of water drops
A water jar is filled:
The sage with merit fills himself,
Gathering it little by little.

6. The Brahmin with a Single Robe

MAKE HASTE TOWARDS THE GOOD ... This instruction was given by the Teacher while he was in residence at Jetavana with reference to the brahmin Little One-Robe, Cūḷa Ekasāṭaka.

For in the dispensation of the Buddha Vipassī there lived a brahmin named Mahā Ekasāṭaka, Big One-robe, and he it was who was reborn in the present dispensation in Sāvatthī as Cūḷa Ekasāṭaka, Little One-robe. For Cūḷa Ekasāṭaka possessed only a single under garment, and his wife possessed only a single under garment, and both of them together possessed only a single upper garment. The result was that whenever either the brahmin or his wife went out of doors, the other had to stay at home. One day an announcement was made that there would be a preaching at the monastery. Said the brahmin to his wife, "Wife, an announcement is made that there will be a preaching at the monastery. Will you go to hear the Dhamma by day or by night? For we do not have enough upper garments between us to go together." The brahmin's wife replied, "Husband, I will go in the daytime." So saying, she put on the upper garment and went.

The brahmin spent the day at home. At night he went to the monastery, seated himself in front of the Teacher, and listened to the Dhamma. As he listened to the Dhamma, the five sorts of joy arose within him, suffusing his body. He greatly desired to do honour to the Teacher, but the following thought restrained him, "If I give this garment to the Teacher, there will be no upper garment left for my wife or me." A thousand selfish thoughts arose within him; then a single believing thought arose within him. Then thought of self arose within him and overmastered the believing thought. Even so did the mighty thought of self seize, as it were, and bind and thrust out the believing thought. "I will give it! No, I will not give it!" said the brahmin to himself.

As he thus reflected, the first watch passed and the second watch arrived. Even then he was not able to bring himself to give the garment to the Teacher. Then the last watch came. Finally the brahmin thought to himself, "While I have been fighting with thoughts of faith and thoughts of self, two watches have elapsed. If these powerful thoughts of self increase, they will not permit me to lift up my head from the four states of suffering.[11] I will therefore give my gift." Thus the brahmin finally overmastered a thousand thoughts of self and followed the lead of a thought of faith. Taking his garment, he laid it at the Teacher's feet and thrice cried out with a loud voice, "I have conquered! I have conquered!"

King Pasenadi of Kosala happened to be listening to the Dhamma. When he heard that cry, he said, "Ask him what he has conquered." The king's men asked the brahmin the question, and the brahmin explained the matter to them. When the king heard the explanation, he said, "It was a hard thing to do what the brahmin did. I will do him a kindness." So he caused a pair of garments to be presented to him. The brahmin presented these garments also to the Tathāgata. Then the king doubled his gift, presenting the brahmin first with two pairs of garments, then with four, then with eight, finally with sixteen. The brahmin presented all these garments also to the Tathāgata. Then the king directed thirty-two pairs of garments to be presented to the brahmin. But to avoid having it said, "The brahmin has not kept a single pair for himself, but has given away every pair he received," he said to the brahmin, "Keep one pair for yourself and give another pair to your wife." So saying he caused the brahmin to keep two pairs and let him give the remaining thirty pairs to the Tathāgata alone. Even had the brahmin given away what he possessed a hundred times, the king would have met his gifts with equal gifts.

(In a former state of existence Mahā Ekasāṭaka kept for himself two pairs of garments out of sixty-four he received; Cūḷa Ekasāṭaka kept two out of thirty-two.)

The king gave orders to his men, "It was indeed a hard thing to do what the brahmin did. Fetch my two blankets into the presence-chamber." They did so. The king presented him with the two blankets, valued at a thousand pieces of money. But the

---

11. Asuras, ghosts, animals, and hell-realm beings.

brahmin said to himself, "I am not worthy to cover my body with these blankets. These are suitable only for the religion of the Buddha." Accordingly he made a canopy of one of the blankets and hung it up in the Perfumed Chamber over the Teacher's bed;[12] likewise he made a canopy of the other blanket and hung it up in his own house over the spot where the monk who resorted to his house for alms took his meals. In the evening the king went to visit the Teacher. Recognizing the blanket, he asked him, "Reverend sir, who was it that honoured you with the gift of this blanket?"— "Ekasāṭaka." Thought the king to himself, "Even as I believe and rejoice in my belief, even so does this brahmin believe and rejoice in his belief." Accordingly he presented to him four elephants, four horses, four thousand pieces of money, four women, four female slaves, and four most excellent villages. Thus therefore did the king cause the brahmin to be given the "gift of fours."

The monks started a discussion in the Hall of Truth: "Oh, how wonderful was the deed of Cūḷa Ekasāṭaka! No sooner done than he received all manner of presents of four! As soon as he did a good deed, straightaway the fruit thereof was given to him." The Teacher approached and asked the monks, "Monks, what are you sitting here now talking about?" When they told him, he said, "Monks, had Ekasāṭaka been able to bring himself to give me his gift in the first watch, he would have received the 'gift of sixteens'; had he been able to do so in the middle watch, he would have received the 'gift of eights'; because it was not until late in the last watch that he gave me his gift, he received only the 'gift of fours.' He who does good works should not put away the impulse to good that arises within him, but should act on the instant. A meritorious deed tardily done brings its reward, but tardy is the reward it brings. Therefore a man should perform a good work the instant the impulse to good arises within him." So saying, he showed the connection, and teaching the Dhamma, pronounced the following stanza:

116. Make haste towards the good
And check one's mind from evil;
If one is slow in making merit,
One's mind delights in evil.

---

12. The "Perfumed Chamber" (*gandhakuṭi*) is the name of the Buddha's personal cottage in Jetavana.

7. Pāṭhika the Naked Ascetic

THE FAULTS OF OTHERS ... This instruction was given by the Teacher while he was in residence at Sāvatthī with reference to Pāṭhika the naked ascetic.[13]

At Sāvatthī, we are told, the wife of a certain householder ministered to the needs of a naked ascetic named Pāṭhika, treating him as she would her own son. Of her nearest neighbours, those who went to hear the Teacher teach the Dhamma returned praising the virtues of the Buddhas in manifold ways, saying, "Oh, how wonderful is the preaching of the Buddhas!" When the woman heard her neighbours thus praise the Buddhas, she desired to go to the monastery and hear the Dhamma. So she put the matter to the naked ascetic, saying, "Noble sir, I desire to go and hear the Buddha." But as often as she made her request, the naked ascetic dissuaded her from going, saying, "Do not go!" The woman thought to herself, "Since this naked ascetic will not permit me to go to the monastery and hear the Dhamma, I will invite the Teacher to my own house and hear the Dhamma right here."

Accordingly, when it was evening, she summoned her own son and sent him to the Teacher, saying to him, "Go and invite the Teacher to accept my hospitality for tomorrow." The boy started out, but went first to the place of residence of the naked ascetic, saluted him, and sat down. "Where are you going?" asked the naked ascetic. "By my mother's direction I am going to invite the Teacher."—"Do not go to him."—"All very well, but I am afraid of my mother. I am going."—"Let the two of us eat the fine things prepared for him. Do not go."—"No, my mother will give me a scolding."—"Well then, go. But when you go and invite the Teacher, do not say to him, 'Our house is situated in such and such a place, in such and such a street, and you may reach it by taking such and such a road.' Instead, act as if you lived nearby, and when you leave, run off as if you intended to take a different road, and come back here."

The boy listened to the instructions of the naked ascetic and then went to the Teacher and delivered the invitation. When he had done everything according to the instructions of the naked

---

13. See Dīgha Nikāya No. 24.

ascetic, he returned to the latter. Said the naked ascetic, "What did you do?" Said the boy, "Everything you told me to do, noble sir."—"You have done very well. Now we shall both of us eat the good things prepared for him." On the following day, very early in the morning the naked ascetic went to that house, taking the boy with him, and the two sat down together in the back room.

The neighbours smeared that house with cow-dung, decked it with the five kinds of flowers, including the *lāja* flower, and prepared a seat of great price, that the Teacher might sit therein. (People who are not familiar with the Buddhas know nothing about the preparation of a seat for them. Nor do the Buddhas ever need a guide to direct them on their way. For on the day of Enlightenment, when they sit under the Bodhi-Tree, causing ten thousand worlds to quake, all paths become plain to them: "This path leads to hell, this path leads to the world of beasts, this path leads to the world of ghosts, this path leads to the world of humans, this path leads to the world of the gods, this path leads to the Deathless, to Great Nibbāna." There is never any need of telling them the way to villages, market-towns, or other places.)

Therefore the Teacher, very early in the morning, took bowl and robe and went straight to the house of the great female lay disciple. She came forth from the house, respectfully bowed down to the Teacher, escorted him into the house, poured the water of donation into his right hand, and gave him the choicest of food, both hard and soft. When the Teacher had finished his meal, the female lay disciple, desiring to have him pronounce words of thanksgiving, took his bowl, and the Teacher with his own sweet voice began the address of rejoicing. The lay disciple listened to the teaching of the Dhamma and applauded the Teacher, saying, "Well said! Well said!"

The naked ascetic, sitting there in the back room, heard the words of applause uttered by the lay disciple as she heard the Teacher teach the Dhamma. Unable to control himself, he remarked, "She is my disciple no longer!" and came out. And he said to the lay disciple, "Hag, you are lost for applauding this man thus." And he reviled both the female lay disciple and the Teacher in all manner of ways, and then ran off.

The lay disciple was so embarrassed by the naked ascetic's insulting words that her mind became completely distraught, and she was unable to concentrate her attention on the Teacher's discourse. The Teacher asked her, "Lay disciple, are you unable to fix your mind on my discourse?"—"Good and reverend sir," she replied, "my mind is completely distraught by the insulting words of this naked ascetic." Said the Teacher, "One should not consider the talk of such a contrary person; one should pay no attention to such as he; one should regard only what one has committed and omitted to do." So saying, he pronounced the following stanza:

50. Not the faults of others,
    Nor what they did and did not;
    But in oneself should be sought
    Things done and left undone.

8. Coppertooth the Thief-killer

THOUGH A THOUSAND SPEECHES ARE MADE OF MEANINGLESS LINES ... This instruction was given by the teacher while he was in residence at Veḷuvana with reference to Coppertooth, a public executioner.

We are told that five hundred thieves less one made a living by plundering villages and other acts of violence. Now a certain man with copper-coloured teeth and tawny skin, his body covered with scars, came to them and said, "Let me also live with you." They took him to the ringleader of the thieves, saying, "This man also wishes to live with us." The ringleader of the thieves looked at the man and thought to himself, "This man's nature is inordinately cruel. He is capable of cutting off the breast of his mother and eating it, or of drawing the blood from the throat of his father and drinking it." Therefore he refused his request, saying, "It will not do for this man to live with us."

Although he had thus been refused admission to the band of thieves, he went and won the favour of a certain pupil of the ringleader by his courteous attention to him. This pupil took the man with him, approached the ringleader of the thieves, and said to him, "Master, this man is a dutiful servant of ours; bestow your favour on him." Having made this request, he turned the man over to the ringleader of the thieves.

One day the citizens joined forces with the king's men, captured those thieves, took them to court, and arraigned them before the lords of justice. The justices ordered their heads to be chopped off with an axe. "Who will put these men to death?" said the citizens. After a thorough search they were unable to find a single man who was willing to put them to death. Finally they said to the ringleader of the thieves, "You put these men to death, and we will spare your life and give you a rich reward besides. You kill them." But because they had lived with him, he also was unwilling to put them to death. In like manner also all of the five hundred less one refused when asked. Last of all they asked that scarred, tawny, coppertooth. "Yes, indeed," said he, consenting. So he put to death all the thieves, and in return received his life and rich gifts besides.

In like manner also they brought in five hundred thieves from the country to the south of the city and arraigned them before the justices. When the justices ordered their heads to be chopped off, they asked each thief, beginning with the ringleader, to put his companions to death, but found not a single one willing to act as executioner. Then they said, "The other day a certain man put five hundred thieves to death. Where is he?"—"We saw him in such and such a place," was the reply. So they summoned him and said to him, "Put these men to death, and you will receive a rich reward."—"Yes, indeed," said he, consenting. So he put them all to death and received his reward.

The citizens consulted together and said, "This is a most excellent man. We will make him permanent executioner of thieves." So saying, they gave him the post. Later on they brought in five hundred thieves also from the west and still later five hundred also from the north, and he put them all to death. Thus he put to death two thousand thieves brought in from each of the four cardinal points. As time went on, and one or two men were brought in each day, he put them all to death. For a period of fifty-five years he acted as public executioner.

In old age he could no longer cut off a man's head with a single blow, but was obliged to deliver two or three blows, causing much unnecessary suffering to the victims. The citizens thought to themselves, "We can get another executioner of thieves. This man subjects his victims to much unnecessary torture. Of what use is he any longer?" Accordingly they removed him from his office. During his term of office as executioner of thieves, he had been accustomed to receive four perquisites: old clothes for him to wear, milk-porridge made with fresh ghee for him to drink, jasmine flowers wherewith to deck himself, and perfumes wherewith to anoint himself. But these four perquisites he received no longer. On the day he was deposed from office he gave orders that milk-porridge should be cooked for him. And taking with him old clothes and jasmine flowers and perfumes, he went to the river and bathed. Having so done, he put on the old clothes, decked himself with garlands, anointed his limbs, and went home and sat down. They set before him milk-porridge made with fresh ghee and water for rinsing the hands.

At that moment the Elder Sāriputta emerged from his meditation. He said to himself, "Where ought I to go today?" Surveying his rounds for alms, he saw milk-porridge in the house of the former executioner. Considering within himself, "Will this man receive me kindly?" he became aware of the following: "This excellent man will receive me kindly and will thereby gain a rich reward." So the elder put on his robe, took his bowl, and showed himself at the door of the former executioner's house.

When the man saw the elder, his heart was filled with joy. He thought to himself, "For a long time I have acted as executioner of thieves, and many are the men I have put to death. Now milk-porridge has been prepared in my house, and the elder has come and stands at my threshold. Now I ought to present alms to his reverence." So he removed the porridge which had been set before him, approached the elder, and paid obeisance to him. And escorting him into his house, he provided him with a seat, poured the milk-porridge into his bowl, spread fresh ghee thereon, and standing beside him, began to fan him.

Now for a long time he had not received milk-porridge, and therefore desired greatly to drink thereof. The elder knowing his desire, said to him, "Lay disciple, drink your own porridge." The man placed the fan in the hand of another and drank the porridge. The elder said to the man who was fanning him, "Go fan the lay disciple instead." So while he was being fanned, the former executioner filled his belly with porridge, and then went and resumed fanning the elder. When the elder had finished his meal, he took his bowl.

When the elder began the words of thanksgiving to his host, the man was not able to fix his mind on the elder's discourse. The elder, observing this, said to him, "Lay disciple, why is it that you are not able to fix your mind on my discourse?"—"Reverend sir, for a long time I have done deeds of cruelty; I have put many men to death. It is because I keep recalling my own past deeds that I am unable to fix my mind on your reverence's discourse." The elder thought to himself, "I will play a trick on him." So he said to the man, "But did you do this of your own free will, or were you made to do it by others?"—"The king made me do it, reverend sir."—"If that is the case, lay disciple, what wrong did you do?" The bewildered disciple thought, "According to what the elder says, I have done no wrong." Said he to the elder, "Very well, reverend sir, continue your discourse."

As the elder pronounced the words of thanksgiving, the man's mind became tranquil; and as he listened to the Dhamma, he developed the quality of patience, and progressed in the direction of the path of stream-entry. When the elder had completed the words of rejoicing, he departed. The lay disciple accompanied him a little way and then turned back. As the lay disciple was returning, an ogress came along in the form of a cow, struck him with her shoulder, and killed him. So he died and was reborn in the world of the Tusita gods.

The monks began a discussion in the Hall of Truth: "He who was an executioner of thieves, he who for fifty-five years committed acts of cruelty, today was relieved of his office, today gave alms to the elder, today met death. Where was he reborn?" The Teacher came in and asked them, "Monks, what are you sitting here now talking about?" When they told him, he said, "Monks, that man has been reborn in the world of the Tusita gods."—"What did you say, reverend sir? He who killed men for so long a time has been reborn in the world of the Tusita gods?"—"Yes, monks. A great and good spiritual counsellor did he receive. He heard Sāriputta teach the Dhamma, and profiting thereby, acquired knowledge. When he departed from this existence, he was reborn in the world of the Tusita gods." So saying, he pronounced the following stanza:

> "He who was executioner of thieves in the city
> Listened to words well spoken.
> Having gained patience accordingly,
> He went to heaven, and is in joy."

"Reverend sir, there is no great power in words of thanksgiving, and this man had done much wrong. How could he gain something special with so little?" The Teacher replied, "Monks, do not measure the Dhamma I have taught as being little or much. One saying possessed of meaning is of surpassing merit." So saying, he instructed them in the Dhamma by pronouncing the following stanza:

100. Though a thousand speeches
　　　Are made of meaningless lines,
　　　Better the single meaningful line
　　　By hearing which one is at peace.

9. Husband-honourer

ONLY GATHERING FLOWERS INDEED ... This instruction was given by the Teacher while he was in residence at Sāvatthī with reference to a woman named Husband-honourer, Patipūjikā. The story begins in the world of the Thirty-three gods.

The story goes that a god named Garland-wearer, Mālabhārī, entered the pleasure-garden in the world of the Thirty-three, accompanied by a thousand celestial nymphs. Five hundred of these nymphs climbed trees and threw down flowers; five hundred others gathered up the flowers that fell and decked the god with them. One of these nymphs, even as she sat on the branch of a tree, passed from that state of existence, her body vanishing like the flame of a lamp, and received a new conception in Sāvatthī in a certain family of station. Born with a recollection of her former states of existence, and remembering that she had been the wife of the god Garland-wearer, she made offerings of perfumes and garlands when she grew up, making the earnest wish to be reborn with her former husband.

When she was sixteen years of age, she married into another family. And even then, whenever she gave the monks ticket-food or fortnightly-food or food for the rainy season,[14] she would say, "May this offering assist me to obtain rebirth with my

---

14. These are special types of meal-offerings that lay people make to the monks.

former husband." Said the monks, "This woman, ever busy and active, yearns only for her husband." Therefore they called her Husband-honourer, Patipūjikā. She cared regularly for the Hall of Assembly, supplied water for drinking, and provided seats for the monks. Whenever others desired to give ticket-food or fortnightly-food, they would bring it and give it to her, saying, "Dear lady, please present these to the Order of Monks." Going to and fro in this manner, she obtained at one and the same time the "fifty-six qualities of goodness." She became pregnant and at the end of ten lunar months gave birth to a son; when her son was old enough to walk, she gave birth to another son, and then to another, until she had four sons.

One day she gave alms, rendered honour to the monks, listened to the Dhamma and undertook the precepts, and at the end of that day died of some sudden sickness and was reborn with her former husband. During all that time the other celestial nymphs were decking the god with flowers. When the god Garland-wearer saw her, he said, "We have not seen you since morning. Where have you been?"—"I passed from this existence, husband."—"What do you say?"—"Precisely so, husband."—"Where were you reborn?"—"In a family of station at Sāvatthī."—"How long a time did you remain there?"—"At the end of the tenth lunar month I issued from the womb of my mother. When I was sixteen years old, I married into another family. I bore four sons, gave alms, and rendered honour to the monks, making an earnest wish to return and be reborn with you, husband."—"How long is the life of men?"—"Only a hundred years."—"So short as that?"—"Yes, husband."—"If men are reborn with so short a time as that to live, do they spend their time asleep and heedless, or do they give alms and render honour?"—"What do you say, husband? Men are ever heedless, as if reborn with an incalculable number of years to live, as if in no way subject to old age and death."

The god Garland-wearer was greatly agitated. Said he, "If, as you say, men are reborn with only a hundred years to live, and if they lie heedless and asleep, when will they ever obtain release from suffering?" (Now a hundred of our years are equivalent to a night and a day in the world of the Thirty-three gods, thirty such nights and days make up a month, twelve such months make up a year, and the length of their lives is a thousand such celestial years;

or, in human reckoning, thirty-six million years. Thus it was that for that god not a single day had passed; nay, not more than a moment of time. Therefore he thought to himself, "If the life of men is so short, it is highly improper for them to give themselves up to a life of heedlessness.")

On the following day the monks, on entering the village, found the Hall of Assembly uncared for, no seats provided, no water supplied for drinking. "Where is Husband-honourer?" they asked. "Reverend sirs, how could you expect to see her? After your reverences had eaten and departed, she died in the evening." Thereupon monks who had not yet attained the fruit of stream-entry, remembering her kindly services to them, were unable to restrain their tears, while monks who had attained arahantship were deeply moved by Dhamma.

After eating their breakfast, they went to the monastery and asked the Teacher, "Reverend sir, Husband-honourer, busy and active, performed all manner of work of merit and yearned only for her husband. Now she is dead. Where was she reborn?"—"Monks, she was reborn with her own husband."—"But, reverend sir, she is not with her husband."—"Monks, she yearned not for that husband. Her husband was the god Garland-wearer in the world of the Thirty-three. She passed from that state of existence while decking him with flowers. Now she has returned to where she was before and has been reborn with him."—"Reverend sir, is what you say true?"—"Yes, monks, what I say is true."—"Oh, how short, reverend sir, is the life of creatures in this world! Early in the morning she served us with food, and in the evening she sickened and died." The Teacher replied, "Yes, monks, the life of creatures in this world is indeed short. Therefore while creatures in this world yet yearn for the things of earth and have not yet satisfied their desires for sensual pleasures, death overpowers them and carries them off wailing and weeping." So saying, he pronounced the following stanza:

48. Only gathering flowers, indeed,
    Insatiate in sensual desire,
    With a mind clinging—just such a man
    Must the Ender bring under his sway.

10. A Certain Monk

THE MIND IS VERY HARD TO CHECK ... This instruction was given by the Teacher while he was in residence at Sāvatthī with reference to a certain monk.

In the country of the king of the Kosalans, it appears, at the foot of a mountain, was a certain thickly settled village named Mātika. Now one day sixty monks, who had received from the Teacher a subject of meditation leading to arahantship, came to this village and entered it for alms. Now the headman of this village was a man named Mātika. When Mātika's mother saw the monks, she provided them with seats, served them with rice-porridge flavoured with all manner of choice flavours, and asked them, "Reverend sirs, where do you desire to go?"—"To some pleasant place, great lay disciple." Knowing that the monks were seeking a place of residence for the season of the rains, she prostrated herself at their feet and said to them, "If the noble monks will reside here during these three months, I will take upon myself the Three Refuges and the Five Precepts and will perform Uposatha-day practices." The monks consented, thinking to themselves, "With her assistance we shall be free from anxiety on account of food and shall be able to effect escape from the round of existence."

Mātika's mother superintended the erection of a monastery to serve as their place of residence, presented it to them, and the monks took up their residence there. On a certain day they met together and admonished each other as follows, "Brethren, it behoves us not to live the life of heedlessness, for before us stand the eight great hells with gates wide open, even as our own houses. Now we have come here thus, having received a subject of meditation from the living Buddha. And the favour of the Buddhas cannot be won by a deceitful person, even though he walk in their very footsteps. Only by doing the will of the Buddhas can their favour be won. Therefore be heedful. Two monks may neither stand nor sit in any one place. In the evening we shall meet together to wait upon the elder, and early in the morning we shall meet together when it is time to go the rounds for alms. At other times two of us must never be together. If, however, a monk is taken sick, let him come to the monastery court and strike the block.[15] At the

---

15. A hollow or solid block of hardwood, still used in Asian monasteries.

signal given by a stroke on the block, we will come together and provide a remedy for him." Having made this agreement, they entered upon residence.

One day, while the monks were in residence, that female disciple took ghee, molasses, and other kinds of medicine and in the evening, accompanied by a retinue of bondsmen and servants, went to the monastery. Seeing no monks, she asked some men, "Where have the noble monks gone?"—"My lady, they must be sitting in their own respective night quarters and day quarters."—"What must I do in order to see them?" Men who knew about the agreement made by the Order of Monks said, "If you strike the block, my lady, they will assemble." So she struck the block. When the monks heard the sound of the block, they thought to themselves, "Someone must be sick." And coming forth from their several quarters, they assembled in the monastery court. No two monks came by the same path.

When the female lay disciple saw them approach one at a time, each from his own quarters, she thought to herself, "My sons must have had a quarrel with each other." So, after paying obeisance to the Order of Monks, she asked them, "Have you had a quarrel, reverend sirs?"—"No, indeed, great lay disciple."—"If, reverend sirs, there is no quarrel among you, how is it that whereas in coming to our house you came all together, today you do not approach in that manner, but instead approach one at a time, each from his own quarters?"—"Great lay disciple, we were sitting each in his own cell engaged in the practice of meditation."—"What do you mean, reverend sirs, by this expression, 'practice of meditation'?"—"We rehearse the thirty-two constituent parts of the body[16] and thus obtain a clear conception of the decay and death inherent in the body, great lay disciple."—"But, reverend sirs, are you alone permitted to rehearse the thirty-two constituent parts of the body and thus obtain a clear conception of the decay and death inherent in the body; or are we also permitted to do this?"—"This practice is forbidden to none, great lay disciple." "Well then, teach me also the thirty-two constituent parts of the body and show me how to obtain a clear conception of the decay

---

16. Beginning: hair of the head, hair of the body, nails, teeth, skin. See *Mirror of the Dhamma* (BPS Wheel No. 54).

and death inherent in the body."—"Very well, lay disciple," said the monks, "learn them." So saying, they taught her all. She began at once to rehearse the thirty-two constituent parts of the body, striving thereby to obtain for herself a clear conception of the decay and death inherent in the body. So successful was she that even in advance of those monks she attained the three paths and the three fruits, and by the same paths won the four analytical knowledges and mundane super-knowledge.[17]

Arising from the bliss of the paths and the fruits, she looked with divine vision and considered within herself, "At what time did my sons attain this state?" Immediately she became aware of the following, "All these monks are still in the bondage of lust, hatred, and delusion. They have not yet, by the practice of deep meditation, induced insight." Then she pondered, "Do my sons possess the dispositions requisite for the attainment of arahantship or do they not?" She perceived, "They do." Then she pondered, "Do they possess suitable lodgings or do they not?" Immediately she perceived that they did. Then she pondered, "Have they proper companions or have they not?" Immediately she perceived that they had. Finally she pondered the question, "Do they receive proper food or do they not?" She perceived, "They do not receive proper food."

From that time on she provided them with various kinds of rice-porridge and with all manner of hard food and with soft food flavoured with various choice flavours. And seating the monks in her house, she offered water of donation[18] and presented the food to them, saying, "Reverend sirs, take and eat whatever you desire."

As the result of the wholesome food they received, their minds became tranquil; and as the result of tranquillity of mind, they developed insight and attained arahantship together with the analytical knowledges. Then the thought occurred to them, "The great female lay disciple has indeed been our support. Had we not received wholesome food, we should never have attained the paths

---

17. That is, she attained the path and fruit of non-returning, accompanied by certain other advanced types of meditative knowledge and psychic powers.
18. She offered the water of donation as a symbol of offering merits to her relatives or other beings born in states of suffering.

and the fruits. As soon as we have completed our residence and done the ceremony of Pavāraṇā[19] let us go and visit the Teacher." Accordingly they took leave of the great female lay disciple, saying, "Lay disciple, we desire to see the Teacher."—"Very well, noble sirs," said she. So she accompanied them on their journey a little way, and then, saying, "Look in on us again, reverend sirs," and many other pleasant words, she returned to her house.

When those monks arrived at Sāvatthī, they paid obeisance to the Teacher and sat down respectfully on one side. The Teacher said to them, "Monks, you have evidently fared well, had plenty to eat, and have not been troubled on account of food." The monks replied, "We have indeed fared well, reverend sir, had plenty to eat, and have by no means been troubled on account of food. For a certain female lay disciple, the mother of Mātika, knew the course of our thoughts, in so much that the moment we thought, 'Oh, that she would prepare such and such food for us!' she prepared the very food we thought of and gave it to us." Thus did they recite her praises.

A certain monk, who heard his fellow monks praise the virtues of their hostess, conceived a desire to go there. So obtaining a subject of meditation from the Teacher, he took leave of the Teacher, saying, "Reverend sir, I intend to go to that village." And departing from Jetavana, he arrived in due course at that village and entered the monastery. On the very day he entered the monastery he thought to himself, "I have heard it said that this female lay disciple knows every thought that passes through the mind of another. Now I have been wearied by my journey and shall not be able to sweep the monastery. Oh, that she would send a man to make ready the monastery for me!" The female lay disciple, sitting in her house, pondering within herself, became aware of this fact and sent a man, saying to him, "Go make ready the monastery and turn it over to him." The man went and swept the monastery and turned it over to him. Then the monk, desiring to have water to drink, thought to himself, "Oh, that she would send me some sweetened water!" Straightaway the female lay disciple sent it. On the following day, early in the morning, he

---

19. A ceremony held at the end of the rains residence, when monks invite admonition from their fellow-monks.

thought to himself, "Let her send me soft rice-porridge with some dainty bits!" The female lay disciple straightway did so. After he had finished drinking the porridge, he thought to himself, "Oh, that she would send me such and such solid food!" The female lay disciple straightaway sent this also to him.

Then he thought to himself, "This female lay disciple has sent me every single thing I have thought of. I should like to see her. Oh, that she would come to me in person, bringing with her soft food seasoned with various choice seasonings!" The female lay disciple thought to herself, "My son wishes to see me, desires me to go to him." So procuring soft food, she went to the monastery and gave it to him. When he had eaten his meal, he asked her, "Lay disciple, is your name Mātika's Mother?"—"Yes, dear son."—"You know the thoughts of another?"—"Why do you ask me, dear son?"—"You have done for me every single thing I have thought of; that is why I ask you."—"Many are the monks who know the thoughts of another, dear son."—"I am not asking anyone else. I am asking you, lay disciple." Even under these circumstances the female lay disciple avoided saying, "I know the thoughts of another," and said instead, "Those who do not know the thoughts of another do thus, my son."

Thereupon the monk thought to himself, "I am in a most embarrassing position. They that are still worldings like me entertain both noble and ignoble thoughts. Were I to entertain a single inappropriate thought, she would doubtless change her attitude towards me, as they seize a thief with the goods by his hair. Therefore I had best run away from here." So he said to the female lay disciple, "Lay disciple, I intend to go away."—"Where are you going, noble sir?"—"To the Teacher, lay disciple."—"Reside here for a while, reverend sir."—"I can no longer reside here, lay disciple. I must positively go away." With these words he departed and went to the Teacher.

The Teacher asked him, "Monk, are you no longer residing there?"—"No, reverend sir, I cannot reside there any longer."—"For what reason, monk?"—"Reverend sir, that female lay disciple knows every single thought that passes through my mind. It occurred to me, 'They that are still worldings like me entertain both noble and ignoble thoughts. Were I to entertain a single inappropriate thought, she would doubtless change her attitude towards me, as they seize a thief with the goods by his hair. That is why I have returned."—"Monk, that is the very place where you ought to reside."—"I cannot, reverend sir. I will not reside there any longer."—"Well then, monk, can you guard just one thing?"—"What do you mean, reverend sir?"—"Guard your thoughts alone, for thoughts are hard to guard. Restrain your thoughts alone. Do not concern yourself with anything else, for thoughts are unruly." So saying, he pronounced the following stanza:

35. The mind is very hard to check
     And swift it falls on what it wants;
     The training of the mind is good,
     A mind so tamed brings happiness.

When the Teacher had admonished that monk, he dismissed him, saying, "Go, monk, concern yourself with nothing else. Resume residence in that same place." And that monk, after being admonished by the Teacher, went to that same place and did not think thoughts concerned with exterior things.

The great female lay disciple looked with divine vision and seeing the elder, she determined by her own knowledge alone the following fact, "My son has now gained a Teacher who gives admonition and has returned once more." And at once she prepared wholesome food and gave it to him. Once having received wholesome food, in but a few days the elder attained arahantship.

As the elder passed his days in the enjoyment of the bliss of the paths and the fruits, he thought to himself, "The great female lay disciple has indeed been a support to me. By her assistance I have gained release from the round of existence." And he considered within himself, "Has she been a support to me in my present state of existence only or has she been a support to me in other states of existence also, as I have passed from one state of existence to another in the round of existences?" With this thought in mind he recalled a hundred states of existence less one. Now in a hundred states of existence less one that female lay disciple had been his wife, and her affections had been set on other men, and she had caused him to be deprived of life. When, therefore, the elder beheld the huge pile of demerit she had accumulated, he thought to himself, "Oh, what wicked deeds this female lay disciple has committed!"

The great female lay disciple also sat in her house, considering within herself the following thought, "Has my son reached the goal of the holy life?" Perceiving that he had attained arahantship, she continued her reflections as follows, "When my son attained arahantship, he thought to himself, 'This female lay disciple has indeed been a powerful support to me.' Then he considered within himself, 'Has she been a support to me in previous states of existence also or has she not?' With this thought in mind he recalled a hundred states of existence less one. Now in a hundred states of existence less one I conspired with other men and deprived him of life. When, therefore, he beheld the huge pile of demerit I thus accumulated, he thought to himself, 'Oh, what wicked deeds this female lay disciple has committed!' Is it not possible that, as I have passed from one state of existence to another in the round of existences, I have rendered assistance to him?"

Considering the matter further, she called up before her mind her hundredth state of existence and became aware of the following: "In my hundredth state of existence I was his wife. On a certain occasion, when I might have deprived him of life, I spared his life. I have indeed rendered great assistance to my son." And still remaining seated in her house she said, "Discern further and consider the matter." By the power of the divine ear the monk immediately heard what she said. Discerning further, he called up before his mind his hundredth state of existence and perceived that in that state of existence she had spared his life. Filled with joy, he thought to himself, "This female lay disciple has indeed rendered great assistance to me." Then and there, reciting the questions relating to the four paths and fruits, he attained the remainderless element of Nibbāna.[20]

---

20. This means, in ordinary terms, that he passed away.

Part II
Doing Evil

11. *The Lay Disciple Atula*

FROM DAYS OF OLD IT HAS BEEN, ATULA ... This instruction was given by the Teacher while he was in residence at Jetavana with reference to the lay disciple Atula.

Atula was a lay disciple who lived at Sāvatthī, and he had a retinue of five hundred other lay disciples. One day he took those lay disciples with him to the monastery to hear the Dhamma. Desiring to hear the Elder Revata teach the Dhamma, he saluted the Elder Revata and sat down respectfully on one side. Now this Elder Revata was a solitary recluse, delighting in solitude even as a lion delights in solitude, and thus he had nothing to say to Atula.

"This elder has nothing to say," thought Atula. Provoked, he arose from his seat, went to the Elder Sāriputta, and took his stand respectfully on one side. "For what reason have you come to me?" asked the Elder Sāriputta. "Reverend sir," replied Atula, "I took these lay disciples of mine to hear the Dhamma and approached the Elder Revata. But he had nothing to say to me; therefore I was provoked at him and have come here. Teach the Dhamma to me."—"Well then, lay disciple," said the Elder Sāriputta, "sit down." And forthwith the Elder Sāriputta expounded the Abhidhamma at great length.

Thought the lay disciple, "The Abhidhamma is exceedingly abstruse, and the elder has expounded this alone to me at great length; of what use is he to us?" Provoked, he took his retinue with him and went to the Elder Ānanda. Said the Elder Ānanda, "What is it, lay disciple?" Atula replied, "Reverend sir, we approached the Elder Revata for the purpose of hearing the Dhamma and got not so much as a syllable from him. Provoked at this, we went to the Elder Sāriputta and he expounded to us at great length the Abhidhamma alone with all its subtleties. 'Of what use is he to us?' we thought to ourselves and provoked at him also, we came here. Teach the Dhamma to us, reverend sir."—"Well then," replied the Elder Ānanda, "sit down and listen." Thereupon the

Elder Ānanda expounded the Dhamma to them very briefly, and making it very easy for them to understand.

But they were provoked at the Elder Ānanda also, and going to the Teacher, saluted him, and sat down respectfully on one side. Said the Teacher to them, "Lay disciples, why have you come here?"—"To hear the Dhamma, reverend sir."—"But you have heard the Dhamma."—"Reverend sir, first we went to the Elder Revata, and he had nothing to say to us; provoked at him, we approached the Elder Sāriputta, and he expounded the Abhidhamma to us at great length; but we were unable to understand his discourse, and provoked at him we approached the Elder Ānanda; the Elder Ānanda, however, expounded the Dhamma to us very briefly, therefore we were provoked at him also and came here."

The Teacher heard what they had to say and then replied, "Atula, from days of old until now it has been the invariable practice of men to blame him who said nothing, him who said much, and him who said little. There is no one who deserves unqualified blame and no one who deserves unqualified praise. Even kings are blamed by some and praised by others. Even the great earth, even the sun and moon, even a Supremely Enlightened Buddha, sitting and speaking in the midst of the fourfold assembly,[21] some blame and others praise. For blame or praise bestowed by utter simpletons is a matter of no account. But he whom a man of learning and intelligence blames or praises—he is blamed or praised indeed." So saying, he pronounced the following stanzas:

227. From days of old it has been, Atula—
This is not only of today:
They blame one who keeps silent,
They blame one who speaks much,
They blame one who says little too—
There is no one in the world unblamed.

228. There never was, and never will be,
Nor is there found at present
A person blamed exclusively
Nor yet one wholly praised.

---

21. Of monks, nuns, laymen, and laywomen.

229. But if the wise praise a man,
After observing him day by day—
One of flawless conduct, astute,
In wisdom and virtue well-composed—

230. Who can blame that worthy one
Like ornament of finest gold?
Even the devas praise him,
By Brahmā, too, he is praised.

12. Ciñcā the Brahmin Girl

THE PERSON OF FALSE SPEECH—TRANSGRESSOR OF ONE PRINCIPLE ... This instruction was given by the Teacher while he was in residence at Jetavana with reference to Ciñcā Mānavikā.

For in the first period after the Enlightenment the disciples of the Master multiplied and innumerable gods and men entered on the plane of the noble ones.[22] And as the glory of his virtues became widely known, rich gain and high honour were bestowed upon him. But as for the sectarians, lost to them were gain and honour alike, even as fireflies lose their brilliance before the coming of the sun. And they gathered in the street and cried out, "Is the monk Gotama the only Buddha? We also are Buddhas! Does that alone which is given to him yield abundant fruit? That which is given to us brings abundant fruit also. Therefore give alms to us; bestow honour upon us." With such words as these did they appeal to the multitude, but for all their appeal they got neither gain nor honour. Accordingly they met together in secret and considered within themselves, "By what means can we cast reproach upon the monk Gotama in public and so put an end to the gain and honour bestowed upon him?"

Now at that time there lived in Sāvatthī a certain wandering nun named Ciñcā Mānavikā. She possessed surpassing beauty and loveliness; a very celestial nymph was she; from her body proceeded forth rays of light. Now a certain harsh counsellor made this proposal, "With the assistance of this woman we shall be able to cast reproach upon the monk Gotama, and so put an

---

22. Meaning that they attained the paths and fruits up to arahantship.

end to the gain and honour bestowed upon him."—"That is the way!" exclaimed the sectarians, agreeing to his proposal.

Ciñcā Mānavikā went to the monastery of the sectarians, saluted them, and stood waiting; but the sectarians had nothing to say to her. Thereupon she said, "What fault do you find in me?" This question she repeated three times; then she said, "Noble sirs, I appeal to you for an answer. Noble sirs, what fault do you find in me? Why do you not speak to me?"—"Sister," replied the sectarians, "Don't you know the monk Gotama, who goes about doing us harm, depriving us of gain and honour alike?"—"No, noble sirs, I do not know him; but is there anything I can do to help you in this matter?"—"Sister, if you wish us well, summon up your resources, contrive to cast reproach upon the monk Gotama, and so put an end to the gain and honour bestowed upon him."—"Very well, noble sirs," replied Ciñcā Mānavikā. "I will take all the responsibility; have no anxiety as to the outcome." So saying, she departed.

From that time on, she employed all of her skill in the arts of a woman to effect her purpose. When the residents of Sāvatthī were returning from Jetavana after listening to the Dhamma, she would put on a cloak the colour of cochineal, and bearing perfumes and garlands in her hands, would walk in the direction of Jetavana. "Where are you going at this time of day?" people would ask her. "What business of yours is it where I am going?" she would reply. She would spend the night near Jetavana at the monastery of the sectarians, and early the following morning, when throngs of lay disciples were coming out of the city for the purpose of rendering the morning greeting to the Teacher, she would wend her way back and re-enter the city. "Where have you spent the night?" people would ask her. "What business of yours is it where I have spent the night?" she would reply.

After the lapse of a month and a half, whenever they asked her this question, she would reply, "I spent the night at Jetavana alone with the monk Gotama in the Perfumed Chamber." And by her answer she caused doubts and misgivings to spring up in the minds of those who were still worldlings. And they said to themselves, "Is this true, or is it false?" When three or four months had gone by she wrapped her belly about with bandages, to create the impression that she was pregnant, and dressing herself in a scarlet cloak, she went about, saying, "I have conceived a child by the monk Gotama." Thus did she deceive utter simpletons.

When eight or nine months had gone by, she fastened a disc of wood to her belly, drew a cloak over it, produced swellings all over her body by pounding her hands and feet and back with the jaw-bone of an ox, and pretending to be physically exhausted, went one evening to the Hall of Truth and stood before the Tathāgata. There, in his gloriously adorned Seat of Truth, sat the Tathāgata teaching the Dhamma. And standing there before him, Ciñcā Mānavikā opened her lips and reviled him, saying, "Mighty monk, mighty is the throng to which you teach the Dhamma; sweet is your voice, soft are your lips. Nevertheless you are the one by whom I have conceived a child, and the time of my delivery is near at hand. But in spite of all this, you make no effort to provide a lying-in chamber for me, nor do you offer to provide me with ghee and oil and such other things as I need. And failing yourself to attend to your duty, neither do you say to any one of your supporters, the king of Kosala, or Anāthapiṇḍika, or Visākhā, your eminent female lay disciple, 'Do for this young woman what should be done for her.' You know well enough how to take your pleasure, but you do not know how to look after the child you have begotten." Thus did she revile the Tathāgata in the midst of the congregation, even as a woman with a mass of dung in her hand might seek to defile the face of the moon.

The Tathāgata stopped his discourse, and like a lion's roar, cried out, "Sister, as to whether what you have said is true or false, that is something which only you and I know." - "Yes, mighty monk, but who is to decide between the truth and the falsehood of what is known only to you and to me?" At that moment Sakka's seat showed signs of heat. Thereupon Sakka pondered the cause and became aware of the following, "Ciñcā Mānavikā is falsely accusing the Tathāgata." Thereupon Sakka said to himself, "I will clear up this matter," and forthwith set out with four deities. The deities turned themselves into little mice. With one bite of their teeth these little mice severed the cords with which the disc of wood was fastened to the belly of the woman. At that moment the wind blew up the cloak which was wrapped about her, and the disc of wood fell upon her feet, cutting off the toes of both her feet.

Thereupon the multitude cried out, "A hag is reviling the Supremely Enlightened One." They spat on her head, and taking clods of earth and sticks in their hands, drove her out of the Jetavana. As she passed out of sight of the Tathāgata, the great earth split apart, an abyss opened under her feet, and flames shot up from the Avīci hell. Thus was she swallowed up, enveloped as it were in a scarlet blanket such as is presented by wealthy families, and reborn in the Avīci hell. From that time the gain and honour of the sectarians decreased, but the offerings presented to the Master increased more and more.

On the following day the monks began a discussion in the Hall of Truth: "Brethren, Ciñcā Mānavikā, because she falsely accused the Possessor of Eminent Virtues, the Foremost Recipient of Offerings, the Supremely Exalted, came to utter ruin." The Teacher approached and asked, "Monks, what are you sitting here now talking about?" When they told him, he said, "Monks, this is not the first time she has falsely accused me and come to utter ruin; she did the same thing in a previous state of existence also." Having thus spoken, he said:

> Unless a king discern clearly
> Fault on the part of another,
> After himself investigating carefully all the facts,
> Both small and great,
> He should not inflict punishment.

So saying, he related in detail this Mahā Paduma Jātaka (Jāt. No. 472).

Story of the Past: The Lewd Woman and the Youth

At that time, it appears, Ciñcā Mānavikā was reborn as one of the chief consorts of the king, fellow-wife of the mother of the Future Buddha, Prince Mahā Paduma. She invited the Great Being[23] to lie with her, and when he refused to do so, disfigured her own body with her own hands, feigned sickness, and told the king, "Your son brought me to this pass because I would not lie with him." The king, hearing this, was filled with rage, and straightaway flung the Great Being down Robbers' Cliff. The deity dwelling

---

23. The Bodhisatta or future Buddha in his earlier existences.

in the mountain chasm cared for him and placed him safe and sound within the hood of the king of the dragons. The king of the dragons carried him to the abode of the dragons and honoured him by conferring upon him half his kingly power. After the Great Being had dwelt there for a year, he conceived a desire to adopt the life of an ascetic. Accordingly he went to the Himalaya country, adopted the life of an ascetic, and in the course of time developed the direct knowledges by the practice of deep meditation.

Now a certain forester happened to see him there and reported the matter to the king. Thereupon the king went to him, exchanged friendly greetings with him, learned what had happened, and offered to bestow his kingdom upon the Great Being. The Great Being, however, declined his offer and admonished him as follows, "For my part, I have no desire to rule. But as for you, you should keep unimpaired the ten royal virtues,[24] avoid evil deeds, and rule your kingdom justly." Thereupon the king arose from his seat in tears and went back to the city. On the way there he asked his ministers, "Through whose fault was I separated from one endowed with such uprightness?"—"Your chief consort was to blame for this, your majesty." Thereupon the king had her taken by the heels and flung head first down Robbers' Cliff. And entering his city, from then on he ruled his kingdom justly. At that time Prince Mahā Paduma was the Great Being, and the fellow-wife of his mother was Ciñcā Mānavikā. (*End of Story of the Past.*)

When the Teacher had made this matter clear, he said, "Monks, in the case of those who have abandoned one thing—the speaking of truth—who have become confirmed in falsehood, who have rid themselves of (the chance of a happy) next world, there is no evil deed which they will not commit." So saying, he pronounced the following stanza:

176. The person of false speech—
 Transgressor of one principle,[25]
 Rejecter of the other world:
 There is no evil he cannot do.

---

24. Giving, virtuous conduct, renunciation, uprightness, gentleness, austerity, non-anger, harmlessness, patience, non-opposition (to the will of the people).
25. Truthfulness is the one necessary principle (*dhamma*).

13. The Black Ogress

NOT BY ENMITY AT ANY TIME ... This instruction was given by the Teacher while he was in residence at Jetavana with reference to a certain barren woman.

It appears that a certain householder's son, on the death of his father, did all the farm and household work by himself alone and took care of his mother as well. Now his mother said to him, "Dear son, I will fetch you a young wife."—"Dear mother, do not speak like that. My sole desire is to take care of you so long as you shall live."—"Dear son, you alone are doing the farm and household work, and I am not satisfied to have it so; let me fetch you a young wife." He protested time and again, and then held his peace.

The mother left the house, intending to go to a certain family and fetch home the daughter of that family. Her son asked her, "To what family are you going?"—"To such and such a family." He would not let her go to the family she had in mind, but told her of a family he liked better. So she went to the family he fancied, selected a wife for her son, and having set the day, installed her in her son's house. The woman turned out to be barren.

Then said the mother to the son, "Son, you had me fetch you a wife you yourself selected. Now she turns out to be barren. Without children a family dies out, and the line is not continued. Therefore let me fetch you another young wife."—"Enough said, dear mother," replied the son; but the mother repeated her request time and again. The barren wife heard the talk and thought to herself, "It is certain that sons cannot disobey the words of their mothers and fathers. Now if she fetches him a wife who is fruitful, they will treat me like a slave. Suppose I were to fetch him a young woman of my own selection?"

So the barren wife went to a certain family and selected a young woman for him. But she immediately encountered the opposition of the young woman's parents, who said to her, "Woman, what are you saying?" The barren wife replied, "I am a barren woman, and without children a family dies out. If your daughter gives birth to a son, she will be mistress of the family and the wealth thereof. Therefore give your daughter to me for my husband." She finally prevailed upon them to grant her request, and taking the young woman with her, installed her in her husband's house.

Then this thought occurred to her, "If my rival gives birth to a son or daughter, she alone will be mistress of the household. I must see to it that she shall not give birth to a child." So the barren wife said to her rival, "As soon as you have conceived a child in your womb, please let me know."—"Very well," replied her rival. In accordance with her promise, as soon as she had conceived, she told her fellow-wife.

Now the barren wife was accustomed to give her rival a meal of rice-porridge regularly every day with her own hand. So along with the food she gave her a drug to cause abortion. The result was that her rival had a miscarriage. Again the second time the fruitful wife conceived a child and informed the barren wife, and again her fellow-wife did as before and brought about a miscarriage.

The women who lived in the neighbourhood asked the fruitful wife, "Is not your rival putting an obstacle in your way?" When she told them the facts, they said to her, "You foolish woman, why did you do this? This woman was afraid you would get the upper hand, so she mixed a preparation to bring about a miscarriage and gave it to you. Do not tell her again." Accordingly the third time the fruitful wife said nothing to her rival. But the barren wife, seeing her belly, said to her, "Why did you not tell me that you had conceived a child?" Said the fruitful wife, "It was you who brought me here, and twice you have caused me to suffer a miscarriage; why should I tell you?"

"Now I am lost," thought the barren wife. From that time on she watched to catch her rival off her guard. When the baby in the womb was fully matured, she took advantage of an opportunity, mixed a drug, and gave it to her. But because the baby in the womb was fully mature, an abortion was out of the question, and the result was that the child lodged across the neck of the womb. Immediately the mother suffered acute pains and feared that her hour had come.

"You have killed me!" she cried. "It was you alone that brought me here; it was you alone that killed my three children. Now I also am going to die. When I have passed out of this existence, may I be reborn as an ogress able to devour your children." And having made this earnest wish, she died, and was reborn in that very house as a cat. The husband seized the barren wife, and saying to her, "It was you who destroyed my family," beat her soundly with elbows, knees, and otherwise. As the result of the beating she received, she sickened and died, and was reborn in that very house as a hen.

So the fruitful wife was reborn as a cat, and the barren wife was reborn as a hen. The hen laid eggs, and the cat came and ate them. This happened three times. Said the hen, "Three times you have eaten my eggs, and now you are seeking an opportunity to eat me too. When I have passed out of this existence, may I be able to eat you and your offspring." And having made this earnest wish, she passed out of that existence, and was reborn as a leopardess. The cat was reborn as a doe.

So the barren wife, at the end of her existence as a hen, was reborn as a leopardess; and the fruitful wife, at the end of her existence as a cat, was reborn as a doe. Thrice the doe brought forth young, and thrice the leopardess went and devoured the doe's offspring. When the doe came to die, she said, "Thrice this beast has devoured my offspring, and now she intends to devour me too. When I have passed out of this existence, may I be able to devour her and her offspring." And having made this earnest wish, she was reborn as an ogress. When the leopardess passed out of that existence, she was reborn in Sāvatthī as a young woman of station.

So the fruitful wife, at the end of her existence as a doe, was reborn as an ogress; and the barren wife, at the end of her existence as a leopardess, was reborn in Sāvatthī as a young woman of station. When the latter grew up, she was married and went to live with her husband's family in a little settlement near the gate of the city. After a time she gave birth to a son. The ogress disguised herself as a dear friend of the young woman and went to see her. "Where is my friend?" said the ogress. "In the inner room; she has just given birth to a child."—"Did she give birth to a son or a daughter? I should like to see her." So saying, the ogress went in. While pretending to be looking at the child, she seized him, devoured him, and then went out. Again a second time she devoured a child of the young wife in the same way.

The third time the young wife was pregnant she addressed her husband, "Husband, in this place an ogress has devoured two sons of mine and escaped. This time I intend to go to the house of my parents to give birth to my child."

Now at this time the ogress was away doing her turn at drawing water. (For Vessavaṇa's ogresses take their turn at drawing water from Lake Anotatta, passing it along from the source.²⁶ At the expiration of four or five months they are released; the others die from exhaustion.) The moment the ogress was released from her turn at drawing water, she went quickly to the young wife's house and inquired, "Where is my friend?"—"Where you will not see her. There is an ogress that devours every child she bears in this house, and therefore she has gone to the house of her parents."—"She may go wherever she likes, but she will not escape from me." Spurred on by an impulse of hatred, the ogress dashed towards the city.

On the day appointed for the naming of the child, the mother bathed him, gave him a name, and then said to her husband, "Husband, now we will go back to our own home." Accordingly she took the boy in her arms and set out with her husband along the path leading through the grounds of the monastery. When they reached the monastery pool, the young wife gave the boy to her husband and bathed in the pool. When she had finished her bath, her husband bathed in the pool. While the husband was bathing, the wife remained near, giving suck to her child.

Just then the ogress drew near. The young wife saw her coming and recognized her. Immediately she screamed with a loud voice, "Husband! Husband! Come quickly! Come quickly! Here is that ogress!" Not daring to wait until her husband came, she turned and dashed into the monastery.

Now at this time the Teacher was teaching the Dhamma in the midst of the Order. The young wife laid her boy at the feet of the Tathāgata and said, "I give you this child; spare the life of my son." The deity Sumana, who resided in the gate, prevented the ogress from entering. The Teacher addressed the Elder Ānanda, saying, "Go, Ānanda, summon that ogress within." The Elder summoned her within. The young wife said, "Here she comes, reverend sir." Said the Teacher, "Let her come; make no noise."

---

26. Vessavaṇa is one of the divine kings in the heaven of the Four Great Kings. He rules over the ogres and ogresses.

When the ogress came and stood before him, the Teacher said: "Why have you done so? Had you not come face to face with a Buddha like me, you would have cherished hatred towards each other for an aeon, like the snake and the mongoose, who trembled and quaked with enmity, like the crows and the owls. Why do you return hatred for hatred? Hatred is quenched by love, not by hatred." And when he had thus spoken, he pronounced the following stanza:

5. Not by enmity at any time
   Are those with enmity allayed:
   They are allayed by amity—
   This is an ancient principle.

At the conclusion of the stanza the ogress was established in the fruit of stream-entry.

The Teacher said to the woman, "Give your child to this ogress."—"I am afraid to, reverend sir."—"Fear not, you have no reason to be alarmed because of her." The young wife gave her child to the ogress. The ogress kissed and caressed him, gave him back again to his mother, and began to weep. The Teacher asked her, "Why do you weep?"—"Reverend sir, in the past I have managed somehow or other to get a living, but I have never had enough to eat. Now how am I to live?" Then the Teacher comforted her, saying, "Do not worry." And turning to the mother, he said, "Take this ogress home with you, let her live in your own house, and feed her with the choicest rice-porridge."

So the young wife took the ogress home with her, lodged her on the back veranda, and fed her with the choicest rice-porridge. Now when the rice was threshed and the flail was raised, she feared that it would strike her head. So she said to her friend, "I shall not be able to live here any longer; lodge me elsewhere." She was lodged successively in the flail-hut, the water hut, the bake-house, the storeroom for nimbs, the dust-heap, and the village gate. But she refused to live in any of these places, saying, "Here the flail rises as if it would split my head in two; here boys empty out slops; here dogs lie down; here boys attend to nature's needs; here they throw away sweepings; here village boys practise fortune-telling." So they lodged her in a quiet place by herself outside of the village, and there they brought her the choicest rice-porridge.

The ogress said to her friend, "This year there will be abundance of rain; therefore plant your crops in a moist place." Other people's crops were destroyed either by excessive moisture or by drought, but the crops of the young wife flourished above measure.

People asked the young wife, "Woman, your crops are destroyed neither by excessive moisture nor by drought. When you plant your crops, you seem to know in advance whether the season will be wet or dry. How is this?" The young wife replied, "I have a friend, an ogress, who tells me whether the season will be wet or dry; and I plant my crops according to her directions on high or low ground. Don't you see? Every day the choicest rice-porridge and other kinds of food are carried out of our house and offered to her. If you also carry the choicest rice-porridge and other kinds of food to her, she will look after your crops also."

Straightaway all the residents of the city rendered honour to her. On her part, from that time forth, she looked after the crops of all. And she received abundant gifts and a large retinue. Subsequently she established the eight tickets for food, which are kept up even to this present day.

14. The Five Laymen

THERE IS NO FIRE LIKE LUST ... This instruction was given by the Teacher while he was in residence at Jetavana with reference to five lay disciples.

The story goes that these five men went to the monastery desiring to hear the Dhamma, and, having saluted the Teacher, sat down respectfully on one side. Now in the case of the Buddhas, no such thought ever enters their mind as the following: "This man is a khattiya, this man is a brahmin, this is a rich man, this is a poor man; I will teach the Dhamma to this man in such a way as to exalt him; I will not do so, however, in the case of this other man." It matters not with reference to what subject the Buddhas teach the Dhamma. They place reverence for the Dhamma before all else, and teach the Dhamma as though they were bringing down the celestial river from the sky.

But though the Tathāgata taught the Dhamma in this way to the five men who sat about him, one of the five, even as he sat there, fell asleep, another sat and dug the earth with his finger, another sat and shook a tree, another gazed at the sky. Only one listened attentively to the Dhamma. As the Elder Ānanda stood there fanning the Teacher, he observed the conduct of the five men and said to the Teacher, "Reverend sir, you are teaching the Dhamma even as thunders the thunder which accompanies a heavy rain, but even as you teach the Dhamma, these men sit doing this and that."—"Ānanda, do you not know these men?"—"No, reverend sir, I do not."

"Of these five men, he that sits there sound asleep was reborn as a snake in five hundred states of existence, and in each of these states of existence he laid his head in his coils and fell asleep; therefore at the present time also he is sound asleep; not a sound I make enters his ear."

"But, reverend sir, tell me, was this in successive states of existence or at intervals?"—"Ānanda, at one time this man was reborn as a human being, at another time as a god, and at another time as a snake. Indeed it would be impossible, even with the knowledge of omniscience, to determine exactly the number of times he has undergone rebirth at intervals. But in five hundred successive states of existence he was reborn as a snake and fell asleep; not even yet is he sated with sleep.

"The man who sits there scratching the earth with his finger was reborn in five hundred successive states of existence as an earthworm and burrowed into the earth; hence he digs the earth at the present time also, and fails to hear my voice.

"The man who sits there shaking a tree was reborn in five hundred successive states of existence as a monkey, and from sheer force of habit acquired in previous states of existence, he still continues to shake a tree, and the sound of my voice does not enter his ears.

"The brahmin who sits there gazing at the sky was reborn in five hundred successive states of existence as an astrologer, and therefore today also he gazes at the sky just the same, and the sound of my voice does not enter his ears.

"The man who sits there listening attentively to the Dhamma was reborn in five hundred successive states of existence as a brahmin versed in the Three Vedas, devoted to the repetition of the sacred texts, and therefore listens attentively today also, as though he were putting together a sacred text."

"But, reverend sir, your teaching of the Dhamma cleaves the skin and penetrates to the marrow of the bones. Why is it that while you are teaching the Dhamma, they do not listen attentively?"—"Ānanda, you evidently imagine that my Dhamma is easy to listen to."—"Why, reverend sir, do you mean that it is difficult to listen to?"—"Precisely so, Ānanda."—"Why is that, reverend sir?"—"Ānanda, these living beings, during countless thousands of cycles of time, never heard of the Buddha, the Dhamma, and the Order, and therefore are unable now to listen to this Dhamma which I teach. In the round of existences without conceivable beginning, these living beings have been accustomed to listen to the speech of animals in its countless forms. Therefore they spend their time in places where men drink and amuse themselves, and therefore sing and dance; it is impossible for them to listen to the Dhamma."—"But, reverend sir, for what reason is it that they are unable to listen to the Dhamma?"

The Teacher answered him as follows: "Ānanda, they are unable to do so by reason of lust, by reason of hatred, by reason of delusion. For there is no fire like the fire of lust, consuming living beings as it does, without leaving so much as ashes behind. To be sure, the world-conflagration which closes an epoch burns up the world without leaving anything behind, but this is a fire which breaks out only on the appearance of the seven suns, and this fire burns only at times and at seasons. But as for the fire of lust, there is no time when the fire of lust does not burn. Therefore I say that there is no fire like the fire of lust, no grip like hatred, no snare like delusion, and no river like craving." So saying, the Teacher pronounced the following stanza:

251. There is no fire like lust,
No captor like aversion;
Unequalled is delusion's net,
No river like craving.

15. *King Pasenadi of Kosala*

A DULLARD DROWSY WITH MUCH GLUTTONY .... This instruction was given by the Teacher while he was in residence at Jetavana with reference to King Pasenadi of Kosala.

At a certain period of his life this king used to eat boiled rice cooked by the bucketful, and sauce and curry in proportion. One day after he had his breakfast, unable to shake off the drowsy feeling occasioned by overeating, he went to see the Teacher and paced back and forth before him with a very weary look. Overcome by drowsiness, unable to lie down and stretch himself out, he sat down on one side. Thereupon the Teacher asked him, "Did you come, great king, before you were well rested?"—"Oh no, reverend sir," replied he king, "but I always suffer greatly after eating a meal." Then said the Teacher to him, "Great king, overeating always brings suffering in its train." So saying, he pronounced the following stanza:

325. A dullard drowsy with much gluttony,
　　　Engrossed in sleep, who wallows as he lies,
　　　Like a great porker stuffed with fattening food,
　　　Comes ever and again unto the womb.[27]

At the conclusion of the lesson the Teacher, desiring to help the king, pronounced the following stanza:

If a man is ever mindful,
If moderate in taking food,
His sufferings will be but slight,
He ages slowly, preserving his life.

The Teacher taught this stanza to Prince Uttara and said to him, "Whenever the king sits down to eat, you must recite this stanza to him, and by this means you must cause him to diminish his food." In these words the Teacher told him just what means to employ. The prince did as he was directed. After a time the king was content with a pint-pot of rice at most, and became lean and cheerful. He established intimate relations with the Teacher and for seven days gave "the gifts beyond compare."[28] When the Teacher pronounced the words of rejoicing for the gifts presented to him by the king, the assembled multitude obtained great spiritual advantage.

---

27. The translation of Ven. Ñāṇamoli Thera from *The Guide* (PTS 1962).
28. "The gifts beyond compare" are described in the Dhammapada Commentary in *Buddhist Legends*, 3:24ff.

16. Great-wealth the Treasurer's Son

HAVING LED NEITHER THE HOLY LIFE NOR RICHES WON WHILE YOUNG .... This instruction was given by the Teacher while he was in residence at Isipatana with reference to Great-wealth, Mahādhana, the treasurer's son.

Great-wealth, it appears, was reborn at Benares in a household worth eighty crores.[29] Now his mother and father thought to themselves, "We have a vast store of wealth in our house, and there is no necessity that our son should do anything else than enjoy himself according to his own good pleasure." Accordingly they had him instructed in singing and in the playing of musical instruments, and that was all the instruction he received. Likewise in that same city, in a household worth eighty crores of treasure, a daughter was reborn. The same thought occurred to her mother and father also, and they had her instructed only in dancing and singing. When the two reached the proper age, they were married with the customary ceremonies. In the course of time both their parents died, and then there were twice eighty crores of treasure in the same house.

It was the custom of the treasurer's son to go thrice a day to wait upon the king. One day a company of knaves who lived in that city thought to themselves, "If this treasurer's son would only get drunk, it would be a fine thing for us. Let us show him how to get drunk." Accordingly they procured strong drink, put roast meat, salt, and sugar in the skirts of their clothing, and taking roots and bulbs, seated themselves in a convenient place, watching the path by which he would approach from the royal palace. When they saw him approaching, they began to drink strong drink, placed particles of salt and sugar in their mouths, and took the roots and bulbs in their teeth and chewed them. And they said, "Live for a hundred years, master treasurer's son! With your help may we be enabled to eat and drink to our heart's content!" Hearing their words, the youth asked the little page who followed him, "What are these men drinking?"—"A certain drink, master."—"Does it taste good?"—"Master, in this world of the living there is no kind of drink to be had comparable to this."—"In that case," said the

---

29. This is a way of saying "multi-millionaire."

youth, "I must have some, too." So he caused the page to bring him first a little, and then a little more, and all this he drank.

Now in no long time those knaves discovered that he had taken up the habit of drinking. Then they flocked around him. As time went on, the crowd that surrounded him increased in numbers. He would spend a hundred or two hundred pieces of money at a time on strong drink. It became a habit with him after a time, wherever he happened to be, to pile up a heap of coins and call out as he drank, "Take this coin and fetch me flowers! Take this coin and fetch me perfumes! This man is clever at dicing, and this man at dancing, and this man at singing, and this man at the playing of musical instruments! Give this man a thousand and this man two thousand!" Thus did he spend his money.

In no long time he squandered all the eighty crores of treasure that formerly belonged to him. Then those knaves said to him, "Master, your wealth is all spent."—"Has my wife no money?"—"Yes, master, she has."—"Well then, fetch that too." And he spent his wife's money in precisely the same way. As time went on, he sold his fields and his parks and his gardens and his carriages. He even disposed of the vessels he used at meals, of his coverlets and his cloaks and couches. All that belonged to him, he sold, and the proceeds he spent in riotous living. In old age he sold his house, the property of his family. And those to whom he sold his house took possession of it and straightaway put him out. Thereupon, taking his wife with him, he found lodging near the house-wall of other people's houses. With a broken potsherd in his hand, he would go about begging alms. Finally he began to eat the leavings of other people's food.

One day he stood at the door of a rest house, receiving leavings of food presented to him by young novices. The Teacher saw him and smiled. Thereupon the Elder Ānanda asked him why he smiled. The Teacher explained the reason for his smile by saying, "Ānanda, just look here at Great-wealth, the treasurer's son! In this very city he has squandered twice eighty crores of treasure. Now, accompanied by his wife, he is begging alms. For if in the prime of life this man had not squandered his wealth, but had applied himself to business, he would have become the principal treasurer in this very city; and if he had retired from the world and become a monk, he would have attained arahantship, and his wife would have been established in the fruit of the third path. If in middle life he had not squandered his wealth, but had applied himself to business, he would have become the second treasurer; and if he had retired from the world and become a monk, he would have attained the fruit of the third path, and his wife would have been established in the fruit of the second path. If in the latter years of his life he had not squandered his wealth, but had applied himself to business, he would have become the third treasurer; and if he had retired from the world and become a monk, he would have attained the fruit of the second path, and his wife would have been established in the fruit of stream-entry. But now he has fallen away from the wealth of a layman and he has likewise fallen away from the estate of an ascetic. He has become like a heron in a dried-up pond." So saying, he pronounced the following stanzas:

155. Having led neither the holy life
 Nor riches won while young,
 They linger on like aged cranes
 Around a fished-out pond.

156. Having led neither the holy life
 Nor riches won while young,
 They lie around like worn-out bows
 Sighing about the past.

Buddhism in Psychotherapy

Two Essays

by

Seymour Boorstein, M.D.
Olaf G. Deatherage, Ph.D.

WHEEL PUBLICATION NO. 290/291

Copyright © Kandy; Buddhist Publication Society, (1982)

Troubled Relationships: Transpersonal and Psychoanalytic Approaches[1]

Seymour Boorstein, M.D.
Kentfield, California

The use of a transpersonal approach in working with couples in a troubled relationship, in addition to facilitating gratifying change within the relationship, may also promote individual changes of a transpersonal nature. Joseph Goldstein (1979), a Vipassanā Buddhist meditation teacher, recently suggested that, whereas in the East a monastic approach is common, in the West the Dharma (i.e., that which is ultimate) may more likely manifest in the working out of the vicissitudes of relationships. The same skills and insights that allow us to soothe the "ruffled feathers" and hurt feelings of a troubled relationship may be the ones that allow us to let go of fetters to spiritual growth.

Psychotherapy of troubled relationships usually involves clarification of communications and learning of constructive communication. In addition, in insight therapy, the fears, angers, and tensions that arise are used to focus on the transference distortions, thus making conscious those forces, usually of an infantile nature, that have been unconscious. Once they become conscious, these forces can usually be dealt with by the more rational and adult aspects of the personality.

An extra, constructive dimension may be added to traditional psychotherapy by incorporating a transpersonal approach. This could involve sharing with one's clients some of the therapist's personal philosophic beliefs via the use of "teaching stories." It might include the suggestion that clients consider beginning a meditative practice if this is not already part of their experience.

---

1. Reprinted by permission from the *Journal of Transpersonal Psychology*, 1979, Volume 11, Number 2. Copyright © Transpersonal Institute, 1979, Box 4437, Stanford, California 94305.

This approach is most readily adopted when a couple is already committed to spiritual goals. In such cases it may be helpful to articulate the idea that, whereas man's basic goal may be the enlightenment state, working on one's relationship may facilitate the elimination of those fetters which prevent us from experiencing this state. Specifically placing the therapeutic work in such a broader context may encourage clients to put maximum effort into the work.

Sharing a transpersonal approach with one's clients may also make the work on relationships a bit less grim. The sense that on some level all of our experience may be a dream or an illusion allows some distance from the situation and enhances the ability to view things from a more balanced perspective. This in no way negates the value of the work which may be seen as an effort to keep the dream from becoming a nightmare. In addition, and perhaps most importantly, developing a stable, loving, caring relationship may ultimately allow the partners to direct their energies towards their spiritual work from a secure rather than an exhausted depressed position. Even with clients who are not particularly aware of or interested in the transpersonal dimension of work on themselves, many of the insights derived from spiritual practice may be incorporated in the work without specifically labeling them as such. For instance, the concept of "attachments" and the pain that often accrues as a result of attachments to people, to things, etc., is understandable in any context. Likewise, the concept of "impermanence," which can be pointed out by focusing attention on any aspect of a person's experience, can diminish the anxiety that people experience about their current unhappy state, thinking that it will last forever.

Before drawing the specific parallels that I see as existing between working on an individual spiritual practice and working on a relationship, I want to delineate a bit more how I think both the traditional and the transpersonal approach may each be particularly appropriate for specific aspects of relationship problems. In actual practice a skilled therapist should be able to move back and forth between both modes.

A major area of relationship difficulty arises as a result of unconscious conflicts that get played out in the arena of transferences and counter transferences in the relationship.

According to Freudian theory, these usually represent unresolved issues stemming from early developmental periods. In couples operating with a relatively high degree of ego functioning, these unconscious conflicts may be dealt with through the use of traditional psychotherapeutic techniques. The insights from uncovering these unconscious motivations may be incorporated into the adult aspects of the couple's personality, thus attenuating the friction between them.

Another major area that often comes into focus in relationship therapy is one in which the conscious and unconscious styles of the partners, stemming probably from identification with early parental figures, are irritating the other partner. A very neat and orderly person whose central values are thrift and hard work may feel threatened and anxious in a relationship with a person with a more relaxed, less intense personality. While the individual styles may not either be pathological, they may nevertheless be abrasive to one another. In such instances a transpersonal approach may be helpful. As each partner becomes more aware of how attached he or she is to the idea that his/her style is "right," it may make it easier to countenance the idea that both are just styles, and neither is "right." The story of the Sufi Master, who is arbitrating a couple's disagreement, is helpful here.

A couple came to the Sufi Master with a disagreement. After listening to the husband's story he says, "You are right." Then following the wife relating her side of the story, he says to her also, "You are right." His aide, a bit bewildered, takes the Sufi Master aside and asks, "How can they both be right?" The Sufi Master turns to him and says, "And you are right, too."

The style of needing to be "right" sometimes reflects character armor, covering fears of a primitive, existential nature. Focusing on these fears which become exposed as the style is threatened may allow the individuals to give up their adversarial stance and consider their own personal motivations. This is not to suggest that putting people in touch with their own existential anxiety makes them feel any better. My sense is, however, that it shifts the emphasis from placing the difficulty in the other person, or in the relationship, to the recognition that one needs ultimately to do one's own inner work.

It goes without saying that neither the approach of insight therapy or transpersonal therapy is appropriate in those situations where self-destructive or abusive behavior is manifest in the relationship. Such behavior usually reflects infantile and/or narcissistic personalities stemming from early life trauma, and attention needs to be given to the ego defects involved. A transpersonal approach may be misinterpreted: "It's her karma, I don't need to be responsible." Nor is insight therapy appropriate: "Do Not Add Insight To Injury." Socialization therapy, Reality therapy, and basic nurturing in whatever ways it can be constructively assimilated would be appropriate.

It is of course crucial in the early stages of therapy that the level of mutual caring be evaluated. If there is not a reasonable amount of caring, in addition to the negativity, then the work to help the couple will probably fail.

In tracing the parallels between spiritual work and relationship work I will use as a reference the five categories of hindrances, derived from the Buddhist tradition (Goldstein, 1976), which are considered to be fetters keeping us from the balanced mind necessary to achieve the enlightened or unity consciousness. Among the many ways to organize the problems of relationships, I chose the "five fetters" approach because of the striking parallels between the hindrances arising in meditation and the impediments to a gratifying relationship. This approach also leads to the conclusion that we may be able to loosen many of our spiritual fetters through working on relationships. *A role of the therapist is therefore to point out how every point of friction or discontent in a relationship actually is highlighting a hindrance, or fetter.* Each partner therefore becomes, rather than an adversary, a trusted, even if challenging, companion. This approach also mitigates in favor of continuing in a relationship, whenever possible, instead of ending it and moving on to another one. In the same way, staying with one meditative practice through its difficult, tedious stages is generally felt to be more fruitful than changing. Where both partners became allies in a mutual agreement to be present as living teachers for each other, consistently and over a long period of time, it becomes more and more difficult to keep up individual systems of self-deception. It is important to stress that "teachings" are not always experienced as loving, but with skillful practice may become more that way.

Although, in actual work with couples, multiple fetters often are present and overlap each other, for purposes of discussion, I will outline them separately. Each of the following categories attempts to correlate a specific hindrance in meditation practice with a specific problem in relationships and also to suggest appropriate psychoanalytic and transpersonal approaches.

Fetter 1: Sense Desire (Lusting After Sense Pleasure)

The fetter of desire as it arises in meditation practice is generally a thought about an attachment to some pleasure available somewhere that would make the meditator more comfortable than his/her current situation. Or, it might manifest in a sense of greed, a desire to have more of a pleasurable experience, either current or remembered. The antithesis of these feelings would be contentment with one's current state, whatever it is. In a relationship, this pattern emerges as the notion, on the part of either or both of the partners that they would be more gratified, and thus more content, with another partner. One or the other partner might become involved with fantasied or actual relationships with other partners, thus removing energy from the ongoing relationship. Or one partner, unable to recognize his/her own unconscious desires, might project these desires onto the partner and then feel hurt or angry over imagined infidelities.

From a psychodynamic point of view, such problems might be approached with insight therapy. The expectation that somewhere there is a partner who would be totally gratifying is often a recreation of an Oedipal expectation. The uncovering of this Oedipal wish often allows individuals to have a more realistic expectation of their real-life partner.

In a transpersonal context, my working assumption would be that each individual is entirely responsible for how he or she experiences their situation. To cite a culturally unfamiliar example, Seikan Hasagawa, in *Essays on Marriage* (1977), indicates that prior to enlightenment we cannot know who would be the "best" partner. He feels that spending time and energy picking a partner is not as important as living the married life skillfully. His view is that it does not matter whom you pick as a partner since you can use the struggles of the relationship for spiritual growth: Although this approach may be inappropriate for our lifestyle and culture, it does seem to have certain advantages insofar as if one's spouse is chosen by others, one may not necessarily or readily perpetuate one's own neurotic propensities in the selection.

The issue of greed usually manifests in relationships in struggles over money, power, and the need to have more things go one's own way rather than accommodating the partner. Traditionally this might be approached by examining the roots, in his or her background of the need to have more, perhaps stemming from some deprivation in an early developmental stage. In a transpersonal context, the emphasis might be on the impossibility of ever satisfying greed, since all things and experiences are by nature impermanent. In addition, perhaps the therapy can uncover and work with some of the existential anxieties (e.g., I won't have enough, I'll die or starve, or I need to be richer, more powerful, etc.) that underlie the need to have more. A helpful illustration is found in the teaching story of how a monkey can be caught:

> A coconut shell is hollowed out, fastened to a tree, and a banana placed inside. The opening is large enough for the monkey to put his opened hand in. On seeing the fruit, desire arises and that monkey reaches inside the coconut shell, grabs the fruit but is unable to remove his clenched hand which is holding the fruit. He sees the hunters coming to kill him, but he wants the fruit, stays trapped and dies. To be free he had only to "let go." We all have so many "bananas" that we clutch at, stay trapped and therefore do not live as fully as we might.

Fetter 2: Anger

When anger arises as a hindrance in meditation it is often difficult to let go of, because it carries such a strong energy charge, thus seducing the mind to stay preoccupied with it. A similar situation prevails in a relationship situation where, once angry feelings have been introduced into the situation, it is difficult for either partner to back off into a position of tolerance and to let go of protecting their own point of view. Thus whatever behavior was originally anger-producing becomes entrenched as the partners become adversaries, each trying to prove that they are "right."

Traditional psychotherapy might be used to expose and explore the fears that lie behind the angers. These fears often reflect unresolved, and/or traumatic infantile or early childhood events. For example an individual angry with a partner over the partner's relaxed attitude towards money may come to see that the anger is masking an underlying fear of lack of enough money, goods or security to survive. Presumably the now more adult ego can practically care for these earlier needs and fears.

In a transpersonal context, the use of "teaching stories" is often a gentle and effective tool. There are stories from the Sufi and the Buddhist traditions, and probably from other traditions as well, that highlight the idea that we really cannot be sure, from our limited world view, of what is "right" and what is "wrong" or what is fortunate, or unfortunate, and that remaining doggedly attached to one point of view prevents our experiencing a wider awareness. One illustration follows:

> The Chinese farmer had a horse and was therefore able to plow many fields and was thus fortunate. One day his horse ran away and he was thus said to be unfortunate since he could not plow his fields. The next day his horse returned, bringing with it a wild horse. Now he was thought to be doubly fortunate: So the next day the farmer's son went to tame the wild horse, was thrown, and broke his leg. Now the farmer is said to be unfortunate again. The next day the King's army came to the farm looking for soldiers to go to war, but were unable to take the son because of his broken leg. So now the farmer was said to be fortunate. And so the story goes on.

In a situation where it is appropriate, a *mettā* or loving-kindness meditation might be suggested. In this meditation one forgives others for their hurtfulness and asks forgiveness for oneself. Along with this, positive wishes for the happiness of others as well as for oneself are made. When introduced into a meditative practice this meditation appears to undercut the fetter of negativity and anger. Partners in an embittered relationship who endeavor to practice this meditation may find that it dissolves feelings of enmity.

Fetter 3: Sloth and Torpor

In classical meditation practice this fetter manifests as lack of energy, and failure to bring enough vigor into the practice to produce any substantial results. A commensurate amount of energy to that needed to realize any spiritual goals is needed to achieve a level of real communion and mutual satisfaction in a relationship. In the West, the media message via TV and movies often gives the impression that quick, often impossibly romantic solutions to relationship problems are possible. This may predispose us as a culture to disillusionment and disappointment when we are confronted with the inevitable shortcomings of a real-life relationship. In addition, the emphasis in the more "new age" elements of the culture seems to be more on "moving on" when a relationship becomes uncomfortable, rather than on working it out.

During the honeymoon phase of a spiritual practice or of a new relationship, there is often a sense of unlimited expectation. Suzuki Roshi (1970) calls this "Beginner's Mind," and cites this as just the element that may be the vital contribution to real spiritual gains. I've counseled Zazen practitioners to try to cultivate this "Beginner's Mind" openness and lack of limiting opinion as a part of their ongoing practice.

Partners in a relationship may work in a similar way to cultivate an ongoing freshness or vitality in their relationship. In situations where a lack of energy input has led to a dullness in the relationship, or inability due to past conditioning to respond to changes in one's partner and a sense of taking each other for granted, the recognition of this fetter can lead to efforts to eliminate it. Specifically, such efforts might include planning on the part of both partners to continually re-clarify communications, to do things that are gratifying for each other, and to remain pleasing and attractive to the other person. Simply developing the awareness that relationships (like meditation practices) do not remain exciting and dynamic on their own but require constant input of renewed energy, may reassure partners that their relationship has not soured because they are unsuitable to each other, but perhaps only because it has been left uncultivated.

One can look at a relationship as a garden that needs constant fertilizing, watering and weeding. If this is not done, there are no flowers or fruits. Even the weeds are reburied in the ground so that their energy can nourish the flowers. Weeding, or working on one's fetters, provides energy which can ultimately be used to nourish the positive aspects of the relationship. Perhaps a prickly cactus garden does not need much tending or weeding, but fruit and flower gardens do.

Fetter 4: Restlessness

In meditation practice this hindrance often manifests as difficulty in staying present, mentally and/or physically, in the meditation situation, and in a sense of terrible boredom with one's current experience. In a relationship this hindrance appears as the "Seven Year Itch." This syndrome, generally associated with couples who have been in a relationship for a number of years, is not associated with a relationship that is painful or unhappy, but rather with a relationship that is reasonably gratifying but nevertheless humdrum. It is not so much that "Familiarity breeds contempt" as "Familiarity breeds boredom." The classical reaction to the syndrome is the search for new partners to relieve the restlessness and satisfy the boredom:

Traditional therapy might focus on unreasonable expectations of enduring gratification in a relationship or on other unconscious motivations such as the need to prove, via a new partner, that one continues to be attractive and alluring. A more transpersonal approach might cultivate the awareness that boredom is not a reflection of an uninteresting situation but rather of an unmindful observer. Fritz Perls (1973) is often quoted as saying that boredom always reflects not paying enough attention. To an observer cultivating mindful awareness, everyday situations can be fascinating. Annie Dillard, the naturalist author of *Pilgrim at Tinker Creek* (1972), describes her awareness of the teeming life that is present in the very small area of seemingly lifeless earth on which she is sitting. Partners in a relationship may perhaps cultivate that awareness which makes even the mundane events of family life interesting. Specifically in terms of the sexual boredom that is implicit in the "Seven Year Itch," it is possible, for couples who are motivated to do so, to recognize that every sexual encounter is a new experience—similar to, undoubtedly, but in some way different from the previous five hundred sexual experiences. A few clinical examples illustrate the above points:

Mr. A, a corporate executive, and Mrs. A. a housewife, a couple in their 40s who have been married for 18 years, came for help because of continuing power struggles centering around decisions regarding money, running the household and sexual contacts.

Despite their great angers, both still cared for the other. In addition, both had been involved previously in spiritual and meditation practices. Part of our work consisted of tracing out the source and effects of a rather hypercritical and punitive early upbringing. These manifested themselves in the (unconscious) transferences to each other and towards me. They were able to see how they were more eager to be right and the winner, rather than be happy—much as a 2-year-old may stay constipated, have a bellyache, but feel pleased that mother could not force him to have a BM.

Mr. B, a 40-year old policeman, and Mrs. B, a 35-year-old childcare worker, came for help as a last ditch measure prior to divorce. Mrs. B felt very dominated and misunderstood by her husband. She collected and saved all of her grievances to then be played out by pouting, always being late and other passive aggressive maneuvers. Some of our work consisted of helping her see how she "selected" unconsciously a husband to duplicate her relationship with her mother whom she also feared and acted out towards passive aggressively. Neither were spiritually oriented in the least, and Mr. B didn't particularly feel any need to change. He just wanted his wife to be more cooperative and pleasant.

By exposing the unconscious compulsion to repeat her relationship with her mother, Mrs. B was able to see her desire for the infantile gratifications which it was now too late to get, and especially her attachment to her anger which she enjoyed greatly and kept alive by collecting grievances, all the while being frightened. In addition, the teaching story of the two monks and the beautiful girl was very helpful to Mrs. B in seeing how she collected grievances, continually mulled them over and enjoyed being upset by them.

> There were two monks waiting on a street corner where there was a good deal of flooding. A beautiful girl was standing there trying to get across but was unable to. One of the

monks seeing the situation quickly picked up the girl, carried her across the water and placed her down on a dry spot. The other monk was the meanwhile thinking—how could he do that—we've taken priestly vows not to look at beautiful women let alone hold them close to our bodies"—and on and on. A few miles down the road the second monk could no longer contain himself and began to berate the first monk who had assisted the girl. After the berating had stopped the first monk turned to the second and said, "I put the girl down three miles back—how come you are still carrying her?" This story is helpful to couples who are grievance collectors.

Thus working on the first two fetters, desire and anger, greatly alleviated the marital tensions, and she was now able to express her adult needs directly, to which the husband more often than not responded—ultimately resulting in greater affection between them.

To further help her when she felt flooded, I taught her mindfulness meditation, without calling it that, so that when she experienced anger or fear she learned how to watch the experience without getting caught up as readily as before by providing time to avoid reacting automatically as she used to do.

Fetter 5: Doubt

The fifth fetter is that of doubt, the recurrent concern that one's chosen meditative path is not a viable one, that the philosophy behind it is false, that one's teachers are inadequate and/or that one will never be able to make any progress anyway. Parallel doubts arise in a relationship. Questions of whether or not one has chosen an appropriate partner, or whether or not it is too late to change to a new partner, arise not only at times of conflict in the situation, but also, as they do in the meditative situation, at times of comparative calm. Traditional therapy might attempt to explore hidden stresses, such as significant birthdays, work promotions or retirements which testify to advancing age, as being reasons to suddenly evaluate whether it is not too late to change to a new partner in order to get more out of this life. A transpersonal approach might suggest that doubt is just one of the many mind states that arise and pass away naturally, on their own timetable, often unrelated to outward circumstances. In meditation practice it is generally accepted that one of the enduring effects of one's first, albeit brief, experience of enlightenment consciousness is that the fetter of doubt disappears forever.

In my own experience I have come to believe that the recurrence of doubt about one's relationship disappears finally at that point in a relationship where enough years of mutual care and mutual struggle, mutual interests and mutual gratifications finally come together in such a way as to suddenly, as in a flash of insight, make it clear to both partners that this is not only the "right" relationship for them to be in, but that the relationship will endure. As in meditation practice, where there is no way of predicting how long it will take for such doubt-dispelling occurrences to happen, there is no way to predict how long it takes for such awareness to occur in a relationship. Perhaps the first ten years of a relationship is the trial cruise and after that the ship might be expected to maintain fairly smooth sailing conditions The challenge is to stay with the difficulties regardless of the number of years, whenever possible, because what is at stake is one of the most fundamental and potentially gratifying situations—an intimate relationship.

References

Dillard, A. *Pilgrim at Tinker Creek.* New York: Bantam, 1975.
Goldstein, J. *The experience of Insight.* Santa Cruz, Ca.: Unity Press, 1976.
Goldstein, Joseph. Personal Communication, 1979.
Hasagawa, S. *Essays on Marriage:* Arlington, Va.: Great Ocean Publ., 1977.
Perls, F. *The Gestalt Approach.* New York: Science and Behavior Books, 1973.
Suzuki, Shunryu. *Zen Mind, Beginner's Mind.* New York: Walker/ Weatherhill, 1970.

Mindfulness Meditation as Psychotherapy

Olaf G. Deatherage, Ph.D.
Creston, British Colombia

Mindfulness meditation, like any other approach, is most powerful when employed as part of an overall program of psychotherapy designed specifically for the individual client. It can be a primary, secondary, or supplementary part of any therapy program, depending upon what is appropriate for the client.

This approach to psychotherapy derives directly from Buddhist teachings. It is therefore relevant to mention the philosophical foundation of the techniques. Buddhist thought and practice have always been directed toward providing the individual with a way to gain insight into life experiences, to perceive more clearly the nature of internal and external realities and the relationships between the two. People continuously and rapidly cycle through a multiplicity of moods and emotional states. This cycling process, *saṃsāra*, is inescapable as long as its motive powers persist, namely greed, hatred, and delusion. But this process can be seen, transformed, and finally stopped, thus providing people with freedom unavailable to others who are unknowingly entrapped in states of psychological distress.

Buddhism uses both philosophy and direct "therapeutic" intervention to accomplish its goal of enlightenment. Therefore the Buddhist approach establishes logical tenets and then provides a way of personally verifying them. For example, the beginning teachings in Buddhism—the Four Noble Truths—observe that everything is impermanent, including one's own life, and that the impermanence of the material world is a primary and direct cause of unhappiness (things and people deteriorate and pass away). Any rational mind can accept the existence of suffering and unhappiness, can perceive the impermanence of the world, and can to some degree accept the relationship between them. There are ways out of this dilemma, however. Buddhism offers a pathway of coming to know the mental processes and of working directly with these processes to gain insight into—and to some degree freedom from—entrapment in the saṃsāric cycling process.

The mindfulness meditation described here, when practiced diligently and progressively, can potentially lead the practitioner to experience directly the ultimate realities described in Buddhist scriptures. Soma (1949), Mahāsi (1975), and Nyanaponika (1972, 1973) describe the Theravada Buddhist mindfulness as *satipaṭṭhāna*: *sati* ("awareness") + *paṭṭhāna* ("keeping present"). These forms of meditation are the basis of the mindfulness meditation that is discussed here. It is designed to enhance mental health. First it allows one to see one's own mental processes; second, it allows one to exert increasing degrees of control over mental processes; and finally, it allows one to gain freedom from unknown and uncontrolled mental processes. This seemingly impossible task is accomplished through what Nyanaponika calls "bare attention" (1972): the accurate, continuous registering at the conscious level of all events occurring in the six sensory modes—seeing, hearing, touching, tasting, smelling, and thinking—without qualitative judgments, evaluation, mental comment, or behavioral act.

Techniques of Bare Attention

How is such an investigation of the mental processes carried out? First, a set of meditative exercises teaches and refines the techniques of bare attention. If one sits quietly with the body comfortable and relaxed, one can practice bare attention through consciously observing the breathing process as one breathes in, pauses, breathes out, pauses longer, and then breathes in again. This concentration on a physical process quickly produces interesting results. Soon, mental events begin to occur and interrupt breath observation. Events external to the body impinge on consciousness—a dog barks, a door closes, the day grows hot, a fly lands on one's face. Awareness of the breathing process is interrupted momentarily as awareness shifts to the sound or other sensation. Awareness arises that breath observation has been interrupted by something particular; breath observation is resumed. Perhaps a memory rises to consciousness, again disrupting the observation process and shifting awareness to the memory for a time; then realizing that a memory interruption has occurred, one resumes breath observation. Awareness of the breathing process may soon be lost again as a fantasy arises and is played out—what to do during vacation, how to ask the boss for a raise; again awareness eventually arises that breath observation has been interrupted, and it is resumed.

After only a few minutes of breath observation, one realizes that a continuous chain of mental events is taking place, that awareness is flipping from what one is intentionally attending to, the act of breathing; to innumerable other things—bodily sensations, external factors, memories, fantasies. This constant losing and regaining of conscious awareness of what one is doing takes place thousands of times a day. The initial observation of breathing, or any other ongoing process on which attention can be focused, clearly demonstrates the frequency with which this shifting takes place.

Through such observation and through neutral, nonjudgmental naming of each interrupting factor (remembering, worrying, hearing, imagining), one begins to see and appreciate that mental events jump from one event to the next with a staccato rapidity that is seemingly random and chaotic, even frightening. Naming the interrupting factors begins to provide insight into one's unique mental processes and identifies the area with which one must work. One person is interrupted again and again by memories from the past; another is plagued by fantasies of performing heroic acts; a third is interrupted by bodily discomfort, sleepiness, or boredom. Becoming aware of one's primary interrupting factors can be diagnostically and therapeutically significant because one can sometimes clearly see unhealthy, habitual mental processes.

Using Mindfulness Training with Neurotic Patients

While mindfulness training is not indicated for psychotic, senile, or brain-damaged clients, it can be useful with the large group of so-called neurotic, anxious, or depressed clients. Buddhist psychology, in fact, views almost everyone as neurotic to some degree. The person seeking psychotherapeutic help is only slightly more neurotic than the one who does not seek help. Neurosis may be characterized by ongoing internal dialogues: "I want to find a new job"; "No, you had better not—you might fail"; "You are probably right, but I hate this one so much". These I's who populate our minds reflect our neuroses, sources of discomfort, hang-ups, and disunity.

Mindfulness training, then, can be used to see and name mental processes in action. What use is this? If we believe that the most powerful way to live is in the present, dealing with each moment and situation effectively, then it follows that excessive mental energy spent remembering the good old days or the bad old days is not available to use in the present, where everything is happening. Mental energy expended in fantasies of other circumstances and other places also takes energy from dealing effectively with the present. These are all varieties of neuroses for which mindfulness training can sometimes be effective. Here is a simple clinical illustration of how mindfulness techniques can be used with a client.

Case 1

A 23-year-old, newly divorced female patient complained that her thoughts about her former husband's bizarre sexual demands were triggering bouts of depression and severe anxiety attacks. She was trained to observe these retrospective thoughts carefully, using *satipaṭṭhāna* techniques, and to label them as "remembering, remembering." Within a few days, she reported that while there was no significant decrease in the frequency of the thoughts, the way they affected her had changed. The labeling process helped her to break the causative relationship between these thoughts and the depression and anxiety attacks, thus allowing the gradual disappearance of those symptoms. What remained at that point were regret about the past and considerable guilt, which were worked on in a traditional group psychotherapy setting in the following weeks.

The Watcher Self

When straightforward breath observation techniques are used with clinical patients, many potentially positive benefits can be gained, one of which involves what we shall call the "watcher self." This is the aspect of one's mental "self" which is discovered through, and carries out, the task of mindfulness. It is the part capable of consciously watching and naming interruptions or bothersome mental habits and events. While it is only one aspect of the total personality, the "watcher" can be useful and important for certain clients because it always behaves with calm strength. The watcher can see the remembering of some painful event and label it objectively without becoming involved in its melodrama. The watcher can therefore put psychological distance between the "me" who experienced the painful event and the "me" who is presently remembering it. The watcher is neutral and can be identified with intentionally. The individual who feels weak, inadequate, indecisive, and defeated can, by intentionally identifying for a time with this watcher, develop new strengths, motivations, and abilities to participate more fully in and benefit from an overall psychotherapy program. Here is a case in point.

Case 2

A 27-year-old divorced woman had been hospitalized for two and a half months for a condition variously diagnosed as manic-depressive psychosis, and schizophrenia. She had responded to psychotropic medication to the extent that she was able to begin group psychotherapy free of psychotic symptoms. However, she still suffered from recurring episodes of depression, anxiety, loss of interest in life, and loss of self-esteem. Several weeks of intensive group psychotherapy failed to produce symptom relief, and she was re-admitted to the hospital suffering from severe depression and thoughts of self-destruction. Her primary concerns, in addition to feelings of depression, were loss of concentration and racing thoughts.

Mindfulness technique was presented to the patient as a "concentration exercise." She was asked to sit quietly, look at the second hand of an electric clock, and try to attend fully to its movement. She was instructed to notice carefully when she lost her concentration on the moving second hand, to identify what constituted the interruption, and to name it. She quickly found her concentration constantly broken by thoughts. On inspection, the nature of the thoughts racing through her mind was always the same—concern with her past, her misfortunes in the relationship with her ex-husband, and her regrets about that situation.

She was instructed simply to label such thoughts, "remembering, remembering." The labeling process seemed to allow her to withdraw some of her involvement in those depressing thoughts about the past and to let her realize that more than just these thoughts was present in her mind; there was also a "she" who could watch and name thoughts. She learned to identify herself as the objective watcher of her disturbing thoughts instead of the depressed thinker, and she began to feel some relief from her psychiatric complaints.

On reflection, the patient reported that, as a result of this psychotherapeutic endeavor, she had come to see more clearly the nature of her former illness. She subjectively perceived that she had become totally immersed in thoughts and regrets about the past, thus becoming less involved in what was happening around her in the present. She consequently lost any involvement in her future as well. Because her thoughts of the past caused her discomfort and depression, even anxiety, she used large amounts of energy to defend herself against them and make them go away. She felt that during her illness all of her energies had been consumed in thinking about the past and simultaneously fighting to stop such thoughts. This left her no energy to run her life. The mindfulness technique of labeling was effective here because it allowed the patient to stop expending energy in fighting the remembering.

After only a few days of using the exercise, the patient reported a significant increase in her concentration span. This increased concentration, accompanied by decreases in frequency and intensity of disturbing thoughts, allowed her to begin reading again, to carry on meaningful personal interchanges without the usual loss of what was happening, and to devote more time and energy to her personal appearance, which had been untidy during her illness.

With the additional benefits coming from the slightly disguised *satipaṭṭhāna* techniques, she could then investigate the nature of the "watcher self" which she had come to identify. This allowed her to come in contact with the calm and peaceful aspects of her own mind—her "center" was how she identified it at the time—and to re-establish some enjoyment and pleasure in her life. These dimensions had been missing for many months, and this, too, helped with her interpersonal relationships. Within a few weeks of these observations, she was able to decide to terminate therapy, after which she moved to another city, where she intended to begin a new life.

All of the "selves", "I's", and "me's", including the neutral "watcher," are of course the products of continuous brain processes. All of these selves are collectively termed the "ego" in Buddhist psychology (not to be confused with Freud's use of "ego"). When we employ mindfulness meditation with clinical patients, it is not our purpose to establish the watcher as anything permanent or "real." The watcher is used only as a tool for grounding some of the patient's mental energies in the present, providing a temporary, psychologically stable center for them to operate from and providing a perspective from which their own psychological functioning can be objectively observed.

Many clinical patients, especially those we would label depressive, anxious, or neurotic, have problems either contacting or controlling emotions. Continued work with mindfulness techniques often yields results in these areas, because emotions and emotional states can be made the object of contemplation. Emotions, too, can be watched and labeled (anger, joy, fear), and when seen objectively, they can be allowed to return to their proper place within a healthier psychological system.

Case 3

During a group therapy session, a 22-year-old married woman who suffered from what had been diagnosed as an endogenous depression expressed despair at her inability to "feel anything anymore," relating a total lack of emotion. The only feeling she could identify was one of gloom and depression. She was asked to begin to get in touch with her feelings, becoming more aware of, and carefully and accurately labeling any emotion she experienced as she sat quietly watching her breathing or even during her normal daily activities.

Over the next few weeks she found herself increasingly naming anger as her predominant emotion, and it became possible to identify the source of that anger in her marital relationship. She then gradually became aware that she had been misinterpreting her emotions over many months, mistakenly believing that she had been experiencing depression whereas strong elements of anger, hostility, self-abasement, and disappointment had also been present. This recognition of the feelings she had been inaccurately labeling depression freed her to identify other feelings as well. Soon she was back in touch with the full spectrum of human emotions. Her depression disappeared and was replaced by a greatly improved self-image and understanding of her feelings.

In a similar way, thoughts, intentions, and even the task in which one is involved can be made the objects of contemplation within the psychotherapeutic setting, yielding insights into psychological processes that can be useful in helping the patient to grow in positive directions.

Case 4

A devout Mormon woman of 29, who was married to a teacher, spent her days at home with her two children: At the beginning of their marriage, both she and her husband had been university students, but soon she quit to take a job. After her husband received his degree, they moved to a city where he had been offered a job, and she did not finish her studies. The husband went out to work each day, and she became a housewife. After only a few years of marriage, a definitely unhealthy pattern emerged in their relationship, the husband becoming more involved in his job and spending more and more time there. In fact, job and church activities left him little time or energy for his wife and family.

She began to suffer the classic symptoms of "housewife's syndrome." She became depressed, edgy, anxious, and had no motivation or energy to care for the children or to do housework. She ceased going out because she felt even more anxiety outside her home. She could not even sit completely through a church service because her anxiety level would increase until she had to flee, usually using her youngest child as an excuse. At home, she could make no decisions of her own, did not want to be left alone with the children, and berated her husband when he went out for any reason. During the day she just sat, not even watching television or listening to the radio, unable even to bring herself to do simple tasks like dishwashing. At the urging of her husband and mother, she finally came under the care of a psychiatrist who placed her in a psychiatric unit. As was that psychiatrist's custom, the patient was referred to group therapy immediately upon admission. She also received psychotropic medication and individual daily sessions with ward staff and her physician. In the group she proved to be remarkably intelligent, verbal, and supportive of others, but initially totally lacking in insight into her own life. She was consistently whiny and often weepy when interacting with ward staff and other patients. After a few group sessions in which she was able to describe her problems as she saw them, and after a session with her and her husband alone in which the family dynamics were well delineated, the therapist decided to use some mindfulness techniques as a supplement to her therapy program. This proved initially difficult. She rebelled against any kind of introspection because it tended to raise her anxiety level. The therapist finally had her imagine she was back home, prior to hospitalization, just sitting during the day as she often had done. Then she was asked to look at the thoughts which had been taking place there and to attempt to relate them to the therapist. Although she accomplished the task with some difficulty, it became quite evident over time that her predominant mental process was imagining. She used all kinds of fantasies to take her away from her anxieties and depression and poured great amounts of energy into that process.

Though we had not established the watcher through the usual set of mindfulness procedures, we had discovered the patient's main interrupting factor. It was then pointed out to her that she was using most of her energies in fantasizing, and she could easily see this. She was then told she would have to work on this if her problems were to be alleviated. Though she expected some mysterious psychological procedure to accomplish such a thing, she was, in fact, instructed to bake a cake mindfully in the treatment center kitchen, trying to attend fully to every detail, to notice when she began to fantasize and to return to full concentration on the task. She did this and found that she could use some of her energies in a present-oriented task, observing when she was interrupted by the persistent fantasies.

A substitute for breath observation, the cake baking routine was used as an example of how she could attempt to attend fully to the present moment, no matter what was happening. She began to work hard at this and slowly improved. She had a mechanism for noticing when fantasies began, and she found that they were decreasing in length and frequency. She could intentionally return to the present, and she learned that, with this intention, she could initiate behaviors, such as cooking, sewing, reading, and piano playing, which she had neglected for some time. She played the piano very well at the treatment center and found music an excellent way to stay grounded in the present.

In group therapy, she worked on relationships between herself and her husband. This was supplemented by family therapy sessions in which he participated fully.

She also worked on her extremely dependent relationship with her mother who constantly told her what to do; she gained independence and confidence, slowly losing her anxieties. She continued group and family therapy for several months after which she was released from hospital. During that time she began to attend church without anxiety, to care for the house and children, and to get out and involve herself in activities that interested her and helped her grow. Although the mindfulness techniques were not the only psychotherapeutic tools employed, and perhaps were not even the primary ones that aided her, they proved to be the key approach in getting her moving and growing in a positive way again.

Suiting Technique to Client

A psychotherapist-as-guru approach is not being advocated here. Neither is sending the client to meditate advocated as the best therapy. The word *meditation* is seldom mentioned to patients. What is being advocated is the adaptation of certain useful techniques of mindfulness meditation to the treatment program for selected clients. Mindfulness training does not work for everyone. To look directly within requires a great effort, and psychotherapists realize that many clients, particularly those just beginning therapy, are not capable of this kind of intense work. As I have pointed out before, mindfulness training is most appropriate for clients with an intact rational component and sufficient motivation to make the effort required. Only with these two factors present will the techniques be successful.

In short-term psychotherapy, breath-observation techniques, or some modification of them, are usually most appropriate. Discussion between client and therapist about insights gained is the primary indicator of the techniques' effectiveness for a given client. In long-term applications of mindfulness techniques, basic breath observation and interruption naming are first accomplished. Then the client can observe mental processes during everyday activities without needing breath observation as the focal point. Emotions, thoughts, and thought subject matter can be observed in any life situation once the watcher is trained. Awareness is then focused directly on what is happening in the present and on the mental processes of perceiving and reacting to external and internal stimuli which are gaining access to consciousness. Insights into the perceptive process—how external events are translated into internal reality—seem to occur if the "meditation" is directed toward seeing the external situation clearly and objectively from the perspective of the watcher self, which does not react emotionally, verbally, or behaviorally but simply sees. The watcher can suddenly see old and persistent patterns of reacting to certain standard problem situations. This frees the client to respond volitionally in new and different ways. The automatic response of fear or anger to a particular set of stimuli—an authority figure perhaps or a frustrating situation—will suddenly be seen occurring, due to concentration on the incoming stimuli of the present moment. These can be valuable, insightful occurrences for the individual who goes to the trouble of practicing and refining the mindfulness techniques. A simple, non-clinical example illustrates this.

If I am driving during rush hour, a dangerous near collision with another car can be a good situation to observe mindfully. The near collision may have been due to the failure of a traffic light, rather than either driver. Yet the other driver directs abuse at me. The other driver's statement is an event external to "me." If I am being mindful, "I" will note that "I" perceive the event in a particular way, namely that the other driver is being unfair and unjust. This perception of the event leads to an immediate intention to reply, to assert "my" point of view. There is great freedom available to me when I see that intention clearly, because many possibilities exist for action or inaction. If I do not see the intention and resultant emotions, like anger and frustration early, I can only react to the situation instead of experiencing its freedom. Seeing the intentional process arising allows a choice of responses: verbal action ("The same to you, fellow!"), physical action (crashing my car into his to teach him a lesson), early cancellation of either the verbal or physical action, thinking vindictive thoughts about the other driver; it even allows for the continuation of mindfulness—operating in the present, continuing to drive mindfully, and letting the negative thoughts and emotions produced by the event dissipate, instead of preserving them in my consciousness and going over and over them in memory. It does not matter whether I choose thoughts, words, actions, or cancellations as long as these things are done at a level of awareness where I can suddenly come to understand and say, "Oh yes, now I see why I always do that." These are everyday insights that come with increased mindfulness.

Mindfulness training, then, can create a space between life's events and the ego's reaction to those events. The ego itself begins to be seen and known. Mental processes basic to the ego are sometimes seen in operation. Slowly one becomes capable of dealing more effectively and intelligently with each life event as it occurs. At this stage of development, the watcher's role begins to shift and diminish. Occasional, total conscious immersion in present events begins to occur without the watcher consciously watching. In this state of total involvement, no mental energy is held back for consciously operating the watcher, and none is used to escape in fantasies or memories; one is functioning at heightened effectiveness. Emotions associated with total involvement are purer. They are uncontaminated by reactions to involuntary memories and fantasies typically projected onto ongoing situations. A state of mental health without the neurotic internal mental dialogue's constant comments and digressions has been temporarily achieved. Total concentration is directed to the task at hand, whether it be washing the dishes; solving a family disagreement, or driving to work. For a time all the "I's" and "me's" are quieted, and the whole person, with all capabilities intact, is allowed to function.

The goal of mindfulness training, then, is to work directly with the ongoing train of experiences, to practice directing "bare attention" to those experiences, to develop patience with and compassion for oneself as well as others, and to deal effectively with neurotic disturbances of mind. This, of course, is asking a great deal. Many clients find it difficult, painful, and even overwhelming to look at their own troublesome and persistent mental processes. A greatly agitated, depressed, or otherwise disturbed individual is not an immediate candidate for such direct therapy, although he or she may later derive great benefit from this approach.

The following case study demonstrates the use of mindfulness techniques with a woman in long-term therapy.

Case 5

A 27-year-old woman, married with two young children, was referred by her psychiatrist for group therapy because of increasing depression and inability to cope with family and life responsibilities. She was an intelligent, beautiful woman who was cool and aloof in interpersonal relationships. She attended group therapy for a few sessions and identified some problems with her husband, who traveled extensively and was away from home on business four or five nights each week. She suspected he was being unfaithful, and he admitted he had had an affair a few weeks earlier with a woman in another city.

After about her third week of group therapy, I received a frantic call from her husband one morning saying she had attempted suicide by overdosing with sleeping pills. She was comatose and in the intensive care unit of the hospital at that time. While we waited for her to regain consciousness, the husband related his understanding of the family problems and stated that the attempted suicide had resulted from his wife's reduced sense of self-worth because of his confessing to the affair. He felt guilty about it, vowed to quit the job, and began to search for another that day.

As she awoke, the woman was upset to learn she had failed in her suicide attempt, and repeatedly said she wanted to die. However, on later learning her behavior had caused serious reconsiderations on her husband's part, she soon agreed to a no-suicide contract and was transferred to the psychiatric ward by her physician. Her temporary but apparently sincere agreement to remain alive left her with little choice but attempt resolution of the conflicts which had brought her to this point.

Although she was still unable to express herself openly in group therapy and soon even refused to attend the group, she proved a willing and capable client in an individual setting. So all subsequent work with her was on a one-to-one basis. She received the usual psychotropic medication for approximately two weeks while in the hospital. She finally admitted in a private session that she had been experiencing strong feelings of friendship, warmth, and perhaps even sexual attraction for an older woman whom she had met a few months earlier. The woman was outgoing, artistic, and in the client's view, everything she was not. She felt guilty and even abnormal about these unwanted feelings. We were able to make some progress in helping her to accept, understand, and work with those feelings during the first days of her hospitalization.

Before leaving the hospital, she began the basic mindfulness practices of thought and feeling observation. She found no difficulty in thought observation because she was a persistent intellectualizer. However, she claimed to be able to identify no feelings at all. Over some weeks after leaving the hospital, she began to identify two feelings. These were not identified during breath observation but only during situations which arose during the day. She was able to identify strong anger at her husband and children at times and fear in certain interpersonal situations, particularly in meeting male strangers in new social settings. She worked hard on the social fear and soon lost much of her former aloofness by consciously trying to be open, attentive, and receptive in social encounters. At that point, with her depression alleviated and some of her problems partly solved, she chose to terminate therapy. She had not yet really looked at her barely repressed homosexual desires toward her friend.

Approximately one year later, she came to my office saying she felt minor recurrences of her old depression and was afraid.

In talking with her, I learned that with her husband home each night, her marriage had slightly improved but was still less than perfect. The friendship with the older woman had developed into a sexual relationship, and she was again feeling guilty about it.

She specifically requested that we continue the mindfulness training she had begun months before. This time we worked, not on breath observation, but on increasing awareness during ordinary life events, especially in stressful situations. She progressed rapidly, finding that her social fears produced a characteristic response of coldness and near withdrawal, which made her seem conceited to others. She was able to see this mechanism coming into play, and thus to stop withdrawing. She began to derive some of the fulfillment from social situations previously denied her, and to accept more fully the bisexual nature of her sexual relationships. Although this channeled some of her energies away from her marriage, she seemed to have more satisfaction from both relationships.

This woman has come to feel very positive about herself; her occasional minor bouts of depression ended, and she has remained apparently symptom-free for a year. Since her hospitalization, she has coped well at home, has grown greatly in personal satisfaction, and has completed two years at the university, something she had previously wanted to do but never felt capable of doing. No further suicide attempts or serious depressions have occurred to date.

This case study is fairly typical of long-term employment of mindfulness training. It takes months, even years, for most of us to grow out of psychological difficulty. It takes persistent application of the techniques to ensure growth, and each person has to grow at his or her own pace. If there is time available, if the therapist can provide the appropriate guidance, and if the client has the motivation and perseverance to work through problems, only then can the mindfulness approach be considered appropriate for a client.

Implications for the Therapist

Mindfulness meditation techniques, when used in psychotherapy, have several things to offer the psychotherapist. First of all, the approach is very client-centered; it allows the client the freedom and dignity to work with himself under the therapist's guidance. This, of course, is efficient because it does not confine therapy to the hours when therapist and client meet. Also, it does not condition, direct, or shape the client's behavior into some preordained pattern decided by the therapist. Instead, the course of therapy is more one of the client's seeing, knowing, and accepting his mental processes and then allowing them to re-form and grow in new ways that are healthy for him. However, it is not a cure-all as is shown in this case.

Case 6

A slightly disguised set of *satipaṭṭhāna* techniques was employed with a 23-year-old male patient who had been hospitalized for extreme periodic aggressiveness, fighting, and alcohol abuse, which had occasionally led to brief periods of amnesial or fugue-like states. This young man, who was married and had young children, had been extremely irritable and explosive at home, often losing his temper over minor events and striking out physically or storming out of the house for up to three days. A typical though infrequent pattern was for him to go to a bar with friends for a few drinks during the evening and become intoxicated. In this condition he would often steal a car, get in a fight, or even threaten homicide, but he failed to have any memory of these acts the next day. He was hospitalized twice after such unlawful behavior.

The second time he was admitted to the psychiatric unit, he proved warm and cooperative but experienced high anxiety levels when the staff wanted to discuss why he was in the hospital. He chose to characterize himself as an alcoholic. After a few days of psychotropic medication, his psychiatrist referred him for group therapy. For the next few weeks, he received a therapeutic program consisting of brief daily visits by the psychiatrist, psychotropic medication, twice-weekly group therapy, a weekly session of conjoint family therapy with the group therapist, and whatever sessions the patient chose to initiate with the psychiatric nursing staff. This program was continued throughout his four weeks in the hospital and four more of outpatient care.

During the initial group and family therapy sessions, numerous identifiable marital problems became evident; these were the focus of the family therapy. Group and individual therapy revealed personal problems of expressing anger, self-image, hostility toward women, and extreme competitiveness with other men.

Since it did not appear that this man would be receptive to the usual mindfulness approach, a modified version was tried. His tendency to deny anger and then express it explosively seemed to be a good place to begin. It was mentioned casually during a group therapy session, when the topic arose naturally, that one could perhaps come to know, quite accurately, the causes of one's behavior. The young man took issue with this, saying he did many things he could not hope to understand. It was suggested that he attempt to look at and name the emotions he experienced during the next few days. He tried that suggestion and reported that what he felt most of the time was fear (of people or sometimes of nothing he could identify) and psychological pain. He was instructed to keep watching and naming emotions. Over some weeks, he began to see anger arising in certain interpersonal situations. He was also able to experience his feelings of irritability and to see what events produced them. Most important, he began to be aware that he did not express anger and often was not even cognizant of it until it had overwhelmed him. He was taught to verbalize his anger, to vent it as he experienced it, and to view anger as something all people normally feel. This seemed to free him for progress in psychotherapy. He stopped seeing his problem as alcoholism and spoke of alcohol intoxication as another way of trying to hide from his anger. Soon he stopped mentioning alcohol at all.

Other mindfulness techniques were then used with this man, particularly thought contemplation, which made him aware of his ineffective and inaccurate self-image. This helped him to start correcting misunderstandings about male-female relationships. At the end of eight weeks of this treatment, he took a job. Ten months later, he was still functioning effectively at home and at work, with no recurrences of drinking, fighting, or fugue-states. The mindfulness techniques used here constituted one part of an overall therapy program which proved to be effective.

A few months after this case history was published, the man again behaved erratically. Even at the behest of his family and friends, he refused to seek help and continued to encounter more problems, primarily with his family and his job. He finally fired a rifle through the window of a house, critically injuring a woman he did not know while apparently trying to injure his wife. At this writing, he is confined awaiting trial.

This case is an isolated but a striking example of a person who did not continue to grow after terminating therapy, but instead slowly lost the benefits he had gained. The psychotherapeutic gains achieved through the use of this technique, like most other forms of therapy, can erode over time if the client ceases to practice mindfulness and stops growing. It is usually a mistake to expect predictable, linear progression through therapy for a patient using mindfulness techniques, as the following case demonstrates.

Case 7

A 21-year-old female sought help for her increasingly frequent anxiety attacks. Although the attacks could come upon her at any time, she was particularly troubled by crowded places such as classrooms. Her case was complicated by her having been previously treated unsuccessfully by two other psychotherapists. One had apparently attempted desensitization procedures, treating her case as a phobic reaction to crowded places; the other had served only as a counselor discussing her problems with her. Both had failed to alleviate the symptom, and she had terminated therapy after a few months in each case.

After some preliminary sessions, we decided to try mindfulness techniques. She was shown the basic breath observation technique of noting interruptions and naming them. After this, most sessions consisted of discussing her experiences with the mindfulness practices. After she had become fairly adept at noting and naming interruptions to breath observation, and after the watcher had been investigated, she began to work on observing emotions. She reported that, as she sat quietly observing interruptions and emotions, fear would arise within her from no detectable source, panic would follow, and she would then have to struggle with that anxiety—effectively ending her observation as she became involved with the anxiety. Slowly she became aware that the watcher could see but did not experience anxiety, and she could sometimes get a little space between the "me" who was so afraid and the watcher.

Suddenly unexpected progress began to occur in our sessions together, progress that seemed to have been impelled by the mindfulness training. The case became almost classically psychoanalytic for a time, with our discussions proceeding backward in time to the point where she discussed a sexual experience with an aggressive older boy when she was 12. From that almost cathartic session, other sessions followed in which she discussed a long period of sexual promiscuity. At that point in therapy, her crowd-induced anxiety attacks began to subside, allowing her to go into places which had been previously troublesome. Then she related in great detail a long-repressed incident that she had mentioned slightly in one of our first sessions. When she was 9 or 10, her father had—at least in her perception of the event—attempted to seduce her. Telling her mother about the incident had caused family difficulties, and she had incurred much guilt about her parents' relationship. All of this poured out as well as her hostility towards males. All her later life had been concerned with rewarding, punishing, and controlling males with her sexuality; at last she began to see this important fact.

By this time her anxiety attacks had grown infrequent and were far less terrifying mainly because she was able to experience them more from the watcher's point of view. The attacks tended to occur only when she was alone, and she felt more capable of dealing with them. Her therapy was finally terminated when she and her husband moved to another city, where she apparently continued with another therapist.

The mindfulness approach to psychotherapy has proven to be compatible with chemotherapies, somatotherapies, and various other psychotherapies. It can provide valuable and timely insights for most clients with whom it is used appropriately, insights that can be deepened and broadened through discussion as therapy progresses.

However, the clinician who plans to use this approach needs first to become personally familiar with the technique. He or she should verify the insights potentially available by practicing the techniques personally before employing them with clients.

People almost never seem to reach a condition of total psychological stability. Change is constantly required of us as we age and encounter new experiences. Mindfulness training can help the client to continue to adapt successfully long after formal therapy has ended.

References

Mahāsi Sayādaw, *The Satipaṭṭhāna Vipassanā Meditation*. San Francisco: Unity Press, 1972.

Nyanaponika Thera, *The Heart of Buddhist Meditation*. New York: Samuel Weiser, 1973.

Nyanaponika Thera, *The Power of Mindfulness*, Santa Cruz, Unity Press, 1972.

Soma Thera, *The Way of Mindfulness*. Kandy: Buddhist Publication Society, 1975.[2]

---

2. The Buddhist Publication Society publishes Mahāsi Sayādaw's *Practical Insight Meditation* and *The Progress of Insight; A Treatise on Buddhist Satipaṭṭhāna Meditation*, as well as Nyanaponika Thera's *The Power of Mindfulness*.

Buddhist Women at the Time of the Buddha

by
Hellmuth Hecker

Translated from the German by
Sister Khemā

WHEEL PUBLICATION NO. 292/293

Copyright © Kandy; Buddhist Publication Society, (1982)

Foreword

The following stories, written by Hellmuth Hecker, have been translated from the German Buddhist magazine, *Wissen und Wandel*, XVIII 3 (1972) and XXII 1/2 (1976). They are published here with their kind permission.

While every effort has been made by the translator to conform to the original writing, some changes had to be made for the sake of clarity.

The stories of Bhaddā Kuṇḍalakesā and Paṭācārā have been enlarged and filled in.

Grateful acknowledgement is made to Ven. Khantipālo for his assistance in improving the style and content of this narrative. His new translations of verses of the Therīgāthā and the Dhammapada from the original Pali have helped to make these stories come alive.

It is hoped that this booklet will serve as an inspiration to all those who are endeavouring to tread in the Buddha's footsteps.

Sister Khemā
Wat Buddha Dhamma
Wisemans Ferry, N.S.W. 2255
Australia
January 1982

The Verses of Final Knowledge of Bhikkhunī Sujātā

With subtle veils adorned,
Garlands and sandal-wood bedecked,
Covered all over with ornaments,
Surrounded by my servants,
Taking with us food and drink,
Eatables of many kinds,
Setting off from the house,
To the forest grove we took it all.

Having enjoyed and sported there,
We turned our feet to home
But on the way I saw and entered
Near Sāketa, a monastery.

Seeing the Light of the World
I drew near, bowed down to him;
Out of compassion the Seeing One
Then taught me Dhamma there.

Hearing the words of the Great Sage,
I penetrated Truth:
The Dhamma passionless,
I touched the Dhamma of Deathlessness.
When the True Dhamma had been known,
I went forth to the homeless life;
The three True Knowledges are attained,
Not empty the Buddha's Teaching!

Therīgāthā, 145–150
Verses of the Elder nuns

Queen Mallikā

At the time of the Buddha, a daughter was born to the foreman of the guild of garland-makers in Sāvatthī. She was beautiful, clever and well behaved and a source of joy to her father. Her name was Mallikā.

One day, when she had just turned sixteen, she went to the public flower gardens with her girlfriends and took three portions of fermented rice along in her basket as the day's sustenance.

When she was just leaving by the city gate, a group of monks came along, who had come down from the monastery on the hill to obtain almsfood in town. The leader among them stood out; one whose grandeur and sublime beauty impressed her so much, that she impulsively offered him all the food in her basket.

He was the Buddha, the Awakened One. He let her put her offering into his alms bowl. After Mallikā—without knowing to whom she had given the food—had prostrated at his feet, she walked on full of joy. The Buddha smiled. Ānanda, his attendant, who knew that the fully Enlightened One does not smile without a reason, asked therefore why he was smiling. The Buddha replied that this girl would reap the benefits of her gift this very same day by becoming the Queen of Kosala.

This sounded unbelievable, how could the Mahārāja of Benares and Kosala elevate a woman of low caste to the rank of Queen? Especially in the India of those days with its very strict caste system, this seemed quite improbable.

The ruler over the united kingdoms of Benares and Kosala in the Ganges Valley was King Pasenadi, the mightiest Mahārāja of his day. At that time he was at war with his neighbour, the King of Magadha. The latter had won a battle and King Pasenadi had been forced to retreat. He was returning to his capital on his horse. Before entering the city, he heard a girl sing in the flower gardens. It was Mallikā, who was singing melodiously because of her joy in meeting the Illustrious Sage. The King was attracted by the song and rode into the gardens; Mallikā did not run away from the strange warrior, but came nearer, took the horse by its reins and looked straight into the King's eyes. He asked her whether she was already married and she replied in the negative. Thereupon he dismounted, lay down with his head in her lap and let her console him about his ill-luck in battle.

After he had recovered, he let her mount his horse behind him and took her back to the house of her parents. In the evening he sent an entourage with much pomp to fetch her and made her his principal wife and Queen.

From then on she was dearly beloved to the King. She was given many loyal servants and in her beauty she resembled a goddess. It became known throughout the whole kingdom that because of her simple gift she had been elevated to the highest position in the State and this induced her subjects to be kind and generous towards their fellow men. Wherever she went, people would joyously proclaim: "That is Queen Mallikā, who gave alms to the Buddha." (J 415)

After she had become Queen, she soon went to visit the Enlightened One to ask him something which was puzzling her: how it came about that one woman could be beautiful, wealthy and of great ability, another beautiful but poor and not very able, yet another ugly, rich and very able, and finally another ugly, poor and with no skills at all. These differences can constantly be observed in daily life. But while the ordinary person is satisfied with such commonplace terms as fate, heredity, coincidence and so on, Queen Mallikā wanted to probe deeper as she was convinced that nothing happens without a cause.

The Buddha explained to her in great detail that all attributes and living conditions of people everywhere were solely dependent on the extent of their moral purity. Beauty was caused by forgiveness and gentleness, prosperity due to generous giving, and skilfulness was caused by never envying others, but rather being joyful and supporting their abilities. Whichever of these three virtues a person had cultivated, that would show up as their 'destiny,' usually in some mixture of all of them. The coming together of all three attributes would be a rarity. After Mallikā had listened to this discourse of the Buddha, she resolved in her heart to be always gentle towards her subjects and never to scold them, to give alms to all monks, brahmins and the poor, and never to envy anyone who was happy.

At the end of the Enlightened One's discourse she took refuge in the Buddha, Dhamma and Saṅgha and remained a faithful disciple for the rest of her life (AN 4:197).

She showed her great generosity not only giving regular alms, but also by building a large, ebony-lined hall for the Saṅgha, which was used for religious discussions (MN 78, DN 9). She exhibited her gentleness by serving her husband with the five qualities of a perfect wife, namely: always rising before him, and going to bed after him, by always obeying his commands, always being polite, and using only kind words. Even the monks praised her gentleness in their discussions about virtue.

Soon she was to prove that she was also free of jealousy. The King had made up his mind to marry a second chief wife and brought a cousin of the Buddha home as his betrothed. Although it is said that it is in the nature of women not to allow a rival into her home, Mallikā related to the other wife without the slightest malice (A VI, 52). Both women lived in peace and harmony at the Court.

Even when the second wife gave birth to a son, the crown prince, and Mallikā had only a daughter, she was not envious. When the King voiced disappointment about the birth of a daughter, the Buddha said to him that a woman was superior to a man if she was clever, virtuous, well-behaved and faithful. Then she could become the wife of a great King and give birth to an almighty Ruler (SN 3:16). When the daughter, Princess Vajirā, had grown up, she became Queen of Magadha and thereby the ancestress of the greatest Indian emperor, Asoka, who ruled Magadha 250 years later.

After Mallikā had become a faithful lay devotee of the Buddha, she also won her husband over to the Dhamma. And that happened in this way. One night the King had a succession of sixteen perturbing dreams during which he heard gruesome, unfathomable sounds from four voices, which uttered: *"Du, Sa, Na, So."* When the King woke up from these dreams, great fear seized him, and sitting upright and trembling, he awaited the sunrise.

When his Brahmin priests asked him whether he had slept well, he related the terror of the night and asked them what one could do to counteract such a menace. The Brahmins declared that one would have to offer great sacrifices and thereby pacify the evil spirits. In his fear the King agreed to that. The Brahmins rejoiced because of the gifts they would surely reap and busily began to make preparations for the great sacrifice. They scurried about, building a sacrificial altar, and tied many animals to posts so they could be killed.

For greater efficacy, they demanded the sacrifice of four human beings and these also awaited their death, tied to posts. When Mallikā became aware of all this activity, she went to the King and asked him why the Brahmins were so busily running about full of joyous expectation. The King replied that she did not pay enough attention to him and did not know his sorrows.

Thereupon he told her of his dreams. Mallikā asked the King whether he had also consulted the first and foremost of Brahmins about the meaning and interpretation. He replied that she first had to tell him who was the first and foremost of Brahmins. She explained that the Buddha was foremost in the world of Gods and men, the first of all Brahmins. King Pasenadi decided to ask the Awakened One's advice and went to Prince Jeta's Grove, Anāthapiṇḍika's Monastery.

He related to the Buddha what had taken place in his dreams and asked him what would happen to him. "Nothing," the Awakened One replied and explained the meaning to him. The sixteen dreams which he had had were prophecies, showing that the living conditions on earth would deteriorate steadily, due to the increasing moral laxity of the kings. In a meditative moment, King Pasenadi had been able to see future occurrences within his sphere of interest because he was a monarch concerned with the well-being of his subjects.

The four voices which he had heard belonged to four men who had lived in Sāvatthī and had been seducers of married women. Because of that they were reborn in hell and for 30,000 years they drowned in red-hot cauldrons, coming nearer and nearer to the fire, which intensified their unbearable suffering. During another 30,000 years they slowly rose up in those iron cauldrons and had now come to the rim, where they could once again at least breathe the air of the human realm.

Each one wanted to speak a verse but, because of the gravity of the deed, could not get past the first syllable. Not even in sighs could they voice their suffering, because they had long lost the gift of speech. The four verses, which start in Pali with *du, sa, na* and *so*, were recognized by the Awakened One as follows:

Du: Dung-like life we lived,
No willingness to give,
Although we could have given much,
We did not make our refuge thus.

Sa: Say, the end is near?
Already 60,000 years have gone.
Without respite the torture is
In this hell realm.

Na: Naught, no end near. Oh, would it end!
No end in sight for us.
Who once did misdeeds here
For me, for you, for both of us.

So: So, could I only leave this place
And raise myself to human realm,
I would be kind and moral too,
And do good deeds abundantly.

After the King had heard these explanations, he became responsive to the request of the compassionate Queen and granted freedom to the imprisoned men and animals. He ordered the sacrificial altar to be destroyed (J 77 & 314).

The King, who had become a devoted lay disciple of the Buddha, visited him one day again and met a wise and well-learned layman there. The King asked him whether he could give some daily Dhamma teaching to his two Queens. The layman replied that the teaching came from the Enlightened One and only one of his immediate disciples could pass it on to the Queens. The King understood this and requested the Buddha to give permission to one of his monks to teach. The Buddha appointed Ānanda for this task. Queen Mallikā learned easily in spite of her uneducated background, but Queen Vasabhakhattiyā, cousin of the Buddha and mother of the crown-prince, was unconcentrated and learned with difficulty (Pāc 3/Vin IV 158).

One day the royal couple looked down upon the river from the palace and saw a group of the Buddha's monks playing about in the water. The king said to Queen Mallikā reproachfully: "Those playing about in the water are supposed to be Arahants?" Such was namely the reputation of this group of the so-called seventeen monks, who were quite young and of good moral conduct. Mallikā replied that she could only explain it thus, that either the Buddha had not made any rules with regard to bathing or that the monks were not acquainted with them, because they were not amongst the rules which were recited regularly.

Both agreed that it would not make a good impression on lay people and on those monks not yet secure, if those in higher training played about in the water and enjoyed themselves in the way of untrained worldly people. But King Pasenadi wanted to avoid blackening those monks' characters and just wanted to give the Buddha a hint, so that he could lay down a firm rule. He conceived the idea to send a special gift to the Buddha to be taken by those monks. They brought the gift and the Buddha asked them on what occasion they had met the King. Then they told him what they had done and the Buddha laid down a corresponding rule (Pāc 53/Vin IV 112).

One day when the King was standing on the parapet of the palace with the Queen and was looking down upon the land, he asked her whether there was anyone in the world she loved more than herself. He expected her to name him, since he flattered himself to have been the one who had raised her to fame and fortune. But although she loved him, she remained truthful and replied that she knew of no one dearer to herself than herself. Then she wanted to know how it was with him: Did he love anyone—possibly her—more than himself? Thereupon the King also had to admit that self-love was always predominant. But he went to the Buddha and recounted the conversation to find out how a *Arahant* would consider this.

The Buddha confirmed his and Mallikā's statements:

I visited all quarters with my mind
Nor found I any dearer than myself;
Self is likewise to every other dear;
Who loves himself may never harm another.

    Ud 5.1; SN 3:8 (translated by Ven. Ñāṇamoli)

One day the Buddha said to a man whose child had died: "Dear ones, those who are dear, bring sorrow, lamentation, pain, grief and despair," the suffering that results from a clinging love. In spite of the clearly visible proof, the man could not understand this. The conversation was reported to the King and he asked his wife whether it was really true that sorrow would result from love. "If the Awakened One has said so, O King, then it is so," she replied devotedly.

The King demurred that she accepted every word of the Buddha like a disciple from a guru. Thereupon she sent a messenger to the Buddha to ask for more details and then passed the explicit answer on to her husband. She asked him whether he loved his daughter, his second wife, the crown-prince, herself and his kingdom? Naturally he confirmed this, these five things were dear to him. But if something happened to these five, Mallikā responded, would he not feel sorrow, lamentation, pain, grief or despair, which comes from loving? Then the King understood and realized how wisely the Buddha could penetrate all existence: "Very well, then Mallikā, continue to venerate him." And the King rose, uncovered his shoulder, prostrated deferentially in the direction where the Blessed One was residing, and greeted him three times with: "Homage to the Blessed One, the Holy One, the fully Awakened One."

But their lives together did not remain quite without conflict. One day an argument arose between the couple about the duties of the Queen. For some reason the King was angry at her and treated her from then on as if she had disappeared into thin air. When the Buddha arrived at the palace the next day for his meal, he asked about the Queen, who had always been present at other times. Pasenadi scowled and said: "What about her? She has gone mad because of her fame." The Buddha replied that he, himself, had raised her up to that position quite unexpectedly and should become reconciled with her. Somewhat reluctantly the King had her called. Thereupon the Buddha praised the blessing of amity and the anger was forgotten, as if it had never happened (J 306).

But later on a new tension arose between the couple. Again the King would not look at the Queen and pretended she did not exist. When the Buddha became aware of this, he asked about her. Pasenadi said that her good fortune had gone to her head. Immediately the Awakened One told an incident from a former life. Both were then heavenly beings, a deva couple, who loved each other dearly. One night they were separated from each other because of the flooding of a stream. They both regretted this irretrievable night, which could never be replaced during their life-span of a thousand years. And during the rest of their lives they never let go of each other's company and always remembered to use this separation as a warning so that their happiness would endure during that whole existence.

The King was moved by this story, and became reconciled to the Queen. Mallikā then spoke this verse to the Buddha:

> With joy I heard your varied words,
> Which spoken were for my well-being;
> With your talk you took away my sorrow
> Verily, you are the joy-bringer amongst the ascetics
> May you live long!
>
> J 504

A third time the Buddha told of an occurrence during one of the former lives of the royal couple. At that time Pasenadi was a crown-prince and Mallikā his wife. When the crown-prince became afflicted with leprosy and could not become King because of that, he resolved to withdraw into the forest by himself, so as not to become a burden to anyone. But his wife did not desert him, and looked after him with touching attention. She resisted the temptation to lead a care-free life in pomp and splendour and remained faithful to her ugly and ill-smelling husband. Through the power of her virtue she was able to effect his recovery. When he ascended to the throne and she became his Queen, he promptly forgot her and enjoyed himself with various dancing girls. It is almost as difficult to find a grateful person, the Buddha said, as it is difficult to find a Holy One (A 3:122).

Only when the King was reminded of the good deeds of his Queen, did he change his ways, ask her forgiveness and live together with her in harmony and virtue (J 519).

Queen Mallikā committed only one deed in this life which had evil results and which led her to the worst rebirth. Immediately after her death, she was reborn in hell, though this lasted only a few days. When she died, the King was just listening to a Dhamma exhortation by the Buddha. When the news reached him there, he was deeply shaken and even the Buddha's reminder that there was nothing in the world that could escape old age, disease, death, decay and destruction could not immediately assuage his grief (AN 5: 49).

His attachment—"from love comes sorrow"—was so strong that he went to the Buddha every day to find out about the future destiny of his wife. If he had to get along without her on earth, at least he wanted to know about her rebirth. But for seven days the Buddha distracted him from his question through fascinating and moving Dhamma discourses, so that he only remembered his question when he arrived home again. Only on the seventh day would the Buddha answer his question and said that Mallikā had been reborn in the "Heaven of the Blissful Devas." He did not mention the seven days she had spent in hell, so as not to add to the King's sorrow.

Even though it was a very short-termed sojourn in the lower realms, one can see that Mallikā had not yet attained stream-entry[1] during her life on earth, since it is one of the signs of a stream-winner that they cannot take rebirth below the human state. However, this experience of hellish suffering together with her knowledge of Dhamma, could have quickened Mallikā's last ripening for the attainment of stream-entry.

Sources: MN 87; AN 5:49, 4:197, 8: 91; SN 3:8 = Ud 5.1; SN 3:16; J 77, 306, 314, 415, 504, 519; Pāc 53, 83; Mil 115, 291; Jtm 3; Divy p.88

---

1. Stream-entry: the first stage of Enlightenment, where the first glimpse of Nibbāna is gained and the first three fetters abandoned.

What Cannot Be Got

The Buddha's Words to King Pasenadi on Queen Mallikā's Death

At one time the Lord was staying near Sāvatthī at the Jeta Grove, Anāthapiṇḍika's Monastery. Then King Pasenadi of Kosala approached the Lord and having done so, paid his respects and sat down nearby. Now at that time Queen Mallikā died. A certain man then approached the King and whispered in his ear: "Your Majesty, Queen Mallikā has died." At those words King Pasenadi was filled with grief and depression, and with shoulders drooping, head down, he sat glum, and with nothing to say. The Lord saw the king sitting there like that and spoke to him in this way:

"Great king, there are these five circumstances not-to-be-got by a monk, brahmin, deva, Māra, Brahma, or by anyone in the world. What are the five?

"That what is of the nature to decay may not decay, is a circumstance not-to-be-got by a monk ... or by anyone in the world. That what is of the nature to be diseased may not be diseased, is a circumstance not-to-be-got by a monk ... or by anyone in the world.

"That what is of the nature to die may not die, is a circumstance not-to-be-got by a monk ... or by anyone in the world.

"That what is of the nature to be exhausted may not be exhausted, is a circumstance not-to-be-got by a monk ... or by anyone in the world.

"That what is of the nature to be destroyed may not be destroyed, is a circumstance, not-to-be-got by a monk ... or by anyone in the world.

"Great king, for an uninstructed ordinary person, what is of the nature to decay does decay, what is of the nature to be diseased does become diseased, what is of the nature to die does die, what is of the nature to be exhausted is exhausted and what is of the nature to be destroyed is destroyed. And when these things happen to him he does not reflect, 'It's not only for me that what is of the nature to decay decays ... that what is of the nature to be destroyed is destroyed, but wherever there are beings, coming and going, dying and being born, for all those beings what is of the nature to decay decays ... what is of the nature to be destroyed is destroyed. And if I, when there is decay in what is of the nature to decay ... when there is destruction in what is of the nature to be destroyed, should grieve, pine, and lament, and crying beat the breast and so fall into delusion, food would not be enjoyed, my body would become haggard, work would not be done and enemies would be pleased, while friends would be depressed.' Then, when there is decay in what is of the nature to decay, disease in what is of the nature to be diseased, death in what is of the nature to die, exhaustion in what is of the nature to be exhausted, destruction in what is of the nature to be destroyed, he grieves, pines and laments, and crying beats his breast and so falls into delusion.

"This is called an uninstructed ordinary person; pierced by the poisoned dart of grief, he just torments himself. Great king, for the instructed Noble Disciple what is of the nature to decay does decay ... and what is of the nature to be destroyed is destroyed ... and when these things happen to him he does reflect, 'It's not only for me that what is of the nature to decay decays ... that what is of the nature to be destroyed, is destroyed, but wherever there are beings, coming and going, dying and being born, for all those beings what is of the nature to decay decays ... what is of the nature to be destroyed is destroyed. And if I, when there is decay in what is of the nature to decay ... when there is destruction in what is of the nature to be destroyed, should grieve, pine and lament, and crying beat the breast and so fall into delusion, food would not be enjoyed, my body would become haggard, work would not be done and enemies would be pleased while friends would be depressed.' Then when there is decay in what is of the nature to decay, disease in what is of the nature to be diseased, death in what is of the nature to die, exhaustion in what is of the nature to be exhausted, destruction in what is of the nature to be destroyed, he does not grieve or pine or lament, he does not beat his breast and fall into delusion.

"This is called an instructed Noble Disciple. Drawn out is the poisoned dart of grief with which the uninstructed ordinary person torments himself. Free of grief, free from the dart, the Noble Disciple has quenched[2] himself completely."

---

2. Or 'become cool,' literally 'nibbāna-ed.'

"Great king, these are the five circumstances not-to-be-got by monk, brahmin, deva, Māra, Brahma, or by anyone in the world.

"Do not grieve, nor should you lament.
Here, what good is gained?—none at all indeed,
and enemies rejoice to see that grief and pain.
But when misfortunes do not shake the wise—
that one who knows well how to seek the good,
then enemies because of that are pained
seeing his face as formerly, not strained.
Where and whatever good may gotten, be
there and just there he should try for that
by study, wisdom and well-spoken words,
unpractised so far, and tradition, too.
But if he knows: 'This good can be got
Neither by me nor any other too'
then ungrieving he should bear it all (and think),
'Now how to use my strength for present work?'"

AN 5:49

Khemā of Great Wisdom

Just as there were two foremost disciples in the order of monks, namely Sāriputta and Moggallāna, likewise the Buddha named two women as his foremost disciples in the Bhikkhunī Saṅgha, the Order of Nuns. These two were Uppalavaṇṇā and Khemā, the former excelling in psychic power, the latter in wisdom (AN 1 Ch. 14). The Buddha held up these two as the models and examples for all the nuns to emulate, the standard against which other nuns could evaluate themselves (SN 17:24).

The name Khemā means well-settled or composed or security and is a synonym for Nibbāna. The nun Khemā belonged to a royal family from the land of Magadha. When she was of marriageable age, she became one of the chief consorts of King Bimbisāra. As beautiful as her appearance was, equally beautiful was her life as the wife of an Indian Mahārāja.

When she heard about the Buddha from her husband, she became interested, but she had a certain reluctance to become involved with his teaching. She felt that the teaching would run counter to her life of sense-pleasures and indulgences. The king, however, knew how he could influence her to listen to the teaching. He described at length the harmony, the peace and beauty of the monastery in the Bamboo Grove, where the Buddha frequently stayed. Because she loved beauty, harmony and peace, she was persuaded to visit there.

Decked out in royal splendour with silk and sandalwood, she went to the monastery. Gradually whe was attracted to the hall where the Buddha was preaching. The Buddha, who read her thoughts, created by his psychic powers a handsome young lady, standing aside fanning him. Khemā admired her beauty. The Buddha made this created image change from youth to middle age and old age, till it finally fell on the ground with broken teeth, grey hair, and wrinkled skin. Only then did she realize the vanity of external beauty and the fleeting nature of life. She thought, "Has such a body come to be wrecked like that? Then so will my body also."

The Buddha read her mind and said:

They who are slaves to lust drift down the stream,
Like to a spider gliding down the web,
He of himself wrought. But the released,
Who all their bonds have snapt in twain,
With thoughts elsewhere intent, forsake the world,
And all delights in sense put far away.

She penetrated this sermon fully and still dressed in royal garments, she attained to enlightenment. Just like the monk, Mahākappina—a former king—through the power of the Buddha's words right on the spot she attained Arahantship together with the analytical knowledges. With her husband's permission she joined the Order of Nuns. Such an attainment, almost like lightning, is only possible however where the seed of wisdom has long been ripening and virtue is fully matured.

An ordinary person, hearing Khemā's story, only sees the wonder of the present happening. A Buddha can see beyond this and knows that this woman did not come to full liberation accidentally. It came about like this: In former times when a Buddha appeared in the world, then Khemā in those past lives also appeared near him, or so it has been recounted. Due to her inner attraction towards the highest Truth, she always came to birth wherever the bearer and proclaimer of such Truth lived. It is said that already innumerable ages ago she had sold her beautiful hair to give alms to the Buddha Padumuttara. During the time of the Buddha Vipassi, ninety-one eons ago, she had been a teacher of Dhamma. Further it is told that during the three Buddhas of our happy eon, which were previous to our Buddha Gotama, she was a lay disciple and gained happiness through building monasteries for the Saṅgha.

While most beings mill around heaven or hell realms during the lifetime of a Buddha, Khemā always tried to be near the source of wisdom. When there was no Buddha appearing in the world, she would be reborn at the time of Pacceka-Buddhas or Bodhisattas. In one birth she was the wife of the Bodhisatta, who always exhorted his peaceful family like this:

> According to what you have got, give alms;
> Observe the Uposatha days, keep the precepts pure;
> Dwell upon the thought of death and be mindful of your mortal state.
> For in the case of beings like ourselves, death is certain, life is uncertain;
> All existing things are transitory and subject to decay.
> Therefore be heedful of your ways day and night.

One day Khemā's only son in this life was suddenly killed by the bite of a poisonous snake, yet she was able to keep total equanimity:

> Uncalled he hither came, without leave departed, too;
> Even as he came, he went. What cause is here for woe?
> No friend's lament can touch the ashes of the dead:
> Why should I grieve? He fares the way he had to tread.
> Though I should fast and weep, how would it profit me?
> My kith and kin, alas, would more unhappy be.
> No friend's lament can touch the ashes of the dead:
> Why should I grieve? He fares the way he had to tread.
>
> J 354

Another time, so it is told, she was the daughter-in-law of the Bodhisatta (J 397); many times too a great Empress who dreamt about receiving teaching from the Bodhisatta and then actually was taught by him (J 501, 502, 534). It is further recounted that as a Queen she was always the wife of he who was later Sāriputta, who said about her:

> Of equal status is the wife,
> Obedient, speaking only loving words,
> With children, beauty, fame, garlanded,
> She always listens to my words.
>
> J 502, 534

This husband in former lives was a righteous king, who upheld the ten royal virtues: Generosity, morality, renunciation, truthfulness, gentleness, patience, amity, harmlessness, humility, justice. Because of these virtues the king lived in happiness and bliss. Khemā, too, lived in accordance with these precepts (J 534).

Only because Khemā had already purified her heart and perfected it in these virtues in many past lives, she was now mature enough, and had such pure and tranquil emotions, that she could accept the ultimate Truth in the twinkling of an eye.

The Buddha praised her as the nun foremost in wisdom. A story goes with that: King Pasenadi was travelling through his country, and one evening he arrived at a small township. He felt like having a conversation about Dhamma and ordered a servant to find out whether there was a wise ascetic or priest in the town. The servant sounded everyone out, but could not find anyone whom his master could converse with. He reported this to the King and added that a nun of the Buddha lived in the town.

It was the saintly Khemā, who was famed everywhere for her wisdom and known to be clever, possessing deep insight, had heard much Dhamma, and was a speaker of renown, knowing always the right retort. Thereupon the king went to the former Queen, greeted her with respect and had the following conversation with her:

Pasenadi: "Does an Awakened One exist after death?"
Khemā: "The Exalted One has not declared that an Awakened One exists after death."
Pasenadi: "Then an Awakened One does not exist after death?"
Khemā: "That too, the Exalted One has not declared"
Pasenadi: "Then the Awakened One exists after death and does not exist?"

Khemā: "Even that, the Exalted One has not declared."
Pasenadi: "Then one must say, the Awakened One neither exists nor does not exists after death?"
Khemā: "That too, the Exalted One has not declared."

Thereupon the King wanted to know why the Buddha had rejected these four questions. First we must try to understand what these questions imply.

The first question corresponds with the view of all those beings whose highest goal is to continue on after death, spurred on by craving for existence. Answering that an Awakened One continues to exist after death is done by all other religions, including later interpretations of Buddhism.

Answering that the Enlightened One does not exist after death would be in keeping with craving for non-existence, i.e., annihilation. Because of an urge for definite knowledge and certainty, a definition is sought which could claim that the five aggregates (*khandha*) of form, feeling, perception, mental formations and consciousness—which make up the sum total of all existence—are completely dissolved and disappear upon the shedding of an Awakened One's body; and that deliverance consisted in that mere fact of dissolution.

Answering that the Awakened One exists after death and does not exist would be a compromise: everything impermanent in an Awakened One would be annihilated, but the permanent aspect, the essence, his actual person, would remain.

Answering by way of formulating a 'neither-nor' situation is an attempt to get out of the predicament by giving a seemingly satisfying answer.[3]

All four questions have been rejected by the Buddha as wrong views. They all presuppose that there is an 'I' distinct from the world, while in reality 'I' and 'world' are part of the experience which arises because of consciousness.

Only the Enlightened Ones can actually see this, or those who have been their disciples, and unless this understanding is awakened, the assumption is made that an 'I,' an essentially permanent 'self,'

---

3. This 'solution' is formulated with the idea that it is something that words/concepts cannot describe, but it still uses 'exist' and 'not exist' and so was not accepted by the Buddha.

is wandering through *saṃsāra*,[4] gradually ascending higher and higher until it is dissolved, which is liberation. This is a belief held by some. Others conclude from this, that the Buddha teaches the destruction of the 'self.' But the Buddha teaches that there is no 'I' or 'self' which can be destroyed, that it has never existed and has never wandered through *saṃsāra*.

What we call 'I' and what we call 'world' are in reality a constantly changing process, always in flux, which always throws up the illusion of 'I' and 'world' born in the present and speculated upon in the past and future. The way to liberation is to stop speculating about the 'I,' to become free from habitual views and formulas, and come to the end of the mind's illusory conjuring.

Not through increasing the thought processes about phenomena, but through mindfulness of the arising of phenomena—which leads to reducing the chatter in the mind— can liberation be attained. Everything we see, hear, smell, taste, touch and think, anything that can be contained in consciousness, no matter how wide-ranging and pure it is, has arisen due to causes; therefore it is impermanent and subject to decay and dissolution.

Everything which is subject to decay and change is not-self. Because the five clung-to aggregates are subject to destruction, they are not 'my' self, are not 'mine.' 'I' cannot prevent their decay, their becoming sick, damaged, faulty and their passing away. The conclusion that the self must then be outside of the five aggregates does not follow either, because it, too, is a thought and therefore belongs to one of the five clung-to aggregates (i.e., mental formations).

Any designation of the Enlightened One after death is therefore an illusion, born out of compulsion for naming, and cannot be appropriate. Whoever has followed the teaching of the Awakened One, as Khemā did, is greatly relieved to see that the Buddha did not teach the destruction of an existing entity nor the annihilation of a self. But, on the contrary, those not instructed by the Exalted One live without exception in a world of perpetual destruction, of uncontrollable transiency in the realm of death. Whatever they look upon as 'I' and 'mine' is constantly vanishing and only by renouncing these things which are unsatisfactory

---

4. *Saṃsāra*: the rounds of birth and death, continually recurring.

because of their impermanence can they reach a refuge of peace and security. Just as the lion's roar of the Exalted One proclaimed: "Open are the doors to the deathless, who has ears to hear, come and listen."

Khemā tried to explain this to the King with a simile. She asked him whether he had a clever mathematician or statistician, who could calculate for him how many hundred, thousand or hundred-thousand grains of sand are contained in the river Ganges. The King replied that that is not possible. The nun then asked him whether he knew of anyone who could figure out how many gallons of water are contained in the great ocean. That, too, the King considered impossible. Khemā asked him why it is not possible. The King replied that the ocean is mighty, deep, unfathomable.

Just so, said Khemā, is the Exalted One. Whoever wished to define the Awakened One could only do so through the five clung-to aggregates and the Buddha no longer clung to them. "Released from clinging to form, feeling, perception, mental formations and consciousness is the Enlightened One, mighty, deep unfathomable as the great ocean."

Therefore it was not appropriate to say he existed or did not exist, or existed and did not exist, nor did he neither exist nor not exist. All these designations could not define what was undefinable. Just that was liberation: liberation from the compulsion to stabilize as 'self' the constant flux of the five aggregates, which are never the same in any given moment, but only appear as a discharge of tensions arising from mental formations.

The King rejoiced in the penetrating explanation of the nun Khemā. Later on he met the Enlightened One and asked him the same four questions. The Buddha explained it exactly as Khemā had done, even using the same words. The King was amazed and recounted his conversation with the wise nun Khemā, the *Arahant* (SN 44:1).

Sources: Commentary to her Thī verses; SN 17:23; 44:1; AN I:24; 2:62; 4:176; 8:91; Th 139–144; J 354, 397, 501, 502, 534, 539; Ap 2:18 (verse 96); Bv 26, 19.

Bhaddā Kuṇḍalakesā

The Former Jain Ascetic

In Rājagaha, the capital of the kingdom of Magadha, lived a girl of good family named Bhaddā. Her parents protected her very carefully, because she had a passionate nature and they were afraid that she would be hurt due to her attraction to men. One day from her window Bhaddā saw how a thief was being led to the place of execution. He was the son of a Brahmin but had a strong tendency towards stealing. She fell in love with him at first sight. She convinced her father that she could not live without him, and so he bribed the guards who let the condemned man escape.

Soon after the wedding the bridegroom became obsessed with the desire to get his wife's jewellery. He told her he had made a vow that he would make an offering to a certain mountain deity if he could escape execution. Through this ruse he managed to get Bhaddā away from his home. He wanted to throw her down from a high cliff to gain possession of her valuable ornaments. When they came to the cliff, he brusquely told her about his intention. Bhaddā, in her distress, likewise resolved to a ruse that enabled her to give him a push so that it was he who fell to his death.

Burdened by the enormity of her deed, she did not want to return to lay life. Sensual pleasures and possessions were no longer tempting for her. She became a wandering ascetic. First she entered the order of Jains and, as a special penance, her hair was torn out by the roots when she ordained. But it grew again and was very curly. Therefore she was called 'Curly-hair' (Kuṇḍalakesā).

The teachings of the Jain sect did not satisfy her, so she became a solitary wanderer. She travelled through India and visited many spiritual teachers, thereby obtaining an excellent knowledge of religious scriptures and philosophies. She became one of the most famous debaters. When she entered a town, she would make a sand-pile and stick a rose-apple branch into it and would announce that whoever would engage in discussion with her should trample upon the sand-pile.

One day she came to Sāvatthī and again erected her little monument. At that time, Venerable Sāriputta—the disciple of the Buddha with the greatest power of analysis—was staying at the Jeta Grove. He heard of the arrival of Bhaddā and as a sign of his willingness for debate, he had several children go and trample on the sand-pile. Thereupon Bhaddā went to the Jeta Grove, to Anāthapiṇḍika's Monastery, accompanied by a large number of people. She was certain of victory, since she had become used to being the winner in all debates.

She put a number of questions to Sāriputta. He answered all of them until she found nothing more to ask. Then Sāriputta questioned her. Already the first question affected Bhaddā profoundly, namely, "What is the One?" She remained silent, unable to discern what the Elder could have been inquiring about. Surely he did not mean 'God,' or 'Brahman' or 'the Infinite,' she pondered. But what was it then? The answer should have been 'nutriment' because all beings are sustained by food.

Although she was unable to find an answer and thereby lost the debate, she knew that here was someone who had found what she had been looking for during her pilgrimage. She chose Venerable Sāriputta as her teacher, but he referred her to the Buddha. The Awakened One preached Dhamma to her at Mount Vulture Peak and concluded with the following verses:

> Though a thousand verses
> are made of meaningless lines,
> better the single meaningful line
> by hearing which one is at peace.
>
> Dhp 101

Just as the wanderer Bāhiya was foremost amongst monks who attained Arahantship faster than anyone else, she was foremost amongst nuns with the same quality. Both grasped the highest Truth so quickly and so deeply that admittance to the Order followed after attainment of Arahantship. The mind and emotions of both of them had long been trained and prepared, so that they could reach the highest attainment very quickly.

Bhaddā's verses have been handed down to us in the Therīgāthā, as she summarizes her life:

I travelled before in a single cloth,
With shaven head, covered in dust,
Thinking of faults in the faultless,
While in the faulty seeing no faults.[5]
When done was the day's abiding,[6]
I went to Mount Vulture Peak
And saw the stainless Buddha
By the Order of Bhikkhus revered.
Then before Him my hands held up[7]
Humbly, I bowed down on my knees.
"Come, Bhaddā," He said to me:
And thus was I ordained.
Debt-free, I travelled for fifty years
In Anga, Magadha and Vajji,
In Kasi and Kosala, too,
Living on the alms of the land.
That lay-supporter—wise man indeed—
May many merits accrue to him!
Who gave a robe to Bhaddā for
Free of all ties is she.

Thī 107–111

Sources: AN I:24; (Commentary on) Thī 107–111; J 509; Ap 2:21 (p.560).

---

5. *Vajja*: fault; it can also mean 'what is obstructive to spiritual progress.'
6. The daytime spent in seclusion for meditation.
7. *Añjali*: hands placed palms to palm respectfully.

Kisāgotamī

The Mother with the Dead Child

There lived in Sāvatthī a girl called Gotami, in poor circumstances, belonging to the lowest caste. Because she was very thin and haggard, a real beanpole, everyone called her the haggard (*kisa*) Gotami. When one saw her walking around, tall and thin, one could not fathom her inner riches. One could truly say about her:

> Her beauty was an inner one
> One could not see its spark outside.

She was despondent because due to her poverty and lack of attractiveness, she was unable to find a husband. But one day it suddenly happened that a rich merchant who appreciated her inner wealth and considered that more important than her outer appearance, married her. However, the husband's family despised her because of her caste, her poverty and her looks. This animosity caused her great unhappiness, especially because of her beloved husband, who found himself in conflict between love for his parents and love for his wife.

But when Kisāgotamī gave birth to a baby boy, the husband's whole clan finally accepted her as the mother of the son and heir. Her relief about this changed attitude was immense and a great burden was taken from her. Now she was totally happy and contented. The boy grew up and soon started playing outside, full of energy and joy. However, one day her happiness showed itself to be based on an illusion. Her little son died suddenly. She did not know how to bear this tragedy. Beyond the usual love of a mother for her child, she had been especially attached to this child, because he was the guarantee for her marital bliss and her peace of mind.

His death made her fear that her husband's family would despise her again and that they would blame her, saying she was karmically unable to have a son. People would say: "Kisāgotamī must have done some very despicable deeds, to have this happen to her." And even her husband might reject her now. All such ideas and imaginings revolved in her mind and a dark cloud descended upon her. Refusing to accept the fact that the child was dead, and became obsessed with the fantasy that her child was only sick and that she had to get medicine for him.

With the dead child in her arms, she ran away from her home and went from house to house asking for medicine for her little son. At every door she begged, "Please give me some medicine for my child." Always the people replied that medicine would not help any more, the child was dead. But she did not understand what they were saying to her, because in her mind she had resolved that the child was only ill. Others laughed at her without compassion. But amongst the many selfish and unsympathetic people, she also met a wise and kind person who recognized that her mind was deranged because of grief. He advised her to visit the best physician, the Buddha of the ten powers, who would know the right remedy.

She immediately followed this advice and ran to Prince Jeta's Grove, Anāthapiṇḍika's Monastery, where the Buddha was staying. She arrived in the middle of a discourse being given by the Buddha to a large congregation. Totally despairing and in tears, with the corpse of the child in her arms, she begged the Buddha, "Master, give me medicine for my son." The Awakened One interrupted his teaching and replied kindly that he knew of a medicine. Hopefully she inquired what that could be.

"Mustard seeds," the Enlightened One replied, astounding everyone present.

Joyfully, Kisāgotamī inquired where she should go to obtain them and what kind to get. The Buddha replied that she need only bring a very small quantity from any house where no one had died. She trusted the Blessed One's words and went to the town. At the first house, she asked whether any mustard seeds were available. "Certainly," was the reply. "Could I have a few seeds?" she inquired. "Of course," she was told, and some seeds were brought to her. But then she asked the second question, which she had not deemed quite as important: whether anyone had died in this house. "But of course," the people told her. And so it went everywhere. In one house someone had died recently, in another house some time ago. She could not find any house where no one had died. The dead ones are more numerous than the living ones, she was told.

Towards evening she finally realized that she was not alone in being stricken by the death of a loved one, but this was the common human fate. What no words had been able to convey to her, her own experience—going from door to door—made clear to her. She understood the law of existence, the law of impermanence and death within the ever-recurring round of becoming. In this way, the Buddha was able to heal her obsession and bring her to an acceptance of reality. Kisāgotamī no longer refused to believe that her child was dead: she understood that death is the destiny of all beings.

Such were the means by which the Buddha could heal grief-stricken people and bring them out of their overpowering delusion, in which the whole world was perceived only in the perspective of their loss. Once, when someone was lamenting the death of his father, the Buddha asked him which father he meant: the father of this life, or the last life, or the one before that. Because if one wanted to grieve, then it would be just as well not only to feel sorrow for the one father (Pv 8, J 352). Another time a grief-stricken person was able to see reality when the Buddha pointed out to him that his son would be reborn and that he was only lamenting for an empty shell (Pv 12, J 354).

After Kisāgotamī had come to her senses, she took the child's lifeless body to the cemetery and returned to the Enlightened One. He asked her whether she had brought any mustard seed. She gratefully explained how she had been cured by the Blessed One. Thereupon the Master spoke the following verse to her:

> In flocks and children finding delight,
> With a mind clinging—just such a man
> Death seizes and carries away,
> As a great flood, a sleeping village.

Dhp 287

Because her mind had matured and she had won insight into reality, it was possible for her to become a stream-winner after hearing the Buddha proclaim just that one verse. She asked for admittance into the Order of Nuns.

After having spent some time as a nun, practicing and studying Dhamma, she watched her lamp one evening and compared the restlessly hissing flames with the ups and downs of life and death.

Thereupon the Blessed One came to her and again spoke a short verse:

> Though one should live a hundred years
> Not seeing the Deathless State,
> Yet better is life for a single day,
> Seeing the Deathless State.
>
> Dhp 114

When she heard these lines, she was able to shed all fetters and became one of the Arahants, the fully Enlightened Ones.

Ninety-two aeons ago, in one of her former lives at the time of the Buddha Phussa, she had been the wife of a Buddha-to-be. During the time of the last Buddha before the Sage of the Sakyas, namely Buddha Kassapa, she had been a King's daughter who became a nun. (J 409)

In her stanzas in the Therīgāthā she describes the great joy the Buddha imparted to her. Therefore she praises friendship with the Noble and Holy Ones:

> The Sage has emphasized and praised
> Noble friendship for the world.
> If one stays with a Noble Friend,
> Even a fool will become a wise person.
> Stay with them of good heart
> for the wisdom of these ever grows.
> And while one is staying with them,
> From every kind of suffering one is freed.
> Suffering one should know well,
> And how suffering arises and ceases,
> And the Eightfold Path,
> And the Four Noble Truths.
>
> Thī 213–215

The compassion of the Buddha, the most noble friend of all, had saved her from all suffering experienced in this and former lives. She used as her model, the heartrending example of the nun Paṭācārā who had also been afflicted with temporary insanity after the death of not only husband and two sons, but also parents and brothers. Because women's longing for men is so deeply ingrained, the Buddha said, "For a man does the woman strive" (AN 6:52).

From this attachment is born the torture of jealousy, the lack of self-reliance, and the despair of loneliness.

Only when one penetrates a woman's suffering in this way can one realize the full impact of Kisāgotamī's gratitude towards the Buddha who showed her the way. So she says:

> "Woman's state is painful,"
> Declares the Trainer of tameable men.
> "A wife with others is painful
> And once having borne a child,
> Some even cut their throats;
> Others of delicate constitution
> Poison take, then pain again;
> And then there's the baby obstructing the birth,
> Killing the mother too."
>
> Thī 216–217

After she attained to Arahantship, she was able to see her past lives and could now say:

> Miserable woman, your kin all dead
> And limitless suffering you've known.
> So many tears have you shed
> in these many thousands of births.
>
> Thī 220

The third part of her verses finalizes her joy in finding liberation and release from all suffering:

> Wholly developed by me is
> the Eightfold Noble Path going to Deathlessness,
> Nibbāna realized,
> I looked into the Mirror of the Dhamma.
> With dart removed am I,
> the burden laid down, done what was to be done.
> The elder nun Kisāgotamī,
> freed in mind and heart, has chanted this.
>
> Thī 222–223

When Māra,[8] as he had done so often before with other nuns, came to tempt her, to distract her from meditation and asked her whether she was lusting for men now that her child was dead. Discerning the ruse, she replied:

> Passed is the time of my child's death
> And I have fully done with men;
> I do not grieve, nor do I weep,
> And I'm not afraid of you, friend.
> Sensual delight in every way is dead,
> For the mass of darkness is destroyed.
> Defeating the soldiery of death,
> I live free from every taint.
>
> SN 5:3

Addressing Māra as 'friend,' she shows her lack of fear and her equanimity. Grumbling sullenly, Māra disappeared just as before when he had tried in vain to fetter other nuns to the realm of birth and death.

The nun Kisāgotamī, rising to holiness from lowliest birth, was praised by the Buddha as one of the seventy-five greatest nuns, foremost among those who wore coarse garments.[9]

Sources: Thī commentary to her verses; AN 1:24; SN 5:3; Thī 213–223; J 438; Dhp Commentary to Dhp 114 (see *Buddhist Stories from the Dhammapada Commentary* Part 4 (Wheel 354/356) Story No. 52; Ap 2:22.

---

8. Mara is traditionally depicted as the 'tempter' or 'temptation.' While here it is made to appear as if 'he' were an outer force, the Buddha taught that temptation arises in one's own heart and mind because of one's own defilements.

9. She was pre-eminent in ascetic habits and was wont to wear garments of rough fibres (AN 1:24).

Soṇā

With Many Children

There was a housewife in Sāvatthī who had ten children. She was always occupied with giving birth, nursing, upbringing, educating and arranging marriages for her children. Her children were her whole life. She was therefore known as "Soṇā with many children." She was rather like Migara's mother of the same city, though the latter had twenty children. We may find such an abundance of offspring in one family somewhat strange today. However, this was not uncommon in Asia and even in some parts of the West.

Soṇā's husband was a lay follower of the Buddha. After having practised moral conduct according to the precepts for several years while living the household life, he decided that the time had come to enter into the holy life, and so he became a monk. It was not easy for Soṇā to accept this decision, yet she did not waste her time with regrets and sorrow but decided to live a more religiously dedicated life. She called her ten children and their husbands and wives together, turned her considerable wealth over to them, and asked them only for support for her necessities. For a while all went well. She had sufficient support and could spend her time in religious activities.

But soon it happened that the old woman became a burden to her children and children-in-law. They had not been in agreement with their father's decision, and even less did they agree with their mother's devout attitude and religious speech. Indeed, they thought of their parents as foolish because they would not indulge in the pleasures their wealth could purchase. They considered their parents mentally unstable, religious fanatics; this attitude made them despise their mother.

They quickly forgot that they owed all their riches to their mother, that she had lavished many years of care and attention on them. Looking only at the present moment, they considered the old woman a nuisance. The words of the Buddha, that a grateful person is as rare in the world as one who becomes a Noble One, proved true again in this case (AN 3:122; 5:143; 5:195).

The increasing disdain by her children was an even greater pain for Soṇā than the separation from her husband. She became aware that waves of bitterness arose in her, that reproaches and accusations intermingled. She realized that what she had taken to be selfless love, pure mother's love, was in reality self love, coupled with expectations. She had been relying on her children completely and had been convinced that she would be supported by them in her old age as a tribute to her long years of solicitude for them, that gratitude, appreciation and participation in their affairs would be her reward. Had she not looked at her children as an investment then, as an insurance against the fear and loneliness of old age? In this manner, she investigated her motives and found the truth of the Enlightened One's words in herself. Namely, that it was a woman's way not to rely on possessions, power and abilities, but solely on her children, while it was the way of the ascetic to rely on virtue alone (A 6:53).

Her reflections brought her to the decision to enter the Order of Nuns so that she could develop the qualities of selfless love and virtue. Why should she remain in her home where she was only reluctantly accepted? She looked upon the household life as a grey existence and pictured that of a nun as brilliant, and so was ready to follow her husband's path. She became a nun, a Bhikkhunī in the order of the Buddha's followers.

But after a while she realized that she had taken her self-love along. The other nuns criticized her behaviour in many small matters. She had entered the Saṅgha as an old woman and had dozens of habits and peculiarities which were obstacles in this new environment. She was used to doing things in a certain way, and the other nuns did them differently.

Soṇā soon realized that it was not easy to reach noble attainments, and that the Order of Nuns was not the paradise she had envisioned—just as she had not found security with her children. She also understood that she was still held fast by her womanly limitations. It was not enough that her weaknesses were abhorrent to her, and that she was longing for more masculine traits. She also had to know what to do to effect the change. She accepted the fact that she had to make tremendous efforts, not only because she was already advanced in years, but also because until now she had only cultivated female virtues. The masculine characteristics which she was lacking were energy and circumspection. Soṇā did not become discouraged, nor thought of the Path as too difficult. She had the same sincerity and steadfastness as her sister-nun Soma, who said:

> What's it to do with a woman's state
> When the mind, well-composed
> With knowledge after knowledge born,
> Sees into Perfect Dhamma clear?
> For who, indeed, conceives it thus:
> A woman am I, a man am I,
> Or what, then indeed, am I?
> Such a one can Māra still address.
>
> SN 5:2

It became clear to Soṇā that she had to develop courage and strength to win victory over her wilfulness and her credulity. She realized that it was necessary to practise mindfulness and self-observation, and to implant into her memory those teachings which could be at her disposal when needed to counteract her emotions.

What use would be all knowledge and vows if she were carried away by her emotions, and her memory fail her when it was most needed? These were the reasons which strengthened Soṇā's determination and will-power to learn the Buddha's discourses. Through many a night thereby she attained the ability to memorize them. Furthermore, she took pains to serve her sister-nuns in a loving way and to apply the teachings constantly. After having practised in this way for some time, she attained not only the assurance of Non-returner, but became an *Arahant*, fully-enlightened, a state she had hardly dared to hope for in this lifetime.

It happened without any special circumstances to herald it. After she had made a whole-hearted commitment to perfect those abilities which she lacked, no matter what the cost, she drew nearer to her goal day by day. One day she was liberated from the very last fetter. The Buddha said about her that she was foremost of the nuns who had energetic courage (AN 1:24).

In the Therīgāthā she describes her life in five verses:

Ten children having borne
From this bodily congeries,
So I, now weak and old,
Approached a Bhikkhunī.

The Dhamma she taught me—
Groups, sense-spheres and elements,[10]
I heard the Dhamma,
And having shaved my hair, went forth.

While still a probationer
I purified the eye divine;
Former lives I knew,
And where I lived before.

One-pointed, well-composed,
The Signless[11] I developed,
Immediately released,
Unclinging now and quenched!

Knowing the five groups well,
They still exist; but with their roots removed.
Unmovable am I,
On a stable basis sure,
Now rebirth is no more.

Thī 102–106

Soṇā's sister-nuns, who had formerly been her severe critics, and who had thought that because of her age she would not be able to change, now apologized to her sincerely and endeavoured to follow her good example.

Sources: AN 1:24; (Commentary to) Thī 102–106; Ap 2:26.

---

10. The five groups (or aggregates), the twelve sense spheres and the eighteen elements—see Buddhist Dictionary, B.P.S. Kandy, for definition.
11. One of the three gates to freedom, the other two being the Desireless and Emptiness.

Nandā

The Half-Sister of the Awakened One

When she was born, Nandā was lovingly welcomed by her parents—the father of the Buddha and his second wife. Her name means joy, contentment, pleasure, and was given when parents were especially joyful about the arrival of a baby.

Nandā was extremely well-bred, graceful and beautiful. To distinguish her from others by the same name, she was later called 'Rūpa-Nandā'—'one of delightful form,' or sometimes 'Sundarī-Nandā,'—'beautiful Nandā.'

In due course many members of her family—the royal house of the Sakyans—left the household for the homeless life, influenced by the amazing fact that one of their clan had become the fully-enlightened Buddha. Amongst them were her brother, her cousins, and finally her mother, together with many other Sakyan ladies. Thereupon Nandā also took this step, but it is recorded that she did not do it out of confidence in the Teacher and the Teaching, but out of love for her relatives and a feeling of belonging with them.

One can easily imagine the love and respect accorded the graceful half-sister of the Buddha and how touched the people were by the sight of the lovely royal daughter, so near in family ties to the Blessed One, wandering amongst them in the garb of a nun.

But it soon became obvious that this was not a good basis for a nun's life. Nandā's thoughts were mainly directed towards her own beauty and her popularity with the people, traits which were resultants of former good actions. These resultants now became dangers to her, since she forgot to reinforce them with new actions. She felt that she was not living up to the high ideals the people envisioned for her, and that she was far from the goal for which so many noble-born men and women had gone into the homeless life. She was sure that the Blessed One would censure her on account of this. Therefore she managed to evade him for a long time.

One day the Buddha requested all the nuns to come to him, one by one, to receive his teaching, but Nandā did not comply. The Master let her be called specially, and then she appeared before him, ashamed and anxious by her demeanour. The Buddha addressed her and appealed to all her positive qualities so that she listened to him willingly and delighted in his words. When the Blessed One knew that the talk had uplifted her, had made her joyful and ready to accept his teaching, he did not immediately explain the noble truths to her, as is often mentioned in other accounts, frequently resulting in noble attainment to his listener.

Because Nandā was so taken up with her physical beauty, the Buddha used his psychic powers to conjure up the vision of an even more beautiful woman, who then aged visibly and relentlessly before her very eyes. Thereby Nandā could see, compressed within a few moments, what otherwise one can only notice in people through decades—and often because of proximity and habit one does not even fully comprehend: the fading away of youth and beauty, the decay, the appearance of wrinkles and grey hair. The vision affected Nandā deeply; she was shaken to the centre of her being.

After having shown her this graphic picture, the Buddha could explain the law of impermanence to her in such a way that she penetrated the truth of it completely, and thereby attained the knowledge of future liberation—Stream-entry. As a meditation subject the Buddha gave her the contemplation of the impermanence and foulness of the body. She persevered for a long time with this practice "faithful and courageous day and night" (Thī 84), as she described in her verses:

> Sick, impure and foul as well,
> Nandā, see this congeries
> With the unlovely,[12] develop mind
> Well-composed to singleness.
>
> As is that, thus will this likewise be.
> Exhaling foulness, evil smells,
> A thing it is enjoyed[13] by fools.

---

12. The meditations on seeing the body as unattractive, either as parts, or in death. See *Bag of Bones*, Wheel 271-272.
13. Play on her own name, Nandā or Joy, and *abhinandita*.

Diligently considering it,
By day and night thus seeing it,
With my own wisdom having seen,
I turned away, dispassionate.

With my diligence, carefully
I examined the body
And saw this as it really is—
Both within and without.

Unlusting and dispassionate
Within this body then was I
By diligence from fetters freed,
Peaceful was I and quite cool.

Thī 82–86

Because Nandā had been so infatuated with her physical appearance, it had been necessary for her to apply the extreme of meditations on bodily unattractiveness as a countermeasure to find equanimity as balance between the two opposites. For beauty and ugliness are just two kinds of impermanence. Nothing can disturb the cool, peaceful heart ever again.

Later the Buddha raised his half-sister as being the foremost amongst nuns who practised absorption-meditation (*jhāna*). This meant that she not only followed the analytical way of insight, but put emphasis on the experience of tranquillity. Enjoying this pure well-being, she no longer needed any lower enjoyments and soon found indestructible peace. Although she had gone into homelessness because of attachment to her relatives, she became totally free and equal to the One she venerated.

Sources: AN 1:24; (Commentary to) Thī 82–86; Ap 2:25 (54 verses).

Queen Sāmāvatī

In the days when India was the fortunate home of an Awakened One, a husband and wife lived within its borders with an only daughter, who was exceedingly beautiful. Their family life was a happy and harmonious one. Then one day pestilence broke out in their hometown. Amongst those fleeing from the disaster area was also this family with their grown-up daughter.

They went to Kosambī, the capital of the kingdom of Vaṃsa in the valley of the Ganges. The municipality had erected a public eating hall for the refugees. There the daughter, Sāmāvatī, went to obtain food. The first day she took three portions, the second day two portions and on the third day only one portion.

Mitta, the man who was distributing the food, could not resist from asking her somewhat ironically, whether she had finally realized the capacity of her stomach. Sāmāvatī replied quite calmly: on the first day her father had died and so she only needed food for two people; on the second day her mother had succumbed to the dreaded disease, and so she only needed food for herself. The official felt ashamed about his sarcastic remark and wholeheartedly begged her forgiveness. A long conversation ensued. When he found out that she was all alone in the world, he proposed to adopt her as his foster child. She was happy to accept and was now relieved of all worries about her livelihood.

Sāmāvatī immediately began helping her foster father with the distribution of the food and the care of the refugees.

Thanks to her efficiency and circumspection, the former chaos became channelled into orderly activity. Nobody tried to get ahead of others any more, nobody quarrelled, and everyone was content.

Soon the finance minister of the king, Ghosaka, became aware that the public food distribution was taking place without noise and tumult. When he expressed his praise and appreciation to the food distributor, the official replied modestly that his foster daughter was mainly responsible for this. In this way Ghosaka met Sāmāvatī and was so impressed with her noble bearing that he decided to adopt her as his own daughter. His manager consented, even if somewhat woefully, because he did not want to be in the way of Sāmāvatī's fortune. So Ghosaka took her into his house and thereby she became heiress of a vast fortune and mixed with the most exalted circles of the land.

The king, who was living in Kosambī at that time, was Udena. He had two chief consorts. One was Vāsuladattā, whom he had married both for political reasons and because she was very beautiful, but these were her only assets. The second one, Māgandiya, was not only very beautiful but also very clever, but cold and self-centred. So the King was not emotionally contented with his two wives.

One day King Udena met the charming, adopted daughter of his finance minister and fell in love with her at first sight. He felt magically attracted by her loving and generous nature. Sāmāvatī had exactly what was missing in both his other wives. King Udena sent a messenger to Ghosaka and asked him to give Sāmāvatī to him in marriage. Ghosaka was thrown into an emotional upheaval. On the one hand, he loved Sāmāvatī above all else, and she had become indispensable to him. She was the delight of his life. On the other hand, he knew his king's temperament and was afraid to deny him his request. But in the end his attachment to Sāmāvatī won, and he thought: "Better to die than to live without her."

As usual, King Udena lost his temper. In his fury he dismissed Ghosaka from his post as finance minister and banned him from his kingdom, and did not allow Sāmāvatī to accompany him. He took over his minister's property and locked up his magnificent mansion. Sāmāvatī was desolate that Ghosaka had to suffer so much on her account and had lost not only her, but also his home and belongings. Out of compassion for her adopted father, to whom she was devoted with great gratitude, she decided to make an end to this dispute by voluntarily becoming the king's wife. She went to the Palace and informed the king of her decision. The king was immediately appeased and restored Ghosaka to his former position, as well as rescinding all other measures against him.

Because Sāmāvatī had great love for everyone, she had so much inner strength that this decision was not a difficult one for her. It was not important to her where she lived: whether in the house of the finance minister as his favourite daughter, or in the palace as the favourite wife of the king, or in obscurity as when she was in the house of her parents, or as a poor refugee—she always found peace in her own heart and was happy regardless of outer circumstances.

Sāmāvatī's life at the royal court fell into a harmonious pattern. Amongst her servants, there was one, named Khujjuttarā, the 'hunch-backed.' Outwardly she was ill-formed, but otherwise very capable. Everyday the Queen gave her eight gold coins to buy flowers for the women's quarters of the palace. But Khujjuttarā always bought only four coins worth and used the rest for herself. One day when she was buying flowers again for her mistress from the gardener, a monk was taking his meal there. He was of majestic appearance. When he gave a discourse to the gardener after the meal, Khujjuttarā listened. The monk was the Buddha. He directed his discourse in such a way that he spoke directly to Khujjuttarā's heart. And his teaching penetrated into her inner being. Just from hearing this one discourse, so well expounded, she attained Stream-entry. Without quite knowing what had happened to her, she was a totally changed person. The whole world, which had seemed so obvious and real to her until now, appeared as a dream, apart from reality. The first thing she did that day was to buy flowers for all of the eight coins. She regretted her former dishonesty deeply.

When the Queen asked her why there were suddenly so many flowers Khujjuttarā fell at the Queen's feet and confessed her theft. When Sāmāvatī forgave her magnanimously, Khujjuttarā told her what was closest to her heart, namely, that she had heard a discourse by the Buddha, which had changed her life. She could not be specific about the contents of the teaching, but Sāmāvatī could see for herself what a wholesome and healing influence the teaching had had on her servant. She made Khujjuttarā her personal attendant and told her to visit the Monastery every day to listen to the Dhamma and then repeat it to her.

Khujjuttarā had an outstanding memory and what she had heard once, she could repeat verbatim. Later on she made a collection of discourses she had heard from the Buddha or one of his enlightened disciples during these days at Kosambī, and this became the book now called *Itivuttaka* ('It-was-said-thus'), composed of 112 small discourses.

When King Udena once again told his beloved Sāmāvatī that she could wish for anything and he would fulfil it, she wished that the Buddha would come to the palace daily to have his food there and propound his teaching. The king's courier took the message of this perpetual invitation to the Buddha, but he declined and instead sent his cousin Ānanda.

From then on the Venerable Ānanda went to the palace daily for his meal and afterwards gave a Dhamma discourse. The Queen had already been well prepared by Khujjuttarā's reports, and within a short time she understood the meaning and attained to Stream-entry, just as her maid-servant had done.

Now, through their common understanding of the Dhamma, the Queen and the maid became equals. Within a short time, the Teaching spread through the whole of the women's quarters and there was hardly anyone who did not become a disciple of the Awakened One. Even Sāmāvatī's stepfather, the finance minister Ghosaka, was deeply touched by the teaching. Similarly to Anāthapiṇḍika, he donated a large monastery in Kosambī to the Saṅgha, so that the monks would have a secure and satisfying shelter. Every time the Buddha visited Kosambī he stayed in this Monastery named Ghositārāma, and other monks and holy people also would find shelter there.

Through the influence of the Dhamma, Sāmāvatī became determined to develop her abilities more intensively. Her most important asset was the way she could feel sympathy for all beings and could penetrate everyone with loving-kindness and compassion. She was able to develop this faculty so strongly that the Buddha called her the woman lay-disciple most skilled in *mettā* (loving-kindness) (AN 1:19).

This all-pervading love was soon to be tested severely. It happened like this. The second main consort of the king, Māgandiyā, was imbued with virulent hatred against everything 'Buddhist.' Once her father had heard the Buddha preach about unconditional love to all beings, and it had seemed to him that the Buddha was the most worthy one to marry his daughter. In his naive ignorance of the rules of the monks, he offered his daughter to the Buddha as his wife. Māgandiyā was very beautiful and had been desired by many suitors already.

The Buddha declined the offer and with a single verse about the unattractiveness of the body caused her father and mother to attain the fruit of Non-returning. This was the Buddha's verse, as recorded in the Suttanipāta (v. 835):

Having seen craving with discontent and lust,[14]
There was not in me any wish for sex;
How then for this, dung-and-urine filled, that
I would not touch her with my foot.

But Māgandiya thought that the Buddha's rejection of her was an insult and therefore hatred against him and his disciples arose in her. Later she became the wife of King Udena. When he took a third wife, she could willingly accept that, as it was the custom in her day. But that Sāmāvatī had become a disciple of the Buddha and had converted the other women in the palace to his Teaching—this she could not tolerate. Her hatred against everything connected with the Buddha now turned against Sāmāvatī as his representative. She thought up one meanness after another, and her sharp intelligence served only to conjure up new misdeeds.

First she told the king that Sāmāvatī was trying to take his life. But the king was well aware of Sāmāvatī's great love for all beings, so that he did not even take this accusation seriously, barely listened to it, and forgot it almost immediately.

Secondly, Māgandiya ordered one of her maid-servants to spread rumours about the Buddha and his monks in Kosambī, so that Sāmāvatī would also be maligned. With this she was more successful. A wave of aversion struck the whole Order to such an extent that Ānanda suggested to the Buddha that they leave town. The Buddha smiled and said that the purity of the monks would silence all rumours within a week. Hardly had King Udena heard the gossip levelled against the Order, then it had already subsided. Māgandiya's second attempt against Sāmāvatī had failed.

Sometime later Māgandiya had eight specially selected chickens sent to the king and suggested that Sāmāvatī should kill them and prepare them for a meal. Sāmāvatī refused to do this, as she would not kill any living beings. Since the king knew of her all-embracing love, he did not lose his temper, but accepted her decision.

Māgandiya then tried for a fourth time to harm Sāmāvatī. Just prior to the week which King Udena was to spend with Sāmāvatī,

---

14. The three beautiful daughters of Māra (the tempter).

Māgandiyā hid a poisonous snake in Sāmāvatī's chambers, but the poison sacs had been removed. When King Udena discovered the snake, all evidence pointed towards Sāmāvatī. His passionate fury made him lose all control. He reached for his bow and arrow and aimed at Sāmāvatī. But the arrow rebounded from her without doing any harm. His hatred could not influence her loving concern for him, which continued to emanate from her.

When King Udena regained his equilibrium and saw the miracle—that his arrow could not harm Sāmāvatī, he was deeply moved. He asked her forgiveness and was even more convinced of her nobility and faithfulness. He became interested in the teaching which had given such strength to his wife.

When a famous monk, named Piṇḍola Bhāradvāja stayed at the Ghosita Monastery, the king visited him and discussed the teaching with him. He inquired how the young monks could live the celibate life joyously and Piṇḍola explained that, according to the Buddha's advice, they did so by regarding women as their mothers, sisters, and daughters. At the end of the discourse, the king was so impressed that he took refuge in the Buddha and became a lay disciple (SN 35:127).

Sāmāvatī had been thinking about the wonders of the Dhamma and the intricacies of karmic influences. One thing had led to another: she had come to Kosambī as a poor refugee; then the food distributor had given her shelter; the finance minister had taken her on as his daughter; then she became the king's wife; her maid-servant had brought the teaching to her; and she became a disciple and Stream-winner. Subsequently she spread the teaching to all the women in the palace, then to Ghosaka and now lastly also to the king. How convincing Truth was! She often thought in this way and then permeated all beings with loving-kindness, wishing them happiness.

The king now tried more determinedly to control his passionate nature and to subdue greed and hate. His talks with Sāmāvatī were very helpful to him in this respect. Slowly this development culminated in his losing all sexual craving when he was in Sāmāvatī's company, as he was trying to attain the feelings towards women of mother, sister and daughter in himself. While he was not free of sexual desire towards his other wives, he was willing to let Sāmāvatī continue on her Path to emancipation unhindered. Soon she attained to the state of Once-returner and drew nearer and nearer to Non-returner, an attainment which many men and women could achieve in lay-life in those days.

Māgandiyā had suspended her attacks for some time, but continued to ponder how to harm the Buddha through Sāmāvatī. After much brooding, she initiated a plan. She won some of her relatives to her point of view and uttered slander against Sāmāvatī to them. Then she proposed to kill her. So that it would not attract attention, but would appear to be an accident, the whole women's palace was to be set on fire. The plan was worked out in all details. Māgandiyā left town some time beforehand, so that no suspicion could fall on her.

This deed of arson resulted in sky-high flames which demolished the wooden palace totally. All the women residing in it were killed, including Sāmāvatī. The news of this disaster spread around town very quickly. No other topic of conversation could be heard there. Several monks who had not been ordained very long were also affected by the agitation and, after their almsround, they went to the Buddha and inquired what would be the future rebirth of these women lay disciples with Sāmāvatī as their leader.

The Awakened One calmed their excited hearts and diverted their curiosity about this most interesting question of rebirth by answering very briefly: "Amongst these women, O monks, there are some disciples who are Stream-winners, some who are Once-returners and some who are Non-returners. None of these lay disciples failed to receive the fruits of their past deeds" (Ud 7. 10).

The Buddha mentioned here the first three fruits of the Dhamma: Stream-entry, Once-returner and Non-returner. All these disciples were safe from rebirth below the human realm, and each one was securely going towards the final goal of total liberation. This was the most important aspect of their lives and deaths, and the Buddha would not elucidate any further details. Once he mentioned to Ānanda that it was a vexation for the Enlightened One to explain the future births of all disciples who died (DN 16.11).

The Buddha later explained to some monks who were discussing how 'unjust' it was that these faithful disciples should die such a terrible death, that the women experienced this because of a joint deed they had committed many life-times ago. Once

Sāmāvatī had been Queen of Benares. She had gone with her ladies-in-waiting to bathe and feeling cold, she asked that a bush be burned to give some warmth. She saw only too late that a monk—a Pacceka Buddha—was sitting immobile within the bush; he was not harmed, however, because one cannot kill Awakened Ones. The women did not know this and feared that they would be blamed for having made a fire without due caution. Thereupon Sāmāvatī had the deluded idea to pour oil over this monk who was sitting in total absorption, so that burning him would obliterate their mistake. This plan could not succeed however, but the bad intention and attempt had to carry karmic resultants. In this lifetime the ripening of the result had taken place.

The Buddha has declared that one of the favourable results of the practice of *mettā* (loving-kindness) is the fact that fire, poison and weapons do no harm to the practitioner. This has to be understood in such a way: during the actual emanation of loving-kindness the one who manifests this radiance cannot be hurt, just as Sāmāvatī proved when the king's arrow did not penetrate her.

But at other times fire could incinerate her body. Sāmāvatī had become a Non-returner, and was therefore free of all sensual desire and hate and no longer identified with her body. Her radiant, soft heart was imbued with love and compassion due to developing the four divine abidings[15] and was unassailable and untouched by the fire. Her inner being could not be burned and that which was burned was the body only. It is a rare happening that one of the Holy Ones is murdered (see Mahāmoggallāna, Kāḷudāyi) or that one of the Buddhas is threatened with murder (see Devadatta's attempt on the Buddha Gotama), and equally rare is it to find that one perfected in *mettā* and attained to Non-returner should die a violent death. All three types of persons, however, have in common that their hearts can no longer be swayed by this violence.

Sāmāvatī's last words were: "It would not be an easy matter, even with the knowledge of a Buddha, to determine exactly the number of times our bodies have thus been burned with fire as we have passed from birth to birth in the round of existences which

---

15. Four divine abidings: loving-kindness, compassion, sympathetic joy and equanimity.

has no conceivable beginning. Therefore, be heedful!" Those ladies meditated on painful feeling and so gained the Noble Paths and Fruits.

Two thousand years after the Parinibbāna of the Buddha, in 1582, soldiers burned a Buddhist Monastery in Japan and all the monks inside were burned to death. The last thing the soldiers heard before everything burned down were the words of the abbot:

> Who has liberated heart and mind,
> For him fire is only a cool wind.

Referring to the tragedy of the fire at Kosambī, the Buddha spoke the following verse to the monks:

> The world is in delusion's grip,
> Its form is seen as real;
> The fool is in the grip of assets,[16]
> Wrapped about with gloom,
> Both seem to last forever
> But nothing is there for one who sees.
>
> (Ud 7.10)

King Udena was overwhelmed with grief at Sāmāvatī's death and kept brooding about who could be the perpetrator of this ghastly deed. He came to the conclusion that it must have been Māgandiya. He did not want to question her directly because she would deny it. So he thought of a ruse. He said to his Ministers: "Until now I have always been apprehensive, because Sāmāvatī was forever seeking an occasion to slay me. But now I shall be able to sleep in peace." The Ministers asked the king who it could have been that had done this deed. "Only someone who really loves me," the king replied. Māgandiya had been standing near and, when she heard that, she came forward and proudly admitted that she alone was responsible for the fire and the death of the women and Sāmāvatī. The king said that he would grant her and all her relatives a boon for this.

---

16. Assets, *Upadhi:* the basis for life and continued birth and death.

When all the relatives were assembled, the king had them burned publicly and then had the earth ploughed under so that all traces of the ashes were destroyed. He had Māgandiyā executed as a mass-murderess, which was his duty and responsibility, but his fury knew no bounds and he still looked for revenge. He had her killed with utmost cruelty. She died an excruciating death, which was only a foretaste of the tortures awaiting her in the nether world, after which she would have to roam in *saṃsāra* for a long, long time to come.

Soon King Udena regretted his revengeful and cruel deed. Again and again he saw Sāmāvatī's face in front of him, full of love for all beings, even for her enemies. He felt that by his violent fury he had removed himself from her, even further than her death had done. He began to control his temper more and more and to follow the Buddha's teachings ardently.

Two women, who had been friends of Sāmāvatī, were so moved by this tragedy and saw the impermanence of all earthly things so clearly, that they entered the Order of Nuns. One of them soon became an *Arahant*, fully enlightened, and the other one attained the goal after twenty-five years of practice (Thī 37 & 39).

Sāmāvatī, however, was reborn in the realm of the Pure Abodes, where she would be able to reach Nibbāna. The different results of love and hate could be seen with exemplary clarity in the lives and deaths of these two queens. When one day the monks were discussing who was alive and who dead, the Buddha said that Māgandiyā, while living was dead already; while Sāmāvatī, though dead, was truly alive, and he spoke these verses:

> Heedfulness—the path to the Deathless,
> Heedlessness—the path to death,
> The heedful ones do not die;
> The heedless are likened to the dead.
>
> The wise then, recognizing this
> As the distinction of heedfulness,
> In heedfulness rejoice, delighting
> In the realm of Noble Ones.

They meditate persistently,
Constantly they firmly strive
The steadfast to reach Nibbāna,
The Unexcelled Security from bonds.

Dhp 21–23

The Buddha declared Sāmāvatī to be foremost among those female lay disciples who dwell in loving-kindness (*mettā*).

Sources: Dhammapada Commentary to vv 21–23; Commentary to Aṅguttara Nikāya Vol. I (on those Foremost); *Path of Purification*, p. 417.

Paṭācārā

Preserver of the Vinaya

Paṭācārā was the beautiful daughter of a very wealthy merchant of Sāvatthī. When she was sixteen years old, her parents put her in a seven-story high tower on the top floor surrounded by guards to prevent her from keeping company with any young man. In spite of this precaution, she became involved in a love affair with a servant in her parents' house.

When her parents arranged a marriage for her with a young man of equal social standing, she decided to elope with her lover. She escaped from the tower by disguising herself, and the young couple went to live in a village far away from Sāvatthī. The husband farmed, and the young wife had to do all the menial chores which formerly had been performed by her parents' servants. Thus she reaped the results of her deed.

When she became pregnant, she begged her husband to take her to her parents' house to give birth there, saying to him that father and mother always have a soft spot in their hearts for their child, no matter what has happened. However, her husband refused on the grounds that her parents would surely subject him to torture or imprisonment. When she realized that he would not give in to her pleas, she decided to make her way to her parents by herself. When the husband found her gone and was told by the neighbours of her decision, he followed her and tried to persuade her to return. However she would not listen to him.

Before they could reach Sāvatthī, the birth pains started, and soon a baby son was born. As there was no more reason to go to her parents' house, they turned back and resumed their family life in the village.

Sometime later she became pregnant again. And again she requested her husband to take her home to her parents. Again he refused, and again she took matters in her own hands and started off, carrying the older child. When her husband followed her and pleaded with her to return with him, she would not listen, but continued on her way. A fearful storm arose, quite out of season, with thunder and lightning and incessant rain. Just then her birth pains started, and she asked her husband to find her some shelter.

The husband went searching for material for a shelter and set about to chop down some saplings. A poisonous snake bit him at that moment and he fell dead instantly. Paṭācārā waited for him in vain and after having suffered birth pains, she gave birth to a second son. Both children screamed at the top of their lungs because of the buffeting of the storm, so the mother protected them with her own body all night long. In the morning she placed the new-born baby on her hip, gave a finger to the older child and set out upon the path her husband had taken with the words: "Come, dear child, your father has left us." After a few steps she found her husband lying dead, his body rigid. She wailed and lamented and blamed herself for his death.

She continued on her journey to her parents' house but when she came to the river Aciravati, it was swollen waist-deep on account of the rain. She was too weak to wade across with both children, so she left the older child on the near bank and carried the baby across to the other side. Then she returned to take the first-born across. When she was mid-stream, an eagle saw the new born baby and mistook it for a piece of meat. It came swooping down and, in spite of Paṭācārā's cries and screams, flew off with the baby in its talons.

The older boy saw his mother stop in the middle of the river and heard her loud yells. He thought she was calling him and started out after her. Immediately, he was swept off by the strong current.

Wailing and lamenting Paṭācārā went on her way, half-crazed by the triple tragedy that had befallen her, losing husband and both sons within one day. As she came nearer to Sāvatthī, she met a traveller who was just coming from the city. She inquired about her family from him but at first he refused to answer her. When she insisted, he finally had to tell her that her parent' house had collapsed in the storm, killing both of them as well as her brother, and that the cremation was just taking place.

When she heard that, the grief was too much to bear and she went mad. She tore off her clothes, wandered around weeping and wailing, not knowing what she was doing or where she was going. People pelted her with stones and rubbish and chased her out of the way.

At that time the Buddha was staying at the Jeta Grove, Anāthapiṇḍika's Monastery. He saw Paṭācārā approaching from afar and recognized that in a past life she had made an earnest resolve to become a nun well versed in the Law. Therefore, he instructed his disciples not to obstruct her, but to let her enter and come near him. As soon as she was close to the Buddha, through his supernormal powers, she regained her right mind. Then she also became aware of being naked and in her shame she crouched upon the ground. One of the lay-followers threw her a cloak and after she had wrapped herself in it, she prostrated at the feet of the Buddha. Then she recounted to him the tragedy that had befallen her.

The Teacher listened to her with compassion and then made it clear to her that these painful experiences she had gone through were only tiny drops in the ocean of impermanence in which all beings drown by their attachment. He told her that all through many existences, she had wept more tears over the loss of dear ones than could be contained in the waters of the four oceans. He said:

> But little water do the oceans four contain,
> Compared with all the tears that man hath shed,
> By sorrow smitten and by suffering distraught.
> Woman, are you still heedless?

This exposition of the Awakened One penetrated her mind so deeply that at that moment she could completely grasp the impermanence of all conditioned things.

When the Enlightened One had finished his teaching she had attained the certainty of future liberation by becoming a Stream-winner. She practised diligently and soon realized final deliverance. She said:

> With ploughs the fields are ploughed;
> With seed the earth is sown;
> Thus wives and children feed;
> So young men win their wealth.

Then why do I, of virtue pure,
Doing the Master's Teaching,
Not lazy nor proud,
Nibbāna not attain?

Having washed my feet,
Then I watched that water,
Noticing the foot-water
Flowing from high to low.
With that the mind was calmed
Just as a noble, thoroughbred horse.

Having taken my lamp,
I went into my hut,
Inspected the sleeping-place,
Then sat upon the couch.

Having taken a pin,
I pushed the wick right down, and
Just as the lamp went out,
So all delusion of the heart went too.

Thī 112–116

It had been enough for her to see the water trickle down the slope, to recognize the whole of existence, each life a longer or shorter trickle in the flood of craving. There were those that lived a short time like her children, those—like her husband—who lived a little longer, or her parents who lived longer yet. But all passed by in constant change, in a never-ending rising and ceasing. This thought process gave her so much detachment, that she attained to total emancipation the following night.

The Buddha said that Paṭācārā was the foremost 'Keeper of the Vinaya' amongst the Nuns. Paṭācārā was thereby the female counterpart of the monk Upali. That she had chosen the 'Rules of Conduct' as her central discipline is easy to understand, because the results of her former indulgences had become bitterly obvious to her.

She learned in the Saṅgha that an intensive study of the rules was necessary and purifying, and brought with it the security and safety of self-discipline; she learned not to become complacent through well-being, or anxious and confused through suffering. Because of her own experiences she had gained a deep understanding for the human predicament and could be of great assistance to her fellow nuns. She was a great comfort to those who came to her in difficulties. The nun Candā said that Paṭācārā showed her the right path out of compassion and helped her to achieve emancipation (Th 125). Another nun, Uttarā II, reported how Paṭācārā spoke to the group of nuns about conduct and discipline:

> Having established mind,
> One-pointed, well-developed,
> Investigate formations
> As other, not as self.
>
> Thī 177

Uttarā took Paṭācārā's words to heart and said:

> When I heard these words—
> Paṭācārā's advice,
> After washing my feet—
> I sat down alone.
>
> Thī 178

Thereby this nun, too, was able to attain to the three 'True Knowledges' (*vijja*) and final liberation. In the Therīgāthā we have a record of Paṭācārā's instructions to the nuns and their resultant gains:

> Having taken flails,
> Young men thresh the corn.
> Thus wives and children feed;
> So young men win their wealth.
>
> So likewise as to Buddha's Teachings,
> From doing which there's no remorse.
> Quickly cleanse your feet
> And sit you down alone.
> Devote yourselves to calm of mind,
> And thus do Buddha's Teachings.
>
> When they heard these words—
> Paṭācārā's instructions,

Having washed their feet,
They sat down, each one alone,
Devoted themselves to calm of mind,
And thus followed the Buddha's Teachings.

In the night's first watch[17]
Past births were remembered;
In the middle watch of the night
The divine eye was purified;
In the night's last watch
They rent asunder the mass of gloom.

Having risen, they bowed at her feet,
Her instructions having done;
We shall live revering you
Like the thirty gods to Indra,
Undefeated in war.
We are with triple knowledge true
And gone are all the taints.

Thī 117–121

Paṭācārā was able to effect the change from a frivolous young girl to a Saṅgha Elder so quickly, because from previous births she had already possessed this faculty. During the previous Buddha's existence, it is said that she had been a nun and had lived the holy life for many, many years. The insights gained thereby had been hidden through her actions in subsequent lives. But when the next Buddha appeared in the world, she quickly found her way to him, the reason unbeknown to herself, spurred on by her suffering. Relentlessly attracted to the Awakened One and his doctrine, she entered into the homeless life and soon attained to eternal freedom.

Sources: AN 1:24; (Commentary to) Thī 112–121, 125, 175, 178; Ap. 2:20; J 547; Dhp Commentary to Dhp 113 (See *Buddhist Stories from the Dhammapada Commentary* Part 4 (*Wheel* 354/356) Story No. 53.)

---

17. First watch of the night: 6–10 pm; middle watch: 10 pm–2 am; last watch: 2–6 am.

The Buddhist Layman

Four essays by
R. Bogoda, Susan Elbaum Jootla,
and M.O'C. Walshe

Copyright © Kandy; Buddhist Publication Society, (1982)

The Lotus-like Lay-follower

Thus spoke the Buddha:

> A lay-follower (*upāsaka*) who has five qualities is a jewel of a lay-follower, is like a lily, like a lotus. What are these five qualities? He has faith; he is virtuous; he is not superstitious; he believes in action (*kamma*) and not in luck or omen; he does not seek outside (of the Order) for those worthy of support and does not attend there first.

—AN 5.175

Ten Virtues of the Lay-follower

> These ten, great King, are the virtues of the lay-follower:
>
> He shares the joys and sorrows of the Order;[1]
> He places the Dhamma first;[2]
> He enjoys giving according to his ability;
> If he sees a decline in the Dispensation of the Teaching of the Buddha, he strives for its strong growth;
> He has right views, disregarding belief in superstitions and omens; he will not accept any other teacher, not even for the sake of his life;
> He guards his deeds and words;
> He loves and cherishes peace and concord;
> He is not envious or jealous;
> He does not live a Buddhist life by way of deception or hypocrisy;
> He has gone for refuge to the Buddha, Dhamma, and Saṅgha.

—Milindapañhā, Ch. IV

---

1. That is, he is concerned about the welfare of the monastic community, with which he is connected.
2. That is, he places the Dhamma before self and worldly considerations; this refers to the three dominant influences (*adhipateyya*), Dhamma being the third, after *atta* (self) and *loka* (world); see AN 3.40.

Principles of Lay Buddhism

by R. Bogoda

Introduction

Buddhism should not be thought to be a teaching for monks only, as it is sometimes wrongly conceived. In a large number of his discourses, the Buddha has given practical guidance for the lay life and sound advice to cope with life's difficulties. Many of our problems and difficulties for which some people blame circumstances and chance, are, if correctly viewed, the result of ignorance or negligence. They could be well avoided or overcome by knowledge and diligence, yet of course, worldly happiness and security are never perfect; they are always a matter of degree, for in the fleeting there is nothing truly firm.

The central problem of a lay Buddhist is how to combine personal progress in worldly matters with moral principles. He strives to achieve this by building his life on the foundation of the Fourth Noble Truth, the Noble Eightfold Path, and to shape his activities in accordance with it. The first step of this Path is Right Understanding; by developing a life style in accordance with it, the other factors of the Path result from it, namely: Right Thoughts, Right Speech, Right Action, Right Livelihood, Right Effort, Right Mindfulness, and Right Concentration. The eight steps of the Path fall into the three divisions of Wisdom (the first two), Morality (the second three), and Mental Culture (the last three). The order of development is, however, Morality (*sīla*), Mental Culture (*samādhi*), and Wisdom (*paññā*). The Path outlines the practice of Buddhism, leading to its ultimate goal—*Nibbāna*.

As a householder, the Buddhist is particularly concerned with Morality. Right Understanding, however, is the prerequisite. Right Effort is the training of the will, and Right Mindfulness, the all-round helper. Progress, to a lay Buddhist, means the development of the whole man in society. It is, therefore, an advance on many fronts—the economic, the moral, and the spiritual, the first, not as an end in itself, but as a means to an end: the full flowing of the human being in the onward-carrying stream of Buddhist ideas and ideals.

A Practical Guide

Right Understanding is the beginning and the end of Buddhism, without which, one's vision is dimmed and the way is lost, all effort misguided and misdirected. Right Understanding, in the context of the layman's Dhamma, provides a sound philosophy of life.

Right Understanding, the first step of the Path, is seeing life as it really is: the objective understanding of the nature of things as it truly is (*yathābhūtañāṇadassana*). All things that have arisen, including the so-called being, are nothing but incessant change (*anicca*), therefore unsatisfactory (*dukkha*) and productive of suffering. It follows then that what is both impermanent and pain-laden cannot conceal within it anything that is solid, substantial, or unchanging—an eternal soul or an imminent abiding principle (*anattā*).

Right Understanding implies further a knowledge of the working of *kamma*—the moral law of cause and effect. We reap what we sow, in proportion to the sowing. Good begets good and evil, evil. Kamma operates objectively, and the results show themselves here or in the hereafter. That is to say, consequences follow causes whether one believes in *kamma* or not, even as a fall from a height will result in injury or even death, irrespective of one's personal belief or disbelief in the force of gravity.

Kamma is intentional or volitional action; *vipāka* is the fruit or result, and every action affects character for good or bad. We know that actions consciously performed again and again tend to become unconscious or automatic habits. They, in turn, whether good or bad, become second nature. They more or less shape or mould the character of a person. Likewise, the unconscious or latent tendencies in us, including inborn human instincts, are merely the results of actions done repeatedly in innumerable past lives extending far beyond childhood and the formative years of the present life. Kamma includes both past and present action. It is neither fate nor predestination.

A Buddhist views life in terms of cause and effect, his own birth included. Existence (life) was not thrust on him by an unseen Deity to whose will he must blindly bend nor by parents, for the mere fusing of two cells from mother and father does not by itself produce life. It was of his own causing of his own choice: the kammic energy generated from the past birth produced life—made real the potential, in the appropriate sperm and ovum of his human parents at the moment of conception, endowing the new life with initial consciousness (*paṭisandhiviññāṇa*), using the mechanism of heredity, duly modified, if necessary.

The arising of a being here then means the passing away of another elsewhere. This changing personality that constitutes "me"—the physical and mental make-up that is "I"—the very environment into which I was born, in which I acted and reacted is more of my own doing, of my own choice, of my own *kamma*, of one's past actions and thoughts. It is just, it is fair, it is right; what is, is the sum of what *was*; effects exactly balance causes. One gets precisely what one deserves, even as the sum of two plus two is four, never more nor less.

Enough of the past that is dead. What remains is the ever-present *now*, not even the future that's still unborn. The past is dead, yet influences the present, but does not determine it. The past and the present, in turn, influence the future that is yet to be. Only the present is real. The responsibility of using the present for good or bad lies with each individual. And the future, still unborn, is one's to shape. The so-called being which, in fact, is merely a conflux of mind and matter, is, therefore, born of, supported by, and heir to, his *kamma*.

One is driven to produce *kamma* by *taṇhā* or desire which itself is threefold. Where there is *taṇhā*, there is ignorance (*avijjā*)—blindness to the real nature of life; and where there is ignorance, there is *taṇhā* or craving. They coexist, just as the heat and light of a flame are inseparable. And the beginning of ignorance (*avijjā*) cannot be known.

Because of this lack of understanding of things as they truly are, we, often unmindful of the rights of others, desire for, grasp at, cling to, the wrong sorts of things: the pleasures that money can buy, power over others, fame and name, wishing to go on living forever. We hope that pleasures will be permanent, satisfying and solid, but find them to be passing, unsatisfying, and empty—as hollow as a bamboo when split. The result is frustration and disappointment, dis-ease and an irritating sense of inadequacy and insufficiency. If we don't get all our wishes, we react with hate or take shelter in a world of delusive unreality or fantasy.

To remedy this, we must correct our understanding and thinking, and see in our own experiences, so near to us, things as they truly are, and first reduce, and finally remove all shades of craving or desire that are the causes of this restlessness and discontent. This is not easy, but when one does so by treading the noble Eightfold path, one reaches a state of perfection and calm (*Nibbāna*) thereby bringing to an end the pain-laden cycle of birth and death.

As long as there is desire, birth leads to death, and death to birth, even as an exit is also an entrance. Each subsequent individual born is not the same as the preceding one, nor is it entirely different (*naca so naca aññ o*) but only a continuity; that is to say, each succeeding birth depends upon, or emerges from, the preceding one. And both, birth and death, are but the two sides of the same coin, life. The opposite of life is not death, as some fondly believe, but rest—the rest and peace of *Nibbāna*, in contrast to the restlessness and turmoil that is life.

Kamma, as we have seen, is volitional action. It implies making choices or decisions between, broadly speaking, skilful (*kusala*) and unskilful (*akusala*) actions. The former are rooted in generosity, loving-kindness, and wisdom leading to happiness and progress, and therefore, to be cultivated again and again in one's life. The good actions are Generosity, Morality, Meditation, Reverence, Service, Transference of merit, Rejoicing in other's good actions, Hearing the Doctrine, Expounding the Doctrine, and Straightening one's views. The unskilled actions are rooted in greed, hate and delusion, leading to pain, grief and decline, and therefore, to be avoided. There are ten such actions: killing, stealing, sexual misconduct, lying, slandering, harsh speech, gossip, covetousness, ill-will and false views. This division of actions is a natural outcome of the Universal Law of Kamma; Kamma is one of the fixed orders of existence.

Life is like a ladder. The human being occupies the middle steps. Above are the celestial worlds of bliss; below, the woeful states of sorrow. With every choice, one moves upward or downward, ascends or descends, for each one is evolved according to one's own actions. Beings are not only owners of *kamma* but also their heirs. Actions fashion not only one's fortune, how one shall be born, dividing beings into inferior or superior, in health, wealth, wisdom, and the like, but also shapes one's future, where one shall be born, whether in the human, heavenly or animal world. In short, one can progress or regress from the human state.

A proper understanding of the Buddhist doctrine of *kamma* and rebirth can, therefore, improve and elevate the character of a person. Buddhism teaches, above all, moral responsibility—to be mindful of one's actions, because of the inevitability of action being followed by reaction. One therefore strives one's best to avoid evil and to do good for one's own welfare, as well as for the benefit of others. This conduct leads to peace within and without. It promotes soberness of mind and habit together with self-respect and self-reliance. Finally, this teaching fosters in us a feeling of all-embracing kindness and tolerance toward all living beings and keeps us away from cruelty, hate, and conflict.

Man, as a whole, has not made a steady progress toward moral and spiritual perfection. But the individual can pursue the ideal of a perfect man—the *Arahant*—free from greed, hate, and delusion, by treading the Noble Eightfold Path comprising Sublime Conduct, Mental Culture and Intuitive Insight (or wisdom). It is the perfection of human living by perfecting one's understanding and purifying one's mind. It is to *know* the Truth, *do* the Truth and *become* the Truth. Such a one has gone beyond the force of *all* rebirth-producing *kamma*, skilful and unskilful. He has attained the highest—*Nibbāna*.

As the Blessed One teaches with incomparable beauty:

Sabbapāpassa akaraṇam,
kusalassa upasampada
Sacittapariyodapanaṃ:
Etam Buddhanusāsanam

To avoid evil,
To do good,
To purify the mind,
This is the advice of all the Buddhas.

This, in brief and simple outline, is the Teaching of the Buddha as it affects the householder's life. It is at once an ideal and a method. As an ideal, it aims at the evolution of a perfect Man—synonymous with the attainment of *Nibbāna*—in this very life itself, by one's own efforts. As a method, it teaches us that the ideal can become real only by the systematic practice and development of the Noble Eightfold Path, at the two levels—that of the monk and that of the layman. Each develops according to his ability and each according to his needs, whereby man, using the instrument of mind, by his own endeavour, comes to *know* himself, *train* himself, and *free* himself from the thraldom of base desire, the blindness of hate, and the mist of a delusive self, to win the highest of all freedoms—freedom from error and ignorance.

In this Noble Teaching, there is no intellectual error, based as it is on reason and, in keeping with the finding of science, no moral blindness; for its ethics are truly lofty, with a rational basis: namely, evolution in terms of *kamma*.

That Buddhism is eminently practicable is clearly shown by the example of the great Indian Emperor Asoka, when Buddhism became the shaping ideal of the State, and Buddhist ideas and ideals were used to build a just and righteous society. Thus ushering in a period of great prosperity, material, moral, and spiritual. It is the only true solution to the manifold problems in the modern world. To this we must now turn.

Social and Economic Aspects

Buddha was a rebel. He rebelled against the way of thought, and the way of life, of his age.

To the philosophical concept of life as dynamic change (*anicca*) of no being but becoming (*bhava*), no thinker but thought, no doer but deed—he added its social equivalent: the doctrine of social fluidity and equality based on nobility of conduct. As the Buddha stated:

> *Not by birth is one an outcaste*
> *Not by birth is one a Brahman.*
> *By deeds is one an outcaste,*
> *By deeds is one a Brahman.*

and again,

A birth no Brahman, nor non-Brahman makes;
'Tis life and doing that mold the Brahman true.
Their lives mould farmers, tradesmen, merchants, serfs;
Their lives mold robbers, soldiers, chaplains, kings.

What matters then is not the womb from which one came nor the societal class into which one was born, but the moral quality of one's actions. As a tree is judged by its fruit, so shall a man be judged by his deeds.

In this way, the doors of the Deathless and of the unconditioned freedom beyond, and of social freedom here on earth, were thrown open to all, regardless of caste, colour, or class. In his teaching all men unite, lose identity, even as do the waters of the rivers that flow into the sea. No caste, class, or race privileges existed among his lay followers or in the Order of the Saṅgha that he founded—a fitting complement to the doctrine of *anattā*.

For the Buddha, all men are one in that they belong to one species. Social classes and castes are nothing but functional or occupational groupings, neither fixed nor inevitable. They are divisions of society, man-made, subject to change and resulting from social and historical factors. A social doctrine based on the alleged superiority of any caste, class, or race, and advocating to keep it dominant by the use of force, must necessarily lead to the perpetuation of social tensions and conflict, and will never bring about harmony and the fraternity of men.

The Buddha's doctrine of equality does not, however, imply that all men are alike physically or mentally. That would be identity. It does mean that each one should be treated equally with human dignity, and given an equal chance to develop the faculties latent in each, as all are capable of moral and spiritual progress, and of human perfection, in view of the common capacity and capability of humanity. Thus the Buddha's teaching of a classless society requires the progressive refinement of man's nature, as shown by his actions, and the development of his character.

The Buddha was not only the first thinker in known history to teach the doctrine of human equality, but also the first humanist who attempted to abolish slavery, in which term is also included the traffic in, and the sale of, females for commercial purposes. In fact, this is a prohibited trade for his followers.

The character of a society depends on the beliefs and practices of its people as well as on its economy. An economic system based on Buddhist ethics and principles, therefore, seems the only alternative. The true nature of man is that he is not only a thinking and feeling creature, but also a striving creature, with higher aspirations and ideals. If he is aggressive and assertive, he is also cooperative and creative. He is forever making not only things, but himself. And the making of oneself by perfecting the art of living, is the noblest of all creative aspirations, yielding the highest happiness and satisfaction in life.

Progress in the material side of life alone is not enough for human happiness, as illustrated by today's affluent societies. The pursuit of material pleasures, in the hope that by multiplying them they will thereby become permanent, is a profitless chase, akin to chasing one's shadow: the faster one runs, the faster it eludes. True happiness, contentment, and harmony come from an emancipated mind. Any economic system is therefore, unsatisfactory, if based on a wrong set of values and attitudes, and will fail in the fulfilment of its promises.

The only effective remedy for the economic and social ills of the modern world is a more rational and balanced economic structure based on Buddhist ideas and ideals. In a Buddhist economic system[3] the people deliberately use the state power to maximize welfare, both economic and social, from a given national income. The methods employed are threefold: economic planning, a suitable fiscal policy, and a comprehensive network of social services. Thus assuring to every member of the community, as a right, and as a badge of citizenship and fellowship, the essentials of civilized living, such as minimum standards of economic security, health care, housing, and education, without which a citizen cannot realize his humanity in full.

In such a system, production, distribution, and values take a different meaning in a new context. Economic activity will be pursued, not as an end in itself, but a means to an end—the all-

---

3. See E.F.S. Schumacher, *Small is Beautiful* (Blond & Briggs, London, 1973), p. 48ff., Buddhist Economics; H.N.S. Karunatilaka, *This Confused Society* (Buddhist Information Centre, Colombo, 1976); Dr. Padmasiri de Silva, *Buddhist Economics* (Bodhi Leaves No. B. 69).

round development of man himself. There should be a revision of values. A person's worth, for instance, ought not be measured in terms of what he *has* but on what he *is*. In short, man or the majority of men in society should be helped to see life in perspective. Knowledge and discipline may transform a society into a workshop or a military camp, but it is the cultivation of a proper sense of values that will make it truly civilized. Perhaps this may be the clue to the paradox of the Western civilization that knows how to go through space and sail across the seas, but not how to live on earth in peace. It is true that such a change of heart and system may, in the present context of the world, take a long time to realize. But what else is the alternative? It is futile to think that reform by revolution will remedy the ills of the world.

In the opening stanza of the Dhammapada the Buddha declared the supremacy of mind over matter: Mind precedes things, dominates them, creates them (*Manopubbaṅgamā dhammā manoseṭṭhā manomayā*).

However, this must not be interpreted to mean that Buddhism is against social and economic reform. It is far from it. Buddhism stands for a society of equals, in which justice and ethical principles shall supplant privilege and chaos. But reform must take place by peaceful persuasion and education, without resorting to violence; worthy aims must be realized by worthy means, even as democracy must be maintained by the methods of democracy.

Buddhism concedes that the economic environment influences character, but denies that it determines it. A person can use his free will, within limits, and act according to his conscience irrespective of the social structure to which he belongs. It all depends on mind and its development.

Society does not stand still. Like any other conditioned phenomenon, it changes constantly and Buddhism teaches us that we cannot change society as something different from its members. Social progress is their progress, social regress their regress. If the individual perfects his life, thinks and acts clearly, lives in accordance with the Dhamma and the moral law of *kamma*, to that extent will there be social order and discipline. Initial improvements from within will result in corresponding changes without. Social order and discipline follow, not precede, the state of mind of the individuals comprising that society. Society reflects the character of its people; the better the people, the better the society. Every society is a projection or extension of the collective personality of its members.

But humanity in the mass can be influenced for good by the example of a few really noble and selfless men with vision and wisdom, with ideas and ideals to live for and to die for. They provide the guiding star round which others, too timid to lead but strong enough to follow, cluster around and become willing followers. It is these few who set the standards for the many at the bottom, and their impact and influence on the way of life, and thought, of the human race can be tremendous. The message they bring carries with it the indelible stamp of truth and is, therefore, never obsolete.

Most outstanding among the great teachers is the Buddha Gotama. It is through his Teachings that all the Buddhist nations, including Sri Lanka, were molded, and into the fabric of national life were woven the strands of his Teaching.

It is then the duty of every genuine Buddhist to help to make known, far and wide, the Teaching of the Buddha in all its many aspects, and thereby make possible tomorrow the seemingly impossible of today—a new and just socio-economic order based on Buddhist ethics, principles, and practices. Such a society will be both democratic and socialistic, with liberty, equality, fraternity, and economic security for all, not as ends in themselves but as means to an end—the full development of man into a well-rounded, happy human being in the setting of the Teaching of Gotama the Buddha, Guide Incomparable to a troubled world.

Buddhism and Daily Life

A follower of the Buddha learns to view life realistically, which enables him to adjust to everything that comes his way. Buddhism tells him the meaning and purpose of existence and his place in the scheme of things. It suggests the lines of conduct, supported by cogent reasons, by which he should live his daily life. It clarifies what his attitude should be to specific matters like self, job, sex, and society. Thus it assists him in the business of living, for to lead a full life four fundamental adjustments have to be made. He must be happily adjusted to himself and the world, his occupation, his family, and his fellow beings.

(a) Himself and the World

A Buddhist tries to see things as they really are. He remembers the instability of everything and understands the inherent danger in expecting to find permanence in existence. In this way, he strives to insulate himself from potential disappointments. So, a discerning lay Buddhist is not unduly elated or upset by the eight worldly conditions of gain and loss, honour and dishonour, praise and blame, pleasure and pain. He does not expect too much from others, nor from life, and recognizes that it is only human to have one's share of life's ups and downs.

He looks at life's events in terms of cause and effect, however unpleasant or painful they may be. An understanding layman accepts *dukkha* as the results of his own *kamma*—probably a past unskilful (*akusala*) action ripening in the present.

He sees the connection between craving and suffering and therefore tries to reduce both the intensity and variety. As the Dhammapada states:

From craving springs grief, from craving springs fear,
For him who is wholly free from craving, there is no grief—
whence fear?

—Dhp 215

Therefore, he is mindful of a scale of values—knowing clearly what is really important to him as a Buddhist layman, what is desirable but not so important, and what is trivial. He tries to eliminate the non-essential and learns to be content with the essential. Such a person soon discovers that to need less is to live better and happier. It is a mark of maturity. It is progress on the path to inner freedom.

One should wisely seek and carefully choose in one's actions and strive to maintain a Buddhist standard of conduct, whatever disappointments life may bring. And when disappointments come, one tries to look at them with some degree of detachment, standing, as it were, apart from them. In this way, a person gains a feeling of inner security and frees himself from fears, anxieties, and many other heavy burdens. This attitude to life and the world brings courage and confidence.

How does a lay Buddhist view himself? In the Buddha Dhamma, the human being is an impersonal combination of ever-changing mind and matter. In the flux is found no unchanging soul or eternal principle. The self or soul is then a piece of fiction invented by the human mind. To believe in such an absurdity is to create another source of unhappiness.

One should therefore see oneself as one truly is—a conflux of mind and matter energized by *taṇhā* or craving, containing immense possibilities for both good and evil, neither overestimating nor underestimating one's capacities and capabilities. One must also take care to recognize one's limitations and not pretend that they do not exist. It is simply a matter of accepting what one is, and deciding to make the most of oneself. With this determination, one's position in this world will be decided by one's efforts. And everyone has a place, however humble it may be, and a contribution to make as well.

Seeing that no two are alike, physically or psychologically, in the light of *kamma*, a wise person should, therefore, avoid comparing himself with others. Such profitless comparison can only lead to unnecessary sorrow and suffering. If he thinks that he is better than others, he may become proud and conceited and develop a superiority feeling—or an inflated I. If the person thinks he is worse than others, he is liable to develop an inferiority feeling—or a deflated I, and to withdraw from the realities and responsibilities of life. If he considers that he is equal to others, there is likelihood of stagnation and disinclination to further effort and progress.

So, instead of keeping pace with, or outdoing others, socially, financially, and in other ways, the understanding layman proceeds to do something more useful. He decides to take stock of himself, to know himself, his true nature in all aspects, as a first step to improving it: the secular (such as his physical, mental, emotional qualities), the moral, and the spiritual, through careful self-examination and observation, by past performance, and by the candid comments of sincere friends. Seeing himself as a whole, he plans for life as a whole in the context of the Noble Eightfold Path. Such a plan when drawn up will include all important events of a normal layman's life including occupation, marriage, and old age. Lay happiness and security lie then in finding out exactly what one *can* do and in actually doing it.

A plan like this brings order into an otherwise aimless and meaningless life, prevents drift and indicates the right direction and drive. A thoughtful lay Buddhist will not simply do what others do. He can resist the pull of the crowd when necessary. He is ever mindful both of ends pursued and the means employed. He does not merely go through life aimlessly; he goes, knowing clearly where he wants to go, with a purpose and a plan based on reality.

To be born as a human being is hard, but made easier in a Buddha Era—that is, an age when his teachings are still remembered and practiced. The more reason then why a lay Buddhist should consciously direct his life for purposeful living with a right end, by right endeavour, to a right plan; this is the quintessence of Buddha's teachings.

(b) Earning a Living

Men work to satisfy the primary or basic urges of hunger, thirst, and sex, as well a host of secondary wants and desires created by a commercial civilization such as ours.

The Buddha's teaching is a teaching of diligence and right effort or exertion. The opposite of diligence is negligence—aimless drift, sloth, and laziness which are hindrances to both material and moral progress. It is the active man who lives purposefully, who blesses the world with wealth and wisdom. So work is essential for happy living. Life without work would be an eternal holiday, which is the hell of boredom.

A large part of our waking life is spent earning a living. So it is easy to appreciate why we should be at least moderately happy in our job. But choosing a suitable career, like choosing a marriage partner, is one of the most important yet one of the most difficult tasks in life.

The economic aspect of a community profoundly affects its other aspects. The Buddha says that society, as with all conditioned phenomena, has no finality of form and therefore changes with the passage of time. The mainsprings of social change are ideology and economics—for men are driven to action by beliefs and desires. Some systems emphasize the latter; the Buddha, the former, for an economic structure can only influence but never determine man's thought.

Man must live and the means of his livelihood are matters of his greatest concern. A hungry man is an angry man. And a man poisoned by discontent is hardly in a fit frame of mind to develop his moral and spiritual life. The spirit may be willing but the flesh may prove to be weak. Unemployment and economic insecurity lead to tension, irritability, and loss of self-respect without which a healthy mental life is impossible. And one of the essential needs of a man is to feel he is wanted in the world.

Of human rights the right of work should, therefore, be assured to all, as a prerequisite for the good life. It is the duty of the state to uphold justice, and provide for the material and spiritual welfare of its subjects.

While Buddhism recognizes that bread is essential for existence, it also stresses that man does not live by bread alone. This is not all. How he earns and why he does it are equally relevant. He should not gain a living by methods detrimental to the welfare of living beings—*anākulā ca kammantā*, a peaceful occupation, as the Discourse on Blessings (Mahāmaṅgala Sutta) has it. So the Buddha forbade five kinds of trade to a lay Buddhist, and refraining from them constitutes Right Livelihood, the seventh step of the Path. They are: trading in arms, human beings, flesh (including the breeding of animals for slaughter), intoxicants and harmful drugs, and poisons. These trades add to the already existing suffering in the world.

Economic activity should also be regarded as a means to an end—the end being the full development of man himself. Work should serve men, not enslave him. He should not be so preoccupied with the business (or, busy-ness, to be more accurate) of earning a living that he has no time to live. While income and wealth through righteous means will bring satisfaction and lay happiness, the mere accumulation of riches for their own sake will only lead to unbridled acquisitiveness and self-indulgence, resulting later in physical and mental suffering. The enjoyment of wealth implies not merely its use for one's own happiness, but also the giving for the welfare of others as well.

The Buddha further says that the progress, prosperity, and happiness of a lay person depends on hard and steady effort— rather discouraging, no doubt, to many people who want something for nothing. Efficiency in work, be it high or humble, makes a useful contribution to the production of socially desirable goods and services. It gives one's work meaning and interest, besides enabling one to support oneself and one's family in comfort. Conservation and improvement of one's resources and talents, acquired or inherited, with balanced living, living within one's income, ensuring freedom from debt is a sure indicator of right seeing or understanding. Lastly, a blameless moral and spiritual life should be the aim of right livelihood.

Life is one and indivisible, and the working life is a part of the whole. The man who is unhappy at work is unhappy at home, too. Unhappiness spreads. Likewise, business life is part of life. The Dhamma of the Blessed One should therefore pervade and permeate one's entire life for only wealth rooted in righteous endeavour can yield true happiness.

(c) Bringing up a Family

In the Mahā-maṅgala Sutta the Buddha teaches us that:

Mother and father well supporting,
Wife and children duly cherishing,
Types of work unconflicting,
This, the Highest Blessing.

—Sn 2.4

The essentials of happy family life are then a partnership of two parents with common aims, attitudes, and ideals who love, respect, and trust each other; who love and understand their children, on whom they, in turn, can depend for the same treatment and sound guidance grounded on true values, living by Right Livelihood, and supporting aged parents. In Buddhism, however, marriage is not a compulsory institution for all lay followers. It is optional. This brings us to the important question of sex.

The sex instinct is a powerful impersonal impulse or force in us all to ensure the preservation of the race. Nature, to make sure of its objective, made the reproductive act of sexual union highly pleasurable so that it is inevitably sought by the individual for its own sake. There is no special mating season for humans, and males and females may find that they are physically attracted at any time.

Sex is an essential part of life. In some form or other it affects us every day, and often ends in choosing a partner for life. It can make or mar a householder's life.

What is the Buddhist attitude to sex? For a lay person, there is nothing sinful or shameful in sex, nor does it carry lifelong burdens of guilt. Sexual desire, in its personal aspect, is just like another form of craving and, as craving, leads to suffering. Sexual desire, too, must be controlled and finally totally eradicated. This happiness[4] arises only at the third stage of Sainthood, that of *Anāgāmī*. When a lay Buddhist becomes an *Anāgāmī*, he leads a celibate life.

But sexual behaviour, in its social context, demands mindfulness of the fact that at least one other person's happiness is at stake and, possibly, that of another—a potential child. And children born of premarital relations, when deprived and unwanted, often develop into juvenile delinquents. Besides, premarital sex may carry with it the risks of venereal infection. A compassionate Buddhist, mindful of his own and others' welfare, acts wisely and responsibly in sexual matters. Misconduct for a layman means sexual union with the wives of others or those under protection of father, mother, sister, brother, or guardian, including one's employees.

Adolescence is a period of stress and strain. It is at this time that the sex instinct becomes active, and sensible parents should guide and help their children to adjust to the changes. This sexual energy could be diverted not merely to outdoor games and sports, but also to creative activities like hand work, gardening, and other constructive activities.

It is not easy for an unmarried adult to practice sexual self-restraint till such time as he is able to marry. No doubt he lives in a sex-drenched commercial civilization where sex is seen, heard, sensed, and thought of most the time. But the ideal of sex only within marriage is something worth aiming at. The Buddhist's ultimate objective is, after all, to be a Perfect Man—not a perfect beast. And a start has to be made some day, somewhere—and now is the best time for it.

At all times in a man's life, it is mind that dominates man's actions. It is mind that makes one what one is. There is no

---

4. Complete freedom from the sexual urge.

doubt about this. Truly, it is an encouraging fact—one tends to become what one wants to be. And, if one wishes to be chaste, one can be. One's life will then move irresistibly in the direction of its fulfilment.

Much can be done by sublimating the instinct by diverting the energy in the sex impulse into other activities. Developing an occupational interest or hobbies or sports can divert the mind and provide suitable outlets. Moderation in eating is helpful. But what is most important is the guarding of thoughts regarding all sexual matters. One must also avoid situations and stimuli likely to excite sexual desires.[5] When sensual desires do arise, the following methods may be tried:

1. Mindfully note the presence of such thoughts without delay; when they tend to arise, merely notice them without allowing yourself to be carried away by these thoughts.
2. Simply neglect such thoughts, turning your mind either to beneficial thoughts or to an activity that absorbs you.
3. Reflect on the possible end results.

Steps should also be taken to foster and maintain all that is wholesome, as for instance, wise friendship, and keeping oneself usefully occupied at all times. If one has succeeded in meditative practice, the happiness derived from it will be a powerful counter-force against sexual desires.

This mindfulness is the only way to achieve self-mastery. It is a hard fight requiring patient and persistent practice; nevertheless, it is a fight worth waging and a goal worth winning.

(d) Social Relationships

A lay Buddhist lives in society. He must adjust himself to other people to get on smoothly with them. Human relationships—the education of the emotions—are the fourth R in education and play an important part in everyday life. So instead of keeping pace with, or outdoing others socially, financially, and in other ways, the understanding layman proceeds to do something more useful.

---

5. To the latter belong films, pictures, and literature which are chiefly intended to provide sexual titillation.

Happiness and security then lie in finding out exactly what one can do, and doing it well.

The lay person who practices morality (*sīla*), by reason of his virtue gives peace of mind to those around him. He controls his deeds and words by following the third, fourth, and fifth steps of the noble Eightfold Path, namely Right Speech, Right Action and Right Livelihood or by observing the Five Precepts (*pañca sīla*).

Such regulated behaviour flows from proper understanding of the Buddhist doctrine of *kamma*, that a man is what he is because of action and the result of action. If one is genuinely trying to tread the path, one's daily life should reflect it. So, the Buddhist avoids killing living beings, stealing, sexual misconduct, drugs, intoxicants, and harmful lying, tale-bearing, harsh words, and idle talk.

The Buddha's attitude toward stupefying drugs and intoxicants is clear and simple: complete abstinence from both. And why? The immediate aim of a Buddhist layman is happiness and security, here and now—in the present existence, while his distant objective is the lasting peace and security of *Nibbāna* and, therewith, freedom from repeated births and deaths, with their attendant frustrations, disappointments, and the pain of temporal life. Now, the one and only tool he has at his disposal to achieve both of these goals is the weapon of the mind, which, under the wise guidance of the Master's teaching, he gradually learns to use with skill, without ill to himself or others. And one of the best ways of impairing the efficiency of this precious mental instrument—to make it dull and blunt, is to partake of intoxicating drinks and drugs. Even when taken in moderation they have a pernicious influence on the mind and on the body, as well as on the character and the moral qualities. Under their baneful effects, mind becomes confused, and the drinker finds it difficult to distinguish between right and wrong, good and bad, the true and false. Such a person, then, wrongs himself, wrongs those who live with him, and wrongs society at large. On the other hand, he who faithfully follows the Buddha's advice and abstains completely from the use of all intoxicants and harmful drugs, is always sober in mind, and is therefore able to exercise physical, mental, and moral control. Such a one has always a clear mind and can easily understand what is going on within, and also without, one's mind.

But what of a Buddhist who, as a rule, refrains from alcoholic drinks and drugs, but occasionally finds himself placed in a delicate situation such as when offered an intoxicating drink at a party given by his superior or at an important occasion? Should he accept or refuse? At least two possible courses are open to him: he could politely decline excusing himself on medical grounds (which are justifiable), and ask instead for a non-alcoholic drink, mindfully noting what is taking place, and impress on his mind that even a single deviation from the ideal of total abstinence is to open the way, even temporarily, to heedlessness, recklessness, and mental confusion. Alcohol does impair the ability to think clearly, to decide wisely, and to perform any work of an exacting nature. If a Buddhist layman, while aiming at absolute perfection occasionally lapses, and is content with approximations, he is free to do so—but at his own grave peril.

Positively, the Buddhist layman is kind and compassionate to all, honest and upright, pure and chaste, sober and heedful in mind. He speaks only that which is true, in accordance with facts, sweet, peaceable, and helpful. Morality is a fence that protects us from the poisons of the outer world. It is, therefore, a prerequisite for higher spiritual aspirations and through it character shines. The development of personality on such lines results in charm, tact, and tolerance—essential qualities to adjust oneself to society, and to get on well with other people.

In the Sigālovāda Sutta, the Buddha explained to young Sigāla the reciprocal relationship that should exist among the members of society. They are worth mentioning in brief; parents have to look after their children, and guide and educate them; children have to respect their parents, perform their duties and maintain family traditions; teachers must train and instruct pupils in the proper way; and pupils in turn must be diligent and dutiful; a husband should be kind, loyal, and respectful of his wife, supply her needs and give her due place in the home, and she in return should be faithful, understanding, efficient, industrious, and economical in the performance of her duties; friends should be generous, sincere, kindly, and helpful to one another, and a sheltering tree in time of need; employers must be considerate to their employees, give adequate wages, ensure satisfactory conditions of work and service and they, in return must work honestly, efficiently and be loyal to their masters; the laity should support and sustain the monks and other holy men who, in turn, should discourage them from doing evil, encourage them to do good, expound the teaching and show the way to happiness.

Buddhist morality is grounded on both thought and feeling. A Buddhist monk does social service when he himself, while not engaging in the worldly life, so teaches the Dhamma that he makes the lay followers better Buddhists, and thereby induces them to take to social work, which is an ideal practical form of the Four Sublime states: loving kindness, compassion, sympathetic joy, and equanimity, besides their practice of these at the meditational levels. They should be the four cornerstones of genuine lay Buddhist life. The Four Sublime States form the foundation of individual and social peace, and combine in them the realism of human nature and the idealism of youth to work for the social betterment, out of natural sympathy and concern for fellow-beings.

But for social work to be of real value it should spring from genuine love, sympathy, and understanding for fellow-men, guided by knowledge and training. It is the living expression of Buddhist brotherhood.

The cultivation of the neglect of these duties is a matter for each one of us, but their promotion will undoubtedly foster healthier interpersonal relationships, decrease social tension and irritability, and appreciably increase social good, stability, and harmony.

Mental Health

Life is full of stress and strain, but we have to live in conditions as they are and make the best of them. Successful adjustment to life in the light of Buddha's teachings will, however, ensure the all-round progress of the lay Buddhist, maximizing happiness and minimizing pain.

The Buddha names four kinds of lay happiness: the happiness of possession as health, wealth, longevity, wife, and children; the enjoyment of such possessions; freedom from debt; and a blameless moral and spiritual life. Yet even the happiest person cannot say when and in what form misfortune may strike him. Against suffering, the externals of life will be of little or no avail. Real happiness and security are then to be sought in one's own mind, to be built up by constant effort, mindfulness, and concentration.

So the wise layman while being *in* this world, will try to be less and less *of* it. He will train his mind to look at life mindfully with detachment, and soon discover that modern civilization is, by and large, a commercial one, for the benefit of a powerful minority at the expense of the unthinking majority, based on the intensification and multiplication of artificial wants, often by arousing and stimulating the undesirable and lower elements of human nature, and that the increasing satisfaction of these wants leads not to peace and stillness of mind, but only to chronic discontent, restlessness, dissatisfaction, and conflict.

He therefore decides to practice voluntary simplicity and finds a new freedom; the less he wants, the happier and freer he is.

Thinking man realizes that there are but four essential needs for the body—pure food, clothing, shelter, and medicine. Corresponding to these, there are four for the mind—right knowledge, virtue, constant guarding of the sense doors, and meditation.

Bhāvanā, or meditation, is the systematic training and culture of the mind with *Nibbāna* as its goal. The emotions are controlled, the will is disciplined, and the instinctive energies are diverted from their natural ends—led along the Four Great Efforts (the sixth step of the path)—to the sublimated ideal of a perfect Man (the *Arahant*) or *Nibbāna*. If there is an urgent felt need, the ideal has the power of drawing out all one's instinctive impulses so that they are sublimated and harmonized, giving satisfaction to the individual, and therefore benefiting the community as well.

Closely connected with our instincts are the emotions. By emotion is meant a feeling which moves us strongly. We get stirred up, as it were. Examples of emotion are fear, anger, and strong sexual passion. When emotion floods the mind, reason retreats or disappears, and we often do things for which we repent later. So some emotional control is necessary, for, without it, character cannot be developed, and moral and spiritual progress is impossible.

Fear is a common emotion that darkens our lives. It is anticipation of deprivations. One tries to live in two periods of time at once—the present and the future. To know how fear arises enables us to take the right steps for its removal. It results from wrong seeing, not understanding things as they really are. Uncertainty and change are the keynotes of life. To each one of us there is only one thing that is truly ours, is us: our character, as shown by our actions. As for the rest, nothing belongs to us. We can visualize everything else being taken away, save this. But this, one's character, nobody and nothing else can deprive one of. Why then go to pieces when all other things that are liable to break, do break? Why fret about the fragility of the frail? Besides, are we so careful of not taking other people's things, as we are of preserving ours? Our past actions of depriving others may only end in others now depriving us. It is only fair and just.

This attitude of detachment to life's storms is the only sound philosophy that can bring one a true security and a true serenity.

Or again, there is no such thing as justifiable anger in Buddhism, for if one is in the right, one should not be angry, and if one is in the wrong, one cannot afford to be angry. Therefore, under any circumstances one should not become angry.

A good way to secure emotional control is to practice noticing mindfully and promptly an incipient hindrance (or any other mental state of mind); then, of its own, it tends to fade away. If done as often as possible, it will be very effective. The five hindrances are undue attachment to: sensual desire; ill-will; laziness and inertia; agitation and worry; and doubt. The last here refers to indecision or unsteadiness in the particular thing that is being done. One must know exactly one's own mind—not be a Hamlet, unable to decide, because one is always mistrusting one's own judgment.

Daily practice is the way to progress. Even a little practice every day, brings a person a little nearer to his object, day by day.

Right Livelihood: The Noble Eightfold Path in the Working Life

by Susan Elbaum Jootla

The question of correct livelihood is of great importance for any practicing lay Buddhist. So also to the many meditators once they have done enough meditation courses, and work on their own, to realize that they must live a Dhamma life. Just what is Right Livelihood—how broad is the category of trades a disciple of the Buddha cannot ply? And how can one best work so that he is developing the other seven Path factors while earning a living? Is work a total waste—just a means to the end of supporting oneself in order to meditate? Or can one's job be used in a more constructive way so that it brings some direct benefit to those around us as well? These and many other related issues come to the mind of anyone who finds himself in the position of the Buddha's teachings, and to a large extent each of us has to determine for himself the details of how to work out the livelihood aspects of his life. In this essay an attempt is made simply to outline how we can try to use the Noble Eightfold Path in relation to our work—whether it is in an office or a factory, in the city or country, whether it is indoors or outdoors, white collar or blue collar or neither. If the meditator succeeds in applying *sīla* (morality), *samādhi* (concentration), and *paññā* (wisdom), the three aspects of the Path, at work as well as in all other life situations, he will be growing in Dhamma even during the part of the day that is apparently devoted to non-Dhamma work, and at the same time he will be doing his job well and sharing his peace of mind and *mettā* (loving-kindness) with those his livelihood brings him into contact with.

> Monks, these five trades ought not to be plied by a lay-disciple. Trade in weapons, trade in human beings, trade in flesh, trade in spirits (intoxicants) and trade in poison.
>
> *Gradual Sayings* III, p. 153 (AN 5.177).

And what, monks, is wrong mode of livelihood? Trickery, cajolery, insinuating, dissembling, rapacity for gain upon gain. And what, monks, is the right side of merit that ripens unto cleaving to a new birth? Herein monks, an ariyan disciple, by getting rid of wrong livelihood, earns his living by a right mode of living.

Middle Length Sayings III, pp. 118-19.

The fields of livelihood which the Buddha prohibited to his lay followers, as listed in the initial quotation above, are limited to those in which the disciple would be directly, on his own responsibility, involved in breaking one or more of the Five Precepts, which are the very basic moral rules for the Buddhist layman. Anyone who is attempting to develop morality, concentration, and wisdom, to grow in compassion and insight, cannot deal in weapons of any sort, at any level of the business because by doing so he would be involving himself in causing harm or injury to others for his own monetary gain. These days the probability of trading in human beings as slaves or for prostitution is limited, but certainly any job with such overtones is to be avoided. Breeding animals for slaughter as meat or for other uses that may be made of the carcasses is not allowed because this obviously implies breaking the First Precept: I shall abstain from killing. Working on someone else's beef ranch or selling packaged meat is acceptable as there is no responsibility for killing involved. Similarly, anyone trying to follow the teachings of the Buddha should avoid hunting and fishing, nor can he be an exterminator of animals. Dealing in alcohol or intoxicating drugs would be making oneself directly responsible for encouraging others to break the Fifth Precept: I shall abstain from all intoxicants. While by no means everyone we meet is trying to keep these precepts, still, to help others directly in breaking any of them is certainly wrong livelihood. If we manufacture, deal in, or use insecticides or other kinds of poisons in our work, we are engaging to some degree in wrong livelihood because here, too, we are breaking the First Precept and directly encouraging others to do so as well. However, the motivation behind the use of such material has a great deal to do with the depth of the *kamma* being created. A doctor rightly gives drugs which are harmful to bacteria and viruses, not because he hates the bugs, but in order to help cure the human being. Here the good more than balances the bad. But if we go about applying poison to rat-holes and cockroaches' hideouts with anger or aversion toward the pests, we would be generating considerably strong bad *kamma*.

But these five are the only ways of earning a living which are to be strictly avoided by one who is walking on the Path. Other fields of endeavour may seem trivial to the meditator investigating the job market, or they may appear to be just helping others to create more *taṇhā* (craving), or they may involve some indirect responsibility in wrong speech or action—but we must find our work within the context of the society from which we come, and within the framework of available job opportunities. It is not possible first to go about setting up the ideal Dhamma community and then find work within it; so we must live in the society and serve its members to the best of our ability. Someone who finds Dhamma in middle age and is settled into a career with little reasonable possibility of shifting to one more strictly in accord with Right Livelihood can—and must—practice Dhamma as it is possible within his context. For example, only rarely does an army officer serve in combat—the rest of the time there is ample scope for him to work wisely, according to *paññā*, in a detached way, giving the necessary commands without being overly harsh. There are a substantial number of police officers in Rajasthan doing *vipassanā* meditation who already are feeling the benefits of meditation in preserving law and order and dealing with criminals and the general public with little anger. Even people whose livelihood is solely dependent on hunting or fishing can at least develop *dāna* (liberality) and other virtues—as Burmese fishermen do—even if it is impossible for them to give up an incorrect mode of earning a living. After all, an important reason for which serious Buddhists become monks is that the householder's life is full of dust, and few positions for lay livelihood can allow one to be completely pure. Due to the interdependence of all phases of society and today's complex economic structures, it is very difficult to live as a layman and keep the perfect *sīla* the meditator strives for—a farmer has to use insecticides, public health workers kill mosquitoes and their larvae, a truck driver may sometimes have to transport arms or poison. Often one is in a position of having to exaggerate one's statements or omit disadvantageous facts, even if one does not like it. So we must earn our livelihood as we have been trained, and as we find a position for ourselves in society while constantly making an effort to grow in Dhamma.

However, if we let the Dhamma slide and allow our daily routine work to take over and become the thing of paramount importance, then we have lost track of the goal we set for ourselves in being dedicated followers of the Buddha, and especially serious *vipassanā* meditators. One cannot use Dhamma for one's increased mundane profit and continue to grow in *paññā* (wisdom) at the same time because then desire for gain (which is *taṇhā*) will be the root of one's very Dhamma practice and a complete distortion of the real purpose of Dhamma—the elimination of craving (*taṇhā*) and so of suffering (*dukkha*). Occupational work is a means to keep alive and to support one's dependents so that one can grow in Dhamma. Trying to use the Dhamma to help one achieve more at work, and ignoring the Noble Eightfold Path, or getting so involved in business that one cannot even sit for meditation an hour in the morning and an hour in the evening is making a farce of Dhamma—perhaps keeping the form but surely losing the essence of the Buddha's teaching. This is the way of *dukkha*, productive of suffering. To alleviate *dukkha* one must live by the Eightfold Path, earning one's livelihood within its context, trying to practice *sīla*, *samādhi*, and *paññā*—morality, concentration, and wisdom—at the workplace as well as while formally sitting in meditation.

Once we have found a suitable job, the more long-range task begins—applying the Buddha's teachings at work. If we can keep *sīla* only during meditation courses what serious benefit have we gained from such training periods? If we lose all our mindfulness, concentration, and wisdom when we are confronted with the vibrations of a big city or the workplace, where is our wisdom? To grow in Dhamma we have to try constantly to apply the whole of the Noble Eightfold Path in all life's circumstances, and some of the more challenging situations we will come across are very likely to be those we meet during working hours. Jobs are particularly important occasions to keep carefully to the Path for a number of reasons: (1) usually we do not have the support of the Saṅgha while at work and so are completely on our own; (2) work tends to arouse all previous thought associations and our deep-seated conditionings of greed, competition, and aversion; (3) so many of our waking hours are inevitably involved in simply earning a living. Yet if we rightly apply the Path factors on the job, we are still assured of moving toward success in the supramundane field, and we are quite apt to find that these factors enable us to do well in our chosen mundane work as well.

Let us first examine the relationship at work between the three *sīla* factors of Right Speech, Right Action and Right Livelihood. Right Livelihood was outlined in the first quotation from the Buddha. But Right Livelihood will not be really pure unless it includes Right Speech and Right Action as well. We have to strive with determination to keep all the Five Precepts while we work at a job, as well as for the rest of the time. The forms of wrong speech and wrong action to be avoided are all those in which lying, backbiting, or harming of others would be involved. If we are honest in our speech and actions, our employers will certainly be pleased with our work and we will be growing in Dhamma by confronting our mind's opposing tendencies; we will note when the mind tries to find the easy way out or to blame others for our own errors. If we are running our own business, we must be scrupulously honest in our dealings with our customers and avoid all trickery, cajolery dissembling. We can make a reasonable profit for services we perform of bringing our commodity to the consumer, but we must not let ourselves get caught up in the businessman's perpetual tendency toward rapacity for gain upon gain. The merchant plays an important role and function in the community, but the meditator-businessman must always keep in mind that his job is to serve the society and provide for the needs of his family—not to make the maximum amount of money with the least effort as he might previously have perceived it.

Whatever our work situation is—in an office, factory, or shop—we will always feel the benefits of keeping *sīla*. If we do not indulge in gossip or slander—office or academic politics— but keep clearly to the side of right and honesty in every situation that arises with other workers or our employers, we will find that we are less often at the receiving end of other people's anger. In fact, if we are really able to keep on the Path at work, we may well find ourselves in the position of peacemaker or mediator between the opposing sides in many a workplace dispute—and in such a role we will certainly be serving others.

To practice Right Action at work we must scrupulously avoid anything even remotely related to stealing for our own personal gain. The less we are involved in anyone else's taking what was not intended for him, the better off we are as well. So it is beneficial to all to dissuade other workers from stealing from the establishment, liberating materials, or otherwise misappropriating the employer's property. On the other hand, the kammic implications for us in occasionally having to exaggerate a bit at the boss's behest, or to do the firm's accounts in a legally dubious way they have always been done, once in a while, are not so severe because the full responsibility for such occasional acts is not with us. However, we do bear some responsibility in these situations and if the job seems to require chronic dishonesty in speech or action, and this situation cannot be altered by discussion with the employer, then it may be necessary to change jobs. But we have to keep a balanced perspective and not keep running after the perfect work—part of the *dukkha* of the householder's life is the necessity to function in an immoral society while keeping one's own mind clear.

So if we have chosen work which does not involve us in killing, or trading in living beings, or poisons, or in dealing in intoxicants, we are earning a Right Livelihood. And if, while on the job we carefully avoid lying, stealing, and the associated forms of wrong speech and action, we are doing our work and simultaneously practicing *sīla* on the Path.

The *samādhi* section of the Path during meditation has effects in the mundane world, for Right Effort, Mindfulness, and Concentration will contribute greatly to our success in our career.

Right Effort at work, as elsewhere, must be neither over-exertion nor laziness, but a Middle Path. For a businessman to spend all his waking hours involved in the concerns of his firm means that he is consumed with some strong *taṇhā* either for making money or for some particular set of circumstances to come about, and this is in direct contradiction with living the Dhamma life. On the other hand, the employee who sees how inane his work is, or how absurd it is to put two pieces into a car on an assembly line for eight hours a day, or that his job just helps people keep revolving in *dukkha*, and so sits back and does only the barest minimum required of him, means to be overcome by defilement of sloth and torpor, and probably ill-will as well. Right Effort at work means doing our best to accomplish the tasks before us—without becoming mindlessly absorbed or involved in them to the point of forgetting equanimity, and without the inertia that comes of a belligerent mind which thinks itself to be superior to the position it is in. Unrelenting effort in the mundane sphere is summarized by the Buddha in a discourse on the householder's life to the lay disciple Dīghajanu (quoted in Meditation and the Householder by Ven. Acharya Buddharakkhita, in *Mahā Bodhi*, January 1976):

> "By whatsoever activity a householder earns his living, whether by farming, by trading, by rearing cattle, by archery, by service under the king, or by any other kind of craft, at that he becomes skilful and tireless. He is endowed with the power of discernment as to the proper ways and means; he is able to arrange and carry out duties. This is called the accomplishment of unrelenting effort."

Sammā sati, Right Mindfulness or Awareness, is the next factor of the *samādhi* section of the Path, and there are several ways in which the mindfulness we gain from *vipassanā* will help us on the job.

> "Herein, Dīghajanu, whatsoever wealth a householder is in possession of, obtained by work and zeal, collected by the strength of this arm, by the sweat of his brow, justly acquired by right means, such he husbands well by guarding and watching so that kings may not seize it, thieves may not steal it, nor fire burn it, nor water carry it off, nor ill-disposed heirs remove. This is the accomplishment of watchfulness."

The quality of mindfulness mentioned by the Buddha here is not the same as the *sammā-sati* of the Noble Eightfold Path, but this watchfulness is a by-product of mindfulness important to the lay-follower. The more the meditator has developed awareness in the supramundane field, the more careful he will be in all situations of life—meditative, household, or work. If one's mindfulness is not Right, however, then one will be apt to take this injunction of the Buddha's as license to indulge in great *upādāna*, that is, in clinging, by all possible means, to what one regards as one's own. This kind of ignorance-based watchfulness will only lead to *dukkha*. What we have to learn to do is care for the possessions we have acquired so that we and our dependents can make best use of them, but without making the error of expecting them to last indefinitely, nor of considering them as a personal possession fully in one's own control. To want only to give away one's hard-earned or inherited goods to anyone who expresses a desire for them is folly. *Dana* or charity can earn us great merit, but only when done in wisdom and when the quality of the recipient also helps to determine how much merit is earned. Material possessions in themselves are not the fetters that keep us in *dukkha*, so having fewer things or more, for that matter, will not necessarily bring more happiness; it is our attachment to them that is the bondage that must be eliminated. So if we apply Right Mindfulness to the proper taking care of our things, we are only intelligently providing for our own welfare and for that of those who are dependent on us, not necessarily generating more *taṇhā* (craving).

Increased awareness or mindfulness is intertwined with improved concentration in enhancing our performance at work. Greater awareness of all the parameters of a situation will enable a businessman to make more accurate decisions, a workman to avoid accidents, and a teacher to really communicate information to his students.

In addition to this mindfulness of external situations, we also have to try to be mindful of our own minds and bodies while we work, as well as the rest of the time, of course. Once we become fairly established in the tradition of *vedanānupassanā* (mindfulness of feelings, as taught in the tradition of Sayaji U Ba Khin), we have acquired a ready technique for keeping mindfulness always with us. Continual change is always going on in our bodies, so at no time can it be said that there are no sensations, since it is the impermanent (*anicca*) nature of the body which causes the sensations. Once we have acquired the skill of feeling these sensations while we are engaged in daily activities, we would do well to keep some degree of awareness of the *anicca* feelings, or of *ānāpāna* (mindfulness of breathing) awake all the time. Then no matter how difficult, or how boring, or how exhausting be the tasks that we are faced with, we will find that we have a relatively equanimous and balanced mind with which to face them, because we will be alternating mind-moments of mindfulness and wisdom, relating to the ultimate nature of our mind-and-body (*nāma-rūpa*), with the mind-moments that are of necessity fully engaged in the mundane work at hand. Meditators engaged in contemplating the feelings (*vedanānupassanā*), who have practiced the technique for some time, find that this mindfulness of the sensations which are caused by the continual flux that is the nature of the body keeps them in a balanced and detached frame of mind in all kinds of trying situations—and certainly work experiences can sometimes be difficult enough to make it well worth our while to develop the skill of keeping the mindfulness of *anicca* (impermanence) always with us.

Concentration, the last of the *samādhi* section of the Path, obviously is vital to anyone in any task he attempts. The meditator will find that *vipassanā* has enhanced his one-pointedness and this skill will be applied in all the spheres of life, including work. But he must be sure that even at work this concentration is not rooted in strong craving or ill-will, otherwise the meditator may fall into the trap of squandering pure Dhamma for material gain, by using the enhanced concentration without the other aspects of the Path, *sīla* and *paññā*, to balance it. Naturally, it is always useful to keep one's mind clearly focused on the job at hand—if the mind is constantly running off in various directions toward irrelevant objects, our work will be slowed down and perhaps inadequately completed. As the mind is trained in *vipassanā* meditation to be detached from, not distracted by, the pleasure and pains of the senses, we will find that when we are working we will have less and less difficulty concentrating on what has to be done at this time and tend to worry less about the past or future. This does not mean that we do not plan our purchases or work schedule or ignore the future implications of decisions taken now. We do all these kinds of activities; we make all needed choices and decisions, but once such action has been taken, the mind settles back down into the job of the present without being hampered and held back by worries about the past or fears of the future.

An artist or mechanic or craftsman is much better at his creating if his concentration is clear and his mind stays firmly with the materials at hand. A doctor's or lawyer's understanding

of his client's situation will be correspondingly increased as
his concentration on what the client describes is improved—
he cannot practice his profession at all without a fair amount
of concentration. Certainly all kinds of teaching and learning
depend on one-pointedness of mind. A merchant or farmer or
businessman will be much better equipped to solve the difficulties
of his work if he can carefully concentrate on all aspects of the
problems at hand, distinguish relevant from tangential issues,
and sort out appropriate solutions. Concentration is one of the
mental factors that is present in any mind-moment, but the degree
to which it is developed varies considerably between individuals.
A *vipassanā* meditator generally has a well-developed faculty of
concentration due to his mental training and if he puts this ability
to appropriate use in the workplace, he will in this way gain
mundane benefits from his meditation.

The remaining sections of the Noble Eightfold Path fall into
the category of wisdom. *Sammā-diṭṭhi*, Right Understanding or
Right View, means the ability to see things as they are in their
true nature by penetrating through the apparent truth. This
means understanding the *anicca*, *dukkha*, and *anattā* nature of all
phenomena, mental and physical, that is their impermanency,
unsatisfactoriness, and egolessness. This understanding should be
applied to everyday life—including our work.

Right Understanding (*sammā diṭṭhi*) also requires a basic
understanding of the Four Noble Truths—of Suffering, its
Cessation, and the path leading to its Cessation; further, of the
Law of Kamma or moral cause and effect, and the Doctrine of
Dependent Origination. By means of Right Thought, *sammā-
saṇkappa*, the remaining Path-and-Wisdom-factor, one considers
all that happens in life with a mind that is free of greed and
of hatred. For this discussion of the Noble Eightfold Path in
the work situation it is not necessary to separate Right Thought
from Right Understanding, as without one the other could not
exist in such situations.

To apply wisdom (*paññā*) at work means always trying to
keep the mind equanimous and detached while it is engaged in the
necessary mundane activities and interaction with other people.
So if the boss gets annoyed and shouts at us, we remind ourselves
that he is at that moment suffering and generating more suffering

for himself. We try to do the right thing if he is pointing out a reasonable fault, and in any case we attempt to send him *mettā* and not let anger arise in reaction to his sparks.

Whenever a businessman or professor or other professional gets so involved in his work that it occupies his mind all the time, keeping it scheming up more plans or solving problems without rest or even time for meditation, he is acting on the basis of ignorance, not of wisdom. He has forgotten that all the phenomena he is dealing with are primarily operating according to laws of cause and effect, and that his own will and decisions can only do one part of any job; the remainder is beyond his control.

One is not seeing *anattā*, the egoless nature of external phenomena, if he develops tremendous craving (*taṇhā*) for the results of his work. *Anicca*, change and decay, is inherent in all phenomena, but we often slip into ignorance of this factor and unreasonably try to prolong favourable business conditions or consider our resources infinite or get attached to any particular situation. If we forget the Four Noble Truths at work, especially the First and Second—*dukkha* and *taṇhā* as the cause of *dukkha*—we will be continuing to generate more and more unhappiness for ourselves as our craving grows in intensity. Job situations, especially since they involve money, are very likely to bring up the strong conditioning for craving we all have from the past, and if this desire is not observed with wisdom, we will be continually digging deeper mental ruts that will inevitably lead to future misery. To avoid this we have to train our minds to see how no situation, however apparently pleasant it may seem to be, is actually desirable because: (1) no situation can last, all are *anicca*; (2) the state of craving is itself one of unhappiness; and (3) all craving must lead in the direction of future *dukkha*. And, of course, the opposite situation in which the mind reacts with aversion to the circumstances, be they work-related or otherwise, is precisely the same—both clinging and aversion are *taṇhā*.

If the market for our product is favourable at present, if our superiors are pleased with our work, if we are getting good grades at the university, or if any other pleasant situation arises in the course of our work, we would do well to recall that this situation, too, is unsatisfactory. Pleasant experiences bring *dukkha* because they cannot last forever, and any mind which still has conditioning of *taṇhā* and *avijjā* (ignorance), will try to cling to what it likes, striving to perpetuate the pleasant feelings. If we keep the First and Second Noble Truths in mind when we encounter both happy and unhappy states on the job, our minds will be able to remain detached and calm and perfectly equanimous—the only kind of happiness that can endure—no matter what vicissitudes we have to face. At any moment we may run into material gain or loss, be famous or infamous, receive praise or blame, experience happiness or pain. But if the mind remains free from clinging, if it has seen *dukkha* in all craving, then none of this can really touch us and we are sure of inner peace, no matter what the outer circumstances may be.

Recalling the law of cause and effect, cultivating this aspect of *paññā* at work, is quite important and useful. To create good *kamma* the mind has to try to remain free of clinging and aversion, so we have to keep a close watch on our reactions if we are not to prolong the misery of *saṃsāra*. We should not, however, expect that just because we have thought of this and are trying to keep ourselves away from *taṇhā* that this freedom will easily come about—this would be forgetting the *anattā* egolessness nature of the mind. Only gradually can we recondition the mind to operate in channels based on wisdom, by reminding ourselves whenever we notice an unwholesome reaction that such actions lead only to *dukkha*, and that nothing at all is worth getting attached to or developing aversion toward. In this way, over a long period of time we will notice how the force of our reactions does diminish. So when our superior yells at us and we in turn get angry, we just note the reaction and the sensations that arise, see their foolishness and as soon as we can, just let go of them. If a business deal is pending, and we are getting more and more tense about it as the days go by, we may not be able to just give up the tension, but if we observe how this particular conditioning of the mind is happening with some part of the mind detached and with the sensations (which will be reflecting the mind-reactions), we are no longer reinforcing the tension *saṇkhāras* and so the next time they arise, they will be weaker. Becoming impatient with the unwholesome tendencies of the mind cannot change them and, in fact, this would be generating more unwholesome tendencies of a slightly different sort. If the aversion to work keeps coming up, never mind; just observe that, too, with the *anicca* sensations, and slowly it will decrease in frequency and intensity.

Paññā can and must be applied in all situations. It may not be as powerfully clear as when we are meditating, but if we neglect it during the part of the day while at work, we are not living by the totality of the Path; and without trying to understand all the situations of life in their ultimate nature, we cannot expect to progress toward the goal of liberation from all suffering.

When we have undertaken the task of removing all the causes of suffering—which is what it means to be a serious *vipassanā* meditator—we have committed ourselves to a full-time job. To grow in the wisdom that can remove *dukkha* one must at all times try to practice all the aspects of the Noble Eightfold Path. This is the Way taught by the Buddha that enables us to find for ourselves real and lasting peace and happiness. When we are engaged in our mundane work of earning a livelihood, we must be sure to keep our *sīla* (morality) as pure as possible. Vipassanā meditation will have increased our *samādhi* (concentration) and we must be sure that it is Right Concentration we apply on the job, along with balanced Effort. Mindfulness of the true nature of the external experiences and internal phenomena we come into contact with when working must be kept alive. And finally, *paññā*, Right Understanding, and Right Thought must be developed with respect to our relationships with our co-workers, the various conditions at the workplace, and the functioning of our minds while engaged in earning a livelihood.

As we practice the Noble Eightfold Path and live the life of a lay-disciple of the Buddha, meditating while working and living in society, we will find ourselves growing in Dhamma while simultaneously serving all those we come into contact with in some fashion or the other. And just this is the essence of the Dhamma life—to eradicate the causes of one's own suffering by purifying the mind, and with the mind thus freed of greed, hatred, and ignorance, full of *mettā* and compassion, help others in their own quest for real happiness.

May All Beings Be Peaceful!

Having Taken the First Step

by M.O'C. Walshe

What does it feel like when one has fairly recently embarked on a course of Buddhism? The answers will vary a great deal, no doubt, but there ought to be some general characteristics and some problems common to the majority of newborn Buddhists in the West. Let us assume that you are a person who has quite recently, or within the last year or so, begun to take Buddhism seriously as a personal way of life. You may by now be just looking round a bit in your new mental surroundings and trying to take stock of what has happened, now that the first novelty of the situation has worn off. You have, I sincerely hope, tried to do a bit of meditation, though it would not surprise me in the least to hear that you have found this difficult and disappointing. If so, I would like to tell you straight away that you should not be discouraged. This is quite the normal thing. Meditation may *seem* disappointing and even almost useless for quite a long time, but if you persevere in it, results are bound to come. But these results may not be at all the sort of thing you expect. And *you* may not even be the person who first becomes aware of them. So press on regardless, and don't *look* for results. If you can see the point of this piece of advice you have already in fact made useful progress. Insights often come very subtly.

People's motives for taking up Buddhism may vary a great deal on the surface. But fundamentally you have probably come to it because, in one way or another, it seems to promise you *security*. If you haven't realized before that this was a good part of your motive, you might usefully use your next meditation period trying to find out whether I was right or not. If you have realized this, then you may agree that you find the formula, "I go to the Buddha, the Dhamma, and the Saṅgha," for refuge strangely comforting. And so it should be in one way, even though fundamentally you have to learn to be a refuge unto yourself. This is perhaps the first of the many paradoxes you will encounter attempting to tread the Buddhist path.

Now if we consider this problem of security a little further, we soon find that we do indeed crave for it. The obvious reason is that we feel life frankly unnerving, in fact, *insecure*. Here, then, we find straight away two of the three Marks of Existence: all things are marked by impermanence and suffering. *Because* they—and we—are impermanent, they are frustrating, and cause us all kinds of anguish. Buddhism offers a way out of this situation by treading the Noble Eightfold Path. I am assuming that, having taken the first step, you are now familiar with the Four Noble Truths and the steps of this Path. So I just want to mention a few points which may arise at this stage. The first step of the path is known as Right Understanding or Right View. This is seeing things as they are. There are large areas of experience which we would much rather know nothing about. This is the origin of repression, to use a Freudian term which is misleadingly translated. The German for repression in the psychoanalytical sense is *Verdrängung*, thrusting away. It is really successful self-deception. Getting rid of our repressions is therefore not doing what we like, as seems to be popularly imagined, but ceasing to deceive ourselves.

Fundamentally, Buddhism is just a technique of self-undeception. This is not easy, though sometimes it may be fun. It needs some study of theory as well as practice. It is perfectly true that you never gain enlightenment by intellectual knowledge alone, but if you haven't studied the theory to some extent you will almost certainly never be able to start properly on the practice. Before you can develop your intuition you must know what it is—or at least what it isn't—and self-deception in this respect seems to come terribly easy to many people. Intuition, or as I much prefer to call it, insight, is not an emotion, but the best way to develop it is by getting to know one's emotions as thoroughly as possible. When these emotions have been really seen for what are, they no longer stand in the light. Now the biggest emotional blockage we have is that which surrounds the ego-idea. Since it is to the ultimate elimination of this idea that the whole Buddhist training is directed, it may be as well to have a good look at it. In so doing we may get a shock.

By the ego (or self) in Buddhism we mean of course the concept of I am, though this is much more a feeling than a purely intellectual concept—which is the very reason why it is so much more difficult to uproot. From the psychological point of view we must take it to include not only what, in Freudian terms, is called the ego, but also the id and even the superego. Though not wholly adequate, the Freudian conception goes a good way toward giving us the basic idea. This ego of ours is a complex and dynamic set of functions which are not by any means all conscious or under any form of normal conscious control. Its nature is in fact blind ignorance and it fights desperately to maintain that ignorance. It is most important for us to realize from the outset that this is the case, because this is the root-cause of all our troubles. The three unhealthy roots of human nature are greed, hatred, and ignorance, and all our suffering is due to these three. Ignorance is the most fundamental, and greed and hate spring from it.

Now the power of ignorance is broken by knowledge, which is seeing correctly. So all we have to do is to learn to see. *avijjā*, "ignorance" or "not seeing," is no mere passive principle—it is an active force which opposes discovery of the truth at every turn. No need to look for an external devil: the Father of Lies is within every one of us. We all know the story of the Emperor's new clothes. In Buddhism the precise opposite of this situation occurs: the clothes go walking in the procession, but there's no emperor inside them. The whole show is laid on for the honour and glory of a character who doesn't really exist. Here, then, is our second paradox, and it is certainly no less startling than the first one: the ego is the most ruthlessly gluttonous all-devouring monster there is, and yet really all the time there's no such thing! All its activities without exception are simply a tale told by an idiot, full of sound and fury, signifying nothing. How can we solve *this* riddle? How can we ever come to grasp the nature of this peculiar monster that has no mouth and no belly, yet gobbles up the entire world (as some old Chinese monk might have said, but probably didn't)?

Clearly there must be a sense in which the self exists and another sense in which it doesn't. Let us first of all have a frank look at it in the sense of something existing. It is not a pretty sight. Underneath all our lofty ideals, our pious thoughts and holy aspirations, we are all alike. *Our* little personal petty self is the really important thing to us. It is out to grab all it can get, whether in the way of affection and admiration and sympathy or of more apparently tangible satisfactions in the way of sex, money, power, nice things to eat and drink and smell and touch and hear—*all* sorts of things and it doesn't care in the very least how it gets them. We don't all want—at least consciously—all of these things perhaps, but we usually want a lot of credit for not wanting some of them or at least doing without them, even if by necessity rather than choice. All these are aspects of greed including the last, which is of course conceit. They are the things the ego fattens on. Equally impressive and perhaps even more horrifying is the list of items under the heading of hate; we are all capable in our minds of murderous rage, sadism, treachery, and disloyalty of every conceivable kind. Until we have found and identified the seeds of *all* these things in our own hearts, we cannot claim to have made much progress in self-knowledge.

Of course most of us will never yield to such impulses, which may only be very faint; but until a higher stage of development has been reached they will not be totally eliminated as tendencies. The most likely way in which they may find some outward expression will be, perhaps, in the form of over-emotive indignation at the acts of hate committed by somebody else.

What can we do about this situation? First, face it. Second, penetrate to its roots. Buddhism is not something airy-fairy or romantic, it is *practical*. It is first and last something to *do*. To penetrate to the roots of greed, hatred, and delusion is not very easy and it requires certain methods or techniques. But the great thing is to keep going and not be diverted by irrelevancies, interesting by-paths, plausible excuses or pseudo-mystical fantasies, born of conceit and ignorance. A certain discipline is required, in fact. This can be summed up in one word—restraint. Restraint is not repression. In its simplest form it can be something as apparently easy as sitting still. It is just not automatically yielding to every impulse that arises while not, on the other hand, pretending that that impulse does not exist. A good part of Buddhism, in modern terms, is sales-resistance: cultivating at least a degree of immunity to the appeals of the outside world which are today constantly attempting, quite deliberately and purposefully, to arouse new desires within us. It is being deaf to the blandishments of the hidden persuaders whether from within or without, or better perhaps, hearing them without reacting. Who is the rich man who, like the camel, cannot pass through the eye of the needle? He is not only the millionaire, the expense-account johnnie, the take-over charlie: he is anybody who has too many *mental* encumbrances, too many *wants*.

Here then is an exercise: sit down with a straight back for ten minutes resolved not to make a single voluntary bodily movement during that time, and just *observe* what happens. You may get some surprises, but whatever happens you are bound to learn something. If you find, as will probably be the case, that a lot of thoughts and mental images arise, try to discover where they come from, to catch them at the very moment of arising. You won't succeed easily, but you will begin to see something of the mechanism of desires and emotions, and this is immensely valuable. Perhaps the most widespread meditational practice in all schools of Buddhism is *ānāpānasati* or mindfulness of breathing. Just watch the ebb and flow of your breath without interfering and, as far as you can manage, with undivided attention. This is the surest way to achieve calm, concentration, self-knowledge, and insight.

There is no Buddhism worthy of the name without practice, but study is also required. This is especially so in the West, where we have not the background of Buddhist thought which exists in Eastern countries. We have to learn as adults what Eastern people have absorbed from childhood. The study of Buddhist theory should therefore not be neglected. Those who deny its necessity do so usually out of conceit, laziness, or ignorance—or a combination of all three.

The obvious problem which arises here is: Where shall I start? There are many schools of Buddhism and their scriptures, even those readily available in English, are voluminous. There is Theravāda and Mahāyāna, in the form of Zen, Tibetan Buddhism and several other varieties. There are numerous books about most of them. Unguided and indiscriminate reading will only lead to mental indigestion. The obvious thing is to get down to basics. If we ask where these basic principles are set out, the answer is in the Pali Canon of the Theravāda school. In fact, the seeds of all later, so-called Mahāyāna developments are there in this basic Buddhism.

The only reason why some people find Theravada Buddhism apparently unsatisfying is its seemingly negative approach. In the Mahāyāna schools there is greater explicit stress on two things: compassion and the higher wisdom. But we need not worry. Compassion grows inevitably as one trains oneself in Buddhism, and the higher wisdom cannot be gained until the lower wisdom has been developed. It is to this task that the basic training is directed. Before we can begin to grasp the nature of Reality, which is transcendental, we must first grasp the nature of the mundane, the phenomenal world as our senses present it to us. This basically means knowing ourselves. Knowing ourselves means facing our own insecurity. Recognizing the equal insecurity of others is compassion.

Why do we feel so insecure? If we can answer this question, we are on the right track. It is due to our recognition that all things are transient. We seek to achieve a stability in the world which, by the very nature of things, cannot be. But Buddhism teaches us more than this: all things are not only transient, they are empty. This applies to our precious selves as much as to anything else. Man, said the Buddha, is a mere compound of five things, the five *khandhas* or aggregates. He has a physical body, feelings, perceptions, emotional reactions, and consciousness. None of these constitutes any sort of a self which is permanent and unchanging, nor is there any such thing outside of them. His consciousness is just a series of states of awareness, conditioned by the other factors, reaching back into a limitless past. All we are actually aware of is the present moment, or rather consciousness *is* just that awareness. There is no separate entity behind it which is *aware*. In the jargon of some modern philosophers, everything about man is contingent or adjectival, not substantival. The further implications of this must be left for study and meditation, but this is a fundamental principle of all Buddhism. The search for a self behind all this is futile. If you don't believe this you can try to take up the Buddha's challenge and find it.

There may well be a strong feeling of resistance to the acceptance of this point. If so, this feeling itself should be very carefully examined. It is the basis of our habitual ego-reactions. We *want* so badly to have a self and we expend a vast amount of energy in trying to build one up and support it in every way we can think of. That, fundamentally, is why we feel insecure in the world. One could usefully devote a good deal of time meditating on this point alone.

The most notable contribution made to psychology by Alfred Adler was his analysis of the inferiority complex. People who, for one reason or another, feel inferior, says Adler, tend to overcompensate and present an appearance of conceit and aggressiveness. Since Adler's psychology is very much one of social adaptation at not, perhaps, a very profound level, he did not pursue this idea as far as he might have done. But as far as it goes it is quite good Buddhism, though we might prefer to rename his complex the insecurity complex. We might even go so far as to say that for the Buddhist everybody's ego practically consists of an inferiority or insecurity complex, for such an assumption certainly explains a great deal. Every form of ostentation we may indulge in is a way of bolstering up the ego, whether in cruder or subtle form. The large car which seems designed as wide as possible is as much an example of ego-boosting as the padded shoulders worn by the tough: indeed the resemblance is sometimes striking. Of course the compensation for insecurity may take a reverse form of exaggerated modesty and simpering sweetness, or of unnecessary and slightly ostentatious self-sacrifice. This latter is a form of compensation we may choose when all else fails, and it has the advantage of making us feel very holy. Martyrdom is in fact the last consolation of a disappointed ego. And the hallmark of a person who has really gone far in the conquest of self is genuine unobtrusiveness.

The formula of Dependent Origination shows by selecting twelve prominent factors how it is that we go round and round the weary circle of rebirths, and how karma operates. It is not a simple formula of causation but rather of conditioning. Ignorance (*avijjā*) is a necessary condition for our being here—hence if we were not ignorant we would not have been reborn. And birth is a necessary condition for death—if we had never been born we could not die. Thus, too, feeling based on sense-impression is a necessary condition for the arising of craving: if there were no such feeling there would be no craving. But we can stop the craving from arising or at least prevent its developing into grasping. *This* is the point at which karma comes into play. Karma is volitional activity born of desire, and as such produces pleasant or unpleasant results in the future. Whatever condition of body and mind we happen to be in now is due to our past karma; it is *vipāka* or karma-resultant. In accordance with the *vipāka* we are liable to act in the future, but if we have understanding we can control our future actions, and thus their future effects.

The aim of Buddhist training, of whatever school, is to break away from the cycle of becoming. This means somehow attaining the Transcendental Reality which is not karma-bound and therefore permanent, secure, and free from suffering. We do not, as unenlightened individuals, know what this is: at best we have a vague intuition of something wholly other. Its true nature is hidden from us by the veils of our ignorance. The state of enlightenment is called Nirvana (*Nibbāna* in Pali), which is, be it noted, selfless (*anattā*). This means that we cannot grasp it as long as the self-concept (or feeling) is operative. It is beyond the realm of duality, which is that of subject and object, or self and other-than-self.

Probably most people have at times had a feeling while in the normal sense wide awake as if really they were dreaming and would soon wake up. This is actually quite true as far as the first part is concerned. Life, as we know it, is in one sense a dream. The Buddha was the Awakened One, and our normal state is perhaps somewhere about half-way between ordinary sleep and true enlightenment, or wakefulness. We can therefore usefully regard the Buddhist training, if we like, as a way of making ourselves wake up. Sometimes in sleep we become aware of being asleep and want to wake up. Eventually we succeed, but it is often a struggle. The struggle to wake up to enlightenment is far greater than this, because the resistance is stronger. The resistance is stronger for a very simple reason: to the ego it seems like death. This is fair enough, since in fact it *is* the death of ego. And since we have no real experience of the egoless state, it is unimaginable and therefore we are sceptical about it, but this scepticism too really springs from fear. We should have to give up all our attachments to attain it, and that is too high a price to pay. We are like the rich young man to whom Christ said, "Sell all that thou hast and give it to the poor." He went sorrowfully away.

What then must we do, now that we have taken the first step and embarked on the course of Buddhism? We need to have a chart and compass to help us on our way. But first we have to know where we are supposed to be going. The goal of Buddhism is Enlightenment or Awakening or Nirvana, the Deathless State, which is the end of all suffering and frustration, the one permanent and supremely desirable thing. Buddhism claims to be a way of attaining this. There are five factors to be developed which, if they are predominant in our minds, will tend increasingly to bring us to the goal. They are Faith, Energy, Mindfulness, Concentration, and Wisdom. The first of these may come as a surprise to some people. I thought, they may say, you didn't have to have *faith* in Buddhism. In fact faith is an important factor to develop. We can call it confidence or trust if we prefer it. But unless we have *some* confidence that there is such a goal as Nirvana, we shall not even start taking Buddhism seriously at all, and we need also to trust the Buddha as the teacher who has shown the way to reach that goal. At the very least we need to be free from the sort of nihilistic scepticism which is so common today and which prevents us from believing wholeheartedly in *anything* worthwhile. When we say I take refuge in the Buddha, the Dhamma, and the Saṅgha we are expressing faith in the Teaching and the Order of monks who have preserved it and handed it on.

If we have faith we next need to put forth effort, so we need energy. Right Effort is a step of the Eightfold Path. It means getting rid of wrong states of mind and developing right ones. Clearly a certain amount of vigour is required to do this, and faith will strengthen our will to persevere. Clearing up our mental muddle calls for increased self-knowledge, and this is gained by Mindfulness. Mindfulness is being aware of one's own nature and observing one's own reactions, being fully cognizant of what one is about all the time. It is developed by training, such exercises as mindfulness on breathing and on walking being especially beneficial. With full mindfulness, self-deception becomes impossible. It is the way of uncovering the subterfuges of the ego. The Buddha described it as the one and only way to the liberation of beings. It is an absolutely indispensable factor in all Buddhist training. Being mindful one is, too, in some degree automatically concentrated, but the practice of mental concentration can be carried further, to *samādhi*, which is mental one-pointness. By a combination of these two factors, the mind can be sharpened to an instrument capable of cutting through the veils of ego-created illusion. The last of the five factors is Wisdom. Wisdom in this connection means discernment. It includes investigation of all mental phenomena to their essence, which is voidness. When this lower, still mundane wisdom has been sufficiently developed, a basis has been created for the arising of the higher Insight-Wisdom, the perfection of which is Enlightenment. When this has been attained, the job is done.

But these factors must be developed in such a manner that they are properly balanced. Faith must be balanced with Wisdom, and Energy with Concentration. Faith without Wisdom can overreach itself and turn into that kind of blind faith which Buddhism does not encourage. On the other hand, Wisdom without Faith is sterile. Energy unaccompanied by Concentration can easily lead to restlessness, while Concentration without sufficient Energy leads to sloth. It is the function of Mindfulness, by watching over the other factors, to see that the proper balance between them is maintained. These five factors are called *indriyas* or ruling factors. This means that they can and should dominate the mind and give it direction. They are the five guides to keep us on the way. Having taken the first step, and with these as guides, but especially under the leadership of Mindfulness, let us walk on.

Detachment

by M.O'C. Walshe

One way of regarding the Buddhist training is to consider it under the aspect of detachment. Detachment is one of those simple things which we discover to be very profound and in its higher stages intensely difficult. By becoming progressively more detached, one gradually penetrates to the heart of Buddhism. Its importance is repeatedly stressed under various aspects throughout the whole range of the Buddhist scriptures. For instance, in the formula describing how one enters the first *jhāna*: "Detached from sensual objects, O monks, detached from unwholesome states of mind, the monk enters into first *jhāna* which is accompanied by initial and sustained application (*vitakka-vicāra*), is born of detachment (*viveka*) and filled with rapture and joy." The second *jhāna* is then said to be born of concentration. We thus see that detachment is a prerequisite for all concentration. The calm and concentrated mind is the detached mind. While this is obvious enough when we stop to think about it, it may help us to realize why it is that, even in purely mundane matters, we so often fail to concentrate our minds. We all know the picture of the man with furiously knitted brows and a wet towel round his head, who is desperately trying to concentrate on some problem. Of course, he usually fails. The reason, surely, is not far to seek: he is going about it precisely the wrong way. He is not detached. He is in fact very much *at*tached. He may be detached from sense-objects for the moment, but not from unwholesome states of mind. His state of mind is probably dominated by *uddhacca-kukkucca*, restlessness and worry, and so long as this remains the case he will probably get nowhere with his problem. His body too, reflecting this mental tension, is probably tense and strained. He should first try to relax, physically as well as mentally, and then he might make some progress.

At this point perhaps we might pause to consider an objection which is not infrequently made to the cultivation of detachment. There are people who positively regard it as morally wrong to be detached. One should not, they say, become detached and aloof from life, but should be actively involved in it—*engagé* as the French say. For them, detachment is the equivalent of that opprobrious term we used to hear so much about—escapism. Their argument is of course a very simple one: there is so much evil in the world of one kind or another that it is our job to go out and fight it. Now I am not going to argue that such people—let us call them as a generic term crusaders as opposed to introspectives—do not on occasion do a lot of good. A society which has a few dedicated crusaders is certainly, in its mundane way, healthier than one that discourages or represses their activities. They often succeed in abolishing, or at least reducing, much genuine evil. Let us take off our hats to them, and perhaps even on occasion join or support them. But let us also consider their position a little more closely. *Why* does the average crusader function as he does—irrespective of the particular cause he elects to take up? What *really* makes him tick? The answer to this question may put the whole matter in a rather different light.

Most of our crusader friends, whether they go in for party politics or for other similar, perhaps semi-political causes they believe in, are convinced that they do so out of love for their fellow-beings, whether human or animal. In part, this is certainly true. They do, passionately, want to help the poor, the sick, the oppressed, the suffering. Yet in fact their motives are usually not quite as pure as they themselves honestly believe them to be. The key to the situation lies, I think, in the word passionately. They are under the sway of emotions, not all of which are, in the Buddhist view, entirely healthy. Conceit often plays a large if probably quite unconscious part. And surprisingly often too they are really moved far more by hate than by loving-kindness. Hatred, even of the oppressor or the criminal, is not really the right motive because it is not grounded in the right view.

I am not seeking to disparage these people or belittle their efforts, but merely to elucidate something of their attitude in the context of my theme, which is detachment. So let us take a concrete example: one where I was and remain wholeheartedly in agreement with their aims. In Britain we have abolished capital punishment, rightly, I believe, though the increase in crime in recent years has led to demands for its reintroduction.

Those who campaign for this even claim to be in the majority, though I doubt if this is true, and I certainly do not share their viewpoint. They too are crusaders, and their reaction is certainly an emotional one. They really seek, without knowing it, a safe or legitimate outlet for their own aggression. These emotions are in turn rooted in their own basic feelings of insecurity. The trouble is, of course, that such emotions as these (and this is a comparatively mild example, in the world today!), when held collectively are always much worse than when merely held by an individual, not only on account of being multiplied, but because of being at a more primitive level.

It is possible, though I hope and believe unlikely, that pressures for the reintroduction of capital punishment in Britain will build up again to a serious point. Should this be the case, those who wish to oppose such a trend will need to be very careful indeed of their own state of mind. They must not let themselves be trapped in an opposite emotional reaction. They will need to find a way of reducing the buildup of emotional tension so that in a calmer atmosphere wiser counsels may have a chance to prevail. Emotional appeals would anyway, in such a situation, probably be useless, since the stronger emotions would be ranged on the other side. If you want, in fact, to abolish capital punishment you must not want to hang the executioner. Supporters of capital punishment often claim that its opponents show too much sympathy for the murderer and not enough for his victim. It does not seem too much to ask that a Buddhist—or a Christian—should be able to feel compassion for both, and even for the hangman as well, for he is certainly not creating much good karma for himself.

I am not at all arguing that a Buddhist should necessarily and always stand aloof from such campaigns as the—now—rather theoretical one mentioned. I *am* arguing that whatever he does he should know his own true motives, his real emotional reasons for either acting or not acting. I would also suggest that it is truly necessary for society as a whole, as for the individual concerned, that there should be those who in fact keep aloof from the current problems that happen to agitate the world at any moment. It is not for our crusading friends to disparage those who are genuinely detached. If the crusader *for*, say, capital punishment is a victim of his own unresolved aggression and insecurity, how often is not his opponent in virtually the same case! A slight shift in viewpoint or circumstances, and sometimes the roles are even reversed

The reformer looks around him and sees something wrong in society. This is usually not difficult, as there are plenty of things wrong with most societies, and it may be almost a matter of chance what particular evil or abuse he happens to pick on. What does he do then? He becomes what is significantly called an agitator. Now you can only agitate others if you yourself are agitated. What has *really* happened to our would-be reformer is that, his own emotions having been suitably stirred up, he feels it his duty to go out and stir up the emotions of other people. I know. I have gone through this phase myself. If you suggest to him that he should first calm his own emotions he is aggrieved, thereby developing some more agitation. He will probably tell you that this is the easy way out, and he may even admit that in any case he doesn't know how to do it—thereby, incidentally, contradicting the notion that it is easy. Of course, if you *can* get him that far it may be possible to indicate to him the contradiction involved. If he cannot help *himself* to that extent, how can he expect to be able to help others? Even in the field of Buddhism there are those who seem to think they can become Bodhisattvas and liberate all beings without first liberating themselves. They should take to heart the words of the great Zen patriarch Hui-neng, who told his pupils to deliver an infinite number of sentient beings of our own mind.

Let us leave world-problems now and turn to the problem of our own minds. What is it that we have to get detached from? In a sense, of course, it is from the outside world. That at least is how it seems to us. Let us not get involved in a metaphysical discussion about whether there really *is* an outside world or not. In point of fact, from the standpoint of the Buddhist training it scarcely matters whether there is or not! Perhaps we just project the whole thing from some mysterious inner centre. In any case, what we have to get rid of is our excessive preoccupation with it—that is to say, with the things of the senses. What actually happens is this: we have an unsatisfactory feeling in the only place we *can* have it—within ourselves (*whatever*, philosophically, that means). This feeling may take many forms, but whatever its precise nature or mode of manifesting, it is something unpleasant, i.e., what in Buddhism is known as *dukkha*. It may be quite vague in character, but we feel it somehow nevertheless. We therefore look out into the world, either to see what it is, out there, that is supposedly causing this *dukkha*, or to help us forget it, by grasping at something which we assume to be pleasant. The result in either case is not really very satisfying, because we are not even looking in the right direction. But creatures of habit as we are, we are strongly conditioned to look outside, and indeed nature has equipped us to looking outside with some remarkably efficient sense-organs for doing so.

With our outward-turned senses we can do various things about the world we see, hear, smell, taste, and touch. We can try to grasp something outside and extract enjoyment from it. We can try to alter what we see in some way to make it conform more to our idea of what it ought to be like. Or, we can vent our ill-temper on it in a fit of destructiveness. There is a lot of this sort of senseless destructiveness about nowadays. There always has been, really, but we have now made it a special problem, the problem of modern youth. The truth is simply that modern youth has in some ways rather more opportunities for being destructive than it used to have. This is due in large measure to the nature and values of the society we live in, a society which has developed more efficient means of destruction than were ever dreamed of before. The fact that it has also developed more wealth and therefore more means of apparent enjoyment, available to more people than ever before, does not seem to have done very much to reduce the general feeling of dissatisfaction each one of us has deep down inside. All this, of course, goes a long way toward confirming the Buddhist analysis of the situation, that the origin of this suffering, this *dukkha*, lies in craving. Our society is built up all along the line. We accordingly have the simultaneous picture of more and more people craving for more and more things, and quite often getting them, and of both society and individuals showing more and more taste for bigger and bigger forms of motiveless destruction. Greed and hate, in fact, are perhaps more nakedly at work in our society than ever before. That means that they are at work in every one of us, and they can only be dealt with in, and by, each one of us individually.

Greed and hate arise from ignorance: from not understanding, not seeing the true situation as it really is. The individual is a microcosm of society, and each one of us reflects this situation, in some form, individually. Now it may be very dreadful, but so far nobody has found a way whereby society can collectively overcome its ignorance, and set itself fundamentally to rights. Even the Buddha did not show a method of bringing this about—and if *he* couldn't find a way, it is unlikely that anybody else will. But for each individual there *is* a way:

Sabbapāpassa akaraṇaṃ,
kusalassa upasampada
sacittapariyodapanaṃ:
etaṃ Buddhanusāsanaṃ

Cease to do evil,
learn to do good.
Purify your own mind:
that is the teaching of all Buddhas.

And one of the prerequisites of purifying one's own mind is the cultivation of detachment. If we ask Detachment from what?—the answer is from the five hindrances: sensual craving and ill-will, sloth, restless worry and indecision. These are things we all know only too well, and though their final conquest is difficult, they are things we can detach our minds from temporarily with a little effort. The first two of these are obviously aspects of greed and hate. Probably we can see that there is a need to cut these down as much as possible. But if we fail to do so it may be, at least in part, because one of the other three hindrances is preventing us: we may be too indolent or too excited, or we may dither in a state of indecision and doubt.

Now the trouble is that we may see quite clearly, in a way, that our emotions of, say, greed or hate or fear are overmastering us and yet feel quite unable to do anything about them. Then we probably dismiss the whole problem with the words, "Oh yes, that's all very well, but I just haven't got the willpower." In fact it is just here that the value of detachment comes in. What we think of as failure of willpower may really be much more a failure of technique. Let us take the case of a man who, as he thinks and as others probably also think, cannot control his temper. The deeper reasons for this may be various, but they will probably include some strong form of frustration or repression. It is not very difficult to see that the chances of gaining control of any situation are likely to be increased the more one understands the situation. Now what is called repression in psychology is really a thrusting away—in other words it is basically a *refusal* to see something, a form of deliberate (even though unconscious) self-deception. In order to gain insight into the situation, we must have some willingness to understand it. So we need to realize here, right at the outset, that there is a form of clinging to ignorance. In order to cope with this there must be a degree of detachment—we must be able to regard the situation coolly and simply learn not to *mind* too much whatever it is we may be about to discover. We must be prepared to stop working on the old and foolish principle, "Where ignorance is bliss, 'tis folly to be wise."

It is possible that even this much of the chain of events may be fairly clear to us, and yet we may still not feel able to go any further. Intellectual awareness of an emotional situation is not in itself enough, though this does not mean it is of no use. It is just a preliminary stage, and it should be strongly emphasized that progress is in stages. The desire for perfection at a single jump is just another obstacle born of impatience and conceit. It is not an all-or-nothing situation, but a case of one step at a time. Perhaps we have already laid a certain foundation on which progress can be made, even without realizing it. For the man who has said to himself I haven't the willpower to correct this fault has at least made one vital admission. He has in some measure accepted his own inadequacy—in fact he is *too much* aware of this. He has to learn that what he really lacks is not necessarily willpower as much as insight. The next step, then, is merely and simply to recognize *this* fact. It will prove more helpful than may at first appear. For in fact seeing ourselves as we are *is* the cure.

The next step, then, is to find out why we do not already see ourselves as we are. The answer is, of course, as already indicated, that we don't want to, that there is a clinging to ignorance. Why this should be so is perhaps after all not hard to see. To the person with normal eyesight, physical blindness is a terrible thing. We can only too well imagine the feeling of helplessness and insecurity the blind person must suffer from. It is therefore not at all nice to think that though our physical eyes may be all right, we suffer from mental blindness. So we prefer to be blind to the blindness.

This is attachment to ignorance with a vengeance. No wonder it is frustrating, for it is a terrible strain to keep up. Most of our unhealthy emotions are nothing but by-products of this tension, caused by deliberately keeping our mental eyes tight shut while all the time pretending they are wide open. Only the practice of mindfulness can help us here.

What is mindfulness? There are professing Buddhists who are extremely vague about what mindfulness really is, and there are even some who are so afraid of it that they go about telling themselves and others that it is not really necessary. In principle, mindfulness is quite simple. It is just detached watching. Watching one's breathing is a method that suits practically everybody. First of all it brings calm, which enables one to watch one's thoughts and emotions more easily, and reduces the fear of what may come up—an important point sometimes. If mindfulness is pursued for a while, some such experience as the following may occur: a kind of unreal feeling may arise in which one seems to be aware of various emotional states (perhaps self-pity, anger, or the like) without being fully involved in them. One may start thinking Am I really having this emotion or not? Am I somehow putting on an act? What is really happening is that feelings are simply being experienced with detachment. And in such a state one can allow many things to come up to the surface which were previously repressed. But being detached, one is not trapped by these emotional states and sees them as mere effects of past conditioning. And in this way they can be harmlessly dissolved.

The interesting thing is that, when such a situation is operative, everything really seems to go on just as before, with only one slight difference: I am not fully in the situation. There may be even a distinct feeling of puzzlement as to precisely where I am anyway. Am I, for instance, the emotion or the watcher? Or neither, or both? By following up this particular clue we may find that the practice leads us on further to a greater degree of understanding of the impersonality of all things—of our own fundamental egolessness, in fact. The point is here simply that by becoming calm and detached we have, so to speak, accepted the unacceptable. As a result of this practice we shall find a reduction in our own feeling of tension, greater calm and, most probably, some increased insight into our own nature and the way things *really* work.

We can now see the practical answer to our ill-tempered friend's problem. He cannot restrain his temper by willpower but by detached mindfulness he can gradually dissolve it. And the same applies, of course, to all our failings and weaknesses. But there is one form of attachment we must guard especially against, because it makes the cure much more difficult. This is conceit. We all have conceit, of course, but if it is strong it is a particularly dangerous obstacle to progress. Conceit is really attachment to a false picture of the ego. Put negatively, it is a refusal to accept oneself as one is. It may manifest in the feeling I cannot possibly have these weaknesses, or I have overcome these weaknesses. Combined with, for instance, sexual repression it may take the form of a sort of purity complex: I am above all these horrid feelings of sex, they no longer exist for me, and the like. Perhaps this particular complex has become less common since greater openness on sexual matters has become usual. In any case, it is clear that for a person who does have this kind of attitude the development of true detachment, and hence mindfulness, will be exceptionally difficult. We must not be ashamed to admit to *ourselves* (if not perhaps necessarily to others) that we possess our full share of *all* the normal human weaknesses.

At this point there comes an interesting and subtle twist. You may say Yes, I suppose that's true. But somehow there *are* a few things down there inside me which I just *can't* bring myself to face. Now this is of course quite different from denying that they are there at all. It means in fact that repression, i.e., self-deception, has *not* been completely successful. Now it may indeed be true that to face up fully to some of the contents of one's unconscious may be too hard to bear. It might be impossible to maintain detachment. Emotional involvement and perhaps even quite serious trouble might result. But there is still a way. What we *can* do is to accept honestly that precise situation: There is a dark corner where I still dare not to look. It is the mental equivalent of saying I have a sore place which I dare not touch. The technique from then on is basically the same as before, only at one remove. There is just a secondary emotion of fear to be dissolved before the primary situation which is the cause of that fear can be investigated. If that secondary fear is treated with the detachment we have used on other and less frightening emotions, it too can be dissolved.

Later we may even look back and wonder why it was that we ever feared to look in that particular dark corner.

To sum up: detachment is not a kind of selfish flight from the world, but the necessary precondition for coping with the world. It is absolutely essential as a means of dealing with our own emotions. Nor is it in any way incompatible with charity or compassion—as indeed any doctor or nurse can tell you. It is no escapism as is sometimes alleged, but its very opposite. The degree of physical detachment and withdrawal which the individual undertakes may vary considerably—obviously it will be much greater for the monk than for the average lay person. There can be no successful higher meditation without detachment from the things of the senses, and it is an essential ingredient of Right Mindfulness. Incidentally it can even be quite fun. By being detached we can observe ourselves with ironic amusement. By so doing we may suddenly discover that some of the things about ourselves that we took with deadly seriousness are in fact extremely funny. In that way we may find that detachment actually enables us to enjoy our own *dukkha*!

ABOUT PARIYATTI

Pariyatti is dedicated to providing affordable access to authentic teachings of the Buddha about the Dhamma theory (*pariyatti*) and practice (*paṭipatti*) of Vipassana meditation. A 501(c)(3) nonprofit charitable organization since 2002, Pariyatti is sustained by contributions from individuals who appreciate and want to share the incalculable value of the Dhamma teachings. We invite you to visit www.pariyatti.org to learn about our programs, services, and ways to support publishing and other undertakings.

Pariyatti Publishing Imprints

Vipassana Research Publications (focus on Vipassana as taught by S.N. Goenka in the tradition of Sayagyi U Ba Khin)
BPS Pariyatti Editions (selected titles from the Buddhist Publication Society, copublished by Pariyatti)
MPA Pariyatti Editions (selected titles from the Myanmar Pitaka Association, copublished by Pariyatti)
Pariyatti Digital Editions (audio and video titles, including discourses)
Pariyatti Press (classic titles returned to print and inspirational writing by contemporary authors)

Pariyatti enriches the world by
- disseminating the words of the Buddha,
- providing sustenance for the seeker's journey,
- illuminating the meditator's path.

www.ingramcontent.com/pod-product-compliance
Lightning Source LLC
Chambersburg PA
CBHW020348170426
43200CB00005B/87